MW00474586

From Exploitation
Back to Empowerment

This book is part of the Peter Lang Education list.
Every volume is peer reviewed and meets
the highest quality standards for content and production.

PETER LANG
New York • Bern • Berlin
Brussels • Vienna • Oxford • Warsaw

Joseph N. Cooper

From Exploitation
Back to Empowerment

Black Male Holistic
(Under)Development
Through Sport
and (Mis)Education

PETER LANG
New York • Bern • Berlin
Brussels • Vienna • Oxford • Warsaw

Library of Congress Cataloging-in-Publication Control Number: 2018044979

Bibliographic information published by **Die Deutsche Nationalbibliothek**.
Die Deutsche Nationalbibliothek lists this publication in the "Deutsche
Nationalbibliografie"; detailed bibliographic data are available
on the Internet at http://dnb.d-nb.de/.

ISBN 978-1-4331-6156-8 (hardcover)
ISBN 978-1-4331-6155-1 (paperback)
ISBN 978-1-4331-6090-5 (ebook pdf)
ISBN 978-1-4331-6091-2 (epub)
ISBN 978-1-4331-6092-9 (mobi)
DOI 10.3726/b14655

© 2019 Peter Lang Publishing, Inc., New York
29 Broadway, 18th floor, New York, NY 10006
www.peterlang.com

All rights reserved.
Reprint or reproduction, even partially, in all forms such as microfilm,
xerography, microfiche, microcard, and offset strictly prohibited.

CONTENTS

FIGURES

FOREWORD

It is a great privilege to write this foreword for Dr. Cooper. I vividly remember meeting him in Chapel Hill, NC, during his days as a graduate student. I was invited to sit on a panel during the College Sport Research Institute's annual conference being held on the campus of UNC and Joe was in attendance. The panel was on some aspect of college sports and it consisted of myself, Jay Bilas, Danny Green, and Burke Mangus, who was then senior vice president, college sports programming for ESPN. The panel was lively as I challenged Jay Bilas and Burke Mangus to realize that the young Black males they covered on ESPN were actually people and not just robots. At lunch later that day, I had the opportunity to talk, debate, and engage with Joe. I knew then that he was the type of professor we needed to change the culture of big-time college sports. Quite frankly, I told him, we need professors who will engage Black student-athletes and who will encourage and challenge them to be more than just ballplayers.

Through his scholarly work, Dr. Cooper investigates the lived experiences of student-athletes of color to help identify major issues impacting their educational experience and develop solutions that will aid in their holistic development and growth. His research is centered around the intersection of sport, race, education, and culture. Dr. Cooper's research directly informs his work with student-athletes in the Collective Uplift program – an evidence-based program designed to empower student-athletes of color to maximize their potential for success on and off the field. Dr. Cooper has also written numerous articles and book chapters on athlete activism and HBCU athletics including an edited volume entitled *The Athletic Experience at Historically Black College and Universities: Past, Present, and Future.*

While this book is a milestone in his career, I am equally as proud of the work he is doing on the ground at UCONN. When he arrived as an assistant professor he immediately started a program to engage Black student-athletes. Collective Uplift does exactly just that. By focusing on behavior modification, athletic identity, leadership, and decision-making, this initiative has quickly become a model across higher education. So, when you read this book understand that this is not solely based on abstract theoretical principles. Rather, it is grounded in his day-to-day work engaging with student-athletes on his campus and across the country.

Dr. Leonard Moore
Associate Vice President of Academic Diversity Initiatives
Professor of History
University of Texas at Austin

ACKNOWLEDGEMENTS

I would first like to acknowledge, thank, and praise God, my Lord and Personal Savior Jesus Christ, and the Holy Spirit that dwells within me. God has blessed me infinitely and everything I do is to honor and glorify Him. Thank you Lord for your endless mercy, grace, and love. I continually seek to draw nearer unto you and fulfill your purposes for my life. I would like to thank my mother, Dr. Jewell Egerton Cooper, for your unconditional and immeasurable love, sacrifices, nurturing, guidance, and support. Throughout my life, you have served as a positive role model and instilled in me timeless values, critical consciousness, and the importance of concerted actions. You role modeled perseverance and determination against challenging odds. I love you and thank you for being the greatest Mom for me and my heroine. To my father, Dr. Armah Jamale Cooper, thank you for loving me, being my father and Dad, and showing how to be a man of faith and perseverance. Your authenticity and growth showed me that life is a journey and the power of forgiveness is transformative. I love you beyond words. To my brother, Adam Roberts Cooper, thank you for always loving, supporting, and being there for me. Life with you as my bigger brother has been a priceless blessing. I love you very much and always seek to make you proud.

To my grandmothers, Mama Jo (Josephine Johnson Egerton Wilkins) and Mama (Izetta Roberts Cooper), I thank and love you for being my spiritual anchors. To my grandfathers, Daddy Walter (Walter Eugene Egerton, Jr.) and Papi (Dr. Henry Nehemiah Cooper), I love you and hope I am making you all and all of our ancestors proud. To my entire family including extended members and kinship, thank you for your support and I love you. To Dr. Harry Edwards, thank you for your courage, passion, intellect, scholarship, and activism. You have set the benchmark for revolutionary Black empowerment and struggle in the field of sport sociology and beyond. To all of my teachers, advisors, and mentors, thank you all for the guidance, support, and lessons taught. I hope this book reflects my appreciation to you all for what you have done. To all my friends, thank you for your support, friendship, and helping me grow personally and professionally. To all my classmates and colleagues, thank you all for sharing your journeys with me and helping me grow as a learner, critical thinker, writer, communicator, scholar, educator, and activist. Last, but certainly not least, to my lovely and amazing wife, Monique Shari Cooper, thank you for being in my life and loving me the way you do. Our love is one of kind and means more to me than words could ever express. You make me a better child of God, person, man, husband, and father. I love our life, marriage, and family.

INTRODUCTION

To really honor the struggles of the past, however, the ultimate goal must be to create a new and better model, not to replace an old form of oppression with a new one

—Rhoden (2006, p. 195)

The Plight of Black Males in the United States: Conditions, Realities, and Complexities In and Through Sport and Beyond

The dire conditions facing and subsequent outcomes associated with Black[1] males in the United States (U.S.) has been well-documented (Curry, 2017; ETS, 2011; Howard, 2014; Jackson & Moore, 2006; Noguera, 2008). These circumstances include high incarceration and juvenile detention rates, school truancy and attrition rates, overrepresentation in special education and concurrent underrepresentation in gifted programs in the K-12 educational system, persistent health issues (e.g., depression, high blood pressure, diagnosed mental disorders, etc.), cyclical economic deprivation and immobility, and higher mortality rates and shorter lifespans compared to peers (within and outside of their own race and gender groups)—collectively, these outcomes reflect "*social symptoms* of a history of oppression" (Majors & Billson, 1992, p. 12). Another alarming, albeit typically perceived as innocuous, trend among Black males is what Edwards' (2000) calls their obsession with sports. According to Edwards (2000), Black males' obsession with sports results in a triple tragedy: (1) a fixated pursuit of a professional sports career a vast majority of them will not attain, (2) overall identity and skill underdevelopment of Black male former athletes, and (3) a lack of optimal improvements within the Black community due to the talent extraction towards sports and away from vital occupational fields such as health, law, business, politics, education, and technology to name a few. Unfortunately in the U.S., there are few spaces where Black males are valued, supported, and celebrated and sport is one of them. For example, it is not uncommon for a local town or city to declare a holiday or rename a street for a former standout athlete, but this same of recognition is seldom if ever applied for non-athletic accomplishments. Although, this practice occurs in communities across racial lines, the implications for Black males is particularly problematic given the previously cited social realities that position them among the most disadvantaged group in a society founded upon and structured by the ideology of White racism capitalism[2] (WRC).

Despite widespread success in sporting realms, namely in football, basketball, and track and field across all levels (e.g., youth, interscholastic, intercollegiate, and professional), many scholars have argued sport serves more as a site for exploitation consistent with the American tradition of commodifying Black male bodies for the financial and entertainment benefits of Whites rather than for the collective racial, social, political, and economic uplift and sustainability of Blacks (Cooper, 2012; Cooper, Macaulay, & Rodriguez, 2017; Edwards, 1969, 1973, 1984, 2000; Hawkins, 2010; Rhoden, 2006; Powell, 2008; Sellers, 2000; Smith, 2009). Polite (2011) defined exploitation as "the unfair treatment or use of, or the practice of taking selfish or unfair advantage of, a person or situation, usually for personal gain" (p. 2). Within the context of the U.S., exploitation and racial discrimination are inextricably linked. Franklin and Resnik (1973) outlined this relationship with the following definition: "Discrimination in the context of the American society, given its racial heritage, involves antipathetic distinctions that are made systematically (in contrast to randomly made-distinctions) by a dominant white majority to the disadvantage of a subordinate black minority" (p. 16). The four mechanisms by which discrimination is institutionalized in society are through state sanctioning (e.g., laws, policies, statutes, etc.), social preferences (both non-violent and violent), stereotyping, and market conditions (Franklin & Resnik, 1973). Each of these four mechanisms operate on multiple levels in society (macro, meso, and micro) and influence the purpose and structure of social institutions such as sport and education. Suffice it to say Black males' presence in organized sports has been contested since their initial involvement dating back to the mid-1800s (Edwards, 1973; Wiggins, 2014; Wiggins & Miller, 2003). Thus, sport has served as both a site for ideological and social reproduction as well as a space for resistance and transformation in regards to race, class, and power relations (Cooper et al., 2017; Edwards, 1969, 1973, 1980, 2016; Hartmann, 2000).

Notwithstanding the aforementioned complexities, previous research and popular discourse on Black male athletes' socialization experiences and outcomes has been conspicuously limited. Consequently, distorted generalizations of these processes have been widely accepted without a critical examination of the heterogeneity among this sub-group (e.g., all Black males being viewed as sport obsessed, academically deficient, economically impoverished, etc.). In disciplines outside of sport sociology, scholars have asserted the danger of promoting and accepting homogenous narratives of entire racial and gender groups (Celious & Oyserman, 2001; Harper & Nichols, 2008). Even when acknowledging negative outcomes associated with Black males, it is important to recall Edwards' (1984) prophetic message: "Dumb jocks are not born, but rather they are systematically created and the system must change" (p. 8). Hence, the aim of this book is to offer a paradigm shift by outlining five models of Black male socialization in and through sport and (mis) education[3] within a comprehensive historical, sociocultural, political, and economic context while offering a modernized blueprint for positive progress centered on holistic development.[4] These socialization models build upon previous literature and address both Edwards' (1984) call for a systems change and Rhoden's (2006) charge of creating new models that challenge rather than reproduce individual holistic underdevelopment and group oppression. The paradigm shift is a call to action to alter sporting and educational spaces from sites of exploitation and miseducation to sites of empowerment and sustained collective vitality for Black male athletes and the broader Black community.

Related to the proposed socialization models and contrary to stereotypical assertions, Black male athletes are not monolithic. Yet, the dominant narratives, popular discourses, and vast majority of scholarly literature on this sub-group has situated them in a narrow scope. These sources have primarily focused on Black male athletes' early socialization into athletics, keen attraction towards sport glory via positive identity affirmation, concurrent academic underperformance, athletic role engulfment and identity foreclosure, career immaturity, financial illiteracy, and overall underdevelopment and exploitation (Adler & Adler, 1991; Beamon, 2008, 2010, 2012; Beamon & Bell, 2002, 2011; Benson, 2000; Brooks & Althouse, 2000, 2013; Eitle & Eitle, 2002; Harris, 1994; Hawkins, 2010; May, 2008; Sellers, 2000; Sellers, Kuperminc, & Waddell, 1991; Singer & May, 2010; Smith, 2009). While the harsh reality of Black male athletes being exploited across all levels (youth to professional) occurs all too frequently, these descriptions only reflect a subset of the lived experiences of the broader group of Black male athletes in and through sport and (mis)education.

A few notable exceptions have highlighted Black male athletes who were politically conscious and engaged in social justice efforts, but this exploration has largely been limited to Black athlete activism during the Civil Rights Movement and more recently post-Colin Kaepernick's symbolic kneeling gesture in the Black Lives Matter (BLM) era (Cooper et al., 2017; Edwards, 1969, 1980, 2016). Moreover, additional noteworthy works have incorporated anti-deficit approaches in the examination of how Black male athletes navigate contested educational terrains and experience high levels of academic and career success beyond sporting spaces (Bimper, 2015, 2016, 2017; Bimper & Harrison, 2011; Cooper, 2016, 2017; Cooper & Cooper, 2015 Cooper & Hawkins, 2014; Harrison, Martin, & Fuller, 2015; Martin, Harrison, Stone, & Lawrence, 2010; Oseguera, 2010; Smith, Clark, & Harrison, 2014). Despite the benefits of these studies, they offer a polar opposite perspective of Black male athletes' experiences in academic and athletic milieu (i.e., "dumbs jocks" vs. scholar athletes). Given the diversity of experiences among Black male athletes, there is a need for more nuanced coverage of their socialization experiences and subsequent life outcomes. Such analyses would provide vital insights for understanding how specific systems, conditions, and processes contribute to Black male athletes' holistic (under)[5] development.

Foundation for Understanding Black Masculinities In and Through Sport and (Mis)Education

Black masculinities is a complex phenomenon that has been explored across various disciplines such as gender studies (Staples, 1978; Summers, 2004), sociology (DuBois, 1903/2003), philosophy (Curry, 2017; Fanon, 1952/2008), cultural studies (Bush & Bush, 2013a, 2013b; Mutua, 2006), urban education (Howard, 2014; Majors & Billson, 1992; Noguera, 2008), postsecondary education (Cuyjet, 2006; Douglas, 2016; Harper, 2012; Harper & Harris, 2010; Harper & Nichols, 2008; Wood & Palmer, 2014), and sport to name a few (Armstrong & Jennings, 2018; Edwards, 1969, 1973; Harrison, Harrison, & Moore, 2002; Hodge, Burden, Robinson, & Bennett, 2008). The aforementioned interdisciplinary attention towards Black masculinities has examined the nuances associated with biology, anatomy, physiology, ecology, ethnology, anthropology, geography, culture, time, psychology, identity, social constructions, and political economies. In concert with these transdisciplinary approaches, I surmise any theory of Black masculinities and corresponding socialization processes must take into account socio-historical and socio-cultural contexts, which shape meanings both internally, externally, temporally, and in perpetuity. Otherwise stated, Black masculinities do not exist or function in a vacuum, but rather in tandem with identity constructions and social realities.[6]

In an examination of scholarship on Black masculinities, Summers (2004) outlined three distinguishable paradigms. The social science paradigm situates Black masculinities in relation to oppressive structures such as educational institutions, criminal justice system, and different economic sectors (e.g., prisons, sports, etc.). Within this paradigm, Black masculinities are characterized by surveillance, control, and exploitation. These works utilize statistical data and anecdotal narratives and stories to illustrate the nature and extent of Black males' identity development and the conditions therein (Summers, 2004). The discursive paradigm explores the identity construction of Black males through representations in the dominant culture with a particular emphasis on power dynamics and race relations. The historical and dichotomous images of Black males as docile sambos or violent brutes in White mainstream media dating back to the early 19th century through the early 21st century are examples of research within this paradigm (Hawkins, 1998a, 1998b; Sailes, 2010).

The historical paradigm focuses on examining Black masculinities within a broader narrative of African Diasporic (including African American) experiences (Summers, 2004). These works explore how Black masculinities were and remain constructed within the socio-cultural and geopolitical contexts across specific eras in human history. The delineation of the era muscular assimilationism during the latter 19th and early 20th century versus the era of cultural nationalism in the early to mid-20th century in the U.S. and their respective influences on Black masculinities within and beyond sport illustrate analyses associated with the historical paradigm (discussed in greater detail in Chapter 1). Throughout this book, each of the three paradigms are strategically incorpo-rated to reflect my social constructivist epistemological stance as well as my pluralistic proclivities when seeking to understand complex phenomena (the concept of theoretical pluralism is discussed in greater detail in Chapter 3).

My Positionality

The inspiration for my research and this book stem from my subjectivities and life experiences as a Black and African American male who grew up in a Southern Baptist household with my mother and older brother (parents were divorced in my pre-teens and my father lived nearby). During my youth, a significant part of my self-identity was connected to my athletic abilities and accomplishments namely in basketball and soccer. In my home state of North Carolina, basketball is a way of life. Numerous Black males aspired to be the next Michael Jordan and play at one of the Tobacco Road schools (Univer-sity of North Carolina, Duke University, North Carolina State University, or Wake Forest University). In fact, it was not a surprise for any of us in the elite basketball circuit to know or be the star who earned a Division I scholarship or make it to the professional ranks (as of 2018, three of the top 10 point guards in the National Basketball Association (NBA) are from North Carolina and they are all 6′4 inches or shorter—Stephen Curry, Chris Paul, and John Wall; thus illustrating the magnitude of basketball talent and emphasis in the state).

It was not until my playing days were over when I experienced a range of psychosocial challenges due to my reduced athletic status that I came to the realization that being an athlete was only a small part of my identity. In my professional experiences working with Black males, I have learned that many of them share similar experiences in regards to primarily self-identifying as an athlete. As a mentor, I personally connected with my mentees when they described their aspirations of becoming professional athletes as well as their frustrations with being treated differently by others because of their race, ethnicity, gender, and athletic status. As a researcher, I also began to identify common themes in the literature and media coverage of Black male athletes. These common themes included experiences with racial discrimina-tion, social isolation, academic neglect, economic deprivation, and limited leadership opportunities (Cooper, 2012). These trends caused me to question the socialization patterns of young Black males in the U.S. I concluded the underlying problem lies in the fact that young Black males are socialized to be athletes at the expense of their holistic development. My affinity for history, sociology, sport, culture, and education grew during my undergraduate years when I majored in Sociology and Recreation Administration. I later earned my Master's degree in Sport Administration and completed my thesis titled "The Relationship Between the Critical Success Factors and Academic and Athletic Success: A Quantitative Case Study of Black Male Football Student-Athletes at a Major Division I Southeastern Institution" (Cooper, 2009). In 2013, I completed my doctorate at the University of Georgia and my dissertation was titled, "A Mixed Methods Exploratory Study of Black Male Student Athletes' Experiences at a Historically Black University" (Cooper, 2013). My first published manuscript was titled, "Personal Troubles and Public Issues: A Sociological Imagination of Black Athletes' Experiences at Predominantly White Institutions in the United States" (Cooper, 2012). Thus, my epistemological, axiological, ontological, theoretical, and methodological orientations underscore my subjectivities and influence my research.

Moreover, I contend the paradox regarding Black male athletes' experiences with athletic identity foreclosure is reflective of broader systemic inequalities within the U.S. society based on historical patterns of racial discrimination, exploitation, and marginalization of Blacks in general and Black males more specifically. Thus, my research interests are a byproduct of the intersections between my personal background, multiple identities, experiences, exposures, resources, and various ecological and socio-historical factors. The fact that I am a Black and African American male plays a significant role in my research interest in Black male athletes. In addition, my experiences as a former athlete provide me with a distinct lens for examining the impact of sport participation on Black male athletes' academic achievement, self-identity, psychosocial well-being, holistic experiences, and post-athletic career outcomes. I fully acknowledge, accept, and embrace my unique positionality as a researcher of Black male athletes. A goal of my research is to empower those who are disadvantaged by current social structures, arrangements, and practices. Consistent with social constructivism, I assert that my subjectivities strengthen my research rather than constrain it.

The Need for Critical Sociological and Ecological Examinations of Black Male Athletes

In order to understand the experiences of Black male athletes, two important foci area must be examined and understood. First, a critical sociological examination of historical, sociocultural, political, economic, and educational occurrences in the U.S. society is required (Chapters 1 and 2). A major omission from popular discourse on Black male athletes is the lack of contextualization regarding their sport involvement and educational (dis)engagement in connection to broader societal realities. Thus, historical research that situates sport and education within a critical sociological apparatus undergirds the five models presented in this text. For example, when analyzing the history of Black athlete activism in the U.S., Edwards (2016) distinguished events based on the era in which they occurred. The four waves of Black athlete activism that coincided with broader social movements included: (a) first wave (1900–1945) focused on gaining legitimacy, (b) second wave (1946–1960s) centered on acquiring political access and diversity, (c) third wave (mid-1960s–1970s) championed demanding dignity and respect, a period of stagnation (1970s–2005) occurred in the late 20th and early 21st century, and (d) fourth wave (2005-present) shifted attention towards securing and transferring power via economic and technological capital. Broader social movements that occurred concurrently during these eras included the Ante-Bellum Period movement (early 1800s–1860s), Black Liberation movement through Reconstruction (1880s–1920s), Harlem Renaissance Era (1920s–1930s), Black Integration movement (1930s–1960s), Civil Rights movement (1960s), Black Power and Black Feminism movements (late 1960s–1980s), and Black Lives Matter (BLM) movement (2010s) (Cooper, Mallery, & Macaulay, forthcoming). Similar to Edwards' (2016) contextualization of Black athlete activism, I assert critical socio-historical analyses are needed for understanding how and why specific experiences and outcomes manifest among different sub-groups of Black male athletes in the U.S.

The second foci area necessary for understanding Black male athletes' socialization experiences and outcomes is a multi-level analysis of sub- (spiritual), chrono- (time, space, and location), macro- (societal/global/national), exo- (mass media and indirect entities), meso- (cultural/organizational/institutional), and micro-system factors (individual/interpersonal/ community/family/peer group) (Bronfenbrenner, 1977, 1986; Bush & Bush, 2013a, 2013b). In order to unpack the interlocking influences of social systems, structures, polices, and practices on individual and group schemas, behaviors, experiences, and outcomes, a socio-ecological systems analysis is imperative (Chapter 3). The ways in which Black males experience sport and traditional educational spaces is predicated on sociocultural factors (i.e.., significance of and support for sport and education within the individuals' family, community, and sub-cultures), economic resources (i.e., access (or lack thereof) to developmental opportunities beyond sport), and individual factors (i.e, personal identity schemas related to sport and non-sport activities) (Chapters 4–8). In addition, the nature and quality of relationships, exposure, interactions, and related socialization factors are also germane to any analysis of variability in terms of lived experiences and outcomes.

In sum, the same society that produces the apolitical consummate capitalist in Michael Jordan on one end and *the revolutionary activist in Dr. Harry Edwards on the other* also simultaneously produces dismal educational outcomes for Black males in the K-20 educational system or more accurately referred to as the miseducation schooling system, *Rhodes Scholars such as Myron Rolle and Caylin Moore*, a prison industrial complex that results in nearly one-third of all inmates being Black males, *numerous exemplar professionals across multiple academic and occupational fields who graduate from historically Black colleges and universities*[7] *(HBCUs) as well as historically White institutions*[8] *(HWIs)*, disconcerting numbers of Black males with psychological trauma, *a plethora of transformative inventors, pioneers, and Black males who overcome and navigate oppressive conditions through formal and informal means*, disproportionate, alarming, and unnecessary perpetual Black male deaths, and *countless upstanding and present husbands, boyfriends, fathers, brothers, uncles, grandfathers, great grandfathers, community members, and leaders*.

Among this list, some of the patterns documented are more commonly recognizable based on mass media coverage and prevailing stereotypical schemas. Whereas, another set of the patterns listed may appear mythical or atypical. Despite these varied outcomes among Black males, there has yet to be a comprehensive examination that takes into account the diverse experiences of those who participate in sport and (mis)education starting from youth through adulthood. This book fills this gap. The critical sociological analysis within this text incorporates transdisciplinary theories, which allows for the exploration of the interplay between individuals and groups within multi-level systems and their corresponding socialization experiences and life outcomes. This approach disrupts the current erroneous miscategorization of Black male athletes as homogenous and fosters the recognition of their heterogeneity as well as allows for the identification of key intervention points for transformative change (Chapter 9).

Notes

1. The terms "Black" and "African American" are used interchangeably based on the source. The former term is used to refer to the racial group of people with African descent and socially classified as Black and thus historically subjected to differential treatment on

the basis of this marker. The latter term refers to African Americans who have familial lineage in the U.S. dating back to the early 17th century (Singer, 2015).

2. The common usage of the term White supremacy is intentionally not used here or throughout the book to challenge the underlying fallacious assumptions embedded in this terminology. Imposed superiority via violence, political exploitation, and other forms of oppression and human indignities have been well documented across various disciplines. Thus, the usage of the term White racism capitalism emphasizes the intertwinement and recursive relationship between the source of these imposed inequalities and the nature of how they are manifested in socially constructed ways via ideologies, structures, institutions, policies, practices, and property. A useful analysis of the problematic usage of the term White supremacy is offered by the renowned intellectual and Hip-Hop pioneer KRS-ONE (Knowledge Rules Supreme Over Nearly Everyone—birth name is Lawrence Parker) (Parker, 2016).

3. The phrase (mis)education and miseducation is used to signify formal policies and informal practices/social norms that are de facto well-intentioned, but in actuality contribute to negative holistic underdevelopment and communal outcomes for Blacks as well as various oppressed groups. The parentheses around the word "mis" is used selectively to emphasize the contextual distinction between detrimental conditions and educational processes versus positive conditions and true well-rounded educational processes that foster Black holistic development, racial uplift, and cultural empowerment.

4. I define holistic development as the recognition and healthy nurturance of multiple identities including intentional behaviors that foster positive outcomes for self and one's own family, community, racial and cultural groups, and a more equitable society.

5. The phrases (under)development and underdevelopment are used to describe negative life outcomes, as a result of oppressive and exploitative conditions and detrimental socializations processes, such as unemployment, career dissatisfaction and interest mismatch, sporadic and chronic depression, mental health issues, financial instability, social isolation/alienation, academic attrition, and engagement in other maladaptive behaviors for self, family, and community. The parentheses around the word "under" is used selectively to emphasize the contextual distinction between negative life outcomes as a result of sport participation and miseducation and positive life outcomes such as holistic development and cultural empowerment as a result of true well-rounded educational processes.

6. Identity constructions referenced here include humanity, sex, gender, race, age, ability, class/socioeconomic status, spiritual identity, and religious identification to name a few. Social realities refer to the conditions people are subjected to experiencing as a result of prevailing dominant ideologies (e.g., White racism, capitalism, heterosexism, etc.) such as poverty, stigmatization, fear, violent and unsafe spaces, etc.

7. The term HBCU is defined as an institution of higher education in the U.S. established prior to 1964 with the primary purpose of providing educational opportunities to Black Americans and whose current student population is at least 50% Black.

8. The term HWI is defined as institution of higher education in the U.S. that historically excluded and/or limited large numbers of Black students from enrollment prior to 1964 and whose current student population is at least 50% White. I assert the term HWI, as opposed to predominantly White institution (PWI), is more reflective of the relationship

between the origins of these institutions and their current enrollment trends, campus climates, and curricula.

References

Adler, P. A., & Adler, P. (1991). *Backboards and blackboards: College athletics and role engulfment.* New York, NY: Columbia University Press.

Armstrong, K. L., & Jennings, M. A. (2018). Race, sport, and sociocognitive "place" in higher education: Black male student athletes as critical theorists. *Journal of Black Studies, 49*(4), 349–369.

Beamon, K. K. (2008). "Used goods": Former African American college student-athletes' perception of exploitation by division I universities. *The Journal of Negro Education, 77*(4), 352–364.

Beamon, K. K. (2010). Are sports overemphasized in the socialization process of African American males?: A qualitative analysis of former collegiate athletes' perception of sport socialization. *Journal of Black Studies, 41*(2), 281–300.

Beamon, K. (2012). "I'm a baller": Athletic identity foreclosure among African American former student-athletes. *Journal of African American Studies, 16*(2), 195–208.

Beamon, K. K., & Bell, P. A. (2002). "Going pro": The differential effects of high aspirations for a professional sports career on African-American student athletes and White student athletes. *Race & Society, 5*(2), 179–191.

Beamon, K. K., & Bell, P. A. (2011). A dream deferred: Narratives of African American male former collegiate athelets' transition out of sports and into the occupational sector. *Journal for the Study of Sport and Athletes in Education, 5*(1), 29–44.

Benson, K. F. (2000). Constructing academic inadequacy: African American athletes' stories of schooling. *The Journal of Higher Education, 71*(2), 223–246.

Bimper, A. Y. (2015). Mentorship of Black student-athletes at a predominately White American university: Critical race theory perspective on student-athlete development. *Sport, Education and Society, 22*, 1–19. doi: 10.1080/13573322.2015.1022524.

Bimper, A. Y. (2016). Capital matters: Social sustaining capital and the development of Black student-athletes. *Journal of Intercollegiate Sport, 9*(1), 106–128.

Bimper, A. Y. (2017). Mentorship of Black student-athletes at a predominately White American university: Critical race theory perspective on student-athlete development. Sport, Education and Society, *22*(2), 175–193.

Bimper, A. Y., Jr., & Harrison, L., Jr. (2011). Meet me at the crossroads: African American athletic and racial identity. *National Association for Kinesiology and Physical Education in Higher Education, 63*(3), 275–288.

Bronfenbrenner, U. (1977). Toward an experimental ecology of human development. *The American Psychologist, 32*(7), 513–531.

Bronfenbrenner, U. (1986). Ecology of the family as a context for human development: Research perspectives. *Developmental Psychology, 22*(6), 723–742.

Brooks, D., & Althouse, R. (2000). *Racism in college athletics: The African American athlete's experience* (2nd ed.). Morgantown, WV: Fitness Information Technology.

Brooks, D. A., & Althouse, R. (2013). *Racism in college athletics: The African American athlete's experience* (3rd ed.). Morgantown, WV: Fitness Information Technology.

Bush, L. V., & Bush, E. C. (2013a). Introducing African American male theory (AAMT). *Journal of African American Males in Education, 4*(1), 6–17.

Bush, L. V., & Bush, E. C. (2013b). God bless the child who got his own: Toward a comprehensive theory for African-American boys and men. *The Western Journal of Black Studies, 37*(1), 1–13.

Celious, A., & Oyserman, D. (2001). Race from the inside: An emerging heterogeneous race model. *Journal of Social Issues, 57*(1), 149–165.

Cooper, J. N. (2009). The relationship between the critical success factors and academic and athletic success: A quantitative case study of Black male football student-athletes at a major division I southeastern institution (Thesis). Chapel Hill, NC: The University of North Carolina at Chapel Hill.

Cooper, J. N. (2012). Personal troubles and public issues: A sociological imagination of Black athletes' experiences at predominantly White institutions in the United States. *Sociology Mind, 2*(3), 261–271.

Cooper, J. N. (2013). A mixed methods exploratory study of Black male student athletes' experiences at a historically Black university (Dissertation). Athens, GA: The University of Georgia.

Cooper, J. N. (2016). "Focus on the bigger picture": An anti-deficit achievement examination of Black male scholar athletes in science and engineering at a historically White university (HWU). *Whiteness & Education, 1*(2), 109–124.

Cooper, J. N. (2017). Strategic navigation: A comparative study of Black male scholar athletes' experiences at a historically Black college/university (HBCU) and historically White university (HWU). *International Journal of Qualitative Studies in Education, 31*(4), 235–256. doi: 10.1080/09518398.2017.1379617.

Cooper, J. N., & Cooper, J. E. (2015). Success in the shadows: (Counter) narratives of achievement from Black scholar athletes at a historically Black college/university (HBCU). *Journal for the Study of Sports and Athletes in Education, 9*(3), 145–171.

Cooper, J. N., & Hawkins, B. (2014). An anti-deficit perspective on Black male student athletes' educational experiences at a historically Black college/university. *Race, Ethnicity and Education, 19*, 1–30. doi: 10.1080/13613324.2014.946491

Cooper, J. N., Macaulay, C., & Rodriguez, S. H. (2017). Race and resistance: A typology of African American sport activism. *International Review for the Sociology of Sport*, 1–31. DOI: 10.1177/1012690217718170.

Cooper, J. N., Mallery, M., & Macaulay, C. D. T. (forthcoming). African American sport activism and broader social movements. In D. Brown (Ed.). *Passing the ball: Sports in African American life and culture* (pp. 35–51). Jefferson, NC: McFarland & Company.

Curry, T. J. (2017). *The man-not: Race, class, genre, and the dilemmas of Black manhood.* Philadelphia, PA: Temple University Press.

Cuyjet, M. J. (2006). *African American men in college.* San Francisco, CA: Jossey-Bass.

Douglas, T. (2016). *Border crossing brothas: Black males navigating race, place, and complex space.* New York, NY: Peter Lang.

DuBois, W. E. B. (1903/2003). *The souls of Black folk.* Chicago, IL: A. C. McClurg.

Edwards, H. (1969). *The revolt of the Black athlete.* New York, NY: Free Press.

Edwards, H. (1973). *Sociology of sport.* Homewood, IL: Dorsey Press.

Edwards, H. (1980). *The struggle that must be: An autobiography.* New York, NY: Macmillan Publishing.

Edwards, H. (1984). The Black "dumb jock:" An American sports tragedy. *College Board Review,* 131, 8–13.

Edwards, H. (2000). Crisis of black athletes on the eve of the 21st century. *Society, 37*(3), 9–13.

Edwards, H. (2016). *The fourth wave: Black athlete protests in the second decade of the 21st century.* Keynote address at the North American Society for the Sociology of Sport (NASSS) conference in Tampa Bay, Florida.

Eitle, T. M., & Eitle, D. J. (2002). Race, cultural capital, and the educational effects of participation in sports. *Sociology of Education, 75*(2), 123–146.

ETS. (2011). *A strong start: Positioning young Black boys for educational success a statistical profile.* Washington, DC: Educational Testing Service

Fanon, F. (1952/2008). *Black skin, White masks.* New York, NY: Grove Press.

Franklin, R. S., & Resnik, S. (1973). *The political economy of racism.* New York, NY: Holt Rinehart and Winston.

Harper, S. R. (2012). *Black male student success in higher education: A report from the national Black male college achievement study.* Philadelphia, PA: University of Pennsylvania, Center for the Study of Race and Equity in Education.

Harper, S. R., Harris, F. III. (2010). *College men and masculinities: Theory, research, and implications for practice.* San Francisco, CA: Jossey-Bass.

Harper, S. R., & Nichols, A. H. (2008). Are they not all the same?: Racial heterogeneity among Black male undergraduates. *Journal of College Student Development, 49*(3), 199–214.

Harris, O. (1994). Race, sport, and social support. *Sociology of Sport Journal, 11*(1), 40–50.

Harrison, C. K., Martin, B. E., & Fuller, R. (2015). "Eagles don't fly with sparrows": Self-determination theory, African Americna male scholar-athletes and peer group influences on motivation. *The Journal of Negro Education, 84*(1), 80–93.

Harrison, L. Jr., Harrison, C. K., & Moore, L. N. (2002). African American racial identity and sport. *Sport, Education & Society, 7*(2), 121–133.

Hartmann, D. (2000). Rethinking the relationship between sport and race in American culture: Golden ghettos and contested terrain. *Sociology of Sport Journal, 17*(3), 229–253.

Hawkins, B. (1998a). The dominant images of black men in America: The representation of O. J. Simpson. In G. Sailes (Ed.), *African Americans in sport* (pp. 39–52). New Brunswick, NJ: Transaction Publishers.

Hawkins, B. (1998b). The White supremacy continuum of images for Black men. *Journal of African American Men, 3*(3), 7–18.

Hawkins, B. (2010). *The new plantation: Black athletes, college sports, and predominantly White NCAA institutions.* New York, NY: Palgrave-MacMillan.

Hodge, S. R., Burden, J. W., Jr., Robinson, L. E., & Bennett, R. A., III. (2008). Theorizing on the stereotyping of Black male student-athletes: Issues and implications. *Journal for the Study of Sports and Athletes in Education, 2*(2), 203–226.

Howard, T. C. (2014). *Black male(d): Peril and promise in the education of African American males:* New York, NY: Teachers College Press.

Jackson, J. F. L., & Moore, J. L. III. (2006). African American males in education: Endangered or ignored?. *The Teachers College Record, 108*(2), 201–205.

Majors, R., & Billson, J. M. (1992). *Cool pose: The dilemmas of Black manhood in America.* New York, NY: Lexington Books.

Martin, B. E., Harrison, C. K., Stone, J., & Lawrence, S. M. (2010). Athletic voices and academic victories: African American male student-athlete experiences in the Pac-Ten. *Journal of Sport & Social Issues, 34*(2), 131–153.

May, R. A. B. (2008). *Living through the hoop: High school basketball, race, and the American Dream.* New York, NY: New York University Press.

Mutua, A. D. (2006). *Progressive Black masculinities.* New York, NY: Routledge.

Noguera, P. A. (2008). *The trouble with Black boys … and other reflections on race, equity, and the future of public education.* San Francisco, CA: Jossey-Bass.

Oseguera, L. (2010). Success despite the image: How African American male student-athletes endure their academic journey amidst negative characterizations. *Journal of the Study of Sports and Athletes in Education, 4*(3), 297–324.

Parker, L. (2016). *KRS ONE drops mind blowing wisdom—Supreme beings.* Retrieved from https://www.youtube.com/watch?v=pM97HS-HDR4

Polite, F. (2011). Introduction: Elevating and liberating the Black athlete: Harry Edwards as a social activist. In F. G. Polite & B. Hawkins (Eds.), *Sport, race, activism, and social change* (pp. 1–8). San Diego, CA: Cognella.

Powell, S. (2008). *Souled out? How Blacks are winning and losing in sports.* Champaign, IL: Human Kinetics.

Rhoden, W. C. (2006). *40 million dollar slaves: The rise, fall, and redemption of the Black athlete.* New York, NY: Crown Publishing Group.

Sailes, G. (2010). The African American athlete: social myths and stereotypes. In G. Sailes (Ed.), *Modern Sport and The African American Athlete Experience* (pp. 55–68). San Diego, CA: Cognella.

Sellers, R. M. (2000). African American student-athletes: Opportunity or exploitation? In D. A. Brooks & R. Althouse (Eds.), *Racism in college athletics: The African American athlete's experience* (2nd ed., pp. 133–154). Morgantown, WV: Fitness Information Technology, Inc.

Sellers, R. M., Kuperminc, G. P., & Waddell, A. S. (1991). Life experiences of African American student athletes in revenue producing sports: A descriptive empirical analysis. *Academic Athletic Journal,* 21–38.

Singer, J. N. (2015). The miseducation of African American male college athletes. In E. Comeaux (Ed.), *Introduction to intercollegiate athletics* (pp. 193–206). Baltimore, MD: Johns Hopkins University Press.

Singer, J. N., & May, R. A. B. (2010). The career trajectory of a Black male high school basketball player: A social reproduction perspective. *International Review for the Sociology of Sport*, 46(3), 299–314.

Smith, E. (2009). *Race, sport and the American dream* (2nd ed.). Durham, NC: Carolina Academic Press.

Smith, M. P., Clark, L. D., & Harrison, L., Jr. (2014). The historical hypocrisy of the Black student-athlete. *Race, Gender & Class*, 21(1–2), 220–235.

Staples, R. (1978). *Black masculinity*. San Francisco, CA: The Black Scholar Press.

Summers, M. (2004). *Manliness & its discontents: The Black middle class & the transformation of masculinity, 1900–1930*. Chapel Hill, NC: The University of North Carolina Press.

Wiggins, D. K. (2014). "Black athletes in White men's games": Race, sport and American national pastimes. *The International Journal of the History of Sport*, 31(1–2), 181–202.

Wiggins, D. K., & Miller, P. B. (2003). *The unlevel playing field: A documentary history of the African-American experience in sport*. Urbana, IL: University of Illinois Press.

Wood, J. L., & Palmer, R. T. (2014). *Black men in higher education: A guide for ensuring student success*. New York, NY: Routledge.

· 1 ·

A SOCIO-HISTORICAL OVERVIEW OF BLACK MALES' SPORT INVOLVEMENT IN THE UNITED STATES

> If the reader has concluded that there is something "wrong" in sport, one further conclusion is inescapable ... what is "wrong" with sport in America reflects America itself—particularly the relationships between contemporary social, political, and economic realities and this nation's value priorities, its attitudes and its perspectives.
>
> —Edwards (1969, p. 361)

Socio-Historical, Socio-Cultural, and Socio-Political Context for Understanding Black Males' Sport Involvement

Black participation in sport has historically mirrored the broader conditions of race relations in the U.S. society (Cooper, 2012; Edwards, 1969, 1973, 2016; Wiggins, 2014; Wiggins & Miller, 2003). For example, prior to the *Emancipation Proclamation of 1865* and subsequent passage of the 13th, 14th, and 15th amendments, Black participation in organized sport in the U.S. was scarce due to the prevailing racist norms of the antebellum era, which prominently included the enslavement and dehumanization of Blacks via chattel slavery[1] (Wiggins & Miller, 2003). Hunting and horse racing were among the few popular sports, particularly in the South, during the antebellum periods (Wiggins, 2014). During the Reconstruction era (1863–1877), limited opportunities for Blacks to participate in mainstream sports were still commonplace (albeit relatively more access than the previous era). Black male athletes such as Bill Richmond (boxing), Tom Molineuax (boxing), Jack Johnson (boxing), John W. "Bud" Fowler (baseball), Moses Fleetwood Walker (baseball), Weldy Wilberforce Walker (baseball), Marshall "Major" Taylor (cycling), and Isaac Murphy (jockeying) were among the select few who were allowed to compete in White controlled sporting spaces during these eras (Harris, 2000; Stewart, 1996; Wiggins, 2014; Wiggins & Miller, 2003). It is important to recall that during the late 19th and early 20th century Blacks were still largely viewed as property and innately inferior to Whites psychologically, intellectually, emotionally, physically, and spiritually. Thus, their sport participation was primarily driven by Whites' desire to demonstrate their supremacy and control over Blacks either via victories and/or using them for entertainment purposes.

For example, prior to Jack Jackson's famous bouts in the early 1900s against Tommy Burns and Jim "The Great White Hope" Jeffries, widespread media accounts cited that his *innate* cerebral deficiencies, *undisciplined* unorthodox boxing style, and *lazy* work ethic would result in his defeat and confirm White superiority (Stewart, 1996; Wiggins & Miller, 2003). These negative attributes were applied to all Blacks during the early 20th century. Much to the chagrin of these racist commentators and fans, Johnson defeated both Burns and Jeffries decisively in 1908 and 1910, respectively. The latter victory against Jeffries resulted in Johnson earning the title as the first Black heavyweight boxing champion of the world (Stewart, 1996). In spite of these victories, Whites still refused to accept the humanity and excellence of Blacks and their involvement in all sports remained significantly restricted. In fact, Johnson's victory spurred an intense White backlash that coincided with domestic terrorism during the early 20th century against Blacks including widespread lynchings of and violent attacks against Blacks, political disenfranchisement, and a range of other insidious practices indicative of the Jim Crow era in the U.S. (Coates, 2017; Curry, 2017; Stewart, 1996; Wells, 1892, 1997). Along the same lines as the racial discrimination against Johnson in the boxing ring, Blacks were also denied access to mainstream White-controlled baseball, America's pastime, from the early 1900s through 1947 due to racist stereotypes that suggested they did not possess "the requisite skills to play the game" (Wiggins, 2014, p. 185). At the turn of the 20th century, the modern day professional football and basketball leagues had not yet been established

(National Football League (NFL) was founded in 1920 and National Basketball Association (NBA) was established in 1946). Nonetheless, wherever organized sports existed and were controlled by Whites (e.g., youth sport leagues, interscholastic leagues, colleges and universities, semi-professional teams, professional teams with various league structures, etc.) Blacks were either outright excluded or nominally included (Harris, 2000).

Even though, a select few talented Black male athletes experienced noteworthy levels of success, their performances were marginalized by the dominant culture and disregarded as illegitimate in order to fit within the White racial framing of the era (Feagin, Vera, & Batur, 2000). In fact, it was during the early 1900s coupled with pseudo-scientific racist theories such as Social Darwinism that ideas of Black innate athletic superiority and intellectual inferiority (also referred to as biological determinism) began to surface as an explanation for their prowess in sport to discredit their hard work, cognitive abilities, and access to resources (or lack thereof) (Edward, 1973; Hodge, Harrison, Burden, & Dixson, 2008; Sailes, 2010; Wiggins, 2014). Remember prior to the turn of the 20th century, Blacks were deemed as inferior holistically to the extent that they were viewed and treated as less than humans (Curry, 2017; Smedley & Smedley, 2005). Explanations such as the mandingo theory (asserts physical prowess of African Americans was based on selective breeding during slavery), survival of the fittest theory (idea purporting only the strongest Africans survived through the middle passage during the transatlantic slave trade), and genetic theory (belief Africans Americans possess more white fast twitch muscle fibers than Whites) were all rooted in racist myths and promulgated via cultural tropes and mass media (Sailes, 2010). Notwithstanding, these theories have long since been debunked as the historical and anthropological origins of race indicate these categorizations are social constructions and biological myths as opposed being scientific facts (Coakley, 2017; Edwards, 1973; Sage, 1998; Smedley & Smedley, 2005).

Moreover, it has yet to be proven how isolated genetic markers (especially given the widespread miscegenation intra- and inter-nationally throughout human existence) could explain athletic ability without taking into account environmental, socio-structural, and cultural factors. Nonetheless, the rationale for promoting these beliefs is to suggest that if social outcomes can be explained by genetic predispositions, then racialized hierarchies are legitimatized as natural and divine as opposed to being socially constructed and oppressive (see Hawkins (1998a) for an extended discussion on ideological hegemony). For example, insidious stereotypes stigmatizing Black males as savages, animalistic, violent, hypersexual, deviant, and criminal have been used to justify their enslavement, incarceration, and genocide (Alexander, 2012; Curry, 2017; DuBois, 1903/2003; Woodson, 1933/1990). More specific to sport, the impetus of Black male participation was a result of an inequitable interest convergence of whereby Whites' economic interests and entertainment benefits superseded Blacks' their personal well-being, professional gains, and collective racial uplift (Harris, 2000; Wiggins & Miller, 2003). Similar to the chattel slavery arrangements, sport involved an unequal power dynamic where Black bodies and talents were exploited for White capitalist gains (Edwards, 1969, 1973, 1980, 2000, 2016; Hawkins, 2010; Rhoden, 2006; Smith, 2009). In many instances, Black male athletes were denied ownership and control of their labor and suffered subsequent health issues including untimely deaths as a byproduct of encountering perpetual forms of racism and discrimination throughout their lives (Cooper, Macaulay, & Rodriguez, 2017; Edwards, 1980; Wiggins & Miller, 2003). Hence, the U.S. society founded upon and structured by WRC reinforced oppressive ideological aims through various social institutions (policies and practices) including sport.

Not ironically and unfortunately, this same arrangement has been reproduced, albeit in an evolved form, through the early part of the 21st century. Wiggins (2014) described one of the troubling aspects of this reality:

> This pattern, in which athletically gifted blacks were able to exhibit their physical skills and realise material benefits, yet were ultimately never able to exert any significant individual or institutional control over the activities they participated in, has continued to the present day ... (p.182).

In contrast to the majority of their Black peers who were not involved in sport, these select Black male athletes experienced social mobility and in some instances were able to earn their freedom from slavery (i.e., Austin Curtis (horseracing)) (Wiggins, 2014). Thus, these circumstances initiated an affinity for sport participation within the Black community in a White-dominated U.S. society. Excelling in sport provided access to previously denied privileges such as access to travel, improved lodging conditions, and food accommodations (Wiggins, 2014). Sport participation, as a *means to achieve some resemblance of humanity and citizenship*, became a mesmerizing prize for Black males during the late 19th and early 20th centuries particularly in comparison to their normalized oppression.

A majority of Blacks during the turn of the 20th century were relegated to intense labor conditions in both the South (i.e., sharecropping) and North (i.e., factory work) albeit to varying extents (Hine, Hine, & Harrold, 2006). More specifically for Black males, the popularity of boxing in the early 20th century illustrated the strong connection between sport and masculinity (Wiggins & Miller, 2003). Since a majority of these sporting opportunities were limited to males, this psychological attachment with Black masculinity is uniquely rooted. The success of Black male athlete pioneers also symbolized racial and cultural pride, which intensified the unique psycho-social relationship between Blackness/racial identity, masculinity/gender identity, sport/athletic identity, and social advancement that remains prevalent in the 21st century (figuratively and literally) (Andrews, 2001; Boyd, 2003; Edwards, 1969, 1973; Harrison, Harrison, & Moore, 2002; Hodge, Burden, Robinson, & Bennett, 2008; Powell, 2008; Rhoden, 2006; Wiggins & Miller, 2003).

In terms of the broader Black community, Wiggins and Miller (2003) described the significance of these sporting spaces when referencing how they "… created a sense of shared values and aspirations; it helped shape a spirit of community" (p. 2). For example, the popularity of the Black baseball during the early to mid-1900s provided a safe space for Black males to express their masculinity and creativity as well as for Black social engagement, entertainment, and sense of belonging in an otherwise racially hostile society.[2] Along the same lines, the famous HBCU football classics, which began in 1892 with the Turkey Day Classic game between Alabama State College (now University) and Tuskegee Institute (now University) in Montgomery, Alabama, attracted thousands of Blacks throughout the South. These classics and other HBCU athletic contests were accompanied by culturally empowering social events and pageantry (Cooper, Cavil, & Cheeks, 2014). The display of Black male athletic prowess was among the centerpieces of these broader socio-cultural events (Cavil, 2015). Another benefit of these sporting organizations and spaces was the opportunity for Blacks to be involved on multiple levels including as participants, coaches, managers, owners, officials, teachers, statisticians, trainers, journalists, commentators, and historians (Henderson, 1939; Lomax, 2003, 2014; Wiggins & Miller, 2003). As such, Black cultural identities, including the connection between masculinity and sport, was constructed within the confines of the socio-structural realities and arrangements in a U.S. society founded upon and structured by WRC.

The Era of Muscular Assimilationism
In and Through Sport

Between the Reconstruction era (1863–1877) through the early 1900s, African Americans adopted a philosophy of muscular assimilationism (Henderson,

1939), which purported that excellence in sport could serve as a means to demonstrate to Whites (primarily those who controlled mainstream institutions) Black self-worth and determination; thus, signifying that Blacks were worthy of equal and fair treatment in all aspects of U.S. society. This idea was also popularly promulgated by emerging groups of the era such as the National Association for the Advancement of Colored People (NAACP) and National Urban League (NUL), which were founded in 1909 and 1910, respectively (Cooper, Macaulay, & Rodriguez, 2017; Cooper, Mallery, & Macaulay, forthcoming; Miller, 1995; Wiggins & Miller, 2003). Wiggins and Miller (2003) described how "muscular assimilationism was a strategy, just as parallel institutions were a necessity—until the day, yet to come, when black Americans could compete with whites on a level playing field" (p. 87). It was during this time when Black controlled organizations such as the Negro Leagues (baseball), HBCU athletic conferences, New York Renaissance Five (also known as the Harlem Rens; basketball), Harlem Globetrotters (basketball), American Tennis Association (ATA), United Golfers Association (UGA), Colored Speedway Association (CSA), and National Negro Bowling Association (NNBA) were established (Cooper et al., 2014; Lomax, 2003, 2014; Wiggins, 2014; Wiggins & Miller, 2003).

As previously mentioned, a majority of Whites in the U.S. endorsed racist pseudoscience ideas regarding the innate inferiority (both intellectually and physically) of Blacks (Hine et al., 2006; Stewart, 1996). As a result, muscular assimilationism during this period was a form of resistance against prevailing White racist norms. Participation in mainstream U.S. sports was a mechanism to shift cultural attitudes and public policies towards human and civil rights for Blacks. These same sentiments were expressed by their Black successors throughout the 20th and early 21st centuries (i.e., Civil Rights activists-athletes) (Cooper, Macaulay, & Rodriguez, 2017; Cooper, Mallery, & Macaulay, forthcoming; Edwards, 2016; Wiggins & Miller, 2003). Exceptional Black male athletes and intellectuals such as Paul Robeson (football), William Henry Lewis (football), Duke Slater (football), Jerome "Brud" Holland (football), and Fritz Pollard (football) challenged racist norms both within and beyond sporting spaces (Smith, Clark, & Harrison, 2014).

Furthermore, the achievements of renowned Black male athletes such as Jesse Owens (track and field) and Joe Louis (boxing) in their respective arenas on the international stage signified broader cultural victories for the Black race in the U.S. as well as globally (Edwards, 2016; Rhoden, 2006). Their success symbolically underscored the dignity, persistence, and prowess of Blacks in the face of widespread racism and discrimination and functioned as an extension of the larger call for social justice and equality. For example, Jesse Owens' four gold medals at the 1936 Olympics in Berlin, Germany debunked Hitler's claims of Aryan superiority. Similarly, Joe Louis' victories over Primo Carnera of Argentina in 1935 and Max Schmeling of Germany in 1938 were emblematic of U.S. triumph over Italian fascism and German Nazism while also being indicative of Black strength and valor (Rhoden, 2006; Wiggins & Miller, 2003). In concert with previous Black male athletic champions such as Jack Johnson and Isaac Murphy, the success of Owens and Louis revealed the potential and promise of Blacks when given the opportunity to compete on a leveled playing field (Wiggins & Miller, 2003).

Later in 1947, Jackie Robinson famously broke Major League Baseball's (MLB) color barrier when he signed with the Brooklyn Dodgers. This event represented Black racial progress in terms of being assimilated (as opposed to integrated – see Cooper et al. (2014) for an extended discussion on this distinction) into mainstream U.S. culture. It is also important to note this significant sporting event occurred nearly a decade before the landmark *Brown v. Board of Education of Topeka* (1954) decision, which illegalized racial segregation in public educational institutions and thus sport served as a vital leverage tool for Blacks' pursuit of civil liberties within the U.S. Within a few years after Jackie Robinson's assimilation into MLB, all major professional sports followed suit by desegregating their leagues and by the 1970s all major intercollegiate athletic conferences had become void of racial segregation in terms of participation access by rule (Harris, 2000).

The Rise and Decline of Cultural Nationalism In and Through Sport

During the 1960s, a large number of Black athletes shifted from the ideology of muscular assimilationism towards cultural nationalism (Bass, 2002; Edwards, 1969, 2016; Hartmann, 1996, 2000; Wiggins & Miller, 2003). In conjunction with the broader Civil Rights Movement, Black athletes, who were recently being assimilated into mainstream U.S. sports at the intercollegiate and professional levels, began to utilize their respective platforms to increase awareness of social injustices (Harris, 2000; Wiggins, 2000). Similar to their same race peers in non-sporting spaces and athlete predecessors who competed in interracial spaces (i.e., barnstorming Negro Leagues and Black basketball teams such as the Harlem Rens), Black athletes in this era experienced wide-spread racial discrimination. Despite the assumption that assimilation would lead to positive race relations, Black athletes learned personal attitudes and deep seated racist beliefs would take more time to change than the passage of the Civil Rights laws of this era. Carmichael (1971/2007) captured the post-Civil Rights era sentiment among Blacks in the U.S., including activist ath-letes, when he said: "integration is a subterfuge for the maintenance of white supremacy" (p. 23). He further explained the sophisticated tactics of WRC in this era when he said: "You can integrate communities, but you assimilate individuals" (Carmichael, 1971/2007, p. 39).

Tokenistic representation and nominal changes in laws did not fully address racial inequalities stemming from capitalism, racism, imperialism, and militarism. More importantly, "integration" or more properly described as assimilation reinforced the notion that Blacks were inferior and needed to be more like Whites in order to be deemed as civilized and worthy of human dignity and rights (Carmichael, 1971/2007). As a result of societal condi-tions during this time, Black masculinity in and through sport was keenly con-nected to socio-political and socio-cultural consciousness and engagement (Cooper, Macaulay, & Rodriguez, 2017; Edwards, 1969, 1980, 2016). This historic period was the first time in U.S. history where a critical mass of Black males participating in racially mixed sporting environments were outspoken about challenging the dominant racist social order. Similar to the early 1900s, Black masculinity was deeply connected to sport whereby prowess and self-worth were pursued. However, in contrast to the early 1900s, a collective of Black male athletes, along with their same race female counterparts, no longer felt compelled to acquiesce to the status quo. In other words, their racial and gender identities in relation to sport were not disconnected from the plight of the broader Black community. This socio-historical context is pivotal for understanding the modern day intersections of race, gender, sport, politics, economics, law, and education where identities collide with social systems and sociological realities.

Post-1960s, Black athlete activism began to decline for several reasons. First, prior to and during the Civil Rights era, there was not a consensus among the Black community in the U.S. regarding what constituted prog-ress (i.e., assimilation or integration vs. separatism) and often the less dis-ruptive conformist approaches were pursued for various reasons (e.g., lack of state and institutional control, economic wealth, adequate military/ protective forces, etc.). The distinction between the tactics of early Civil

Rights Movement and the Student Non-Violent Coordinating Committee (SNCC) led by Dr. Martin Luther King, Jr. compared to the tenor of the Nation of Islam led by Malcolm X (also supported by Muhammad Ali) along with the newly formed Black Panther Party initially started by Stokely Carmichael (Kwame Ture) and later led by Huey P. Newton and Bobby Seale signified the sharp divide in the Black community concerning pacifist negotiations with the White power structure versus direct confrontation with and deconstruction of it via political, economic, cultural, and militaristic means (Hine, Hine, & Harrold, 2006). This divide did not start in the 1960s and in fact dates back on U.S. soil at least to the 17th century when all Blacks who were enslaved did not directly challenge the status quo with counter-violence compared to individuals like Nat Turner and those of a similar mind who confronted their oppressors with revolutionary violence (Smith, 1994; Stewart, 1996).

This schism continued throughout the early 1900s with the contrasting perspectives articulated by race leaders such as William Edward Burghardt (W. E. B.) DuBois, Booker Taliaferro (T.) Washington, and Marcus Mosiah Garvey regarding whether the cultivation of the talented tenth through the intellectual efforts for racial progress (DuBois) or an industrial, agricultural, and vocational based education that fostered self-determination and assimilation (Washington) or a Pan-African cultural nationalist and separatist approach (Garvey) was the best pathway to Black liberation and empowerment (DuBois, 1903/2003; Hine, Hine, & Harrold, 2006; Woodson, 1933/1990). More specific to Black male athletes, the critical views of U.S. capitalism and militarism expressed by activists such as Paul Robeson (who was associated with the Communist Party during the early 1900s) and Muhammad Ali of the Nation of Islam in 1960s starkly differed from the American assimilationist stances of Jesse Owens, Joe Louis, and Jackie Robinson (later in Robinson's life he became more outwardly critical of the American status quo). As such, the perspectives on the means and ends by which racial progress can and should be attained have historically been (and continue to be) complex and not monolithic. Consequently, limited synchronous counter-hegemonic efforts within and across the race both in the U.S. and globally have been a major inhibitor to collective progress (Carmichael, 1971/2007; Fanon, 1952/2008). Since sport was and remains a microcosm of society, Black athletes during and after the 1960s, similar to their peers in the broader U.S. society, faced the challenge of establishing and sustaining long-term coordinated efforts for the deconstruction of WRC.

Another reason for the decline of Black athlete activism during the 1970s was the popular illusion that Civil Rights legislations would eliminate the race problem in the U.S. (Bell, 1980, 1992; Harris, 1993). In conjunction with this illusion, strategic adjustments by White controlled sport organizations and corporate sponsors diffused the connectivity between Blacks across different socioeconomic statuses, educational levels, occupations, political affiliations, religious identifications, etc. (Bass, 2002; Edwards, 2016; Hartmann, 2000). In particular, these entities utilized the nominal representation of Black athletes as figure heads for their own agendas grounded in WRC. This arrangement reflected the idea that as long as Black athletes were apolitical and silent on systemic inequalities and injustices impacting the Black community (e.g., Orenthal James (O. J.) Simpson, Carl Lewis, Earvin "Magic" Johnson, Bo Jackson, Michael Jordan, and Tiger Woods) they would be rewarded financially and socially in a society founded upon and structured by WRC (Bass, 2002; Cooper, Macaulay, & Rodriguez, 2017; Hartmann, 1996; Hawkins, 1998b; Rhoden, 2006). Nearly 25 years after Jackie Robinson broke the color barrier in MLB in 1947, the 1970s marked a significant turning point in the history of American sport whereby previous Black male labor, aesthetic, and prowess was now being targeted for commodification in the sporting realm at unprecedented levels (Edwards, 1980; Leonard & King, 2012; Powell, 2008; Rhoden, 2006). Several talented Black male athletes' success shifted this discourse:

(a) In 1961, Ernie Davis of Syracuse University became the first African American to win the coveted Heisman Trophy.

(b) In 1966, Texas Western (now the University of Texas-El Paso) men's basketball team became the first all-Black starting five at a HWI to win a National Collegiate Athletic Association (NCAA) championship against the all-White University of Kentucky Wildcats led by Hall of Fame coach Adolph Rupp.

(c) In 1968, O. J. Simpson of the University of Southern California won the Heisman Trophy and later went on to have a Hall of Fame career in the NFL from 1969–1979 and became the symbol for the apolitical capitalist athlete with his major endorsement deals (i.e., famous Hertz Rent-A-Car commercials in the mid to late 1970s).

(d) In 1970, Sam "Bam" Cunningham of the University of Southern California displayed his athletic prowess by rushing for over 135 yards and scoring two touchdowns against the dominant all-White University of Alabama football team led by Hall of Fame coach Paul "Bear" Bryant.

(e) In 1970, 135 athletes from 31 HBCUs were selected in the NFL.

(f) In 1979, the world witnessed the rise of Earvin "Magic" Johnson from Michigan State University who won the NCAA championship (highest rated televised game in college basketball history) and later with the Showtime Los Angeles Lakers in the 1980s against his White arch rival Larry Bird, which undoubtedly elevated the NBA into an unprecedented economic and brand marketing stratosphere.

(g) In 1983, Michael Jordan of the University of North Carolina made the game-winning shot to lead his Tar Heel men's basketball team to the NCAA championship over John Thompson's Georgetown Hoyas led by Hall of Fame coach John Thompson II and future Hall of Fame player Patrick Ewing. Following this hallmark shot, Michael Jordan later went to become arguably the greatest basketball player in the history of the game by winning six NBA championships in the 1990s, playing on the legendary U.S. Olympic Dream Team who won the gold medal in 1992 in Barcelona Spain, securing the highest Nike shoe endorsement deal in the 1980s, and later became the first Black athlete billionaire and first Black majority owner of a mainstream professional franchise (Andrews, 2001; Cooper et al., 2014; Hodge, Collins, & Bennett, 2013; Leonard & King, 2012; Powell, 2008; Rhoden, 2006; Wiggins & Miller, 2003).

Collectively, these accomplishments mirrored efforts in the broader society in the post-Civil Rights era in terms of increasing Black access to mainstream U.S. culture via assimilation and had a profound impact on the sport industry's relationship with Black athletes from the 1970s into the early 21st century (Cooper, Macaulay, & Rodriguez, 2017; Edwards, 2016).

It was during this era when the presence of lucrative televised college and professional games intensified race-based stereotypic beliefs among Black males, the Black community, and the American public at large (Hodge, Burden, Robinson, & Bennett, 2008). Countless images of Black male athletes celebrating championships and living seemingly luxurious care free lifestyles stood in stark contrast to the harsh realities facing a majority of Blacks in the U.S. (Edwards, 1969, 1980, 2000, 2016). Thus, the historical legacy of sport serving as a space where Black masculinity is revered while simultaneously White racist stereotypes and power arrangements remain intact persists today in the early 21st century. As previously noted, the problematic intersection between Black masculinity being intertwined with White-sanctioned sporting spaces reproduces and exacerbates insidious psychological, social, educational, and economic outcomes for many Black male athletes and the broader Black community. The promulgation of images of a minute number of Black males who excel in sports and earn exorbitant salaries (even though often times temporarily) functions as a social engineering tool to preserve the dominant racist social order in a tacit yet seemingly innocuous manner (also referred to ideological hegemony and discussed in greater detail later in this chapter) (Hawkins, 1998b; Sage, 1998; Sage & Eitzen, 2013). The afore-mentioned historical coverage provides a necessary context for understanding how and why sport participation and success are deeply interconnected with psychological, cultural, political, legal, social, educational, and economic *conditions that precede and influence* Black male athletes' perceptions, behaviors, and processes. As such, *Black males have been psychologically, socially, physically, and economically conditioned for nearly a century and a half to view sport as a panacea for gaining human dignity, positive identity affirmation (particularly racially and masculinity wise), and economic mobility* (Cooper, 2012; Cooper et al., 2014; Cooper, Macaulay, & Rodriguez, 2017; Edwards, 1969, 1973, 1984, 2000; Hawkins, 2010; Howard, 2014; Lomax, 2003, 2014; May, 2008; Powell, 2008; Rhoden, 2006; Smith, 2009). Understanding the historical origins of this phenomenon facilitate the cultivation of effective counter-actions for the holistic development of positive Black masculinities in and through sport and education as well as collective racial uplift for the broader Black community.

Performative Black Masculinities In and Through Sport

In the critically acclaimed book, *Cool Pose: The Dilemmas of Black Manhood in America*, Majors and Billson (1992) conceptualized prevalent mentalities and behaviors among Black males in response to oppressive conditions in the U.S. that deprive them of traditional characteristics of masculine identity (e.g., breadwinner, provider, protector, etc.). Majors and Billson (1992) describe the *cool pose* as "a ritualized form of masculinity that entails behaviors, scripts, physical posturing, impression management and carefully crafted performances that deliver a single, critical message: pride, strength, and control" (p. 4). In a capitalistic society where wealth acquisition is the primary marker of power and control, *Black males as a collective are systematically deprived of obtaining this type of power*. Thus, engaging in behaviors that are deemed "cool" serve as accessible coping mechanisms for Black males. Along the same lines, in an earlier analysis, Staples (1982) described this responsive behavior among Black males as the "manhood mystique" whereby neoliberal conceptions of success (e.g., individualism, materialism, etc.) combined with the realities and feelings of "alienation, cynicism, and hopelessness" are more intensely internalized among disadvantaged groups such as Black males who face the most insurmountable odds of attaining this type of status through legal and socially acceptable means (p. 144). More specifically, sports and music (i.e., Hip-Hop) are central sources of Black masculine expression because they require few resources, provide a space where Blackness is uniquely celebrated, place a premium on improvisation, and offer real and perceived opportunities for increased social status and economic mobility (Boyd, 2003).

Facing said conditions many impressionable young Black males perceive and personify manhood in terms of being heterosexual, sexually promiscuous, aggressive, knowledgeable about how to acquire money by any means necessary (legally or illegally), and confident particularly when confronted with challenging situations (May, 2008). Black males who grow up in certain environments such those with poverty and/or with similar negative pressures (e.g., violence, drug usage, vandalism, etc.) are particularly susceptible to reproducing this type of masculinity where "drug-dealing "hustlas" and slam-dunking "hoopas"" are perceived as role models possessing control and influence (May, 2008, p. 128). In contrast, White males in a society founded upon and structured by WRC are able to secure positive identity affirmation via educational attainment or at a minimum status enhancement and protection as a result of their race, gender, class, occupational mobility, and/or income procurement. (Harris, 1993; Majors & Billson, 1992). Hence, the construction of masculinity for Black males in the U.S., who by no fault of their own are forced to encounter systemic oppression, is heavily shaped by unfavorable sociostructural conditions (e.g., environmental, educational, psychological, social, economic, political, legal, health, etc.).

Given limited access to opportunities for upward mobility in society more broadly, sports have been one of the few pathways where Black males have been able to express their masculinity and be celebrated.[3] In sports, Black masculinity continues to be expressed via the *Black aesthetic* (George, 1992). In his book titled, *Elevating the Game: Black Men in Basketball*, George (1992) explained how the uniqueness, resonance, and marketability of the *Black aesthetic* as cultural expressions in style, music, art, and sport are rooted in Black culture and fetishized and commodified by mainstream society. Dating back to the spiritual hymns and dances of the antebellum era through the Harlem

Renaissance in 1920s to the Motown era in 1950s and 1960s to the emergence of Hip-Hop in the 1980s, Blacks have used distinct forms of expression as a means of resistance against White normative values and ways of thinking (Boyd, 2003; George, 1992; Lomax, 2003, 2014; Powell, 2008; Rhoden, 2006; Wiggins & Miller, 2003). Colorful attire, rhythmic dances, soulful music (e.g., Gospel, rhythm and blues (R&B), jazz, hip-hop, etc.) were all birthed out of the "souls of Black folks" (Dubois, 1903/2003) as a means to validate their humanity in an oppressive U.S. society as well as to maintain a level of connectivity to their African cultural heritages. Given their historic exclusion and tokenistic inclusion in mainstream U.S. sports prior to the mid-20th century, the limited number of Blacks who were granted access to sport utilized their agency to not only display their athletic prowess, but also to disrupt White hegemonic norms through their activation of the *Black aesthetic* (also referred to as agentic resistance – see Cooper, Mallery, and Macaulay, forthcoming).

An example of this type Black masculine expression is reflected in the life of Jack Johnson, the first Black heavyweight boxing champion in the U.S. Beyond his dominance in the ring, Johnson possessed an unorthodox boxing style, a boisterous personality, unflappable confidence, and wore flamboyant attire outside of the ring (Rhoden, 2006). Collectively, these characteristics and behaviors challenged the White dominant status quo that positioned Black males as sambos who primarily sought to please the interests of Whites with little to no desire to challenge their subordinate status or exhibit any individual thinking beyond prescribed racist stereotypes (Hawkins, 1998a). Another example of the *Black aesthetic* is found in the legendary Black baseball teams of the late 1800s and early 1900s (Lomax, 2003). One of the unique aspects of these Black baseball teams (which later evolved with the creation of the Negro Leagues in the early 1900s) was their entertaining brand of baseball, which involved animated displays of athleticism and verbal engagement with opposing teams and fans (Lomax, 2003). This type of exuberant expression is more commonly referred to as a trash talking or jockeying in the modern era (Boyd, 2003; George, 1992; Leonard & King, 2012). More recent examples of the *Black aesthetic* include the legendary Michael Jordan and his acrobatic style of play on the basketball court, innovative and widely popular shoes, and longer and baggier shorts which he began wearing in the early 1990s; the famous Michigan Fab Five black socks and baggy shorts in the early 1990s; Allen Iverson's iconic braids, tattoos, hip-hop attire, personal swag, relentless playing style, and defiant persona as well as numerous celebratory dances, styles of play, and forms of communication performed by Black athletes across all levels of sport and entertainment.

Consequently, the popular appeal of the *cool pose* and *Black aesthetic* has been commodified by nearly every facet of the entertainment industry (also referred as Blaxploitation) and led to increased global consumption of music (Hip-Hop, Jazz, and R&B specifically and a notable ripple influence on genres such as Pop) as well as of sports such as basketball, football, and track and field (Andrews, 2001; Boyd, 2003; George, 1992; Leonard & King, 2012; Powell, 2008; Rhoden, 2006). In connection to the historical context offered earlier in this chapter, Edwards (1973) outlined the sociological apparatus that funnels Black males into the sport and entertainment industry:

> In American society, black people are relegated, as a consequence of the social and political realities symbolized by the phenotypical role and status signs of race, to the lowest priority in terms of having access to the full range of alternative means to obtaining goods and services ... Hence, a situation arises wherein whites, being the dominant group in the society, have greater potential access to all means of achieving valuables—prestige, wealth, feelings of self-adequacy, and so forth. Blacks, on the other hand, are channeled by racism and discrimination in the general society and by a heightened value on sports participation in the black subculture, into the one or two prestige endeavors known to be open to them—sports, and to a lesser degree, other forms of entertainment, particularly music. (p. 201)

The *Black aesthetic* and the *cool pose* involve the performative nature of being "charismatic, suave, debonair, and entertaining" (Majors & Billson, 1992, p. 2). Unfortunately, for far too long Black progress in sport has been measured by participation and accolades (referred to as illusionary success – discussed in greater detail in Chapter 4), while the overarching racial power structure that exploits them remains intact (Edwards, 1969, 1980, 2000; Hawkins, 2010; Wiggins, 2014).

The intersection of limited paths for economic mobility and masculine ideals in society founded upon and structured by WRC consequently complicate the healthy development of Black masculinities. For example, Messner (1990) found that White males from higher status backgrounds were more like to make conscious decisions to focus on career goals aside from sport during high school. In contrast, for males from lower status backgrounds including Minority males, sports was found to be the only means by which positive masculine status could be attained. From this analysis, the author concluded that "the choice to pursue or not to pursue an athletic career is explicable as an individual's rational assessment of the available means to achieve a respected masculine identity" (Messner, 1990, p. 106). Hence, the convergence of Black males' racial, gender, and athletic identities results in what Brown (2016) described as the "Blathlete" phenomenon. Although, this convergence can yield positive benefits such as those associated with the athletic manifest destiny model (Coakley, 2017), it more often contributes to identity foreclosure and holistic underdevelopment due to the myopic socialization of viewing positive racial and masculine identities as only being accessible through sport participation and performance. As a result, once one's athletic identity and career begin to decline so too does their sense of self, which leads to maladaptive psychological and social processes (Beamon, 2008, 2010, 2012; Edwards, 1984, 2000; Northcutt, 2013). Hence, any examination of Black masculinities in and through sport must take into account sociological and ecological factors.

Ideological Hegemony and Mass Mediated Constructions of Black Masculinities In and Through Sport

Ideological or cultural hegemony refers to the maintenance and normalization of inequitable arrangements and exploitative structures within capitalist state relations (Gramsci, 1971, 1990). This ideological hegemony is institutionalized through various mechanisms such as mass media propaganda, political and economic control, educational systems, and violence to name a few. Gramsci's (1971, 1990) conception of ideological or cultural hegemony has been applied to the structure and function of sport in capitalist societies particularly in regards to its role as ideological outposts for the masses (Coakley, 2017; Sage, 1998). Sage (1998) offered a cogent description of how sport is embedded in the hegemonic social order in societies such as the U.S.:

> [M]odern sport, rather than being merely a diversionary entertainment, is considered to be an important cultural practice upon which dominant ideologies are constructed, maintained, and reproduced; sport, thus plays a broad social reproductive role in American society. (p. 30)

As it pertains to U.S. sporting practices, these spaces often reinforce prevailing hegemonic ideologies related to race (White racism), gender (patriarchy), and class (capitalism/classism). Citing Gramsci's seminal work (1971, 1990), Hawkins (1998a) explained how ideological hegemony in sport impacts Black male athletes. The appeal of the *cool pose* and *Black aesthetic* has been so lucrative that numerous domestic and international corporate sponsors have appropriated Black cultural assets (also referred to as swag) for the purpose of increasing their profits (e.g., Nike, major record label companies, mainstream clothing lines such as Polo, Google, Apple, major television networks, etc.) (Andrews,

2001; Boyd, 2003; Leonard, 2010; Leonard & King, 2012). Despite constituting a majority of the participants in the multi-billion dollar professional football and basketball leagues in the U.S., nearly all of these sport franchises, corporate partners, and governmental entities are owned and controlled by Whites (Cooper, 2012; Rhoden, 2006). Even worse, Black males' participation and success in sport has had little impact on eliminating the systemic oppression facing Black people as a collective in the U.S. and in many ways (both subtle and overt) has strengthened and validated WRC (Edwards, 1980, 2000).

In addition to being commodified and exploited, another consequence of the Black male *cool pose* and *aesthetic* within WRC ideological hegemonic contexts is the problematic association between these performative masculinities and maladaptive behaviors such as academic disengagement, substance abuse, criminal activities, and a range of other actions detrimental to the Black community at large (Majors & Billson, 1992; May, 2008). Unfortunately, these behaviors and trends undergird the central discourse of Black male athletes as well (Hawkins, 1998a, 1998b; Leonard, 2006, 2010; Leonard & King, 2012). Hawkins (1998a) explained the historical origins of stereotypical images of Black males and their function within the U.S. society:

> ... black heterosexual masculinity has been strategically defined and black men have conveniently had their identities pre-arranged for them ... They are based upon certain historical roles of the sambo and the brute nigger that were ascribed to black men to maintain the social order during the ante-bellum and post-ante-bellum periods. This safeguarding of the public order is continued today in the representation of black men in the mass media. (p. 39)

These simplistic and generalized labels do not reflect the complexity of Black males' personalities and idiosyncrasies and even more disturbingly they are contrived to justify the oppressive aims of WRC. Relatedly, Howard (2014) noted how Black males are subjected to the stereotypes of being anti-intellectual, hypersexual, criminally inclined, and/or a pimp or street hustler. Therefore, *societal conditions foster the congruency between such labels and observable life outcomes* (e.g., proliferation of criminal images along with concurrent environmental and economic violence, racist laws, and enforcement against Blacks males that lead to their disproportionate incarceration and death, underrepresentation in gifted programs and overrepresentation in special education, disparate suspension and expulsion rates along with widespread misdiagnoses of certain psychological disorders, increased likelihood of experiencing sub-standard P-12 educational experiences and resources, etc.) *as opposed to the fallacious assertions attributing these realities to genetic predispositions or solely individual agency* (Cooper, 2012; ETS, 2011; Howard, 2014; Noguera, 2008). As previously noted, Black males' attraction to sport is not an isolated phenomenon, but rather interconnected to their access (or lack thereof) to positive identity validation and upward mobility opportunities in a society founded upon and structured by WRC. In other words, the institution and structure of sport as it relates to Black masculinities remains true to its ideological hegemonic purpose, which was and remains to *control, surveillance, commodify, exploit,* and *holistically under develop* Black males (Cooper, 2012; Cooper, Macaulay, & Rodriguez, 2017; Cooper, Mallery, & Macaulay, forthcoming; Curry, 2017; Edwards, 1969, 1980, 2000, 2016; Rhoden, 2006).

Moreover, within the gendered racist continuum, Black males are positioned as either harmless threats who are content with being subordinate to Whites (sambo) or imminent threats to the dominant social order who must be tamed, controlled, and/or eliminated if necessary (brute) (Hawkins, 1998a, 1998a). Historically, Black male athletes such as Joe Louis, Jesse Owens, Jackie Robinson, O. J. Simpson, and Michael Jordan were viewed as sambos and Jack Johnson, Paul Robeson, Muhammad Ali, Jim Brown, and Mike Tyson were labeled as brutes (Hawkins, 1998a; Leonard & King, 2012). Hawkins (1998a) further explained how the concurrent prevalence of Blacks in the prison industrial complex (PIC) along with their overrepresentation on NFL and NBA teams is not by happenstance. He argues this intentional arrangement is a direct result of the increased privatization of prisons and sport organizations in the U.S., which fulfills capitalist aims and serves as an effort to preserve WRC ideological hegemony (Hawkins, 1998a). Similar critiques are abound in the literature on Black male athletes and highlight the damaging effects of White neoliberalism on their ability to acquire healthy masculinities (Cooper, 2012, 2016a; Edwards, 1969, 1973, 1980, 2000; Hartmann, 2000; Leonard, 2006, 2010; Leonard & King, 2012; May, 2008; Sage, 1998). Understanding the interplay between dominant ideologies, societal structures, internalized beliefs and attitudes, and lived experiences is critical for addressing the problems of Black males' holistic underdevelopment.

White Gazes with Phobic and Erotic Obsessions: Connections to Black Masculinities In and Through Sport

In another text germane to the current analysis, in his book titled, *The Man-Not: Race, Class, Genre, and the Dilemmas of Black Manhood,* Curry (2017) offers an in-depth ethnological analysis of how Black males have been historically and systematically denied access to traditional rights and privileges associated with White masculinity. In contrast to dominant hegemonic and feminist epistemologies, Curry (2017) contends Black males as well as males from other subordinated groups represent the largest threat to WRC and consequently they are the most targeted, disadvantaged, and oppressed groups in societies grounded in these oppressive ideologies. Rather than being aspiring patriarchs or benefitting from patriarchal norms as asserted in feminist literatures, Curry (2017) highlights the frequency by which Black males have been lynched, castrated, raped, murdered, incarcerated, mutilated, oppressed, and dehumanized to illustrate the extent White males along with their White female accomplices are willing to go to preserve their power. Instead of seeking to be like their oppressors, he argues Black males have always possessed different ideals of masculinities rooted in Black and African Diasporic cultural foundations (Curry, 2017).

In regards to Whites, Curry (2017) conceptualizes their violent and domineering actions as an expression of a deeper "phobic obsession" of the Black male body particularly the phallus (p. 147). Boyd (2003) echoes this sentiment when he said: "Black culture has always been positioned between the poles of fear and entertainment in its relationship to the White mainstream ... controlled by the dominant White gaze ..." (p. 14). These analyses reinforce Hawkins' (1998a, 1998b) juxtaposition of the sambo and brute images attributed to Black males including athletes. Related to modern day sport, this White gaze is reflected in the fact that during the 2016–2017 season, 59, 942 football and 10, 588 basketball fans, a majority of which are White, attended Power 5 conference home games while Black males constituted 55% and 56% of the football and men's basketball teams, respectively (Harper, 2018). In relationship to Black masculinity, Curry (2017) posits that White masculinity is defined by its fear of and ability to control and dominate the *threatening* Black male body. These conceptions not only shape societal arrangements, but also have a profound impact on Black masculine identity development within these social milieu (Baldwin, 1961, 1963, 1965; Curry, 2017).

Both Dubois (1903/2003) and Baldwin (1961, 1963, 1965) articulated the psychological strife Black males in the U.S. confront as a result of systemic gendered racism, economic deprivation, and a dislocation of their identities and dignities as humans and as Black men of African descent existing in America (e.g., double consciousness, constant state of rage, foreigner in a strange land, etc.). In order to cultivate healthy Black masculinities, Black males must intentionally counter oppressive conditions imposed upon them based on their race and gender in a society founded upon and structured by WRC. Leonard and King (2012) incorporated the terms "commodified" and "criminalized" in the title of their book to draw parallels between the ways in which Black males are portrayed by the mass media and treated in both the broader society and more specifically in sporting spaces. These descriptions connect closely with historical depictions of Black male athletes who are labeled as brutes (Hawkins, 1998a, 1998b) and thus sport serves as another social institution where Black males are controlled and exploited to fulfill the needs of oppressive Whites. The perpetual use of the plantation and slave analogies to describe the historical and contemporary relationship, power dynamics, and property ownership between the primary benefactors of WRC and Black males remains applicable (Hawkins, 2010; Edwards, 1984, 2000; Oates, 2007; Powell, 2008; Rhoden, 2006). Although, not explicit in Curry's (2017) text, I surmise this dual erotic and phobic obsession of Black males explains the prevailing structure of sport across all levels (youth, interscholastic, intercollegiate, and professional) where controlling Whites exploit, sanction, surveillance, enjoy, and exercise their desires over Black male athletes. Since Blacks were viewed and treated as property before and at the founding of the U.S. (Harris, 1993), Whites through collective memory, formal laws, informal practices, and social expectations have created and reproduced conditions that position them as superior and Blacks as inferior. It is important to reiterate these arrangements are socially constructed and not a byproduct of divine intentions or natural human order (Smedley & Smedley, 2005).

Moreover, the homoeroticism of Black males from White males (Baldwin, 1961; Curry, 2017) is prevalent starting at the grassroots levels where White sport organizers, coaches, and scouts are entranced with young Black male athletes' physiques and prowess.[4] This White gaze has roots dating back at least to the early 17th century when it was normalized for Whites (both males and females) to sexually violate Blacks (both males and females) for their demonic erotic pleasures (Curry, 2017). The most prominent place where this homoeroticism is displayed is at the annual NFL draft combine where Black males are required to strip down to near nakedness and every aspect of their body is closely scrutinized (Oates, 2007). Various body parts are measured and assessed such as their hands, thighs, glutes, feet, torso, backs, chests, legs, waists, heads, and necks by numerous White onlookers. This process eerily resembles 17th to 19th century slave auction blocks where White economic exploiters would sell Blacks as property to the highest bidder for slave labor and other unjust purposes (Curry, 2017; DeGruy, 2005; Hine, Hine, &

Harrold, 2006). In a critical analysis of the NFL draft process, Oates (2007) described this spectacle:

> ... the process of the NFL draft as an erotic problem, as a cultural site where the admiration of male bodies by men can circulate with remarkable openness. This openness not only satisfies desires that are in the most other arenas strictly policed by taboos, but serves to affirm inter-male dominance based on a hierarchy of race by referencing a gender hierarchy. Draftees are positioned as the objects of the erotic gaze, which allows for the pursuit of long-sublimated desires while offering the prospects a disempowered role traditionally occupied by women. (p. 75)

The author further asserted that the commodification of Black male bodies serves both political and sexual aims (Oates, 2007). The social construction of Black masculinity within a society founded upon and structured by WRC involves a psychological paradox for Black males in terms of whether they acquiesce to prescribed oppressed roles for self-preservation or resist at the risk of losing their life, harm to their families, alienation, sabotage, economic deprivation, imprisonment, and/or death. The fact that it is common for Black males to participate in these routine practices suggest the preference for conformity based on economic dependency and a psychological, sociological, and intellectual disconnection from the racist history against Blacks in this society is more popular. Whereas, those who have resisted these oppressive forces have been swiftly isolated, ostracized, and penalized (Bass, 2002; Cooper, Macaulay, & Rodriguez, 2017; Edwards, 1973; Hartmann, 2000).

Prior to the professional ranks, this process of homoeroticism and commodification of the Black male body is present at the high school and intercollegiate levels in sports like football, basketball, and track and field where the institutional prestige via athletic success is heightened and the stakes for earning coveted college scholarships is paramount for Black males who have limited upward mobility opportunities in a society founded upon and structured by WRC (Donnor, 2005; Rhoden, 2006). Several journalistic exposes and films have detailed the insidious nature of this arrangement and the damaging impact it has on Black males, their families, and the Black community (Araton, 2012; Dohrmann, 2010; James & Marx, 1994; Robbins, Tollin, Laiter, & Wiley, 1999; White & Ridley, 2016). These negative impacts include short- and long-term psychological trauma, economic exploitation, academic devaluation, and personal and professional underdevelopment (Cooper, 2012, 2016b; Edwards, 1984, 2000). Thus, Black masculinity in the U.S. including in sporting contexts is a byproduct of direct confrontation with WRC while

White masculinity is constructed within the same ideological apparatus that necessitates the conquest of Black bodies.

Black Male Literal and Figurative Death In and Through Sport

The historical and current structure of sport in concert with broader societal arrangements (ETS, 2011) suggest many White sport owners and organizers along with causal fans contribute to the normalized fetishizing of Black male athletes so as long as they do not challenge the structure and norms of WRC (Edwards, 1973, 1980, 1984, 2000; Hawkins, 2010; Hawkins et al., 2017; Rhoden, 2006). Comparatively, there is far less concern for the post-sport participation hardships many Black male athletes endure. Common explanations for Black male athletes' decline after their athletic careers conclude are deficit-laden (e.g., *they* had the educational opportunity and did not take advantage of it, *they* frivolously wasted their money, *they* made bad decisions and must suffer the consequences, etc.) and *disregard socio-structural, historical, and ecological factors* (e.g., systemic racism, gendered racist oppression, academic neglect, detrimental athletic-centric cultures, economic deprivation, dehumanization and criminalization via law enforcement, malnutrition, inattentiveness to intergenerational psychological trauma and needs, the destruction of the Black family, exposure to perpetual violence, etc.) that greatly contribute to the manifestation of these outcomes (Cooper, 2012; Curry, 2017; DeGruy, 2005). In other words, Black male death or suffocation (literal and figurative) in and through sport involves the creation and reproduction of systems that nurture their athletic entertainer/dramatic spectacle identities while simultaneously stifling their holistic consciousness, empowerment, and identity development (Cooper, 2016b). As such, the death of their holistic identities results in the sustainment of the racialized status quo while the illusions of liberalism distract the masses, and in large part the Black community, who continue to either fuel this system actively and/or passively.

In an effort to challenge this status quo, several standout Black male athlete social justice champions such as Muhammad Ali, Tommie Smith, John Carlos, and more recently Colin Kaepernick have engaged in courageous activism. However, each of them along with their fellow activist athlete counterparts experienced subsequent backlash from the protectors of WRC, which reveals the extent to which the power structure is willing to go in order to preserve their privilege and property. As Hawkins (1998a) professed, Black male athletes who are threats to the sporting establishment, which is an extension of the broader system of WRC, are labeled as troublemakers and through social conditioning their figurative (i.e., career) and at times actual physical deaths are deemed as justifiable. The ideological hegemony in sport and society creates conditions that result in detrimental outcomes for Black male athletes not the least of which is their holistic underdevelopment. Some examples of these systemic tragedies are listed below and discussed in greater detail in Chapters 4 and 5:

(a) *Literal death of Black males as a result of societal conditions, negative impacts associated with the collective hubris of sport participation, and concurrent inattention to various health needs* (e.g., Len Bias tragedy in the 1986, Jovan Belcher's tragic family murder and suicide in 2012, Jordan McNair's alarming death in 2018, etc.) (Cooper, 2016b; Cooper, Corral et al., 2018, Cooper & Harris, 2018; Delsohn, 2014; Edwards, 1984, 2000; Schuppe, 2016);

(b) *Post-athletic career figurative deaths* also referred to by Edwards (1984) as "disengagement trauma" (p. 9) (e.g., Jesse Owen's post-Olympic glory life challenges in 1940s–1980s, Kevin Ross's story post-Creighton University involving an suicide attempt in the early 1990s, Lenny Cooke's story of life transitional challenges after his heralded high school basketball career in the early 2000s, etc.) (Araton, 2012; Bass, 2002; Donnor, 2005; Edwards, 1969, 1984, 2000);

(c) *Figurative deaths via academic neglect throughout their K-20 miseducation schooling experiences* (e.g., Dexter Manley's story of being illiterate after attending Oklahoma State University in late 1970s and early 1980s, James Brooks' story of being illiterate after attending Auburn University in the late 1970s and early 1980s, and countless other Black males who either did not matriculate through school with a meaningful education or they formally graduated through a process of schooling that still leaves them underprepared for life after sports) (Beamon, 2008; Benson, 2000; Brooks & Althouse, 2000, 2013; Cooper, 2012; Donnor, 2005; Sellers, 2000; Smith & Willingham, 2015);

(d) *Literal career deaths and suffocation of Black male athletes who choose to engage in activist actions against the dominant hegemonic social order* (e.g., Muhammad Ali (formerly Cassius Clay), Mahmoud Abdul-Rauf (formerly Chris Jackson), Colin Kaepernick, etc.) *and perpetual violation of Black athletes' rights* (e.g., lack of negotiation power and representation at the intercollegiate level, lack of exclusively Black athlete coalitions and labor union groups, etc.) (Cooper, Macaulay, & Rodriguez, 2017; Cooper, Nwadike, & Macaulay, 2017; Edwards, 2016; Hartmann, 1996, 2000);

(e) *Literal economic death due to a lack of sound financial literacy, advice, and supports* (i.e., the bankruptcy experiences of Andre Rison, Antoine Walker, Terrell Owens, Michael Vick, and numerous others) (Corben, 2012; Fedlam, 2015)

(f) *Literal career death and suffocation via limited leadership opportunities within sport beyond participation level* (e.g., denied ownership, management, and coaching positions – demise of the Negro Leagues, persistent marginalization of HBCU athletic programs, and underrepresentation at all levels of sport leadership) (Cooper, 2012; Cooper et al., 2014; Cunningham, 2010; Lomax, 2003, 2014)

(g) *Literal and figurative death and suffocation of the broader Black community as a result of Black male talent drain*, which is described by Edwards (2000) as the triple tragedy.

By design, the White sporting power structure seeks to foster apolitical, colorblind, Afrocentric-less, and disconnected Black males who are not only physically removed from the Black community, but even worse psychologically detached from the plight of collective racial and cultural uplift (Edwards, 2000; Rhoden, 2006). I likened this condition to what the popular film by Jordan Peele, *Get Out* (2017), describes as a being in a "sunken place," whereby awareness of and intentional counter-action against the oppressive forces of WRC are stagnated and/or eliminated.

There is also a connection between the unjust literal deaths of Black males throughout the broader U.S. society via lynchings, homicides, death penalties, etc. and the figurative death of Black males' holistic development through the athletic industrial complex (AIC; Hawkins, 2010; Smith, 2009), athletic seasoning complex (ASC; Howard, 2014), Conveyor Belt (Rhoden, 2006), and PIC (Hawkins, 2010). Both literal and figurative deaths are contrived through systemic efforts. As such, in concert with Edwards (1980, 2000), I argue the same level of seriousness must be applied to all areas of society where Black exploitation, oppression, and death occur and this includes in and through sport. The ideological hegemony in the U.S. seeks to use sport participation as a controlling mechanism to produce complicit Black athletes as role models. This process not only suppresses revolutionary action, but also reinforces the illusion of racial harmony, equity, and meritocracy (i.e., the corporate monies provided to apolitical Black male athletes such as Michael Jordan, Barry Bonds, Kobe Bryant, and Tiger Woods and concurrent economic alienation and mischaracterization of Black male activist athletes such as Tommie Smith, John Carlos, Mahmoud Abdul-Rauf (formerly Chris Jackson), Craig Hodges, Ed O'Bannon, and Colin Kaepernick are prime examples of the system at work) (Bass, 2002; Cooper, Macaulay, & Rodriguez, 2017; Edwards, 2016; Hartmann, 1996; Hawkins, 1998a, 1998b; Rhoden, 2006). The lack of critical analysis of the complex interplay between the aforementioned sociological realities and their influence on Black masculine identity development in and through sport and (mis)education highlights the needs for the proposed models in this text.

Chapter Summary

In this chapter, foundational conditions for understanding the complex relationship between Blackness, masculinity, and sport involvement were presented. As noted, dating back to the late 18th century, Black males' involvement in sport resulted in preferential treatment compared to their same race peers (e.g., access to travel away from plantations, healthier food, improved temporary living conditions, and at a maximum freedom from slavery altogether) (Wiggins, 2014). Excelling in sport albeit for the pleasure of powerful Whites, served as a means for attaining a level of humanity and masculinity denied to Black males during chattel slavery and in the postbellum era. Similar to the lasting effects of the post traumatic slave syndrome (PTSS; DeGruy, 2005), the intergenerational influence of Black males' relationship with sport in a society founded upon and structured by WRC has had a profound residual impact on their identity development (e.g., racially, gender, athletically, academically, etc.). In a society, where being a Black male is deemed as troublesome, unworthy, criminal, and inhuman, sport has been a space where some resemblance of humanity, dignity, positive identity affirmation, multi-racial adoration, and economic mobility is granted even if transient.

The aforementioned impetus for sport involvement is pivotal for understanding the depth of psychological attraction, affinity, and attachment many Black males in the U.S. place on being valued for their athletic prowess and the subsequent impact on their identity development and at times disconnection from the broader Black community. In other words, the current analysis of the intersection of race, gender, sport, and (mis)education is predicated on the notion that sport must be analyzed as "a cultural practice embedded in political, economic, and ideological formations" (Sage, 1998, p. 11). A critical analysis of history reveals Black male athletes have never been monolithic (e.g., Paul Robeson compared to Joe Louis, Jesse Owens compared to Muhammad Ali, Mahmoud Abdul Rauf (formerly Chris Jackson) compared to Michael Jordan, Colin Kaepernick compared to Dak Prescott, etc.) and their experiences and outcomes in and through sport vary based on a range of factors (e.g., access to non-sporting opportunities, socio-political consciousness, family backgrounds, exposure to social capital beyond sport, etc.). As a result, this book seeks to take into account the interplay of socio-ecological factors such as sub-, chrono-, macro-, exo-, meso-, and micro-level factors and outline the heterogeneity among Black male athletes' experiences and outcomes with holistic (under)development in and through sport and (mis)education.

Notes

1. It is important to acknowledge that the history of African people who were enslaved on U.S. soil did not begin in 17th century. The rich legacy of African people extends back centuries as documented in great detail in previous texts (Asante, 1990; Diop, 1974; Hilliard, 1998; Karenga, 1978; Williams, 1974, 1987). The detailed coverage of this pre-U.S. history is beyond the scope of this book; however, the overarching theme of back to empowerment reflects my Afrocentric foundational epistemology, ontology, and axiology whereby the reclamation of our collectivist roots is directly connected to the origins of African people dating back the beginning of the world through the modern day.
2. See Cooper, Mallery, and Macaulay (forthcoming) for an extended discussion on additional areas for Black expressiveness in music and art especially during the Harlem Renaissance.
3. Although Black male athletes are celebrated in sport, they are also disparately penalized at the same time (see Leonard (2006, 2010) and Leonard and King (2012) for expansive analyses on this topic).
4. The following films illustrate the prevalence of this obsession: *The Program* (Goldwyn, Henderson, Rothman, & Ward, 1993), *Hoop Dreams* (James & Marx, 1994), *Varsity Blues* (Robbins, Tollin, Laiter, &Wiley, 1999), *Blue Chips* (Friedkin, 1994), *He Got Game* (Lee, 1998), *The Blind Side* (Hancock, 2009), *Last Chance U* (Whitely & Ridley, 2016), *The Lenny Cooke Story* (Araton, 2012), and *More Than a Game* (Belman, Mason, Mann, & Perniciaro, 2008) to name a few. The book titled, *Play Their Hearts Out* (Dohrmann, 2010) offers another detailed example of this phenomenon.

References

Alexander, M. (2012). *The new Jim Crow: Mass incarceration in the age of colorblindness*. New York, NY: The New Press.

Andrews, D. L. (2001). *Michael Jordan, inc: Corporate sport, media culture, and late modern America*. Albany, NY: SUNY Press.

Araton, H. (2012, March 3). Star-to-be who never was. *The New York Times*. Retrieved from http://www.nytimes.com/2012/03/04/sports/basketball/lenny-cooke-star-to-be-who-never-was.html

Asante, M. K. (1990). *Kemet, Afrocentricity and knowledge*. Trenton, NJ: Africa World Press.

Baldwin, J. (1961). *Nobody knows my name*. New York, NY: Dial Press.

Baldwin, J. (1963). *The fire next time*. New York, NY: Dial Press.

Baldwin, J. (1965). *Going to meet the man* [Short Stories]. New York, NY: Vintage Books.

Bass, A. (2002). *Not the triumph but the struggle: The 1968 Olympics and the making of the Black athlete*. Minneapolis, MN: University of Minnesota Press.

Beamon, K. K. (2008). "Used goods": Former African American college student-athletes' perception of exploitation by division I universities. *The Journal of Negro Education, 77*(4), 352–364.

Beamon, K. K. (2010). Are sports overemphasized in the socialization process of African American males?: A qualitative analysis of former collegiate athletes' perception of sport socialization. *Journal of Black Studies, 41*(2), 281–300.

Beamon, K. (2012). "I'm a baller:" Athletic identity foreclosure among African American former student-athletes. *Journal of African American Studies, 16*(2), 195–208.

Bell, D. A. (1980). Brown v. Board of Education and the interest convergence dilemma. *Harvard Law Review, 93*(3), 518–533.

Bell, D. A. (1992). *Faces at the bottom of the well: The permanence of racism*. New York, NY: Basic Books.

Belman, K., Mason, H., Jr., Mann, K., & Perniciaro, M. (2008). *More than a game*. [Documentary]. Harvey Mason Media. St. V., Spring Hill Entertainment.

Benson, K. F. (2000). Constructing academic inadequacy: African American athletes' stories of schooling. *The Journal of Higher Education, 71*(2), 223–246.

Boyd, T. (2003). *Young, Black, rich, and famous: The rise of the NBA, the hip-hop invasion, and the transformation of American culture*. New York, NY: Doubleday.

Brown, D. (2016, November 4). *Blathlete: Black-identity development among Black male student-athletes*. Paper presentation at the North American Society for the Sociology of Sport (NASSS) conference in Tampa, Florida.

Brooks, D., & Althouse, R. (2000). *Racism in college athletics: The African American athlete's experience* (2nd ed.). Morgantown, WV: Fitness Information Technology.

Brooks, D. A., & Althouse, R. (2013). *Racism in college athletics: The African American athlete's experience* (3rd ed.). Morgantown, WV: Fitness Information Technology.

Carmichael, S. (1971/2007). *Stokely speaks: From Black power to Pan-Africanism*. Chicago, IL: Chicago Review Press.

Cavil, J. K. (2015). Early athletic experiences at HBCUs: The creation of conferences. In B. Hawkins, J. N. Cooper, A. R. Carter-Francique, & J. K. Cavil (Eds.), *The athletic experience at historically Black colleges and universities: Past, present, and persistence* (pp. 19–58). Lanham, MD: Rowman & Littlefield.

Coakley, J. (2017). *Sports in society: Issues and controversies* (12th ed.). New York, NY: McGraw-Hill Education.

Coates, T. (2017). *We were eight years in power: An American tragedy*. New York, NY: One World.

Cooper, J. N. (2012). Personal troubles and public issues: A sociological imagination of Black athletes' experiences at predominantly White institutions in the United States. *Sociology Mind*, 2(3), 261–271.

Cooper, J. N. (2016a). "Focus on the bigger picture:" An anti-deficit achievement examination of Black male scholar athletes in science and engineering at a Division I historically White university (HWU). *Whiteness & Education*, 1(2), 109–124.

Cooper, J. N. (2016b). Excellence beyond athletics: Best practices for enhancing Black male student athletes' educational experiences and outcomes. *Equity & Excellence in Education*, 49(3), 267–283.

Cooper, J. N., Cavil, J. K., & Cheeks, G. (2014). The state of intercollegiate athletics at historically Black colleges and universities (HBCUs): Past, present, & persistence. *Journal of Issues in Intercollegiate Athletics*, 7, 307–332.

Cooper, J. N., Corral, M. D., Macaulay, C. D. T., Cooper, M. S., Nwadike, A., & Mallery, Jr., M. (2018). Collective uplift: The impact of a holistic development support program on Black male former college athletes' experiences and outcomes. *International Journal of Qualitative Studies in Education*, DOI: 10.1080/09518398.2018.1522011.

Cooper, J. N., & Harris, J. (2018). DJ Durkin's firing won't solve college football's deepest problems. The Conversation. Retrieved from https://theconversation.com/dj-durkins-firing-wont-solve-college-footballs-deepest-problems-106118

Cooper, J. N., Macaulay, C., & Rodriguez, S. H. (2017). Race and resistance: A typology of African American sport activism. *International Review for the Sociology of Sport*, 1–31. DOI: 10.1177/1012690217718170.

Cooper, J. N., Mallery, M., & Macaulay, C. D. T. (forthcoming). African American sport activism and broader social movements. In D. Brown (Ed.). *Passing the ball: Sports in African American life and culture* (pp. 35–51). Jefferson, NC: McFarland & Company.

Cooper, J. N., Nwadike, A., & Macaulay, C. (2017). A critical race theory analysis of big-time college sports: Implications for culturally responsive and race-conscious sport leadership. *Journal of Issues in Intercollegiate Athletics*, 10, 204–233.

Corben, B. (2012). *Broke*. [Documentary]. ESPN Films (Distributor). Invincible Pictures. Rakontur.

Cunningham, G. B. (2010). Understanding the under-representation of African American coaches: A multilevel perspective. *Sport Management Review*, 13(4), 395–406.

Curry, T. J. (2017). *The man-not: Race, class, genre, and the dilemmas of Black manhood*. Philadelphia, PA: Temple University Press.

DeGruy, J. (2005). *Post-traumatic slave syndrome: America's legacy of enduring injury & healing*. Milwaukie, OR: Uptone Press.

Delsohn, S. (2014, September 30). OTL: Belcher's brain had CTE signs. ESPN. Retrieved from http://www.espn.com/espn/otl/story/_/id/11612386/jovan-belcher-brain-showed-signs-cte-doctor-says-report

Diop, C. A. (1974). *The African origin of civilization: Myth or reality*. Westport, CT: Lawrence Hill.

Dohrmann, G. (2010). *Play their hearts out: A coach, his star recruit, and the youth basketball machine*. New York, NY: Ballantine Books.

Donnor J. K. (2005). Towards and interest-convergence in the education of African-American football student athletes in major college sports. *Race, Ethnicity and Education, 8*(1), 45–67.

DuBois, W. E. B. (1903/2003). *The souls of Black folk*. Chicago, IL: A. C. McClurg.

Edwards, H. (1969). *The revolt of the Black athlete*. New York, NY: Free Press.

Edwards, H. (1973). *Sociology of sport*. Homewood, IL: Dorsey Press.

Edwards, H. (1980). *The struggle that must be: An autobiography*. New York, NY: Macmillan Publishing.

Edwards, H. (1984). The Black "dumb jock:" An American sports tragedy. *College Board Review*, 131, 8–13.

Edwards, H. (2000). Crisis of black athletes on the eve of the 21st century. *Society, 37*(3), 9–13.

Edwards, H. (2016). *The fourth wave: Black athlete protests in the second decade of the 21st century*. Keynote address at the North American Society for the Sociology of Sport (NASSS) conference in Tampa Bay, Florida.

ETS. (2011). *A strong start: Positioning young Black boys for educational success a statistical profile*. Washington, DC: Educational Testing Service

Fanon, F. (1952/2008). *Black skin, White masks*. New York, NY: Grove Press.

Fedlam, L. (2015, January 9). *Post-career issues*. Panel presentation at the Black Student-Athlete Conference at the University of Texas at Austin in Austin, Texas.

Friedkin, W. (1994). *Blue chips* [movie]. Paramount Pictures.

George, N. (1992). *Elevating the game: Black men and basketball*. New York, NY: HarperCollins.

Goldwyn, S., Jr., Henderson, D., Rothman, T., & Ward, D. S. (1993). *The program* [Film]. United States Touchstone Pictures. The Samuel Goldwyn Company.

Gramsci A. (1971). *Selections from the prison notebooks*. Q. Hoare & G. N. Smith (Eds. and Trans.). New York, NY: International Publishers.

Gramsci A. (1990). Culture and ideological hegemony. In J. C. Alexander & S. Seidman (Eds.) *Culture and Society: Contemporary Debates* (pp. 47–54). New York, NY: Cambridge University Press.

Hancock, J. L. (2009). *The blind side* [Film]. United States: Alcon Entertainment..

Harper, S. R. (2018). *Black male student-athletes and racial inequities in NCAA Division I college sports: 2018 edition*. Los Angeles, CA: University of Southern California, Race and Equity Center.

Harris, C. (1993). Whiteness as property. *Harvard Law Review, 106*(8), 1707–1791.

Harris, O. (2000). African American predominance in sport. In D. Brooks & R. Althouse (Eds.), *Racism in college athletics: The African Amerian athlete's experience* (2nd ed., pp. 37–52). Morgantown, WV: Fitness Information Technology.

Harrison., L. Jr., Harrison, C. K., & Moore, L. N. (2002). African American racial identity and sport. *Sport, Education & Society, 7*(2), 121–133.

Hartmann, D. (1996). *Race, culture, and the revolt of the Black athlete: The 1968 Olympic protests and their aftermath*. Chicago, IL: The University of Chicago Press.

Hartmann, D. (2000). Rethinking the relationships between sport and race in American culture: Golden ghettos and contested terrain. *Sociology of Sport Journal, 17*(3), 229–253.

Hawkins, B. (1998a). The dominant images of black men in America: The representation of O. J. Simpson. In G. Sailes (Ed.), *African Americans in sport* (pp. 39–52). New Brunswick, NJ: Transaction Publishers.

Hawkins, B. (1998b). The White supremacy continuum of images for Black men. *Journal of African American Men, 3*(3), 7–18.

Hawkins, B. (2010). *The new plantation: Black athletes, college sports, and predominantly White NCAA institutions*. New York, NY: Palgrave MacMillan.

Hawkins, B., Carter-Francique, A. R., & Cooper, J. N. (2017). *Critical race theory: Black athletic sporting experiences in the United States*. New York, NY: Palgrave Macmillan.

Henderson, E. B. (1939). *The Negro in sports*. Washington, DC: The Associated Publishers.

Hilliard, A., III, (1998). *SBA: The reawakening of the African mind*. Gainesville, FL: Makare Publishing.

Hine, D. C., Hine, W. C., & Harrold, S. (2006). *The African-American odyssey: Since 1965* (Third ed. Vol. Two). Upper Saddle River, NJ: Pearson Prentice Hall.

Hodge, S. R., Burden, J. W., Jr., Robinson, L. E., & Bennett, R. A., III. (2008). Theorizing on the stereotyping of Black male student-athletes: Issues and implications. *Journal for the Study of Sports and Athletes in Education, 2*(2), 203–226.

Hodge, S. R., Collins, F. G., & Bennett, R. A., III, (2013). The journey of the Black athlete on the HBCU playing field. In D. Brooks & R. Althouse (Eds.), *Racism in college athletics* (pp. 105–134). Morgantown, WV: Fitness Information Technology.

Hodge, S. R., Harrison, L., Jr., Burden, J. W., Jr., & Dixson, A. D. (2008). Brown in Black and White – Then and now: A question of educating or sporting African American males in America. *American Behavioral Scientist, 51*(7), 928–952.

Howard, T. C. (2014). *Black male(d): Peril and promise in the education of African American males*. New York, NY: Teachers College Press.

James, S., & Marx, F. (1994). *Hoop dreams* [documentary]. Minneapolis, MN: Kartemquin Films.

Karenga, M. (1978). *Essays on struggle: Position and analysis*. San Diego, CA: Kawaida Publications.

Lee, S. (1998). *He got game* [Film]. Touchstone Pictures. 40 Acres & A Mule Filmworks.

Leonard, D. J. (2006). The real color of money: Controlling Black bodies in the NBA. *Journal of Sport and Social Issues, 30*(2), 158–179.

Leonard, D. J. (2010). Jumping the gun: Sporting cultures and the criminalization of Black masculinity. *Journal of Sport and Social Issues, 34*(2), 252–262.

Leonard, D. J., & King, C. R. (2012). *Commodified and criminalized: New racism and African Americans in contemporary sports*. Lanham, MD: Rowman & Littlefield.

Lomax, M. E. (2003) *Black baseball entrepreneurs, 1860–1901: Operating by any means necessary*. Syracuse, NY: Syracuse University Press.

Lomax, M. E. (2014). *Black baseball entrepreneurs, 1902–1931: The Negro National and Eastern Colored Leagues*. Syracuse, NY: Syracuse University Press.

Majors, R., & Billson, J. M. (1992). *Cool pose: The dilemmas of Black manhood in America*. New York, NY: Lexington Books.

May, R. A. B. (2008). *Living through the hoop: High school basketball, race, and the American Dream*. New York, NY: New York University Press.

Messner, M. (1990). Masculinities and athletic careers: Bonding and status differences. In D. Sabo & M. Messner (Eds.), *Sport, men, and the gender order: Critical feminist perspectives* (pp. 97–108). Champaign, IL: Human Kinetics.

Miller, P. B. (1995). To bring the race along rapidly: Sport, student culture, and educational mission at historically Black colleges during the interwar years. *History of Education Quarterly, 35*(2), 111–133.

Noguera, P. A. (2008). *The trouble with Black boys ... and other reflections on race, equity, and the future of public education*. San Francisco, CA: Jossey-Bass.

Northcutt, K. J. (2013). *The dilemma: career transition of African American male football players at Division I institutions* (Dissertation). University of Mississippi.

Oates, T. P. (2007). The erotic gaze in the NFL draft. *Communication and Critical/Cultural Studies, 4*(1), 74–90.

Peele, J. (Director). (2017). *Get out* [movie]. Universal Pictures. Blumhouse Productions. QC Entertainment.

Powell, S. (2008). *Souled out? How Blacks are winning and losing in sports*. Champaign, IL: Human Kinetics.

Rhoden, W. C. (2006). *40 million dollar slaves: The rise, fall, and redemption of the Black athlete*. New York, NY: Crown Publishing Group.

Robbins, B., Tollin, M., Laiter T., & Wiley, M. (1999). *Varsity blues* [Film]. United States: MTV Films. Paramount Pictures. Tollin/Robbins Productions.

Sage, G. H. (1998). *Power and ideology in American sport* (2nd ed.). Champaign, IL: Human Kinetics.

Sage, G. H., & Eitzen, D. S. (2013). *Sociology of North American sport*. New York, NY: Oxford University Press.

Sailes, G. (2010). The African American athlete: Social myths and stereotypes. In G. Sailes (Ed.), *Modern sport and the African American athlete experience* (pp. 55–68). San Diego, CA: Cognella.

Schuppe, J. (2016, June). 30 years after basketball star Len Bias' death, its drug war impact endures. NBC News. Retrieved from https://www.nbcnews.com/news/us-news/30-years-after-basketball-star-len-bias-death-its-drug-n593731

Sellers, R. M. (2000). African American student-athletes: Opportunity or exploitation? In D. A. Brooks, R. (Ed.), *Racism in college athletics: The African American athlete's experience* (2nd ed., pp. 133–154). Morgantown, WV: Fitness Information Technology, Inc.

Smedley, A., & Smedley, B. D. (2005). Race as biology is fiction, racism as a social problem is real: Anthropological and historical perspectives on the social construction of race. *American Psychologist, 60*(1), 16–26.

Smith, E. (2009). *Race, sport and the American dream* (2nd ed.). Durham, NC: Carolina Academic Press.

Smith, J. C. (1994). *Black firsts: 2, 000 years of extraordinary achievement*. Detroit, MI: Visible Ink Press.

Smith, M. P., Clark, L. D., & Harrison, L., Jr. (2014). The historical hypocrisy of the Black student-athlete. *Race, Gender & Class, 21*(1–2), 220–235.

Smith, J. M., & Willingham, M. (2015). *Cheated: The UNC scandal, the education of athletes, and the future of big-time college sports*. Omaha, NE: University of Nebraska Press.

Staples, R. (1982). *Black masculinity*. San Francisco, CA: The Black Scholar Press.

Stewart, J. C. (1996). *1001 things everyone should know about African American history*. New York, NY: Doubleday Dell Publishing Group.

Wells, I. B. (1892; 1997). *Southern horrors: Lynch law and all its phases*. In Royster, J. J. (Ed.), *Southern horrors and other writings: The antilynching campaign of Ida B. Wells, 1892–1900* (pp. 49–72). Boston, MA: Bedford Books.

Whitely, G., & Ridley, A. (2016). Last chance U [Documentary Series]. *Condé Nast Entertainment*. Netflix. https://www.netflix.com/title/80091742

Wiggins, D. K. (2000). Critical events affecting racism in athletics. In D. Brooks, & R. Althouse (Eds.), *Racism in college athletics: The African American athlete's experience* (2nd ed., pp. 15–36). Morgantown, WV: Fitness Information Technology.

Wiggins, D. K. (2014). 'Black athlete in White men's games': Race, sport and American national pastimes. *The International Journal of the History of Sport, 31*(1–2), 181–202.

Wiggins, D. K., & Miller, P. (2003). *The unlevel playing field: A documentary history of the African-American experience in sport*. Urbana, IL: University of Illinois Press.

Williams, C. (1974/1987). *The destruction of Black civilization: Great issues of a race from 4500 B. C. to 2000 A. D.* Chicago, IL: Third World Press.

Woodson, C. G. (1933/2010). *The mis-education of the Negro*. New York, NY: SoHoBooks.

2

SYSTEMIC MISEDUCATION THROUGH SCHOOLING AND SPORT

... although many people blame the student-athletes for their academic short-comings, they fail to analyze the macro-level issues of how the athletic complex functions creating athletic juggernauts and expediting academic ineptness ... Yet, what occurs at the middle-school level illuminates how mismatched identities and "mis-education" is facilitated at the college level because the ground work has already been laid.

—Harrison, Bimper, Smith, & Logan (2017, p. 63)

Miseducation, Schooling, and Black Males

In the U.S. educational system, Black males have been disproportionately underserved, undervalued, and miseducated. These terms are interconnected because the notion of being underserved or undervalued refers to the fact that Black males' educational, developmental, and holistic needs are persistently unmet by dominant social institutions. More specifically, I define miseducation as the confluence of schooling processes that systematically produce a lack of critical analysis and understanding of Blacks' true history including African heritages, the oppressive systems in which they exist as a result of White rac-ism capitalism (WRC), and ways in which they can alter these dismal realities as opposed to reproducing them. Singer (2015) offered another definition of miseducation as "the process that often occurs when one is given wrong or faulty education and where, oftentimes, external forces restrict or impair students' ability to explore the totality of who they are, what they are, and their options and possibilities in various life domains (Marks, 2000)" (p. 193). Both definitions of miseducation indicate an intentional and systematic effort to undermine the holistic development of Black males. From a historical standpoint, Hodge, Harrison, Burden, and Dixson (2008) highlighted how prior to *Brown v. Board of Education of Topeka* (1954) decision social institutions including education and sport were "racially segregated and unequal due mostly to legalized and moralized injustices based on the social construction of race" (p. 944). Unfortunately, little has changed since this milestone legislation as deep racist residue remains embedded in U.S. societal arrangements in the early 21st century. Renowned African American historian, Ibram X. Kendi, echoed the sentiment of previous critical race theorists (Bell, 1980, 1992; Crenshaw, Gotanda, Peller, & Thomas, 1995; Ladson-Billings & Tate, 1995) when he asserted that governments cannot legislate attitudes (O'Neil, 2017). Thus, when Whites who benefit from privilege, including those who oversee K-20 miseducation schooling and sporting systems, prioritize self-interests over racial equality and altruistic morals negative outcomes manifest for Blacks and various subordinate groups in a society founded upon and structured by WRC.

An illustration of this reality is the miscalculated belief that Civil Rights legislations of the 1950s and 1960s and racial assimilation (often mislabeled as integration) would result in reduced racism and improve equity in terms of life outcomes across all racial groups (Bell, 1980, 1992). This misguided assumption was largely based on the public persuasion of Allport's (1954) intergroup contact hypothesis (Hodge et al., 2008) and myths rooted in abstract liberalism (Bonilla-Silva, 2010), which underestimate the impact of power and privilege dynamics between unjustly enriched (i.e., Whites) and unjustly impoverished groups (i.e., Blacks) (Fanon, 1952/2008, 1963/2004; Feagin, 2006; Freire, 1968). Another limitation of *Brown v. Board of Education of Topeka* (1954) was the shift towards the new measure of discrimination being intent rather than outcome (Kendi, 2017). The post-*Brown v. Board of Education of Topeka* (1954) outcomes for Black students in the U.S. K-20 miseducation schooling system have indicated the magnitude of this fallacy (e.g., Black male students graduating at the lowest rates among all sub-groups at the secondary and postsecondary levels, Black males perpetually being less likely to enroll in college compared to their peers, Black males being more likely to be suspended or expelled than their peers, Black males being more likely be referred to special education and less likely to be admitted into gifted education programs, etc.) (Children's Defense Fund, 2012; ETS, 2011; Schott Foundation for Public Education, 2010, 2015). Understanding how oppressive ideologies manifest through systemic policies, practices, and outcomes is imperative for creating effective reform measures as opposed to passing symbolic legislations and implementing surface-level programs that essentially maintain the status quo.

Moreover, scholars have also noted the distinct difference between schooling and education. When discussing these two concepts and drawing from previous scholarly insights (Akbar, 1982; Foster, 1993; Shujaa, 1994), Bush (1997) conceptualized schooling as "the process that trains them to maintain White hegemonic control" whereas education is "the process that leaves them more capable of expressing who they are as defined by their culture and community" (p. 98). The underserving, undervaluing, and miseducation of Black males in the K-20 schooling system is a byproduct of interlocking systems of oppression designed to oppress Blacks as a collective group (Bell, 1980, 1992; Crenshaw et al., 1995; Howard, 2014; Ladson-Billings & Tate, 1995; Noguera, 2008; Woodson, 1903/1990). From the founding of the U.S. until the present day the racial hierarchy, which places Blacks at the bottom, is an American tradition or more accurately described as an unjustifiable travesty and inexcusable moral failure (Bell, 1992; DuBois, 1903/2003; Hine, Hine, & Harrold, 2006; Woodson, 1903/1990).

An example of the sustainment of this racial hierarchy is found in recent data from the Schott Foundation for Public Education (2010) report on Black males. During the 2007–2008 school year, the graduation rates for Black males was 31 percentage points lower than White males, 47% and 78%, respectively (Schott Foundation for Public Education, 2010). The fact that one out of every two Black males will not matriculate past the secondary level reflects a broader societal issue regarding the neglect and stigmatization of Black males' academic prowess and holistic potential (Howard, 2014; Noguera, 2008). Several factors have been identified as causes for Black males' schooling outcomes. Notable factors include economic deprivation and subsequent effects on family structure and health outcomes, cultural mismatch between teachers, curricula, and Black males, and differential treatment with regards to academic learning capabilities and behavior enforcement (Children's Defense Fund, 2012; ETS, 2011; Schott Foundation for Public Education, 2010, 2015). In order to address these issues, it is important to conceptualize the nature of this societal problem using palatable theoretical concepts such as structural intersectionality and education debt.

Structural Intersectionality and Education Debt

Contrary to popular literature, which promulgates deficit-laden recommendations as solutions for improving academic outcomes among Black males (e.g., grit, resilience, motivation, etc.), I concur with scholars who adopt a critical sociological and ecological perspective towards identifying ways to support and nurture the holistic development of Black males (Bush & Bush, 2013a, 2013b; Harper, 2012; Howard, 2014; Wood & Palmer, 2014). The problems facing Black males as well as the Black community more broadly are not isolated occurrences, but rather a result of systemic racism. Howard (2014) explained the interlocking nature of oppressive forces facing Black males in the U.S.:

> Structural intersectionality refers to the creation, operation, maintenance, and synthesis of various systems and structures in society that maintain privilege for some groups or individuals, while restricting or denying the rights and privileges of others (Swanson, Cunningham, & Spencer, 2003). Structural intersectionality also encompasses the political, economic, representational, and institutional forms of discrimination, oppression, exploitation, and domination; highlights the connectedness of systems and structures in society; and helps us understand how each system affects or impacts others. (Wilson, 2009, p. 45)

This notion of structural intersectionality is vital for understanding how specified outcomes manifest for Black males. More importantly, structural intersectionality enables stakeholders to effectively identify and create key areas of intervention for reversing said trends. Within a structural intersectional analysis, race, gender, class, and related factors are examined with a level of complexity in contrast to the mainstream generalizations and simplifications of Black males' lived experiences.

Howard (2014) further noted how it is important to analyze Black males within their respective environments and avoid the pathological temptation of attributing their challenges to their exclusive factors (i.e., social class) without taking into account the intersection of different systems, conditions, psychological schemas, and identities. For example, the ways in which gendered racism intersects with social class can impact Black males in similar *and* distinct ways. Thus, asserting that Black males who are subjected to living in poverty and the challenges therein accurately depicts all of the problems facing this population ignores the lived realities of all Black males who experience these conditions as well as the realities of those who do not grow up in poverty, but still face consequences stemming from their positioning in a society founded upon and structured by WRC. More specifically, in the

U.S., Black males are disproportionately stigmatized, penalized, marginalized, underserved, undervalued, miseducated, and unjustly murdered as a result of academic neglect, economic and occupational deprivation, social isolation, racial discrimination, and limited access to leadership positions and ownership in various societal sectors (Alexander, 2012; Cooper, 2012; Curry, 2017; Howard, 2014; Noguera, 2008). Understanding the impact of multi-level systems on the Black community aids in elucidating the ways in which sport and miseducation also contribute to Black male athletes' holistic underdevelopment.

Another major explanation for Black males' schooling outcomes and a common theme throughout the Black collective experience in the U.S. is the reality of perpetual economic exploitation and deprivation, which is reflective in intergenerational wealth and poverty gaps (DeGruy, 2005; Feagin, 2006; Franklin & Resnik, 1973; Frazier, 1957). According to a Children's Defense Fund report (2012), in 2009, 42% of Black children were born poor compared to 8% of White children, out of those who were born poor 69% of Black children will remain poor throughout their childhoods, and consequently they are more than two times as likely to be persistently poor compared to their White counterparts (31%) (Ratcliffe & McKernan, 2010). These economic conditions have a direct adverse impact on family structure and functioning. In 2009, the median income for White families with children ($61, 775) was nearly twice the median income for Black families with children ($31, 915) (Children's Defense Fund, 2012). Economic disadvantages also often result in less access to vital cultural capital associated with navigating traditional K-12 schooling settings. For example, Eitle and Eitle (2002) found Black male high school students were more likely to grow up in families with significantly lower economic and household resources and subsequently less likely to have exposure to cultural capital such as visits to museums or participate in art, music, or dance classes when compared to White male students. These types of exposure can enhance cognitive processes and performance on culturally based (and biased) standardized assessments in K-12 schooling systems, which have a disparate impact on Black students (Howard, 2014; Noguera, 2008).

Furthermore, the aforementioned disparities are not only a result of racial inequalities in terms of education, occupational attainment, salaries, and wages, but also a consequence of the disruption of two-parent households within the Black community. Less than 40% of Black children live in two parent households compared to 75% of White children, Black children are four times more likely than White children to grow up in foster care, and seven times more likely to have a parent in prison (Children's Defense Fund, 2012). However, it is important to note that living arrangements do not accurately reflect the extent to which Black parents including fathers are actively present or not in their children's lives. In fact, even though many Black fathers are not physically living in the same house as their children and/or the mother, research has highlighted how they are equally if not more likely to be actively involved in their children's lives in terms of attending events, financial contributions, and psycho-emotional support (Bass, 2016). Nonetheless, critical sociological examinations for how and why Black male fathers are physically and at times psycho-emotionally and financially absent from their children's lives is imperative for understanding subsequent impacts on Black male identity development from youth through adulthood. In Michelle Alexander's groundbreaking book titled, *The New Jim Crow: Mass Incarceration in the Era of Colorblindness*, the author details how racist laws and discriminatory enforcement disproportionately imprison and disenfranchise Black males, which contributes to the lack of physically and financially present Black fathers, husbands, brothers, and community members and severely restricts employment opportunities once released from prison (Alexander, 2012). Despite constituting roughly 13.3% of the U.S. population, Blacks account for nearly 37.9% of all inmates (Federal Bureau of Prisons, 2018; U.S. Census Bureau, 2017). The criminalization and subsequent absence of Black males from the Black community has an immeasurable economic, psychological, social, and political impact on Black males' socialization experiences and outcomes.

Beyond economic conditions, racial and cultural identities matter in schooling contexts as well. A national educational report revealed in 2011–2012 Black students constituted 16% of all primary and secondary students while 82% of all public school teachers were White compared to 7% whom were Black (U.S. Department of Education, 2016). In terms of administrator leadership in 2011–2012, 80% of all public school principals were White compared to 10% whom were Black (U.S. Department of Education, 2016). These racial disparities cannot be understated or minimized. This cultural incongruence often leads to mislabeling and misinterpreting Black students' (including males) competencies and behaviors as deficient, deviant, and incompatible with learning environments. For example, in 2006, Black students accounted for only 17% of the public school student population, but accounted for 35.6% of the students who were subjected to corporal punishment, 37.4% of the students who were suspended, and 37.9% of the students who were expelled (Children's Defense Fund, 2012). Regarding cognitive and behavioral perceptions, Black children are half as likely to be placed in gifted and talented classes compared to White children whereas they are twice as likely be labeled as mentally retarded and one and a half times as likely to be removed from their primary class to be in a class designed for students with emotional challenges (Children's Defense Fund, 2012). Scholars have argued this arrangement contributes to negative academic outcomes including lower performance levels and higher levels of disengagement among Black males (Howard, 2014; Noguera, 2008). In addition, when Black males do not see teachers who reflect themselves throughout their K-12 schooling experiences it can perpetuate the message that these traditional spaces and related labels (e.g., intelligence, gifted, smart, etc.) are associated with Whiteness (Fordham & Ogbu, 1986; Majors & Billson, 1992). Furthermore, at the postsecondary level, systemic racist policies and practices at HWIs frequently result in Black students' encounters with racial microaggressions (Sue et al., 2007) and racial battle fatigue (see Smith, Allen, & Danley, 2007 for an expansive discussion on this topic with regards to African American males), which contributes to a range of adverse psychosocial (e.g., trauma, depression, emotional distress, etc.) and educational (e.g., lower graduation rates, lack of institutional commitment and attachment, etc.) outcomes.

Moreover, the miseducation process is deeply embedded within U.S. social structures where the same foundational principles that enslaved Blacks and deem them as property are perpetuated in a multitude of ways in the 21st century including through resource deprivation (ETS, 2011), academic exploitation (Oseguera, 2010), and athletic commodification within educational institutions (Cooper, 2012). Citing Professor Emeritus and economist Robert Haveman, Ladson-Billings (2006) described the education debt:

> The education debt is the foregone schooling resources that we could have (should have) been investing in (primarily) low income kids, which deficit leads to a variety of social problems (e.g., crime, low productivity, low wages, low labor force participation) that require on-going public investment. This required investment sucks away resources that could go to reducing the achievement gap. Without the education debt, we could narrow the achievement debt. (p. 5)

Ladson-Billings (2006) explained how this education debt is a culmination of historical, economic, sociopolitical, and immoral policies and practices that create and maintain social stratification along the lines of race and class. The intentional economic divestment from public education and concurrent increase in the privatization of K-12 schools underscores the erosion of the social contract via public goods while reinforcing the prevailing ideology of neoliberalism. The aforementioned ideology and conditions strengthened the privileging of Whiteness (unjust enrichment) and oppresses Blacks and various racialized groups (unjust impoverishment) (Feagin, 2006). An example of this education debt manifesting itself in early childhood is found in the

ETS (2011) report that revealed 61% of Black children were enrolled in low-quality home based care compared to 20% of White children. A widely known fact within the field of education is when cognitive developmental gaps exist early in childhood they are often exacerbated throughout adolescence and young adulthood (ETS, 2011; Noguera, 2008).

Another research report revealed that by the fourth grade 85% of Black youth are not proficient in reading or math at grade level, by the eighth grade 87% are not reading at grade level and 88% are not performing in math at grade level, and by the twelfth grade 84% are not reading at grade level and 94% are not performing in math at grade level (Children's Defense Fund, 2012). Even worse, for the 2007–2008 school year, 38% of Black students did not complete high school compared to 19% for White students (ETS, 2011). In 19 (out of 50) states the Black male graduation rates for the 2007–2008 academic year were less than 50% and in 16 states the rates were between 50–59% (Schott Foundation for Public Education, 2010). The ten lowest school districts were Jefferson Parish (Louisiana), Pinellas County (Florida), Dade County (Florida), Palm Beach County (Florida), Duval County (Florida), Charleston County (South Carolina), Detroit (Michigan), Cleveland (Michigan), Buffalo (New York), and New York City (New York) (Schott Foundation for Public Education, 2010).

Related to the education debt, these significant gaps in reading and math proficiency are a direct result of systemic racism and economic deprivation that limits the intellectual development and learning skill acquisition among a disproportionate number of Black youth who grow up in economically disadvantaged and educationally underserved neighborhoods. Since Blacks in these environments are not viewed as worthy investments for educational resources, their miseducation is justified and maintained within WRC. Compounding this reality is increased federal education standards such as the *No Child Left Behind Act* (2002), which disparately impacts and reduces resources for predominantly Black schools in economically disadvantaged neighborhoods that do not meet ahistorical, colorblind racist, and inequitable standards (Borman et al., 2004; Hodge et al., 2008; Schott Foundation for Public Education, 2010). The irony of the aforementioned trends is that many of these same municipalities and others with similar demographics are consistent purveyors of Black male athletic talent to top Division I athletic programs at HWIs and subsequently White-controlled professional sport leagues; thus, illustrating the interplay between schooling and sporting systems in the exploitation and underdevelopment of Black males and the broader Black community (Cooper, 2012; Hawkins, 2010; Macaulay, 2017; Rhoden, 2006).

The Miseducation of Black Males Through Youth and Interscholastic Sport

In concert with structural intersectionality (Howard, 2014) and education debt (Ladson-Billings, 2006), the stereotypical Black male athlete label and related socialization influences are yet another way by which Black males experience miseducation at an early age in and through sport and schooling. Hodge et al (2008) articulated the pervasive nature of racism at the intersection of sport and education for Black males:

> For example, when teachers, coaches, and other sport professionals knowingly or unknowingly perpetuate stereotypic beliefs about athletic superiority and intellectual inferiority as a function of race, they do harm to the minds of impressionable youth in their charge. In educational context, this may result in academic disassociation, particularly for Black males. (p. 210)

As noted in Chapter 1, Black male athletes throughout history have been assimilated into a dominant social order that commodifies and conditions them to internalize their primary purpose in a society founded upon and structured by WRC is to serve the needs of Whites (Woodson, 1903/1990). Black male athletes across gender groups are deemed as either inferior beings, athletic entertainers, and/or as prisoners within the U.S. prison industrial complex (PIC) and athletic industrial complex (AIC) (Alexander, 2012; Edwards, 2000; Hawkins, 2010; Smith, 2009). More specific to miseducation, although Black males persistently perform at lower levels academically than their peers, these outcomes have little to no impact on their presence on both school sanctioned (i.e., varsity sports) and non-school athletic teams (e.g., Pop Warner football, Amateur Athletic Union (AAU) basketball, etc.). Howard (2014) described this outcome as the athletic seasoning complex (ASC), which involves the socialization of Black male youth to intensely focus their energies on developing athletically in hopes of earning a coveted college athletic scholarship and securing a professional sport career at expense of their academic development. This early and intense socialization is important to examine and contextualize in order to acquire a better understanding Black males' experiences and outcomes in and through sport and (mis)education.

Black Male Early Socialization In and Through Sport

A majority of the previous theoretical and conceptual frameworks examining Black males athletes' experiences and outcomes has focused on systems level exploitation (Hawkins, 2010; Hawkins, Carter-Francique, & Cooper, 2017; Hylton, 2009; Singer, 2015; Smith, 2009). Although, these analyses are beneficial (and necessary) for understanding systemic and contextual factors impacting Black male athletes' experiences and outcomes, there is a lack of in-depth examinations of their socialization processes and the heterogeneity therein. For example, despite the fact Black male socialization has been explored from scholars across disciplines such as gender studies (Staples, 1978; Summers, 2004), philosophy (Curry, 2017; Fanon, 1952/2008), cultural studies (Bush & Bush, 2013a, 2013b; Mutua, 2006), urban education (Howard, 2014; Majors & Billson, 1992; Noguera, 2008), and postsecondary education (Cuyjet, 2006; Douglas, 2016; Harper, 2012; Harper & Harris, 2010; Harper & Nichols, 2008; Wood & Palmer, 2014), scholarly attention towards the lifespan socialization processes among Black male athletes that accounts for the heterogeneity among this sub-group is conspicuously scare.

Sport participation and socialization processes involve exposure to and support/affirmation from multiple socializing agents including family, community members, peers, and mass media throughout an individual's life (Beamon, 2008, 2010, 2012; Beamon & Bell, 2002, 2006; 2011; Castine & Roberts, 1974; Cooper, Gawrysiak, & Hawkins, 2012; Johnson & Migliaccio, 2009; Singer & May, 2010). Utilizing a social learning theory approach, Castine and Roberts (1974) found that family, peer group, and coaches had significant influence on Black youth's sport participation behaviors. Additional findings from their study revealed Black youth are most influenced by same race sport role models during early childhood compared to adolescence and adulthood. The authors explained the impact of this type of early exposure to sport:

> Socialization in this sense may be viewed as the process in which certain skills, traits, dispositions, and attitudes associated with performing certain sport roles are instilled during childhood. Black youths try to emulate visible Black athletes and thus concentrate upon positions in which Blacks are more prominent. (Castine & Roberts, 1974, p. 61)

These findings have been corroborated in subsequent research that has highlighted the power of social imitation theory and social reproduction theory (discussed in greater detail later in this chapter) where Black males are particularly impressionable when exposed to a preponderance of Black male athlete images from family, community, and the broader society (Beamon, 2008, 2010; 2012; Singer & May, 2010). Reiterating these findings, I along with my colleagues found the sport participation choices of Black baseball players at

HBCUs was influenced by family history and early involvement opportunities (Cooper, Gawrysiak, & Hawkins, 2012). Several of the participants explained how their fathers, older brothers, and other positive Black male role models in their neighborhoods played baseball and coached them, which created a special bond and connection to the sport. Both of these studies offer insight into the ways in which familial influences, early exposure to same race and gender role models, and access to participation opportunities contribute to sport affinity and participation choices.

With regards to social support for sport participation, Harris (1994) found that African American male youth basketball players were four times more likely to perceive social support for playing basketball from coaches, friends, and teachers than their White counterparts and this support was statistically associated with professional sport aspirations for Blacks, but not Whites. Additional findings revealed African American male youth basketball players were more likely to grow up in low-income father-absent households with formal education at or below a high school diploma, more likely to attend public and mostly Black schools, and play for predominantly Black teams. Each of these factors connects to the impacts of systemic racism in the U.S. society whereby Black males from economically disadvantaged neighborhoods are more susceptible to the allure of sport being a perceived (and at times real) means for upward mobility and thus a primary source of identity for them. Related to access, Eitle and Eitle (2002) found economic status influenced sport participation for different racial groups where Whites were more likely to participate in expensive sports such as swimming, baseball, and soccer and Blacks more likely to participate in less costly sports such as football and basketball. These findings support Edwards' (2000) argument that social constraints via limited educational and occupational opportunities for working class Black families fosters Black males' obsession with sports.

In another study, Johnson and Migliaccio (2009) documented how young African American boys are often socialized to view becoming a professional athlete as a tangible "African American Dream" and this aspiration is intensified by the reality of limited opportunities for career mobility in many predominantly African American communities (p. 102). The participants and their parents overwhelmingly conceptualized success in neoliberal terms such as material wealth, fame, and money with an emphasis on acquiring these aspirations via sport. The authors outlined the socialization process whereby African American boys develop strong athletic identities:

As a result of socialization, societal pressures and social experiences, the children in this study see themselves as athletes; they accept the role of what it means to be an athlete. These boys understand the social implications and the recognition as they evolve into adulthood and athletes. They are now not only understanding and accepting the idea of what an athlete is they immerse themselves in the role, they begin to define themselves by the role ... Sport was how they defined their future, and themselves. An athlete is who they are. (Johnson & Migliaccio, 2009, p. 107)

This four part process of athletic identity development among African American boys involves 1) access and introduction to sport at an early age via family, peers, community, and media (sport initiation process – model behavior with an understanding and internalization of the importance of being an athlete), 2) reference group exposure (professional athletes as role models), 3) social recognition (socialization agents), and 4) identity specialization (full immersion of athletic identity) (Johnson & Migliaccio, 2009). These findings are buttressed by Howard's (2014) work where he suggested Black males' engulfment in the athletic seasoning complex (ASC) involves: 1) early and ongoing exposure to sports, 2) significant time commitments devoted to sport through youth and adolescence, 3) "the holdback phenomenon" (discussed in greater detail later in this chapter), and 4) "the save the family syndrome" (p. 78). Hence, Black male athlete identity centrality is a result of specific socialization processes *in tandem with* societal conditions in a hegemonic culture rooted in the exploitation of the Black populace.

Relatedly, scholars have utilized social reproduction theory as a useful analytic lens to examine and explain how Black males have been exploited through sport and schooling in the U.S. (Singer & May, 2010). For example, Singer and May (2010) outlined how macro, meso, and micro level conditions influenced a African American male high school basketball player's singular aspirations of pursuing a professional sports career. With a particular emphasis on race and class, the authors highlighted how the participant experienced the "'double bind of marginality against mobility," which reflects the challenging conditions associated with growing up in public housing while seeking to overcome systemic oppression (Singer & May, 2010, p. 311). Hence, sport for Black males from economically disadvantaged neighborhoods operates as a real and perceived lifeline for upward mobility, which in turn influences their self-identity, sense of purpose, and perceptions of career options beyond sport. These findings echo Eitle and Eitle's (2002) study where African American male high school athletes from lower socioeconomic backgrounds with less access to educational and cultural capital were more likely to participate in football and basketball.

Akin to previous studies (Beamon & Bell, 2002, 2006; Harris, 1994; Johnson & Migliaccio, 2009), for the African American male high school basketball player in Singer and May's (2010) study sport was encouraged from an early age by family members particularly parents who through intergenerational economic deprivation were not able to experience the benefits of attending and graduating from college. The authors expounded upon the problematic nature of this disconcerting trend among African Americans who grow up in working class environments: "The temptation associated with immediate gratification typically supports the reproduction of one's social class position" (Singer & May, 2010, p. 307). As a result of these unfavorable conditions, the participant did not attend college, he was unable to pass qualification tests to enroll in the military, and subsequently worked "odd jobs" in his native community (Singer & May, 2010, p. 309). Unfortunately, his reality was not an outlier, but rather emblematic of numerous African American males who grow up in similar circumstances and experience the cycle of social class stagnation. The conditions under which his family lived preceded his interest and experiences in sport and therefore any efforts to improve Black males' lived experiences and outcomes must account for the interplay between multi-level ecological factors (e.g., access to quality educational resources, family socioeconomic status, etc.).

The Conveyor Belt

The current structural arrangements undergirding the multi-billion dollar U.S. sport industry, in particular intercollegiate and professional football and men's basketball, is predicated on the psychological attachment and athletic identity centrality of young talented Black males. In his critically acclaimed book titled, *Forty Million Dollar Slaves: The Rise, Fall, and Redemption of the Black Athlete*, Rhoden (2006) conceptualizes the societal arrangement that results in the youth to professional sport obsession for Black male athletes who are exploited by sport organizations and affiliate sponsors. Rhoden (2006) defined the Conveyor Belt as:

> ... a process by which athletic gold is mined and distributed largely to the benefit of white institutions and individuals in the billion-dollar sports industry. The "Belt" creates young African American millionaires but reinforces a "white is right" mentality that prevents athletes from galvanizing their power. (p. 170)

The Conveyor Belt is a tool of WRC that masks exploitation by propagandizing the illusion of colorblind meritocracy in and through sport. This ideology and supporting propaganda suggests that if visible Black males are able to secure multi-million dollar professional sport contracts and endorsement deals, then racism no longer exists in society and hard work and talent explain all societal outcomes within and beyond sport.

In fact, the Conveyor Belt and its corresponding ideological hegemony assert that sport serves as a progressive space in the U.S. society where Black males are afforded upward mobility opportunities unrelated to their race despite the fact less than a fraction of Black males experience this outcome. For example, the chances of becoming a professional athlete for Black males is 2 out of 100, 000 or .00002 percent (Leonard & Reyman, 1988). Stated another way, there are roughly 21.5 million Black men in the U.S. and less than 1, 500 Black males on NBA and NFL rosters on any given year, which would mean that the percentage of Black males in the NBA and NFL out of the entire Black male U.S. population is .000000005 (U.S. Census Bureau, 2017). Despite this reality, mass media coverage would suggests a majority of adult Black males in the U.S. society are professional athletes, which is an egregious and fallacious assertion. More recent data from the NCAA (2018) indicate the chances of any male college athlete in football and basketball (not just Black males) securing a professional sports career is 1.6% and 1.2%, respectively. Interestingly the two sports were Black males are overrepresented have the lowest probabilities of professional career attainment compared to baseball and hockey, where Black males are grossly underrepresented, the percentages are noticeably higher at 9.5% and 6.4%, respectively (NCAA, 2018). As noted earlier in the chapter, related to structural intersectionality (Howard, 2014) and education debt (Ladson-Billings, 2006), researchers have found that Black males from lower socioeconomic statuses are particularly susceptible to view sport as a conduit for accessing vital forms of capital (social, cultural, and economic) denied via other avenues (e.g., traditional schooling, professional associations, elite social clubs, etc.) (Eitle & Eitle, 2002). The interplay between class exploitation and racial oppression has been inextricably linked throughout U.S. history (DuBois, 1903/2003; Hine et al., 2006; Woodson, 1933/1990) and contrary to mainstream propaganda sport has been a valuable site for reproducing these inequities in a disguised manner (Edwards, 1969, 1973, 1980, 2000; Powell, 2008; Rhoden, 2006; Smith, 2009).

Moreover, Rhoden (2006) outlined how the Conveyor Belt is a sophisticated system of networks involving capitalist corporate sponsors in partnership with youth (e.g., leagues, camps, clubs, clinics, and organizations), interscholastic (e.g., associations, camps, showcases, etc.), intercollegiate (e.g., NCAA and athletic conferences), and professional sport leagues (e.g., NFL, NBA, etc.). The feeder systems benefit from the hopes and dreams of aspiring young athletes and their families and provide a platform for skill development for participants and talent identification for coaches and corporate sponsors. In essence, the Conveyor Belt reflects the growing trend of neoliberalism whereby sport specialization, competitive cultures within youth sport, and the value therein (e.g., individualism, meritocracy, The Great Sport Myth, etc.) are indoctrinated to athletes at an early age (Beyer & Hannah, 2000; Coakley, 2017; Sage, 1998). The economic stakes for identifying and cultivating talented athletes who can generate large sums of money and brand equity for White-controlled colleges and universities, professional sport leagues, and corporate sponsors has led to a scrupulous youth sport culture where coaches, parents, scouts, and agents engage in a range of unethical practices to win and profit off young athletes' talents (e.g., pay-for-play at the youth sport level, deceitful recruiting tactics, openly defiant rule breaking, and abusive treatment of athletes emotionally and physically, economic exploitation, etc.) (Coakley, 2017; Dohrmann, 2010; Sage & Eitzen, 2013; Rhoden, 2006).

Despite the fallacy of sport being a ahistorical, apolitical, colorblind, and meritocratic space, the creators and managers of the Conveyor Belt understand the power of sport within the Black community as well as in the broader society (also discussed in greater detail in Chapter 4 with the illusion of singular success model (ISSM)). For example, in the film *Schooled: The Price of College Sport* (Finkel & Martin, 2013), Sonny Vacarro, a famous sport marketer for Nike and co-founder of the legendary Dapper Dan Roundball Classic, detailed how major shoe companies seeking to enhance their brand equity and profit margins, intentionally targeted grassroots basketball organizations such as the Amateur Athletic Union (AAU) and athletic-centric youth and interscholastic programs along with eager big-time college athletic departments as partners to carry out the exploitation of talented basketball players (a majority of which were and remain Black). As discussed throughout this book, historically Blacks' sport involvement has been less about an innate interest in these types of physical activities, but rather a space where they felt accepted, welcomed, and valued even if often times disingenuously. In other words, Black male athletes by design within WRC were and are granted access to privileges that a majority of Blacks who are non-athletes in the broader U.S. were and are not (Wiggins, 2014). Rhoden (2006) asserted sport serves as an ideological symbol for America as well as an integral aspect of the U.S. economy; hence, the creation of the Conveyor Belt is designed to streamline the extraction of talented Black male athletes from Black communities to White-controlled, -identified, and -dominated sporting spaces. Otherwise stated, *sport involvement for Blacks has continuously been deeply tied to a desire to be treated and viewed as a human with positive identity affirmation whereas for White power wielders sport is viewed as a means to maintain the broader power apparatus that enables them to control labor production while maximizing their own economic gains and preserving the social hierarchy/stratified status quo (racial, gender, and class).* Thus, Black sport involvement without critical consciousness and collective empowerment does not yield any significant threat to the system of WRC and in fact it strengthens it.

Furthermore, there are additional alarming issues and outcomes associated with the Conveyor Belt (Rhoden, 2006). For athletes on the Conveyor Belt, this culture produces a level of internalized entitlement, which contributes to expectations of preferential treatment in academic environments (i.e., academic fraud via grade inflation or cheating) and social spaces (i.e., not having to pay for items or feeling entitled to engage in sexual behaviors independent of another person's preference/choice). This type of conditioning is problematic for all athletes (irrespective of race, gender, and class—see Coakley (2017) for an extended discussion on the detrimental impacts of this collective hubris), but it has a distinct adverse impact on Black males who exist in a society that criminalizes them and seeks to capitalize on their demise once their purpose and value to WRC is no longer profitable (e.g., due to injury, activism, etc.) (Alexander, 2012; Cooper, Macaulay, & Rodriguez, 2017; Curry, 2017; Edwards, 1980, 1984, 2000; Howard, 2014; Noguera, 2008). The Conveyor Belt also conditions Black male athletes to be apolitical, colorblind, and disassociated with the plight of the broader Black community (Rhoden, 2006). Inherently and importantly, the WRC hegemonic system is dependent upon the uncritical acceptance of the singularly focused and talented Black male athlete image because this internalization detracts attention away from a deeper history and knowledge of the diverse and multi-faceted skill sets possessed and exhibited by Black males over centuries. This lack of exposure to the rich history of African American male athletes' excellence in areas beyond sport as well as their courageous acts of resistance against White racist norms in social and political spaces is a powerful tool of the miseducation machine (Cooper, Macaulay, & Rodriguez, 2017; Harrison et al., 2017). For example, Smith, Clark, and Harrison (2014) highlighted how the stories of talented African American scholar athletes such as William Henry Lewis, Duke Salter, Jerome "Brud" Holland, Fritz Pollard, and Paul Robeson in fields such as law, politics, education, theater, and civil rights are too often unbeknownst to young Black male athletes whereas Kobe Bryant, Cam Newton, Le'Veon Bell, Kevin Durant, and Stephen Curry to name a few are not only well known, but detailed information about their statistics and personal lives are memorized as well. Thus, awareness of Black male athletes' accomplishments beyond sport is one way to mitigate miseducation practices that condition them to believe their most prized trait as a human being is their athletic abilities (Smith, Clark, & Harrison, 2014).

Once placed on the Conveyor Belt, Black male athletes learn that being complicit with the White-controlled sporting system can result in tremendous benefits such as shoes, apparel, athletic scholarships, favorable treatment from adoring White fans, coaches, and organizers, a heightened social status, and the possibility of securing multi-million dollar professional sport contracts and endorsements. These potential benefits are particularly persuasive for impressionable young Black males who have limited access to positive identity affirmation and viable opportunities for upward mobility in a society founded upon and structured by WRC. In exchange for these privileges, Black male athletes must view and conduct themselves as separate and distinct/different from the broader Black community. Rhoden (2006) outlines the significant racial, political, cultural, and emotional implications of this arrangement:

> The major difference with black athletes is the cultural dislocation and isolation the Belt encourages, and the infantilizing effect this has on the athletes themselves and the wasted opportunity it represents for the communities they come from. In the black athlete's quest for power, the Conveyor Belt represents an especially serious impediment. (p. 180)

Throughout history, a key ingredient for the success of WRC has been the physical and psychological separation of Blacks who if galvanized could directly undermine the system. The Conveyor Belt fosters the acceptance of the White savior complex (Hughey, 2014) by which Black male athletes view Whites as the conduits for capitalistic goal attainment without fully understanding how they are being exploited and the Black community at large is being oppressed and underdeveloped throughout this process. In addition, Black male athletes on the Conveyor Belt view escaping and never coming back to their native Black communities as the goal as opposed to understanding the impacts of systemic racism and being committed to championing and improving their native Black communities.[1] The Conveyor Belt thus serves as a powerful mechanism for maintaining WRC and not uplifting the Black race as a whole (versus a limited number of Black males and their families). The Conveyor Belt operates primarily in the sporting realm, but it exists in tandem with other oppressive forces such as gendered racism in and through the miseducation schooling system.

Athletic-Centric Prep and Private Schools

A recent phenomenon that has capitalized on the ASC (Howard, 2014) and Conveyor Belt (Rhoden, 2006) trends has been the growth of athletic-centric prep schools or more commonly known as diploma mill academies (Brennan, 2011; Daza & Gonzalez, 2017; Thamel, 2006; Wolverton, 2014). Prep schools have been around for over two centuries, but the sport-specific prep schools became more popular during the latter part of the 20th and early 21st century (Wolverton, 2014). With little oversight from NCAA and high school athletic governing bodies, these schools operate under their own rules and often take advantage of young athletes (and their families) who have hopes of making it to the next level. Since the early 2000s, numerous Black male athletes (as well as those from different races) who have either struggled to meet the academic eligibility requirements to compete as a freshman at an NCAA institution and/or seeking to improve athletically by competing against college level talent have opted to attend prep schools (Brennan, 2011). Notable prep school attendees who later became first round NBA draft picks include Kevin Durant, Carmelo Anthony, Jerry Stackhouse, Ty Lawson, Brandon Jennings, Michael Beasley, Andrew Wiggins, Rajon Rondo, Ovinton J'Anthony (O. J.) Mayo, Avery Bradley, and Tristan Thompson to name a few. Even though, academic remediation is cited as a primary aim of many of these prep and/or private "schools," many of them are not accredited by reputable educational entities. In fact, several of these prep schools outsource their academic services whereby few if any face-to-face courses are held at the main campus (Thamel, 2006). At many of these schools, it is not uncommon for a majority the school to be comprised of athletes and class attendance is either optional or minimal. Players can be awarded necessary academic credits in order to boost their grade point averages (GPAs) and/or meet course requirements for NCAA eligibility. Yet, in many cases no teaching, learning, or completion of assignments is taking place. Thus, the academic exploitation and fraud at the interscholastic level involves the use of sport as bait to lure vulnerable Black male athletes away from their native communities and educational spaces that could potentially meet their academic needs at a more satisfactorily level.

Regarding traditional private schools, countless Black males have also experienced athletic success through these routes. Examples of standout Black male athletes who attended private high schools include Kobe Bryant, Tracy McGrady, LeBron James, Anthony Davis, A'mare Stoudemire, and Dwight

Howard. A common pattern across prep and traditional private schools is the prioritization of athletics over academics as it pertains to Black males via their selective recruitment and subsequent valuation based on their athletic performance versus their academic enrichment and intellectual gains. For example, a relevant indication of the pervasive nature of the miseducation of Black male athletes through schooling and interscholastic sport is evident in what Howard (2014) describes as the "holdback phenomenon," which is commonly exercised via the prep and/or private school route (p. 81). It is commonplace for talented Black male athletes to either be held back a year for athletic purposes or enroll in a private or prep school especially in sports such as basketball (Wolverton, 2014). In other sports such as football, several schools engage in questionable ethics involving transfer student strategies and adjustments to academic classifications for Black males to procure their athletic services to bolster a school's reputation (Macaulay, 2017). The core problem with these trends lie in the fact that the athletic-centric decision making process involves little to no concern for these Black males' life outcomes beyond sport particularly if (and in many cases when) they are unable to attain either an athletic scholarship at the college level and/or a sustainable professional sports career (Cooper, Corral, et al., 2018).

Moreover, the prep school diploma mills are located all across the U.S. in states such as New York, Philadelphia, Florida, Mississippi, North Carolina, Illinois, California, and Texas to name a few (Thamel, 2006). In addition to academic fraud, a number of other ethical and legal issues have been associated with these diploma mills including the physical abuse of athletes, sub-standard housing conditions, and embezzlement on behalf of administrators, staff, and coaches (Brennan, 2011; Wolverton, 2014). At one academy called 22ft in Anderson, South Carolina, players were forced to live in a converted barn and garage where they were exposed to various animals including "mice, possums, and roaches" (Daza & Gonzalez, 2017, p. 1). Two of the players were bitten by spiders, experienced skin aversions, and required significant medical care. The founders of the academy, Mike and Brenda Rawson, were subsequently indicted on federal charges (Daza & Gonzalez, 2017). Aside from avoiding the rules of mainstream public high school athletic associations, there are significant financial opportunities for prep and traditional private schools who seek to exploit the system. For example, after Tracy McGrady, former standout high school player at Mount Zion Christian Academy in Durham, North Carolina and first round lottery pick (#9) in the 1997 NBA draft, signed an endorsement deal with Adidas and the shoe company gave $300, 000 to the traditional private Christian school and close to $1 million to the head coach (Thamel, 2006). Another potential benefit for the high school coaches involves the opportunity to be hired onto a college coaching staff along with the recruitment of a star player. Given exorbitant salaries for Division I head and assistant coaches as well as directors of player development, this arrangement is enticing for secondary and grassroots coaches seeking upward mobility and a heightened social status (Dohrmann, 2010).

In addition, college coaches also benefit greatly from prep diploma mills and athletic-centric private schools. Since each year coaches have a limited number of scholarships to offer, they can encourage talented prospects to attend one of these schools for a year and then offer them a scholarship the following year (Wolverton, 2014). The coaches can preserve the athletes' four-years of college eligibility, stay within their scholarship restrictions, and know the athlete will compete against college level talent during that year at a prep or private school. One of the main problems with this arrangement is the racist foundation that prioritizes White economic desires over Black male athletes' holistic well-being. The ubiquitous nature of the concocted prep and private school scene and corresponding lack of in-depth intervention on behalf of the NCAA, NBA, NFL, United States Olympic Committee (USOC), and related sport governing bodies highlight the systemic racism embedded in these exploitative miseducation schooling and sporting systems. As a result, the miseducation of Black male athletes in the K-12 schooling system convinces them that their athletic abilities, not their holistic identity, potential, and prowess, is their most valuable asset.

The Miseducation of Black Males Through College Sport: Institutionalized Exploitation

Athletic Role Engulfment and Identity Foreclosure

Rooted in social psychology theories (Tajfel, 1981, 2010; Turner, 1975), identity development theories (Erickson, 1959), and social cognitive theory (Bandura, 1986; 2001), role theory explains the interplay between systems, environments, processes, and individual and group outcomes. More specific to sport, in a seminal study, Adler and Adler (1991) utilized role theory as an explanatory tool to understand the complex socialization experiences of elite male basketball players at a Division I HWI. A majority of the participants in their study were Black, which is consistent with their overrepresentation in men's basketball at the Division I level from the latter 20th century through the early 21st century (Harper, 2018). Using ethnographic approaches, the authors closely examined the institutional culture including the athletic sub-culture at the HWI and its subsequent impact on the identity development of the male basketball players. Several key theoretical concepts were identified from their data analysis including statuses, roles, identities, self, role-set members, role expectations, role conflict, role domination, role abandonment, and role engulfment (Adler & Adler, 1991).

An influential aspect of the players' experiences and identity development was their socially constructed statuses. Adler and Adler (1991) described statuses as positions in a group or system connected to other positions via cultural and organizational norms. In the case of the participants, their athletic status was coupled with heightened visibility, privilege, and reverence within the campus community. This social status created a sense of entitlement and attachment to their athletic abilities. The concept of roles refers to specific activities individuals who possess a certain status will perform to fulfill normative expectations. For the participants in this study, a normative expectation for the male basketball players was to prioritize athletic goals over academic aspirations. As a result, the authors noted how many of the participants initially possessed high academic idealism, but over time their exposure to the athletic sub-culture at the institution and related pressures reduced these motivations. Relatedly, identities refers to personal conceptions or internalizations developed while an individual fulfills a status and performs a role. As noted, within the context of a big-time college sports culture, athletes are encouraged to associate themselves more intensely with their athletic identities over their holistic identities such as their race, gender, family, academic, and other social identities. Hence, the common self-identification reference among Black males as being an "athlete-student" versus a student-athlete (Beamon, 2008; Singer, 2009). The fourth individualized role theory concept is the self. According to the authors, self is conceptualized as the "more global, multirole, core conception of the real person" (Adler & Adler, 1991, p. 28). Despite the importance of the self and the dominant societal narrative that purports sport participation inherently cultivates the development of this aspect of an athletes' identity, Adler and Adler (1991) found the collective hubris, media coverage, public glorification, and money associated with big-time college sports stifled the growth and internalization of male basketball players' sense of self.

Moving beyond individual conceptions, Adler & Adler (1991) analyzed the influence of intergroup social relations. In particular, the authors identified three distinct role-set members or groups: a) academic, b) athletic, and c) social. Academic role-set members are professors, academic advisors, tutors, and classmates. Due to the participants' social statuses as athletes, and related expectations including intense athletic time commitments, the nature of their relationships with their academic role-set members was challenging on multiple levels. Adverse stereotypes about their academic abilities and motivations were ubiquitous (i.e., prevalence of the dumb jock label). Furthermore, they were often steered by their coaches and academic advisors to enroll in faculty-friendly or easy courses where minimal academic effort was expected. Regarding athletic role-set members, their relationships with coaches and athletic staff were ambivalent and often times based on their most recent athletic performance. The social role-set members included significant others and peers who were non-athletes. The heightened social status as athletes created a level of admiration from their peers. The problem with these temporal relationships was the fact that they were primarily based on participants' athletic identities and abilities versus their true self.

When examining participants' environment and subsequent individual outcomes, Adler and Adler (1991) offered five theoretical concepts to explain these processes: a) role expectations, b) role conflict, c) role domination, d) role abandonment, and e) role engulfment (Adler & Adler, 1991). Role expectations refer to an individual's perceptions of their roles prior to enrolling or being immersed into a specific milieu (i.e., big-time college sports at HWIs). The role expectations for participants' in Adler and Adler's (1991) study involved a balanced approach towards academics and athletics. Consequently, after enrolling and being exposed to the HWI environment, participants' learned their academic idealism was not congruent with the athletic-centric culture on campus. This incongruence resulted in role conflict (Adler & Adler, 1991) or also referred to as role strain (Snyder, 1985). Role conflict ensues as a result of incompatible personal and cultural/organizational expectations regarding time, focus, and energy towards academics, athletics, and social interests. Participants initially sought to have a more balanced college experience, but once they encountered role conflict they subsequently engaged in identity and role adjustments. These mental and behavioral shifts were largely due to the fact that their coaches' controlled their scholarships and schedules. These adjustments are described as the role engulfment process whereby the gradual primacy of athletic identity and related tasks (role domination) emerge and concurrent detraction of time, focus, energy, desire, and identification with non-athletic activities and aspirations wane (role abandonment). The net outcome of the athletic role engulfment process includes unfulfilled academic goals, a deflated sense of self at the conclusion of one's athletic career, and negative post-athletic career transitional challenges. This seminal theoretical contribution offered a useful lens to examine how, when, and why athletes (including numerous Black males) strongly identify with their athletic identities to the detriment of their holistic identities (Adler & Adler, 1991).

Building on the works of Erickson (1959) and Marcia (1966), Brewer and Petitpas (2017) expanded on this athletic role engulfment process by defining athletic identity foreclosure as a "commitment to the athlete role in the absence of exploration of occupational or ideological alternatives" (p. 118). Using data on athletes from youth through late adolescence and young adulthood, the authors asserted the socialization process including social, psychological, academic, cognitive, and emotional components in competitive sport contributes to athletic identity foreclosure. Brewer and Petitpas (2017) explained in greater detail how and why this occurs:

> … when athletes get enmeshed in the sport system, they may not engage in exploratory behavior because of the time commitment required for sport participation, the approval they receive from peers from participating in sport, and the intrinsic and extrinsic rewards accrued from athletic accomplishments. (p. 119)

The purpose, meaning, and structure of youth and adolescent sports as well as one's exposure and access (or a lack thereof) to non-sport identity and career development options also influences the prevalence of athletic identity foreclosure (Coakley, 2017). In particular, the intersections of sport participation and masculine identity within a patriarchal society has resulted in male athletes being more susceptible to athletic identity foreclosure compared to their female counterparts (Murphy, Petitpas, & Brewer, 1996). More germane to the current analysis of Black male athletes, understanding the conditions including antecedents, moderators, mediators, and outcomes associated with athletic identity foreclosure as well as the inverse of this process (holistic identity development—see Cooper (2016b) for a detailed discussion on this phenomenon) enables Black males, their families, coaches, teachers, advisors, administrators, and all key stakeholders to better understand how to create and maintain positive supports for holistic development before, during, and after their athletic careers.

Black Male Athletic Identity Foreclosure and Role Engulfment: A Theory of Gendered Racism In and Through Sport and Miseducation

It has been well-documented in the sport and education literature the extent to which athletes from various identity groups and sport types experience levels of athletic role conflict, engulfment, and post-career transitional challenges (Adler & Adler, 1991; Brewer & Petitpas, 2017; Coakley, 2017; Murphy et al., 1996). However, based on a review of relevant literature on Black male athletes (Beamon, 2008, 2010, 2012; Benson, 2000; Bimper, 2016; Cooper & Cooper, 2015; Douglas, Ivey, & Bishop, 2015; Singer, 2005, 2009), I propose the need for a theory that more fully captures the distinct impact of these processes and conditions on this sub-group. More specifically, I surmise the uniqueness of the plight of Blacks in the U.S. and their historical and contemporary connections to sport result in distinct experiences and outcomes among Black male athletes both during and after their athletic careers conclude. The rationale for this theoretical delineation is rooted in the following distinct characteristics:

(a) Since the inception of the U.S., Black males are the only group of males as a collective to be legally viewed and treated as less than human (sub-human concept) inter-generationally (Cooper, 2012; Edwards, 1969, 1973);

(b) Historically, pseudo-science has purported that their race (Black) and gender (male/masculinity) were genetically predisposed for arduous labor for the economic benefits of Whites (e.g., chattel slavery, modern day football, super-human concept, etc.), which correspond with the myth of intellectual inferiority (Edwards, 1969, 1973, 2000; Harrison, Harrison, & Moore, 2002; Hawkins, 1998a, 1998b, 2010; Sailes, 2010)—this concept is also referred to as anti-Black misandry and gendered racism against Black males more broadly—see Curry (2017) and Mutua (2006) for detailed analyses;

(c) They are perpetually overrepresented in two highest revenue-generating sports at the intercollegiate level and highly visible professional sports (football and basketball) while concurrently being underrepresented in the general student body at postsecondary institutions, leadership positions in sport (e.g., ownership, management, coaching, media, etc.), and numerous occupational fields (i.e., education) (Hodge, Collins, & Bennett, 2013; Cooper, 2012; Hawkins, 2010; Harper, 2018);

(d) They experience disparate surveillance as a highly visible racialized male group with the stigmatization of innate criminality, deviance, and savagery in historically White educational and sporting spaces as well as in the broader society (Gill, 2015; Hawkins, 1998a, 1998b; Leonard & King, 2012);

(e) They are more likely to be admitted into college academically underprepared via special admissions (American Institutes for Research, 1989; Cooper, 2012; Harrison, Comeaux, & Plecha, 2006; Nwadike, Baker, Brackebush, & Hawkins, 2016);

(f) They persistently experience the lowest academic performance outcomes among all college athletes (Bennett, Hodge, Graham, & Moore, 2015; Harper, 2018; NCAA, 2017a, 2017b)

(g) As a collective group, they experience cyclical oppression in areas such as shorter lifetime expectancy/higher mortality rates, increased unemployment, lack of home ownership, limited access to quality health care, exposure to miseducation schooling, higher incarceration rates, higher homicides, increased mental health issues, and scarce wealth acquisition compared to their peers across racial, gender, and socioeconomic status groups (Alexander, 2012; Children's Defense Fund, 2012; Cooper, 2012; Curry, 2017; ETS, 2011; Howard, 2014; Noguera, 2008; Majors & Billson, 1992; Schott Foundation for Public Education, 2010, 2015)

Collectively, the aforementioned multi-level systemic factors influence Black male athletes who experience the athletic role engulfment process in distinctive ways from their peers (i.e., their identity foreclosure and holistic underdevelopment combined with cumulative effects of systemic gendered racism exacerbate transitional challenges psychologically and occupationally as a collective group). As discussed in Chapter 1, given the historical nature of their initial access to mainstream organized sport in the U.S. dating back to the late 19th century (Wiggins & Miller, 2003), Black males' involvement in these activities was and remains one of the few spaces where they systematically experience a resemblance of human dignity (albeit ambiguously) and positive identity affirmation. In contrast, Whites historically have used sport participation as a leisure activity for entertainment, social engagement, gender socialization, and character development (Coakley, 2017; Eitle & Eitle, 2002). *Hence, if one's humanity (not simply their identity) is rooted in their sport participation and performance, then the intensity and impact of athletic identity foreclosure and role engulfment as well as post-athletic life transitional processes must be labeled and examined differently.* The proposed model discussed in Chapter 4 builds on previous literature and offers in-depth insight into the socialization phases whereby this process occurs for Black male athletes.

Furthermore, the current body of literature on Black male former athletes' post-athletic career outcomes unequivocally illustrates the significant transitional experiences among this sub-group, which range from loss of identity to extensive depression (Beamon, 2008, 2010, 2012; Northcutt, 2013; Singer, 2009). In a society where Blackness, masculinity, and sport are dangerously synonymous, and societal arrangements are structured to convince this sub-group that their primary human value is based on their athletic abilities, the reconceptualization of role theory (unlike its initial conception in Adler and Adler's (1991) study) must take into account the intersecting effects of systemic racism, gendered racist stigmatization (i.e., concurrent sub- and super-human stereotypical schemata placed upon Black males particularly those involved in sport), and class dynamics. In particular, I argue the sub- and super-human stereotypes placed upon Black males in general and Black male athletes more specifically serves as means to dehumanize them since being viewed as less or more than human justifies their mistreatment and prevents them receiving dignity and rights attributed to those deemed as humans. Self-conceptions (identities, statuses, roles, and self), socialization agents (role-set members), and athletic-related identity processes (role conflict and role engulfment) for Black males are distinct because they are nested within multi-level systems, socio-historical realities, and sociological trends that are unique to their positionality within the U.S. social hierarchy (Cooper, 2012). Thus, each of the proposed models in this book illustrate how conditions surrounding Black males either foster or prevent Black male athletic identity foreclosure and role engulfment. Otherwise stated, the proposed models offer an expansive ecological systems analysis of factors that contribute to their holistic (under)development in and through sport and (mis)education.

Junior Colleges (JUCOs)

Akin to academically fraudulent prep schools, junior colleges (JUCOs) are another site where Black male athletes in many instances experience academic and athletic exploitation.[2] Related to the Conveyor Belt (Rhoden, 2006), Edwards (1984) explained the nature of these exploitative sporting systems:

> Many of these young men eventually end up in what is called, appropriately enough, the "slave trade"—a nationwide phenomenon involving independent scouts (some

would call them "flesh peddlers") who, for a fee (usually paid by a four-year college) search out talented but academically "high risk" black athletes and place them in an accommodating junior college where their athletic skills are further honed through participation in sports. (p. 9)

The critically acclaimed Netflix documentary, *Last Chance U* (Whitely & Ridley, 2016), offers vivid insights into the world of JUCO athletics. The series follows the lives of players, staff, and coaches at a prominent JUCO program, East Mississippi Community College (EMCC). Throughout the series, the harsh realities of the JUCO world are revealed. The athletes in the documentary experience academic underpreparedness, psychological issues, family challenges, financial problems, and various obstacles associated with a high pressure athletic environment where the chances of making it to the next level are not guaranteed. Numerous Black male athletes at JUCOs have Division I level talent, but for reasons ranging from a lack of athletic exposure to academic issues compel them to attend these two-year institutions. In the *Last Chance U* series, the EMCC football coach, Buddy Stephens, acknowledges the goal for him and his players is to get them to the next level athletically as soon as possible (Bembry, 2016). Thus, investment in academic development beyond minimal eligibility standards or career preparation for life after sports is not a focal point at many JUCOs with athletic programs. Consequently, several of the Black male athletes in the documentary experience academic disengagement. In concert with broader societal norms rooted in the neoliberal meritocracy myth, the documentary frames the problems facing Black male athletes as being primarily within their control so as long as they make "good choices" and follow the guidance of "seemingly well-intentioned" Whites in leadership and supportive roles (see Hughey (2014) for an extended discussion on the problematic issues with the White savior complex and narrative promoted in U.S. media). However, a conspicuous omission from the documentary is a critical analysis of the ecological factors that contribute to Black male athletes' academic underpreparedness, lower academic self-efficacy, disengagement, and underachievement. The depiction and internalization among Black male athletes of deficit-based explanations for their negative life outcomes is misleading and do not take into account how miseducation manifests through systemic oppression and ideological hegemony.

Another distinct feature of JUCOs is their geographical and cultural locations. Many of these schools particularly in the Southern and Midwestern U.S. are located in remote predominantly White rural areas. This physical separation from Black communities where many Black males grow up reflects what Hawkins (2010) described as an oscillating migrant experience. Within this arrangement, Black male JUCO athletes are subjected to social and cultural marginalization whereby their athletic identity and performance is the primary marker of validation and acceptance (Cooper & Hawkins, 2014). Similar to Black male athletes' exploitation at the Division I level, the major benefactors of these arrangements are White-controlled institutions, athletic programs, sponsors, and local municipalities. In order to better serve Black male college athletes' educational and personal needs, Hawkins (2010) suggested the campus climates at these HWIs must "not only be inviting and accepting for the athletic talents of these students ... but they must be accommodating of the social and cultural backgrounds ..." (p. 131). The lack of concerted efforts to address this cultural mistrust at HWIs is commonplace in the literature on Black male college athletes (Beamon, 2008; Cooper & Hawkins, 2014; Melendez, 2008; Singer, 2005).

Unfortunately, there is limited national data on the transfer rates of Black male JUCO athletes. Using a small sample size, Harper (2009) noted transfer rate disparities along racial lines between Black and White male JUCO athletes at the following schools in 2008: a) 47% gap at Pima Community College District of Arizona with the football team (Black males—17% compared to White males—63%), b) 31% gap at Dixie State College in Utah with the basketball team (Black males—25% compared to White males—56%), c) 25% gap at Enterprise-Ozark Community College in Alabama with the basketball team (Black males—25% compared to White males—50%), and d) 67% at Gadsden State Community College in Georgia with the basketball team (Black males—0% compared to White males—67%). Although, the transfer rates to four-year colleges among Black male college athletes is less publicized, research on Black males students (including non-athletes and athletes) who attend community colleges highlights the top reasons for their lack of persistence and transfer outcomes include family responsibilities, program dissatisfaction, and other reasons (e.g., issues with faculty and staff, goal adjustment, lack of perception of degree utility, etc.) (Wood, 2012). Hence, when Black males who attend JUCOs for athletic purposes *do not* earn their associate's degree, *do not* transfer to four-year colleges, and/ or *do not* earn a bachelor's degree they often leave school with dejection that is exacerbated by unfulfilled sport aspirations. This outcome means they have been properly miseducated and underserved by the schooling and sporting systems in the U.S.

Special Admissions, Academic Underpreparedness, and Problematic Enrollment Trends

Another form of academic exploitation at the postsecondary level is through a process called special admissions (Barker, 2012; Cooper, Nwadike, & Macaulay, 2017; Nwadike, Baker, Brackenbusch, & Hawkins, 2016). Special admissions involve the enrollment of students whose academic readiness for college is significantly lower than the average student accepted at a given institution. Although, special admissions are not limited to athletes, at many big-time sport institutions athletes constitute a disproportionate number of special admissions (Nwadike et al., 2016). For example, research on the six major Bowl Championship Series (BCS) conferences in 2008 revealed the average Scholastic Aptitude Test (SAT) scores for incoming first-year students (1, 161) was 124 points higher than the average for all college athletes (1037), 220 points higher than football players (941), and 227 points higher than basketball players (934) (Lederman, 2008). The latter two sports with the largest gaps are the teams where Black males are persistently overrepresented (Harper, 2018). Although, the SAT has been deemed culturally bias and has a disparate impact on Blacks, it is important to acknowledge and understand that the same epistemological racism (Scheurich & Young, 1997) and White Anglo-Saxon Eurocentric middle class values system (Lareau, 2002) undergirding the SAT also inform a majority of the curricula at K-20 schools including HWIs in the U.S. Thus, the gaps in SAT scores should not be interpreted as deficits in intelligence or cognitive abilities, but rather differences in culturally and socially constructed standards of knowledge rooted in White normative ways of knowing where Blacks particularly those from working class backgrounds are at inherent disadvantage (Feagin Vera, & Batur, 2000). Along the same lines, Barker (2012) found the incoming average high school grade point averages (GPAs) for the freshman class at Georgia Institute of Technology (Georgia Tech) was 3.9, which was nearly 2.0 GPA points higher than a group of 21 special admit football players whose average GPA was 2.19.

In 2014, national attention was shifted to the University of North Carolina at Chapel Hill (UNC-CH), when Mary Willingham, a former Learning Specialist with the athletics department, revealed through her research several unethical practices relating to the neglect of Black male college athletes' academic needs. In a research study for her doctoral program at the University of North Carolina at Greensboro (UNCG), Willingham examined the reading comprehension skills of 183 football and basketball players at UNC-CH over an eight year period (2004–2012). Findings from her study indicated over half of the participants read between fourth and eighth grade levels and nearly 10% of participants read below third grade levels (Smith & Willingham, 2015). The alarming findings illustrate the extent to which K-12 schooling and special admissions processes at the postsecondary level disadvantage Black male college athletes. Imagine the feeling of sitting in a classroom with peers whose academic prowess earned them acceptance into elite colleges and universities while many Black males recruited for athletic purposes possess insecurities and deficiencies with academic skills such as literacy. Aside from expected academic challenges, these types of experiences can result in short- and/or long-term psychological trauma (see the case of Kevin Ross from Creighton University and additional examples highlighted in Chapter 4).

At the 2016 *Black Student Athlete Summit* at the University of Texas at Austin, following a panel of Division I athletic academic advisors who shared insights on how they support Black male college athletes who are grossly underprepared for college courses I posed two important questions. The first question I asked was *if the skill sets were reversed, would a Black male who possessed athletic skills at a fourth grade level be offered a scholarship to participate on a Division I athletic team and asked to perform immediately or on par with their peers (which is the case when the scenario is academic in nature)?* In a sport such as football, conventional logic would deem this decision as posing a serious health risk for the player. For basketball, the likelihood of a player developing significantly over a four-year period with limited skills is low and also presents a major risk for the player (in terms of psychological and at times physical well-being) and the program especially when the financial stakes for winning are so high at the Division I level for coaches' job security and institutional revenue generation and prestige. As such, the logic of accepting underprepared/underserved Black males largely applies only when the circumstance involves athletics for exploitative purposes, which underscores the unethical nature of big-time college sports in the U.S. (Cooper, Nwadike, & Macaulay, 2017).

The second question I posed to the panel was *how many Black males who are not athletes and read at a fourth grade reading level would be admitted to prestigious Division I institutions where the admissions standards for the general student body are highly competitive and selective?* The answer is very few to zero. Therefore, it seems that Black males who significantly lack academic readiness to excel in college can only (or primarily) access prestigious Division I institutions or rather they are only *worthy to be admitted* so as long as they provide an economic and entertaining service to White stakeholders via athletics (Donnor,

2005; Edwards, 1984; Singer, 2015). This reality harkens to Black males' initial entry into mainstream sports during the postbellum period outlined in Chapter 1 and thus the racist residue through sport and schooling systems remains prominent in the 21st century albeit in an evolved form. Moreover, this often described "educational opportunity" ignores the fact that intercollegiate athletics involves significant time commitments akin to a full-time job, which greatly restricts the amount of time spent on academic remediation and development as well as contributes to a range of psychological, physical, and social stressors (Cooper & Cooper, 2015; Edwards, 1984; Sellers, 2000; Singer, 2009). Unfortunately, this educational malfeasance (Smith, 2009), educational malpractice (Davis, 1992), and academic exploitation (Oseguera, 2010; Sellers, 2000) is not uncommon among postsecondary institutions particularly at big-time college sport schools who continue the age-old American tradition of treating Black males as commodities for their physical labor and devalue their intellectual abilities, holistic development, and overall personal well-being (Cooper, 2012, 2016b; Cooper & Cooper, 2015; Hawkins, 2010; Smith, 2009).

The aforementioned data corroborates previous research that found Black male athletes are more likely than their peers to be admitted into college academically underprepared (Cooper, 2012; Cooper, Nwadike, & Macaulay, 2017; Harrison et al., 2006). As noted in earlier in this chapter, these academic readiness gaps or rather the educational debt (Ladson-Billings, 2006) is established well before the postsecondary level and often worsens over time. The tragedy is too often talented Black male athletes are allowed to persist to the next grade and even be admitted to some of the most renowned colleges and universities in the country while their academic skills (not necessarily their intellectual capabilities) are well below their peers (e.g., reading comprehension, mathematical deduction, critical thinking and problem solving with schooling assignments, etc.) (Pascarella, Bohr, Nora, & Terenzini, 1995; Pascarella et al., 1999). The practice of special admissions has a disparate impact on Black male athletes, many of which will not advance to the professional level in their sport. Thus, after being properly miseducated they are discarded by these institutions and faced with the task of pursuing gainful employment despite lacking career readiness and often coping with undetected psychological trauma (Beamon, 2008, 2012; Beamon & Bell, 2011; Donnor, 2005; Edwards, 1984, 2000; Smith & Willingham, 2015).

The special admissions process and related tactics also results in problematic enrollment trends that are prevalent at several prominent HWIs. For example,

Harper (2018) indicated in a report on racial inequities in big-time college sports that in 2016–2017 Black males comprised 55% of Division I Power 5 football teams and 56% of Division I Power 5 basketball teams while only constituting 2.4% of the total undergraduate student population. The inverse relationship between these trends associated with enrollment and special admissions illustrate how these institutions primarily value Black males for their athletic prowess and not for their academic promise. These trends exacerbate the prevalence of the Black dumb jock stereotype and underscore how these neoliberal HWIs underserve and undervalue the holistic development of Black male athletes (Beamon, 2008; Benson, 2000; Cooper, 2012, 2016b; Donnor, 2005; Edwards, 1984; Singer, 2005, 2015). As a result, the trends of special admissions, academic underpreparedness, and disconcerting enrollment trends highlight how both K-12 schools *and* postsecondary institutions are culpable of the underserving Black males in general and particularly those who participate in athletics.

Academic Clustering

Another questionable practice documented in the literature is the trend of academic clustering or commonly referred to as majoring in eligibility (Beamon, 2008; Benson, 2000; Cooper & Cooper, 2015; Fountain & Finley, 2009; Oseguera, 2010; Singer, 2005, 2009). Academic clustering refers to the enrollment of 25% or more members of a team within a single academic major (Case, Greer, & Brown, 1987; Fountain & Finley, 2009). Oseguera (2010) described clustering as a form of academic exploitation. According to the author, academic exploitation refers to "practices that perpetuate inequitable academic outcomes such as discouragement from enrolling in 'tough' majors or placement in courses that do not advance students towards a degree" (Oseguera, 2010, p. 301). At the conclusion of the 2006 football season, Fountain and Finley (2009) examined the frequency of academic clustering among Atlantic Coast Conference (ACC) schools and found Minority football players were more likely to be clustered into two majors compared to their White football counterparts. Additional findings revealed Minority football players were more likely to be clustered in General Studies or Social and Political Science majors whereas White football players were more likely to be clustered in Business majors. The authors concluded that clustering occurred as a means to preserve eligibility and accommodate athletic schedules. In addition to this explanation, I assert academic clustering serves as a means to reproduce racist beliefs about Black males' academic propensities and interests. The agency to explore and choose one's major is an important aspect of the educational experience at the postsecondary level. The fact that many college athletes including several Black males are denied this right due to the controlling nature of athletics is egregious and an indictment on higher education.

Relating back to UNC-CH, Smith and Willingham (2015) disclosed in their book how multiple Black male college athletes over a 18-year time span were systematically clustered into less rigorous academic majors and enrolled in a series of independent study courses where they were awarded high marks for completing minimal or no work (also referred to as paper classes). These corroborating findings added credibility to concerns about the compromised academic integrity at big-time college sport institutions. In another previous study, my colleague and I examined two groups of Black male college athletes at a Division I HWI and participants explained how they were forced to change their major from what they were interested in to another major that was more accommodative of their athletic practice schedules (Cooper & Cooper, 2015). Similar findings were revealed in Benson's (2000) study with African American football players at another Division I HWI where she argued that institutional practices such as academic clustering facilitated detrimental enabling and student underdevelopment. One participant in her study described his experiences with racial stereotyping and subsequent academic clustering at the HWI when he said: "They're just like, 'Well, he's dumb, so let's put him in this easy class to get his GPA back up,' ... And you're like, 'Well, I don't want to take that' ... *So you feel like*—Like, you have no control, and that's not letting you grow up ... You'll be lost once you have to do it for yourself" (p. 230). One of the most disturbing aspects of this scenario is the lack of consideration for Black males' academic and career interests. Benson (2000) noted how the process of devaluing academic development and achievement is initiated during recruitment and intensified throughout the participants' enrollment experiences. Similar to Adler and Adler's (1991) seminal study and Beamon's (2008, 2010, 2012) more recent work on African American male college athletes, Benson's (2000) findings demonstrate how athletic-centric sub-cultures along with covert and overt racist policies and practices not only contribute to athletic role engulfment, but even worse they produce a deflated sense of self and low internal locus of control.

Gendered Racial Gaps with Academic Progress Rates and Graduation Success Rates

Since 2003, the NCAA's Academic Performance Program (APP) instituted academic progress rate (APR) and graduation success rate (GSR) standards for athletic departments. The APR is a metric that assesses institutional effectiveness in terms of eligibility and retention of college athletes on a yearly basis. The APR formula divides the number of eligible and retained college athletes on a team in a given year by the total number of college athletes on the team and multiplies this number by 1000 to produce a score. An APR score of 930 indicates that the school is on track to graduate at least 50% of its college athletes on a particular team (NCAA, 2014). The GSR is a metric that calculates the percentage of college athletes who graduate within a six-year window from an institution divided by the total number of college athletes enrolled at the institution for the same period (NCAA, 2014). These standards were intended to redress the issue of academic underpreparedness among college athletes (namely males in football and basketball) and increase institutional accountability for supporting college athletes towards and through graduation.

Even though these measures have led to documented increases in graduation rates among college athletes (albeit questionable to what extent based on current metrics—see Southall, Nagel, Wallace, & Sexton (2016) for a critical analysis of the GSR metric), since their inception Black male college athletes have experienced the lowest rates among all college athletes. For example, in 2002, the Division I GSR for Black male basketball players (46%) was 30 percentage points lower than White male basketball players (76%); in 2017, the double digit GSR gap was 14 percentage points between Black male and White male basketball players, 78% and 92%, respectively (NCAA, 2017a). For Football Bowl Subdivision (FBS) schools, in 2002, the gap between Black male football players (53%) and White male football players (76%) was 23 percentage points and in 2017 the double digit gap between the same subgroups was 14 percentage points with the GSRs for Black male and White male football players being 73% and 87%, respectively (NCAA, 2017a). At the University of California at Berkeley, one of the nation's most prestigious public universities, the graduation rates for Black male college athletes (39%) was 26 percentage points lower than their Black male non-athlete peers (65%), 31 percentage points lower than all college athletes (70%), and 52 percentage points lower than the general student body (91%) (Harper, 2018). Similar trends were identified among Power 5 institutions with strong academic reputations such as the University of Texas at Austin, The Ohio State University, University of Illinois at Urbana-Champaign, University of North Carolina at Chapel Hill, University of Virginia, University of Georgia, University of Florida, and Texas Agricultural and Mechanical (A&M) University to name a few (Harper, 2018). Even though, the GSR was only established in 2004, research over the past three and half decades has indicated that the trend of Black male college athletes earning lower GPAs and graduating at lower levels compared to their peers is a norm across a majority of NCAA Division I schools (American Institutes for Research, 1989; Purdy, Eitzen, & Hufnagel, 1982; Sellers, Kuperminc, & Waddell, 1991; Sellers, 1992, 2000).

Harrison et al (2017) described these patterns and embedded athletic sub-cultures at the intercollegiate level (i.e., expectations and demands for excess time, energy, and focus spent on athletics) as "the hidden curriculum" that signals to Black males, the campus community, and society more broadly that their primary purpose at these *institutions of higher education* is centered on their athletic ability and performance (p. 63). Regarding APR, football and men's basketball have consistently posted the lowest APRs. In the first year the APR was assessed, men's basketball was 929, football was 930, baseball was 933, and women's basketball was 959 (NCAA, 2017c). These scores indicated that on average men's basketball and football were graduating 50% or less of the college athletes on these teams. Keep in mind these are the two sports where Black males are overrepresented and graduation is viewed as one of the primary purposes of higher education. Over a decade later, in year 13 of the APP program, the average APRs for men's basketball was 966, football was 964, baseball was 975, and women's basketball was 981 (NCAA, 2017c). On the surface, the reduction in racial gaps in GSRs and sport gaps in APRs appear to signify progress as touted by the NCAA. However, scholars have highlighted the scrupulous practices utilized by well-resourced NCAA member institutions to avoid penalization such as the overuse of summer course enrollment, strategic use of NCAA waivers and exemptions for progress toward degree requirements, the recruitment of former players to complete their degree for GSR purposes, creative advising and academic support to assist with the sustainment of athletic eligibility, and the misleading communication of GSR as an accurate tool for comparing college athletes to their peers who are non-athletes (Gurney & Southall, 2012).

In addition, the abuse of the transfer rule associated with JUCO athletes also allows schools to academically exploit Black male college athletes by focusing on eligibility as opposed to providing a well-rounded education and career readiness beyond sport (Bembry, 2016; Cooper & Hawkins, 2014; Harper, 2009). JUCO athletes can bypass initial eligibility standards so as long as they have satisfactory records at their respective schools, which often involve similar unethical practices such as grade inflation and paper classes.

Furthermore, a primary reason for these continued academic performance gaps (GSR and APR) lies in the color-blind racism embedded in NCAA policies and practices (Cooper, Nwadike, & Macaulay, 2017). As long as special admissions and related practices are widespread and institutional cultures rooted in White Anglo-Saxon Eurocentric middle class norms remain commonplace, increasing academic standards alone does not address interrelated issues facing Black male college athletes. These issues include, but not limited to encounters with stereotype threat in academic spaces (Steele, 2010; Steele & Aronson, 1995; Stone, Harrison, & Mottley, 2012), imposter syndrome (Cooper, 2017; Peteet, Montgomery, & Weekes, 2015), experiences with negative stereotypes and differential treatment from faculty (Comeaux & Harrison, 2007), excessive time spent on athletics (Cooper & Cooper, 2015; Sellers, 2000; Singer, 2009), emotional mistrust with coaches and athletic staff (Cooper & Cooper, 2015; Beamon, 2008, 2012; Singer, 2005), and feelings of cultural marginalization and isolation on campus and in the local community (Cooper, 2012; Cooper & Hawkins, 2014; Melendez, 2008).

The Myth of the Collegiate Model and "Student"- Athlete

Despite the magnitude of the aforementioned academically fraudulent behavior on behalf of athletic department staff and academic faculty, these types of actions should be expected given the multi-billion dollar nature of the college sports industry. The revenue driving this industry is largely derived from Black male labor in basketball and football (Hawkins, 2010). Concurrently, this is the same system that compensates football and men's basketball coaches (a majority of which are White) with significantly higher salaries than university faculty, administrators, and presidents. For example, at the University of Alabama, head football coach Nick Saban grosses $11.1 million annually, which is over 14 times as much as the University of Alabama president, Stuart Bell, who earns roughly $755, 000 annually (Stevenson, 2017). Three of Saban's assistant coaches (Jeremy Pruitt (Defensive Coordinator), Brian Daboll (Offensive Coordinator), and Tosh Lupio (Co-Defensive Coordinator/ Outside Linebackers Coach)) also earned salaries of at least $950, 000 (Stevenson, 2017). In fact, data from business researchers indicated that in 39 out of 50 states a head football or basketball coach at a Division I school is the highest paid state employee (Gaines, 2016). It is important to keep in mind we are referencing *institutions of higher education* and not professional sport leagues such as the NFL and NBA. Also, recall Black males constitute a majority of

participants particularly starters and star players in these two-highest revenue generating sports; hence, resembling the plantation arrangement dating
back to the 17th century on U.S. soil where Black labor fuels White wealth
(Anderson, 1994; Harper, 2018; Hawkins, 2010; Smith, 2009).

In an effort to protect the exploitative nature of the collegiate model
(Southall & Nagel, 2010; Southall & Staurowsky, 2013), the NCAA and
its member institutions engage in a range of propaganda and spin tactics to
promote rhetoric such as eligibility, graduation, and a majority of "student-
athletes" going pro in something other than sports to mask foundational
injustices that belie the colorblind racist system, ubiquitous exploitation and
fraud, and lack of deliverance of quality well-rounded educational experiences
for all college athletes across all racial and gender groups (Cooper, 2016a;
Cooper, Nwadike, & Macaulay, 2017). More specific to Black male college
athletes, dating back to the 1980s research has indicated they experience
the lowest graduation rates among all college athletes (American Institutes
for Research, 1988, 1989; Eitzen & Purdy, 1986; Purdy et al., 1982; Sellers,
1992). Using data from the American Institutes for Research (1988, 1989)
studies, Hawkins (1999) highlighted how Black male college athletes, particularly those in revenue-generating sports, were less likely to feel they had
control over their lives and more likely to experience racial discrimination
and social isolation. More recent research has highlighted how the intense
time demands, inattention to their unique psychosocial and cultural needs,
and perpetual encounters with racism (both overt and covert) has had a detrimental impact on their educational experiences and outcomes (Beamon,
2008, 2010, 2012; Benson, 2000; Cooper & Cooper, 2015; Melendez, 2008;
Singer, 2005, 2008, 2009). Furthermore, the disparate enrollment trends
mentioned earlier in this chapter further illustrate the insidious practices at
these institutions that value these Black males for their athletic prowess at
the expense of their academic and personal development (Edwards, 1984,
2000; Hawkins, 2010; Smith, 2009). As such it is no surprise that researchers
have documented how Black male college athletes feel the term "athlete-
student" most accurately describes their roles, priorities, and treatment in
college versus the often cited and NCAA endorsed term of "student-athlete"
(Beamon, 2008; Northcutt, 2013; Singer, 2009).

Relatedly, critics have noted that even though the NCAA touts
improvement in graduation rates among Black male college athletes these
numbers do not necessarily translate into a well-rounded education and/or
career readiness beyond sport. For example, Sellers (2000) differentiated the

idea of earning a college degree (graduating) from acquiring a well-rounded education. He asserted earning a degree simply means an individual has been recognized by the university for completing a set of courses whereas a meaningful education for African American college athletes must include enhanced personal competency (interpersonal and intrapersonal skills), upward social mobility, and a college degree (Sellers, 2000). Similarly, Bimper (2016) posited that purposeful pedagogy for African American males must involve sociocultural and sociopolitical consciousness, social capital expansion, and culturally rooted competencies. Thus, a proper education, not schooling, for Black male athletes must cultivate a heightened level of critical consciousness of the gendered racist, classist, and neoliberal systems in which they exist (Bimper, 2016; Bimper, Harrison, & Clark, 2012; Harrison et al., 2017; Cooper, 2016a, 2016b, 2017; Cooper & Cooper, 2015; Singer, 2015). Following this consciousness, internalized empowerment, and catalytic engagement in counter-actions must occur whether it be in the form of agency, advocacy, and/or activism for the transformation of miseducation systems and its damaging effects on Black males' life outcomes and the underdevelopment of the Black community at large (Cooper, 2016a, 2016b, 2017; Cooper & Cooper, 2015; Cooper, Macaulay, & Rodriguez, 2017; Edwards, 2000).

Chapter Summary

The U.S. miseducation schooling system was not created with Blacks' holistic well-being' in mind and thus since its inception Black males have faced significant challenges inside and outside of the traditional classroom. The schooling environment from the primary through postsecondary level is entrenched in gendered racist beliefs and norms that have disparate impacts on Black males' cognitive development and educational attainment. The miseducation schooling system has also used sport as a means for exploitation. Instead of cultivating holistic development for Black males, sport has been utilized to meet White-controlled institutional aims of increasing revenue and visibility under the guise of providing quality educational opportunities for Black males. Unfortunately, these "opportunities" are often smoke screens for academic neglect and athletic exploitation. As a microcosm of the broader U.S. society, the miseducation schooling system is yet another social institution that reifies the devaluation of Black humanity and overall well-being.

Notes

1. It is important to acknowledge that this trend of leaving one's native communities without consideration of giving back is not unique to Black males who experience the Conveyor Belt, as it applies to a number of individuals and groups who internalize and embody neoliberal aims (see Frazier (1957) for a detailed discussion of the Black bourgeoisie who neglect the broader Black community in an effort to assimilate in society founded upon and structured by WRC).
2. It is important to note that I am not suggesting all JUCOs engage in academic and athletic exploitation of athletes, but there are numerous ones that do not prioritize the academic, intellectual, and career readiness of college athletes beyond athletics.

References

Adler, P. A., & Adler, P. (1991). *Backboards and blackboards: College athletes and role engulfment.* New York, NY: Columbia University Press.

Akbar, N. (1982). *Miseducation to education.* Jersey City, NJ: New Mind Productions.

Alexander, M. (2012). *The new Jim Crow: Mass incarceration in the age of colorblindness.* New York, NY: The New Press.

Allport, G. W. (1954). *The nature of prejudice.* Cambridge, MA: Addison-Wesley.

American Institutes for Research. (1988). Summary results from the 1987–1988 National Study of Intercollegiate Athletics. *Studies in Intercollegiate Athletics.* Palo Alto, CA: Center for the Study of Athletics.

American Institutes for Research. (1989). The experiences of Black intercollegiate athletes at NCAA Division I institutions. *Studies in Intercollegiate Athletics.* Palo Alto, CA: Center for the Study of Athletics.

Anderson, C. (1994). *Black labor, White wealth: The search for power and economic justice.* Bethesda, MD: PowerNomics Corporation of America, Inc.

Bandura, A. (1986). *Social foundations of thought and action: A social cognitive theory.* Englewood Cliffs, NJ: Prentice-Hall.

Bandura, A. (2001). Social cognitive theory: An agentic perspective. *Annual Review of Psychology, 52,* 1–26.

Barker, J. (2012, December 22). "Special admissions" bring colleges top athletes, educational challenges. *Baltimore Sun.* Retrieved from http://articles.baltimoresun.com/2012-12-22/sports/bs-sp-acc-sports-special-admits-20121222_1_athletes-graduation-success-rate-college-courses/2

Bass, L. (2016). *Black mask-ulinity: A framework for Black masculine caring.* New York, NY: Peter Lang.

Beamon, K. K. (2008). "Used goods": Former African American college student-athletes' perception of exploitation by division I universities. *The Journal of Negro Education, 77*(4), 352–364.

Beamon, K. (2010). Are sports overemphasized in the socialization process of African American males?: A qualitative analysis of former collegiate athletes' perception of sport socialization. *Journal of Black Studies, 41*(2), 281–300.

Beamon, K. (2012). "I'm a baller:" Athletic identity foreclosure among African American former student-athletes. *Journal of African American Studies, 16*(2), 195–208.

Beamon, K., & Bell, P. A. (2002). "Going pro": The deferential effects of high aspirations for a professional sports career on African-American student athletes and White student athletes. *Race & Society, 5*(2), 179–191.

Beamon, K., & Bell, P. A. (2006). Academic versus athletics: An examination of the effects of background and socalization on African American male student athletes. *The Social Science Journal, 43*(3), 393–403.

Beamon, K., & Bell, P. (2011). Adream deferred: Narratives of African-American male former collegiate athletes' transition out of sports and into the occupational sector. *Journal for the Study of Sports and Athletes in Education, 5*(1), 29–44.

Bell, D. A. (1980). Brown v. Board of Education and the interest convergence dilemma. *Harvard Law Review, 93*(3), 518–533.

Bell, D. A. (1992). *Faces at the bottom of the well: The permanence of racism.* New York, NY: Basic Books.

Bembry, J. (2016, July 29). "Last chance U" is compelling and brutal: Netflix documentary follows a junior college football team as it aims for a national championship. *ESPN's The Undefeated.* Retrieved from https://theundefeated.com/features/netflix-documentary-last-chance-u-follows-east-mississippi-junior-college-football-team/

Benson, K. F. (2000). Constructing academic inadequacy: African American athletes' stories of schooling. *The Journal of Higher Education, 71*(2), 223–246.

Beyer, J. M., & Hannah, D. R. (2000). The cultural significance of athletics in US higher education. *Journal of Sport Management, 14*(2), 105–132. doi:10.1123/jsm.14.2.105

Bimper, A. Y. (2016). Capital matters: Social sustaining capital and the development of Black student-athletes. *Journal of Intercollegiate Sport, 9*(1), 106–128.

Bimper, A. Y., Harrison, L., & Clark, L. (2012). Diamonds in the rough: Examining a case of succesful Black male student athletes in college sport. *Journal of Black Psychology,* 1–24.

Bonilla-Silva, E. (2010). *Racism without racists: Color-blind racism and the persistence of racial inequality in the United States* (3rd ed.). Lanham, MD: Rowman & Littlefield.

Borman, K. M., Eitle, T. M., Michael, D., Eitle, D. J., Lee, R., Johnson, L., Cobb-Roberts, D., Dorn, S., & Shircliffe, B., (2004). Accountability in a postdesegregation era: The continuing significance of racial segregation in Florida's schools. *American Educational Research Journal, 41*(3), 605–631.

Brennan, E. (2011, September 6). Prep school scam strands duped prospects. ESPN. Retrieved from http://www.espn.com/blog/collegebasketballnation/post/_/id/34939/prep-school-scam-strands-duped-prospects

Brewer, B. W., & Petitpas, A. J. (2017). Athletic identity foreclosure. *Current Opinion in Psychology, 16*, 118–122.

Brown v. Board of Education of Topeka, 347 U.S. 483 (1954).

Bush, L. (1997). Independent Black institutions in America: A rejection of schooling, an opportunity for education. *Urban Education, 32*(1), 98–116.

Bush, L. V., & Bush, E. C. (2013a). Introducing African American male theory (AAMT). *Journal of African American Males in Education*, 4(1), 6–17.

Bush, L. V., & Bush, E. (2013b). God bless the child who got his own: Toward a comprehensive theory for African-American boys and men. *The Western Journal of Black Studies*, 37(1), 1–13.

Case, B., Greer, S., & Brown, J. (1987). Academic clustering in athletics: Myth or reality? *Arena Review*, 11(2), 48–56.

Castine, S. C., & Roberts, G. C. (1974). Modeling in the socialization process of the black athlete. *International Review for the Sociology of Sport*, 9(3), 59–74.

Children's Defense Fund (2012). Portrait of inequality 2012: Black children in America. Retrieved from https://www.childrensdefense.org/wp-content/uploads/2018/08/portrait-of-inequality-2012.pdf

Coakley, J. (2017). *Sports in society: Issues and controversies* (12th ed.). New York, NY: McGraw-Hill Education.

Comeaux, E., & Harrison, C. K. (2007). Faculty and male student-athletes: Racial differences in the environmental predictors of academic achievement. *Race, Ethnicity, and Education*, 10(2), 199–214.

Cooper, J. N. (2012). Personal troubles and public issues: A sociological imagination of Black athletes' experiences at predominantly White institutions in the United States. *Sociology Mind*, 2(3), 261–271.

Cooper, J. N. (2016a). "Focus on the bigger picture:" An anti-deficit achievement examination of Black male scholar athletes in science and engineering at a Division I historically White university (HWU). *Whiteness & Education*, 1(2), 109–124.

Cooper, J. N. (2016b). Excellence beyond athletics: Best practices for enhancing Black male student athletes' educational experiences and outcomes. *Equity & Excellence in Education*, 49(3), 267–283.

Cooper, J. N. (2017). Strategic navigation: A comparative study of Black male scholar athletes' experiences at a historically Black college/university (HBCU) and historically White institution (HWI). *International Journal of Qualitative Studies in Education*, 31(4), 235–256. doi: 10.1080/09518398.2017.1379617.

Cooper, J. N., & Cooper, J. E. (2015). "I'm running so you can be happy and I can keep my scholarship": A comparative study of Black male college athletes' experiences with role conflict. *Journal of Intercollegiate Sport*, 8(2), 131–152.

Cooper, J. N., Corral, M. D., Macaulay, C. D. T., Cooper, M. S., Nwadike, A., & Mallery, Jr., M. (2018). Collective uplift: The impact of a holistic development support program on Black male former college athletes' experiences and outcomes. *International Journal of Qualitative Studies in Education*, DOI: 10.1080/09518398.2018.1522011.

Cooper, J. N., Gawrysiak, J., & Hawkins, B. (2012). Racial perceptions of baseball at historically Black colleges and universities. *Journal of Sport and Social Issues*, 37(2), 196–221.

Cooper, J. N., & Hawkins, B. (2014). The transfer effect: A critical race theory examination of Black male transfer student athletes' experiences. *Journal of Intercollegiate Sport* 7(1), 80–104.

Cooper, J. N., Macaulay, C., & Rodriguez, S. H. (2017). Race and resistance: A typology of African American sport activism. *International Review for the Sociology of Sport*, 131. DOI: 10.1177/1012690217718170.

Cooper, J. N., Nwadike, A., & Macaulay, C. (2017). A critical race theory analysis of big-time college sports: Implications for culturally responsive and race-conscious sport leadership. *Journal of Issues in Intercollegiate Athletics, 10*, 204–233.

Crenshaw, K., Gotanda, N., Peller, G., & Thomas, K. (1995). *Critical race theory: The key writings that formed the movement.* New York, NY: The New Press.

Curry, T. J. (2017). *The man-not: Race, class, genre, and the dilemmas of Black manhood.* Philadelphia, PA: Temple University Press.

Cuyjet, M. J. (2006). *African American men in college.* San Francisco, CA: Jossey-Bass.

Davis, T. (1992). Examining educational malpractice jurisprudence: Should a cause of action be created for student-athletes? *Denver University Law Review, 64*, 57–96.

Daza, R., & Gonzalez, A. (2017, November 20). How a bootleg prep school profited by ripping off teens with NBA dreams. Deadspin, Retrieved from https://deadspin.com/how-a-bootleg-prep-school-profited-by-ripping-off-teens-1820603652

DeGruy, J. (2005). *Post-traumatic slave syndrome: America's legacy of enduring injury and healing.* Milwaukie, OR: Uptone Press.

Dohrmann, G. (2010). *Play their hearts out: A coach, his star recruit, and the youth basketball machine.* New York, NY: Ballantine Books.

Donnor J. K. (2005). Towards an interest-convergence in the education of African-American football student athletes in major college sports. *Race, Ethnicity and Education, 8*(1), 45–67.

Douglas, T. (2016). *Border crossing brothas: Black males navigating race, place, and complex space.* New York, NY: Peter Lang.

Douglas, T. Ivey, P., & Bishop, K. (2015). Identity, leadership, and success: A study of Black male student-athletes at the University of Missouri. National Collegiate Athletic Association (NCAA) Innovations Grant. Final Report. Retrieved from https://www.ncaa.org/sites/default/files/Douglas%2C%20Ivey%2C%20Bishop%2C%20NCAA%20Final%20Report%2C%20Black%20Male%20Student%20Athlete%20Study%2C%201.4.2016%2C%20submitted.pdf

DuBois, W. E. B. (1903/2003). *The souls of Black folk.* Chicago, IL: A. C. McClurg.

Edwards, H. (1969). *The revolt of the Black athlete.* New York, NY: Free Press.

Edwards, H. (1973). *Sociology of sport.* Homewood, IL: Dorsey Press.

Edwards, H. (1980). *The struggle that must be: An autobiography.* New York, NY: Macmillan Publishing.

Edwards, H. (1984). The Black "dumb jock": An American sports tragedy. *College Board Review, 131*, 8–13.

Edwards, H. (2000). Crisis of black athletes on the eve of the 21st century. *Society, 37*, 9–13.

Eitle, T. M., & Eitle, D. J. (2002). Race, cultural capital, and the educational effects of participation in sports. *Sociology of Education, 75*(2), 123–146.

Eitzen, D. S., & Purdy, D. A. (1986). The academic preparation and achievement of Black and White collegiate athletes. *Journal of Sport and Social Issues, 10*(1), 15–29.

Erickson, E. H. (1959). Identity and the life cycle: Selected papers. *Psychological Issues, 1*, 18–164.

ETS. (2011). *A strong start: Positioning young Black boys for educational success a statistical profile.* Washington, DC: Educational Testing Service

Fanon, F. (1952/2008). *Black skin, White masks*. New York, NY: Grove Press.

Fanon, F. (1963/2004). *The wretched of the earth*. New York, NY: Grove Press.

Feagin, J. (2006). *Systemic racism: A theory of oppression*. New York, NY: Routledge.

Feagin, J., Vera, H., & Batur, P. (2000). *White racism* (2nd ed.). New York, NY: Routledge.

Federal Bureau of Prisons (2018). *Inmate statistics*. Retrieved from https://www.bop.gov/about/statistics/statistics_inmate_race.jsp

Finkel, R., Martin, T., & Paley, J. (Director). (2013). *Schooled: The price of college sports*. [Documentary]. Strand Releasing (Distributor), Makuhari Media.

Fordham, S., & Ogbu, J. (1986). Black students' school success: Coping with the burden of acting White. *Urban Review, 18*(3), 176–206.

Foster, M. (1993). Educating for competence in community and culture: Exploring the views of exemplary African American teachers. *Urban Education, 27*(4), 370–394.

Fountain, J. J., & Finley, P. S. (2009). Academic majors of upperclassmen football players in the Atlantic Coast Conference: An analysis of academic clustering comparing White and Minority players. *Journal of Issues in Intercollegiate Athletics, 2*, 1–13.

Franklin, S., & Resnik, S. (1973). *The political economy of racism*. New York, NY: Holt Rinehart and Winston.

Frazier, E. F. (1957). *Black bourgeoisie*. New York, NY: Free Press.

Freire, P. (1968). *Pedagogy of the oppressed*. New York, NY: The Seabury Press.

Gaines, C. (2016, September 22). The highest-paid public employee in 39 US states is either a football or men's basketball coach. Business Insider. Retrieved from http://www.businessinsider.com/us-states-highest-paid-public-employee-college-coach-2016–9

Gill, E. (2015). *NCAA enforcement and Black male student athletes*. Paper presented at the The Black Student Athlete Conference: Challenges and Opporutnities. Austin, Texas: University of Texas at Austin.

Gurney, G. S., & Southall, R. M. (2012, August 9). College sports' bait and switch. *ESPN*. Retrieved from http://espn.go.com/college-sports/story/_/id/8248046/college-sports-programs-find-multitude-ways-game-ncaa-apr

Harper, S. R. (2009). Race, interest convergence, and transfer outcomes for Black male student-athletes. New Directions for Community Colleges, 147, 29–37.

Harper, S. R. (2010). An anti-deficit achievement framework for research on students of Color in STEM. *New Directions for Institutional Research, 148*, 63–74.

Harper, S. R. (2012). *Black male student success in higher education: A report from the national Black male college achievement study*. Philadelphia, PA: University of Pennsylvania, Center for the Study of Race and Equity in Education.

Harper, S. R. (2018). *Black male student-athletes and racial inequities in NCAA Division I college sports: 2018 edition*. Los Angeles, CA: University of Southern California, Race and Equity Center.

Harper, S. R., & Harris, F., III. (2010). *College men and masculinities: Theory, research, and implications for practice*. San Francisco, CA: Jossey-Bass.

Harper, S. R., & Nichols, A. H. (2008). Are they not all the same?: Racial heterogeneity among Black male undergraduates. *Journal of College Student Development, 49*(3), 199–214.

Harris, O. (1994). Race, sport, and social support. *Sociology of Sport Journal, 11*(1), 40–50.

Harrison, C. K., Comeaux, E., & Plecha, M. (2006). Faculty and male football and basketball players on university campuses: An empirical investigation of the 'intellectual' as mentor to the student-athlete. *Research Quarterly for Exercise and Sport, 77*(2), 277–284.

Harrison, L., Jr., Bimper. A. Y., Jr., Smith, M. P., & Logan, A. D. (2017). The mis-education of the African American student-athlete. *Kinesiology Review,* 6(1), 60–69.

Harrison., L. Jr., Harrison, C. K., & Moore, L. N. (2002). African American racial identity and sport. *Sport, Education & Society, 7*(2), 121–133.

Hawkins, B. (1998a). The dominant images of black men in America: The representation of O. J. Simpson. In G. Sailes (Ed.), *African Americans in sport* (pp. 39–52). New Brunswick, NJ: Transaction Publishers.

Hawkins, B. (1998b). The White supremacy continuum of images for Black men. *Journal of African American Men, 3*(3), 7–18.

Hawkins, B. (1999).Black student-athletes at predominantly White National Collegiate Athletic Association (NCAA) division I institutions and the pattern of oscillating migrant laborers. *The Western Journal of Black Studies,* 23(1), 1–9.

Hawkins, B. (2010). *The new plantation: Black athletes, college sports, and predominantly White NCAA institutions.* New York, NY: Palgrave MacMillan.

Hawkins, B., Carter-Francique, A. R., & Cooper, J. N. (2017). *Critical race theory: Black athletic sporting experiences in the United States.* New York, NY: Palgrave Macmillan.

Hine, D. C., Hine, W. C., & Harrold, S. (2006). *The African-American odyssey: Since 1965* (3rd ed., Vol. 2). Upper Saddle River, NJ: Pearson Prentice Hall.

Hodge, S. R., Collins, F. G., & Bennett, R. A., III, (2013). The journey of the Black athlete on the HBCU playing field. In D. Brooks & R. Althouse (Eds.), *Racism in college athletics* (pp. 105–134). Morgantown, WV: Fitness Information Technology.

Hodge, S. R., Harrison, L., Jr., Burden, J., Jr., & Dixson, A. D. (2008). Brown in Black and White—Then and now: A question of educating or sporting African American males in America. *American Behavioral Scientist, 51*(7), 928–952.

Howard, T. C. (2014). *Black male(d): Peril and promise in the education of African American males:* New York, NY: Teachers College Press.

Hughey, M. W. (2014). *The White savior film: Content, critics, and consumption.* Philadelphia, PA: University of Temple Press.

Hylton, K. (2009). *"Race" and sport: Critical race theory.* New York, NY: Routledge.

Johnson, T. S., & Migliaccio, T. A. (2009). The social construction of an athlete: African American boys' experience in sport. *The Western Journal of Black Studies, 33*(2), 98–109.

Kendi, I. X. (2017).The Civil Rights Act was a victory against racism, but racists also won. *Washington Post.* Retrieved from https://www.washingtonpost.com/news/made-by-history/wp/2017/07/02/the-civil-rights-act-was-a-victory-against-racism-but-racists-also-won/?utm_term=.0e2bda534e37

Ladson-Billings, G., & Tate, W. F. (1995). Toward a critical race theory of education. *Teachers College Record,* 97(1), 47–68.

Ladson-Billings, G. (2006). From the achievement gap to the education debt: Understanding achievement in U.S. schools. *Educational Researcher, 35*(7), 3–12.

Lareau, A. (2002). Invisible Inequality: Social class and childrearing in Black families and White families. *American Sociological Review, 67*(5), 747–776.

Lederman, D. (2008, December 29). The admissions gap for big-time athletes. *Inside Higher Ed.* Retrieved from https://www.insidehighered.com/news/2008/12/29/admit

Leonard, D. J., & King, C. R. (2012). *Commodified and criminalized: New racism and African Americans in contemporary sports.* Lanham, MD: Rowman & Littlefield.

Leonard, W. M., II, & Reyman, J. E. (1988). The odds of attaining professional athlete status: Refining the computations. *Sociology of Sport Journal, 5*(2), 162–169.

Macaulay, C. D. T. (2017). *The manufacturing of high school football recruits in the United States (U.S.): An examination of the high school football landscape as an economic sub-sector* (Unpublished thesis). Storrs, CT: University of Connecticut.

Majors, R., & Billson, J. M. (1992). *Cool pose: The dilemmas of Black manhood in America.* New York, NY: Lexington Books.

Marcia, J. E. (1966). Development and validation of ego-identity status. *Journal of Personality and Social Psychology, 3*(5), 551–558.

Marks, B. T. (2000). The miseducation of the negro revisited: African American racial identity, historically Black institutions, and historically White institutions. In L. Jones (Ed.), *Brothers of the Academy* (pp. 53–69). Sterling, VA: Stylus.

Melendez, M. C. (2008). Black football players on a predominantly White college campus: Psychosocial and emotional realities of the Black college athlete experience. *Journal of Black Psychology, 34*(4), 423–451.

Murphy, G. M., Petitpas, A. J., & Brewer, B. W. (1996). Identity foreclosure, athletic identity, and career maturity in intercollegiate athletes. *The Sport Psychologist, 10*(3), 239–246.

Mutua, A. D. (2006). *Progressive Black masculinities.* New York, NY: Routledge.

NCAA (2014, October 28). NCAA graduation rates: A quarter-century of tracking academic success. *NCAA.* Retrieved from http://www.ncaa.org/about/resources/research/ncaa-graduation-rates-quarter-century-tracking-academic-success

NCAA (2017a). Trends in graduation success rates and federal graduation rates at NCAA Division I institutions. *NCAA.* Retrieved from https://www.ncaa.org/sites/default/files/2017D1RES_Grad_Rate_Trends_FINAL_20171108.pdf

NCAA (2017b). Trends in academic success rates and federal graduation rates at NCAA Division II institutions. *NCAA.* Retrieved from https://www.ncaa.org/sites/default/files/2017RES_D2_Grad_Rate_Trends_FINAL_20171108.pdf

NCAA (2017c). National and sport-group APR averages and trends. *NCAA.* Retrieved from https://www.ncaa.org/sites/default/files/May2017APR_public-release-pres_20170509.pdf

NCAA (2018, April 20). Estimated probability of competing in professional athletics. *NCAA.* Retrieved from http://www.ncaa.org/about/resources/research/estimated-probability-competing-professional-athletics *No Child Left Behind Act of 2001, P.L. 107–110, 20 U.S.C. § 6319 (2002).*

Noguera, P. A. (2008). *The trouble with Black boys … and other reflections on race, equity, and the future of public education.* San Francisco, CA: Jossey-Bass.

Northcutt, J. (2013). *The dilemma: Career transition of African American male football players at Division I institutions* (Dissertation). University of Mississippi.

Nwadike, A. C. Baker, A. R., Brackebusch, V. B., & Hawkins, B. J. (2016). Institutional Racism in the NCAA and the racial implications of the "2.3 or take a knee" legislation. *Marquette Sports Law Review, 26*(2), 523–543.

O'Neil, L. (2017, September 20). Ibram Kendi, one of the nation's leading scholars of racism, says education and love are not the answer. *ESPN's The Undefeated.* Retrieved from https://theundefeated.com/features/ibram-kendi-leading-scholar-of-racism-says-education-and-love-are-not-the-answer/

Oseguera, L. (2010). Success despite the image: How African American male student-athletes endure their academic journey amidst negative characterizations. *Journal for the Study of Sports and Athletes in Education, 4*(3), 297–324.

Pascarella, E. T., Bohr, L., Nora, A., & Terenzini, P. (1995). Intercollegiate athletic participation and freshman-year cognitive outcomes. *The Journal of Higher Education, 66*(4), 369–387.

Pascarella, E. T., Truckenmiller, R., Nora, A., Terenzini, P. T., Edison, M., & Hagedorn, L. S. (1999). Cognitive impacts of intercollegiate athletic participation: Some further evidence. *The Journal of Higher Education, 70*(1), 1–26.

Peteet, B. J., Montgomery, L., & Weekes, J. C. (2015). Predictors of imposter phenomenon among talented ethnic minority undergraduate students. *The Journal of Negro Education, 84*(2), 175–186.

Powell, S. (2008). *Souled out? How Blacks are winning and losing in sports.* Champaign, IL: Human Kinetics.

Purdy, D. A., Eitzen, D. S., & Hufnagel, R. (1982). Are athletes also students? The educational attainment of college athletes. In D. Chu, J. O. Segrave & B. J. Becker (Eds.), *Sport and Higher Education* (pp. 221–234). Champaign, IL: Human Kinetics

Ratcliffe, C., & McKernan, S. (2010, June 29). Childhood poverty persistence: Facts and consequences. Perspectives on Low-Income Working Families Report. *The Urban Institute, Brief 14,* 1–10.

Rhoden, W. C. (2006). *40 million dollar slaves: The rise, fall, and redemption of the Black athlete.* New York, NY: Crown Publishing Group.

Sage, G. H. (1998). *Power and ideology in American sport* (2nd ed.). Champaign, IL: Human Kinetics.

Sage, G. H., & Eitzen, D. S. (2013). *Sociology of North American sport.* New York, NY: Oxford University Press.

Sailes, G. (2010). The African American athlete: Social myths and stereotypes. In G. Sailes (Ed.), *Modern Sport and the African American athlete experience* (pp. 55–68). San Diego, CA: Cognella.

Scheurich, J. J., & Young, M. D. (1997). Coloring epistemologies: Are our research epistemologies racially biased? *Educational Researcher, 26*(4), 4–16.

Schott Foundation for Public Education (2010). *Yes we can: The Schott 50 state report on public education and Black males* (pp. 1–44). Cambridge, MA: Schott Foundation for Public Education. Retrieved from http://schottfoundation.org/resources/yes-we-can-schott-50-state-report-public-education-and-black-males

Schott Foundation for Public Education. (2015). Black lives matter: The Schott 50 state report on public education and Black males. In A. Beaudry (Ed.), *The Metropolitan Center for Research on Equity and the Transformation of Schools* at New York University (pp. 1–68). Retrieved from http://www.blackboysreport.org/2015-black-boys-report.pdf

Sellers, R. M. (1992). Racial differences in the predictors for academic achievement of student-athletes in Division I revenue producing sports. *Sociology of Sport Journal, 9*(1), 48–59.

Sellers, R. M. (2000). African American student-athletes: Opportunity or exploitation? In D. A. Brooks & R. Althouse (Eds.), *Racism in college athletics: The African American athlete's experience* (2nd ed., pp. 133–154). Morgantown, WV: Fitness Information Technology, Inc.

Sellers, R. M., Kuperminc, G. P., & Waddell, A. S. (1991). Life experiences of black student athletes in revenue producing sports: A descriptive empirical analysis. *Academic Athletic Journal*, 21–38.

Shujaa, M. J. (1994). *Too much schooling, too little education: A paradox of Black life in White societies.* Trenton, NJ: Africa World Press.

Singer, J. N. (2005). Understanding racism through the eyes of African-American male student athletes. *Race, Ethnicity and Education, 8*(4), 365–386.

Singer, J. N. (2008). Benefits and detriments of African American male athletes' participation in a big-time college football program. *International Review for the Sociology of Sport, 43*(4), 399–408.

Singer, J. N. (2009). African American football athletes' perspectives on institutional integrity in college sport. *Research Quarterly for Exercise and Sport, 80*(1), 102–116.

Singer, J. N. (2015). The miseducation of African American male college athletes. In E. Comeaux (Ed.), *Introduction to intercollegiate athletics* (pp. 193–206). Baltimore, MD: Johns Hopkins University Press.

Singer, J. N., & May, R. A. B. (2010). The career trajectory of a Black male high school basketball player: A social reproduction perspective. International Review for the *Sociology of Sport, 46*(3), 299–314.

Smith, E. (2009). *Race, sport and the American dream* (2nd ed.). Durham, NC: Carolina Academic Press.

Smith, W. A., Allen, W. R., & Danley, L. L. (2007). "Assume the position … you fit the description" Psychosocial experiences and racial battle fatigue among African American male college students. *American Behavioral Scientist, 51*(4), 551–578.

Smith, M. P., Clark, L. D., Harrison, L., Jr. (2014). The historical hypocrisy of the Black student-athlete. *Race, Gender & Class, 21*(1–2), 220–235.

Smith, J. M., & Willingham, M. (2015). *Cheated: The UNC scandal, the education of athletes, and the future of big-time college sports.* Omaha, NE: University of Nebraska Press.

Snyder, E. E. (1985). A theoretical analysis of academic and athletic roles. *Sociology of Sport Journal, 2*(3), 210–217.

Southall, R., & Nagel, M. S. (2010). Institutional logics theory: Examining big-time college sport. In E. Smith (Ed.), *Sociology of sport and social theory* (pp. 67–79). Champaign, IL: Human Kinetics.

Southall, R. M., Nagel, M. S., Wallace, A., & Sexton, M. (2016, October 19). *2016 Adjusted graduation gap report: NCAA FBS football. College Sport Research Institute.* Retrieved from http://csri-sc.org/wp-content/uploads/2016/10/2016-Football-AGG-Report_Publish_Final_10-19-2016.pdf

Southall, R. M., & Staurowsky, E. (2013). Cheering on the collegiate model: Creating, disseminating, and imbedding the NCAA's redefinition of amateurism. *Journal of Sport and Social Issues, 37*(4), 403–429.

Steele, C. M. (2010). *Whistling vivaldi: And other clues to how stereotypes affect us.* New York, NY: W. W. Norton & Company.

Steele, C. M., & Aronson, J. (1995). Stereotype threat and the intellectual test performance of African Americans. *Journal of Personality and Social Psychology, 69*(5), 797–811.

Stevenson, S. (2017, September 01). Alabama coaches pay offers another example of college football insanity. *Star-Telegram.* Retrieved from http://www.star-telegram.com/sports/college/big-12/texas-christian-university/article170740262.html

Stone, J., Harrison, C. K., & Mottley, J. (2012). "Don't call me a student-athlete": The effect of identity priming on stereotype threat for academically engaged African American college athletes. *Basic and Applied Social Psychology, 34,* 99–106. Sue, D. W., Capodilupo, C. M., Torino, G. C., Bucceri, J. M., Holder, A. M. B., Nadal, K. L., & Esquilin, M. (2007). Racial microaggressions in everyday life: Implications for clinical practice. *The American Psychologist, 62,* 271–286.

Swanson, D. P., Cunningham, M., & Spencer, M. B. (2003). Black males' structural conditions, achievement patterns, normative needs, and "opportunities." *Urban Education Journal, 38*(5), 608–633.

Tajfel, H. (1981). *Human groups and social categories. Studies in social psychology.* Cambridge, England. Cambridge University Press.

Tajfel, H. (2010). *Social identity and intergroup relations.* Cambridge, England: Cambridge University Press.

Thamel, P. (2006, February 25). Schools where the only real test is basketball. *The New York Times.* Retrieved from https://www.nytimes.com/2006/02/25/sports/ncaabasketball/schools-where-the-only-real-test-is-basketball.html

Turner, J. C. (1975). Social comparison and social identity: Some prospects for intergroup behaviour. *European Journal of Social Psychology, 5,* 5–34.

U.S. Census Bureau (2017). Population estimates. Retrieved from https://www.census.gov/quickfacts/fact/table/US/PST045217

U.S. Department of Education (2016). The state of racial diversity in the educator workforce. Retrieved from https://www2.ed.gov/rschstat/eval/highered/racial-diversity/state-racial-diversity-workforce.pdf

Whitely, G., & Ridley, A. (2016). *Last chance U* [Documentary Series]. *Condé Nast Entertainment.* Netflix. https://www.netflix.com/title/80091742

Wiggins, D. K. (2014). "Black athlete in White men's games": Race, sport and American national pastimes. *The International Journal of the History of Sport, 31*(1–2), 181–202.

Wiggins, D. K., & Miller, P. B. (2003). *The unlevel playing field: A documentary history of the African-American experience in sport.* Urbana, IL: University of Illinois Press.

Wilson, W. J. (2009). *More than just race: Being Black and poor in the inner city.* New York, NY: Norton & Simon.

Wolverton, B. (2014, March 30). Basketball academy's empty promises. *Chronicle of Higher Education*. Retrieved from https://www.chronicle.com/article/Basketball-Academys-Empty/145597

Wood, J. L. (2012). Leaving the 2-year college: Predictors of Black male collegian departure. *Journal of Black Studies, 43*(3), 303–326.

Wood, J. L., & Palmer, R. T. (2014). *Black men in higher education: A guide to ensuring student success*. New York, NY: Routledge.

Woodson, C. G. (1933/1990). *The mis-education of the Negro*. Trenton, NJ: Africa World Press.

3

TOWARDS A FRAMEWORK FOR BLACK MALE HOLISTIC (UNDER)DEVELOPMENT THROUGH SPORT AND (MIS)EDUCATION

Fortunately, what we have systemically created we can oftentimes systematically reconstruct in a more productive and humane guise.

—Edwards (1984, p. 10)

Theoretical Issues and Pluralistic Counter-Approaches

Across various disciplines, I have identified three alarming trends regarding the study of Black males in general and Black male athletes more specifically. First, there is a gross and conspicuous under theorization of Black males' lived experiences and outcomes. From a historical standpoint, Curry (2017) argued that since Black males (as well as females) have been deemed as inhuman, dating back to the early 17th century when chattel slavery of Black Africans on American soil was initiated, the efforts to theorize their lived experiences and outcomes have been either significantly lacking or simplistic at best. A vast majority of psychological and sociological theories either do not take Black males into account and/or relegate them to the bottom of any racial hierarchies without a deeper historical analysis of their lived experiences in various contexts. For example, Douglas (2016) surmised that theories of

Black masculinities within the U.S. often reinforce hegemonic masculine assumptions without examining how Black males develop their masculinity in pre-colonized and Afrocentric contexts. In other words, Douglas (2016) posits Black masculinity and Black existence did not start during slavery contrary to modern day theorizations. Both Curry (2017) and Douglas (2016) problematize the taken-for-granted notion in many popularized theories (i.e., feminism) that suggest Black males in hegemonic societies are seeking to mimic their White male oppressors and be patriarchs. I agree with this assertion as well as the ideas promulgated by Afrocentric theorists who argue any theorizing of Black males across the African Diaspora must connect to their original cultural foundations (Asante, 1990, 2003; Asante & Mazama, 2005; Hilliard, 1998; Jackson & Sears, 1992; Karenga, 1978; Mazama, 2001). Yet, there is a dearth of mainstream scholarly contributions that account for these histories, realities, and complexes.

The second disconcerting theme across the literatures on Black males is the preponderance of deficit-based theories. The *cool pose* (Majors & Billson, 1992), *dumb jock theory* (Sailes, 2010), stereotype threat (Steele & Aronson, 1995), social reproduction theory (Beamon, 2008; May, 2008; Singer & May, 2010), athletic role engulfment (Adler & Adler, 1991), and identity foreclosure (Beamon, 2012; Brewer & Petitpas, 2017; Murphy, Petitpas, & Brewer, 1996) as well as a range of similar theories (many of which were originally based on studies of individuals and groups who are not Black males) are a few notable examples of such theories. Black males' experiences have been primarily grounded in gendered racist ideologies that stigmatize their intellect, temperament, academic capabilities, personal motivations and interests, individual agency, criminal orientation, family backgrounds, and athletic abilities. These theories purport that Black males are passive reproducers of pathological beliefs imposed upon them from a society founded upon and structured by WRC. According to the aforementioned theories, Black males are innately or passively willing to be deviant, criminal, hypersexual, athletically gifted, academically inept, misogynistic, incapable of being effective members of society without surveillance, and such a threat to society that their marginalization at a minimum and extermination at a maximum is always justifiable. Moreover, these theories suggest Black males seldom if ever resist and/or challenge these negative stereotypes in productive manners. Although, there are works that have directly challenged these assertions, the lack of anti-deficit based framing (Cuyjet, 2006; Douglas, 2016; Harper, 2012; Harper & Harris, 2012; Harper & Wood, 2015; Wood & Palmer, 2014) and critical sociological inquiry grounded in historical and empirical data (Curry, 2017) underscores the prevalence of epistemological gendered racism against Black males across academic disciplines and in scholarly work (Cooper, 2016a). Notwithstanding, these theories also inform the proposed socialization models in this book to extent that they help explain the complex interplay between Black males and ecological systems and the subsequent impacts on their lived experiences and outcomes.

The third disturbing theme in the literature on Black males is the lack of heterogeneity. Blacks in the U.S. live in and come from vastly different socio-political, geographical, economic, and socio-cultural spaces. Not to mention, post-assimilation era, the shift in job markets has led to various migration patterns whereby not all Blacks live the same environments and experience similar opportunities. Black males' relocation through their lifespan particularly their childhood often results in what Douglas (2016) describes as "border crossing," which also influences their lived experiences and outcomes (p. 3). Yet, current theorizations of Black males do not account for this heterogeneity. Furthermore, not all Black males either fail out of school or graduate with honors, but deficit and anti-deficit perspectives (including in my own work) have been susceptible to perpetuating notions of Black male exceptionality. A limitation of these works is the lack of exploration of their complexity including strengths/prowess as well as shortcomings/areas of improvement from a micro-, meso-, and macro-systems level approach. *I posit that all Black males are gifted and talented and each of them navigate the miseducation schooling systems differently.* Therefore, the labeling of some Black males as talented and others as deficit or deviant reinforces damaging pathological ideas and ignores the variability in their lived experiences over a lifespan and across different sub-groups. More specific to sport, a vast majority of extant literature has focused on Black male athletes' experiences with negative stereotypes and personal downfalls within systems founded upon and structured by WRC (Adler & Adler, 1991; Beamon, 2008, 2010, 2012; Benson, 2000; May, 2008). Acknowledging and examining these experiences are important, but it is also necessary to explore a wider range of Black male athletes' experiences to better understand how, why, when, and where specific outcomes manifest.

As such, within this chapter, I present a range of theories to contextualize the heterogeneous socialization experiences of Black male athletes in the U.S. In contrast to previous theorizing that has relied on one discipline or a single theoretical framework (e.g., role theory, social reproduction theory, critical race theory, social imitation theory, etc.), I adopt a pluralistic approach to understanding the complex identities and socialization processes of Black male athletes. These theories include race-based, gender-based, ecological, sociological, psychological, and athletic-based foci. I do not claim the theories presented here are exhaustive, but rather I assert that the concurrent application of these theories advance previous conceptions and expand our collective understandings of Black males in general and Black male athletes more specifically. I also argue Black male athletes' experiences in and through sport and (mis)education in the U.S. as well as in global contexts (although the latter is beyond the scope of this current book) require more critical analyses with nuanced specificities regarding theorizing beyond deficit-based assertions. It is my hope the reader will gain an appreciation for multi-faceted perspectives and acquire a more comprehensive understanding of the heterogeneity that exists among Black male athletes.

Critical Race Theory in Education and Sport

In the 1970s, legal scholars Derrick Bell, Alan Freeman, Richard Delgado, and Kimberle Crenshaw developed critical race theory (CRT) as an analytical tool to examine and redress systemic racist laws and enforcement throughout the U.S. judicial system. These scholars argued the legal system, similar to all aspects of U.S. society, was grossly flawed by racist beliefs, assumptions, and values. In the development of CRT, three core tenets were presented including the reality that race and racism are endemic in U.S. social institutions, property rights are central to understanding U.S. social arrangements, and the intersection between race, racism, and property are vital for critical discourses on justice and equity minded efforts (Bell, 1992; Crenshaw, Gotanda, Peller, Thomas, 1995; Delgado, 1995; Delgado & Stefancic, 2001; Ladson-Billings & Tate, 1995). Over time CRT was adapted to disciplines beyond law including in education, cultural studies, gender studies, sociology, and psychology to name a few. With this expanded application, additional CRT tenets and extended sub-theories have emerged:

(a) (counter) storytelling/centrality of experiential knowledge (DeCuir & Dixson, 2004; Delgado, 1989; Delgado & Stefancic, 2001; Matsuda, 1995; Solórzano & Yosso, 2002),
(b) permanence of racism (Bell, 1992; Lawrence, 1995),
(c) Whiteness as property norm (Harris, 1993),
(d) interest convergence (Bell, 1980, 1992),
(e) critique of liberalism (Crenshaw et al., 1995; DeCuir & Dixson, 2004; Taylor, Gillborn, & Ladson-Billings, 2009),

(f) intersection of race and other forms of subordination and intersectionality (Crenshaw, 1989; 1991; Solórzano & Yosso, 2002),

(g) challenges to dominant ideology (Delgado Bernal, 2002; Solórzano & Yosso, 2002)

(h) commitment to social justice (Delgado Bernal, 2002; Matsuda, 1995; Solórzano & Yosso, 2002)

(i) transdisciplinary perspective (Delgado Bernal 2002; Harris, 1993; Solórzano & Yosso, 2002)

(j) community cultural wealth (Yosso, 2005)

(j) strategic responsiveness to interest convergence (Cooper & Cooper, 2015b)

Additionally, the sub-fields of sport management, sport studies, and sport sociology have also incorporated CRT as a useful mechanism for exploring the impact of race and racism within sporting structures, policies, and practices (Bimper, 2016, 2017; Bimper, Harrison, Clark, 2012; Cooper & Hawkins, 2014a; Hawkins, Carter-Francique, & Cooper, 2017; Hylton, 2009; Singer, 2005, 2009). In particular, my colleague and I used data from our study of Black male athletes' educational and sporting experiences to develop a CRT sub-theory called strategic responsiveness to interest convergence (SRIC; Cooper & Cooper, 2015b). Within this section, each of the aforementioned tenets and sub-theories are presented and discussed in relation to their influence on the socialization models of Black male holistic (under)development through sport and (mis)education.

Counter Storytelling, Counter Narratives, and Centrality of Experiential Knowledge

The tenet of counter storytelling/counter narratives and centrality of experiential knowledge refers to the process of centralizing and magnifying the voices and experiences of historically marginalized groups such as people of African, Latinx, Indigenous, and Asian racial and ethnic backgrounds (Delgado & Stefancic, 2001; Solórzano & Yosso, 2002). Within the U.S., the dominant ideological, epistemological, axiological, ontological, and paradigmatic frameworks are rooted in White, Anglo-Saxon/Eurocentric, heteronormative, middle class, and Protestant Christian values and practices. Regarding Black male athletes, the dominant narrative depicts them as innately athletically gifted, intellectually inferior, academically apathetic, and socially deviant (Cooper, 2017; Edwards, 1973, 1980, 1984, 2000; Sailes, 2010). Similar to the literature on Black males in the general society (Majors & Billson, 1992), much of the research on Black male athletes has reinforced these deficit-laden perspectives (Hoberman, 1997; Simons, Rheenen, & Covington, 1999). Aside from deficit-based research, another fairly large segment of scholarly literature has focused on Black male athletes' challenges and shortcomings within sporting and educational spaces (Beamon, 2008, 2010, 2012; Benson, 2000; Melendez, 2008; Singer, 2005) whereas an emerging body of literature has incorporated anti-deficit lenses to examine Black male athletes who excel academically, socially, and professionally while defying negative stereotypes (Bimper, 2015; Bimper, Harrison, & Clark, 2012; Cooper, 2016a, 2016b, 2017; Cooper & Cooper, 2015a; Cooper & Hawkins, 2014a; Martin & Harris, 2006; Martin, Harrison, Stone, & Lawrence, 2010; Oseguera, 2010).

Sport education scholars who have utilized the tenet of critical race methodology (CRM; Solórzano & Yosso, 2002) in the form of counter storytelling challenge dominant narratives or master scripts by spotlighting Black male athletes' diverse lived experiences with confronting racism on micro, meso, and macro levels (Bimper, 2016, 2017; Cooper, 2017; Cooper & Cooper, 2015b; Oseguera, 2010; Smith, Clark, & Harrison, 2014). Celious and Oyserman (2001) outlined how Blacks are not homogenous and their experiences in society vary based on numerous factors including, but not limited to social class, skin color, and gender. Similarly, Harper and Nichols (2008) highlighted how Black male undergraduates' experiences differed based on social identities such as being athletes, fraternity members, socially disengaged, campus leaders and activists, and pre-college geographical and demographic backgrounds (e.g., urban vs. rural, predominantly Black vs. White native communities, etc.). The authors concluded: "Simply because Black male students share the same racial categorization, it would be wrong to assume they all perceive or experience Blackness the same way" (Harper & Nichols, p. 12, 2008). Given the heterogeneity among Black male athletes (as opposed to the current dichotomous framing in the literature—academically challenged and disengaged vs. academically prepared and high-performing), counter storytelling serves as a powerful tool for gaining a better understanding of the interplay between distinct contextual conditions (e.g., culture, resources, history, etc.) and individual perceptions, behaviors, and outcomes.

Permanence of Racism

The permanence of racism tenet refers to the notion that racist ideologies are deeply embedded in cultural institutions and ways of knowing and will continue to influence individual and group outcomes in perpetuity (Bell, 1992). CRT pioneer Derrick Bell (1992) described this perspective as a racial realism. As outlined in Chapter 1, racism is the foundational to the U.S. social, economic, political, and cultural fabric and identity. In fact, modern day capitalism would not exist without racist chattel (inhumane) slavery against Black Africans in the Western hemisphere (namely the U.S., Caribbean Islands, Central America, and South America) from the early 17th century through the late 19th century (and arguably continuing today in various forms such as prison labor—see Alexander, 2012 for extended discussion on this topic). Related to sport, the current multi-billion dollar professional, intercollegiate, interscholastic, and youth football and basketball industries in the U.S. are similarly rooted in the economic exploitation of Black male athletic labor (Hawkins, 2010; Powell, 2008; Rhoden, 2006; Smith, 2009). Hence, it is imperative to examine the ways in which racist structures, policies, and practices have influenced Black males' experiences, opportunities (or lack thereof), and outcomes in and through sport and (mis)education (Cooper, 2012).

Whiteness as Property Norm

Related to racial realism, the Whiteness as property norm tenet asserts the U.S. was founded on property rights. In fact, the crux of the Civil War in the mid to late 1800s was a result of economic disputes centered on property ownership and related rights between Union states in the North and Confederate states in the South (Hine, Hine, & Harrold, 2006). According to Harris (1993), Whiteness as property includes rights of disposition, rights of use and enjoyment, reputation, and status property, and absolute right to exclude. The representation of Whites in influential political, business, legal, health, and educational positions coupled with the foundational racist principles of the U.S. underscore how White privilege and Black oppression reflect the inequitable allocation of property rights based on race (Cooper, 2012).

The institutions of sport and miseducation schooling in the U.S. are both comprised of Black male athletes participating in largely White-owned, managed, and controlled spaces. Notable exceptions include HBCU athletic programs and similar predominantly Black controlled sporting and educational entities (Cooper, Cavil, & Cheeks, 2014; Hawkins, Cooper, Carter-Francique, & Cavil, 2015). Furthermore, the lack of Black ownership across all levels of sport also indicates how they are commodified as property and labor whereas elite Whites control the broader apparatus of economics throughout society (Cooper, 2012; Edwards, 1973; Franklin & Resnik, 1973; Hartmann,

2000; Hawkins, 2010; Lapchick & Balasundaram, 2017; Lapchick Malveaux, Davison, Grant , 2016; Leonard & King, 2012; Powell, 2008; Rhoden, 2006; Smith, 2009). The lack of access to property rights has greatly shaped Black male athletes' experiences within and perceptions of sport and (mis)education as well as their subsequent actions (or in many cases inactions) of resistance (e.g., *cool pose*, *Black aesthetic*, African American sport activism, etc.). The Black male athlete socialization models presented here account for this influence.

Interest Convergence

The CRT tenet of interest convergence refers to inequitable arrangements involving gains experienced by an oppressed group occurring only when it serves the needs and wants of the hegemonic group (Bell, 1980, 1992). In a critical analysis of jurisprudence cases, CRT pioneers identified racist patterns in legal enforcement against Blacks, which served the interests of Whites in maintaining the racial hierarchy in society and a means to suppress Black revolution (Bell, 1980, 1992; Crenshaw et al., 1995; Delgado & Stefancic, 2001). Even landmark decisions such as *Brown v. Board of Education of Topeka* (1954) and Civil Rights Laws of the 1960s have been retroactively scrutinized as being an evolution of WRC rather than a transformation or reduction of it (Bell, 1980, 1992; Crenshaw et al., 1995; Kendi, 2017; Ladson-Billings, 2006).

Within sport and (mis)education, the assimilation of Blacks into White mainstream institutions, leagues, and associations was a result of interest convergence. For Black athletes, it provided access to previously prohibited resources and visibility whereas for Whites it resulted in increased revenue streams, entertainment spectacles, and a more subtle means of maintaining racial control (Donnor, 2005; Hawkins et al., 2017). Within the proposed socialization models, the diversity in perspectives of and actions within the aforementioned interest convergence arrangement in sporting and (mis)educational spaces are highlighted. More importantly, explanations are offered for how, when, and why some Black males experience net positive outcomes in terms of holistic development within these unfavorable arrangements and conditions and different groups of Black males experience net negative outcomes.

Critique of Liberalism

The critique of liberalism tenet posits that the dominant ideas of color-blindness, objectivity/neutrality, meritocracy, and gradual change are myths and employed to preserve White racism (Crenshaw et al., 1995; DeCuir & Dixson, 2004). Both sport and miseducation schooling have been touted as great equalizers for racial groups subjected to oppression so as long as they are willing to adhere to meritocratic principles. The organizers and leaders of these industries suggest we live in a post-racial society where landmark Civil Rights Acts have been passed, the first Black president of the U.S. has been elected, and multiple Blacks possess majority or minority owner-ship in major sport franchises (e.g., Michael Jordan of the Charlotte Hor-nets, Magic Johnson of the Los Angeles Dodgers, Grant Hill of the Atlanta Hawks, etc.). However, CRT debunks this myth by highlighting patterns within both institutions as well as society at large whereby Blacks in partic-ular Black males continue to be among the most disenfranchised and dis-advantaged groups by nearly every societal index (e.g., incarceration rates, home and business ownership, political underrepresentation, etc.) (Alexan-der, 2012; Children's Defense Fund, 2012; Curry, 2017; ETS, 2011; Howard, 2014; Noguera, 2008; Schott Foundation for Public Education, 2010, 2015). Challenging liberalism heightens the visibility of the ways in which race and racism work in conjunction with social class, gender, religion, nation-ality, ethnicity, sexual identity, age, ability, political affiliation, geography, and various identity categories to facilitate differential outcomes for Black males in and through sport and (mis)education (read: disrupts ideological hegemony).

Intercentricity of Racism with Other Forms of Subordination

Another tenet of CRT is the intercentricity of racism with other forms of subordination (Crenshaw et al., 1995; Solórzano & Yosso, 2002). This tenet states that racism does not operate in isolation, but rather in tandem and flu-idity with oppressive ideologies such as sexism and patriarchy, heterosexism and homophobia, capitalism, ableism, ageism, White nationalism, religious exclusivity, xenophobia, etc. In concert with this tenet, I assert the social-ization experiences and outcomes of Black male athletes must be examined by taking into account how these interlocking systems of oppression and intersecting identities impact their lived experiences and outcomes as well as the conditions of their native communities. In contrast to popular ideas that suggest Black males in general, and Black male athletes specifically, are privileged by virtue of patriarchy I posit if we view athletes as property (owned by another person or entity) then sport participation even at the professional level cannot be viewed solely as a privilege. Although, there are clear benefits acquired in certain contexts albeit often transient (i.e., increased economic standing), given the prevailing racial hierarchies of power (i.e., differences in ownership vs. labor) along with the vast disadvantages associated with being a Black male in the U.S. historically and contemporarily (e.g., high mortality rates, high incarceration rates, etc.) the net analysis does not result in overarching privilege for the collective group.

In addition, I argue Black male athletes' disadvantages as a collective group outweigh any suggested privileges experienced by a select few; the latter circumstance is a direct byproduct of ideological hegemony. Collective disadvantages as a result of their intersecting oppressions include the pervasiveness of the myth of innate athletic ability (dismisses their humanity, hard work, time, and dedication) (Hoberman, 1997), perceived intellectual inferiority and cognitive deficiencies (justifies their overrepresentation in special education and underrepresentation in gifted programs and post-secondary institutions) (Edwards, 1984), and their positionality as major threats to WRC (violently and otherwise—thus justifying their enslavement, incarceration, surveillance, control, and death) (Edwards, 1980; Hawkins, 1998a, 1998b; Sailes, 2010). Not to mention, Blacks as a collective group have faced dehumanization, marginalization, and oppression in every facet of U.S. society for the past four centuries (Curry, 2017; Du Bois, 1903/2003; DeGruy, 2005; Hine et al., 2006; Woodson, 1933/1990). As a result, the proposed socialization models account for the aforementioned fluidity and variability in terms of the impact of various ideologies and conditions on Black male athletes.

Challenge to Dominant Ideology

The challenge to dominant ideology tenet of CRT refers to direct confrontations with oppressive forces in society (Delgado Bernal, 2002; Solórzano & Yosso, 2002). For example, the proposed socialization models challenge the dominant ideology of the dichotomous Black male athlete. As noted earlier, Black male athletes are largely viewed in simplistic terms such as being either troublesome brutes, complicit sambos, dumb jocks, or an exceptional scholar athletes (Edwards, 1984, 2000; Hawkins, 1998a, 1998b; Sailes, 2010; Smith et al., 2014). The lack of complexity in analyses within scholarly literature and popular discourse reflect the ubiquitous nature of the dominant ideology that positions Black male athletes in a limited scope. The theoretical pluralism and nuanced analyses within the proposed models enable taken-for-granted ideas of Black masculinities in and through sport and (mis)education to be effectively challenged.

Commitment to Social Justice

Along the same lines as the challenge to the dominant ideology, the commitment to social justice tenets refers to ideological, theoretical, methodological, and empirical approaches that seek to redress injustices in society (Delgado Bernal, 2002; Matsuda, 1995; Solórzano & Yosso, 2002). Any and all efforts to liberate Blacks from the vicissitudes of WRC reflects a commitment to social justice. As such, any socialization models of Black male athletes must move beyond simply explaining how and why they experience negative outcomes within WRC to also exploring how, when, where, and why they challenge, disrupt, and navigate these systems of oppression and experience positive developmental outcomes. The proposed models accomplish this aim.

Transdisciplinary Perspective

In the vein of theoretical pluralism, I believe any socialization models of Black male athletes are also greatly enhanced by incorporating transdisciplinary perspectives (Delgado, 1995; Delgado Bernal 2002; Solórzano & Yosso, 2002). The intricacy of Black male athletes' intersecting identities, lived experiences, varied contextual conditions, and diverse outcomes require insights from different disciplines. The proposed models are influenced by the following range of interdisciplinary theories and frameworks:

(a) law (Bell, 1980, 1992; Crenshaw et al., 1995; Delgado, 1995; Delgado & Stefancic, 2001; Harris, 1993),
(b) education (DeCuir & Dixson, 2004; Delgado Bernal, 2002; Douglas, 2016; Harper, 2012; Ladson-Billings, 2006; Ladson-Billings & Tate, 1995; Solórzano & Yosso, 2002; Yosso, 2005)
(c) philosophy (Curry, 2017; Fanon, 1952/2008, 1963/2004)
(d) cultural studies (Boyd, 2003; Majors & Billson, 1992)
(e) urban education (Howard, 2014; Noguera, 2008; Stevenson, 1994)
(f) gender studies (Martin & Harris, 2006; Mutua, 2006)
(g) psychology (Adler & Adler, 1991; Moore, Madison-Colmore, & Smith, 2003; Steele, 2010; Steele & Aronson, 1995; Sue et al., 2007)

(h) Africana studies (Asante, 1990, 2003; Asante & Mazama, 2005; Boy-kin, 1986; Murrell, 2002)
(i) African American male studies (Bush & Bush, 2013a, 2013b)
(j) ecology (Brofenbrenner, 1977, 1986)
(k) sociology (Cooper, Macaulay, & Rodriguez, 2017, Cooper, Mallery, & Macaulay, forthcoming; Mills, 1959;)
(l) sport, race, and education (Beamon, 2012; Bimper, 2016; Cooper, 2009, 2012, 2016a; Cooper & Cooper, 2015b; Donnor, 2005; Edwards, 1973; Harrison, Bimper, Smith, & Logan, 2017; Hawkins, 2010; Hodge, Burden, Robinson, & Bennett, 2008; Singer, 2005, 2009, 2015; Smith, 2009)

For example, in previous work I highlighted the parellels between Black male athletes' experiences at HWIs and broader Black experiences in the U.S. society using Mills' (1959) sociological imagination (Cooper, 2012). Within this analysis, common experiences related to racial discrimation/social isolation, academic neglect, economic deprivation, and limited leadership opportunities revealed connections between the personal troubles of Black male athletes and the public issues facing Blacks in the broader U.S. Hence, the incorporation of theoretical perspectives that incorporate a range of sensitivities related to historical, social, political, economic, cultural, sociological, and ecological factors is pertinent for engaging in a comprehensive analysis and acquiring a more holistic understanding of the systems, contexts, and conditions influencing Black males' socialization experiences in and through sport and (mis)education.

Community Cultural Wealth

A sub-theory of CRT is Yosso's (2005) community cultural wealth (CCW). In an effort to explain the ways in which groups who have been oppressed overcome unfavorable conditions in society, Yosso (2005) posited these groups possess and activate different types of capital. Similar to CRT, CCW has roots in transdisciplinary fields including sociology, economics, ethnic and cultural studies, history, women's studies, and law (Crenshaw et al., 1995; Yosso, 2005). Yosso (2005) defined CCW as "an array of knowledge, skills, abilities, and contacts possessed and utilized by Communities of Color to survive and resist macro and micro-forms of oppression" (p. 77). Dominant ideologies in the U.S. suggest Whites possess all the power and resources to impose their will on "subordinate" racial groups. Although, widespread inequities and inequalities exist in the U.S. as a result of domestic terrorism and inhumane atrocities such as chattel slavery, Jim Crow, colonialization, and imperialism, Yosso (2005) argued people of Color[1] utilize their respective ingenuity and resources to counter these oppressive forces. The six types of CCW capital are aspirational, navigational, social, linguistic, familial, and resistant. Aspirational capital involves the internalized belief and actualized perseverance towards specific goals while existing as the targets of an oppressive system. Black male athletes who grow up in economically disadvantaged backgrounds often rely on aspirational capital to excel academically at HWIs particularly when the conditions on these campuses are geared toward fostering athletic role engulfment and identity foreclosure. Navigational capital refers to context specific skills and knowledge that facilate individual growth and/or group progress within a given environment. My previous work on Black male athlets has revealed how they identify and activate various forms of navigational capital from resources including athletic academic support, financial aid offices, etc. (Cooper, 2016a, 2017; Cooper & Cooper, 2015b).

Social capital refers to the presence of meaningful relationships that contribute to positive developmental outcomes (e.g., educationally, occupationally, etc.). One of the benefits of being an athlete is heighten visibility and connections to indivduals from different walks of life who have an affinity for sport. As a result, several Black male athletes both during and after their athletic careers have access to social capital that can enhance their life outcomes. Linguistic capital refers to distinct language, dialect, and communication skills and knowledge individuals and groups possess that demonstrate cultural heritage and cognitive sophiscation. Throughout history, African cultures have utilized unique communication styles to express themselves, preserve their heritages, and navigate contested milieu. Familial capital refers to information, resources, and relationships connected to family lineage that enhance sense of self, belonging, purpose, and possibility. Research on Black male athletes has highlighted the vital role of family support particularly emotional, psychological, and social even more so than technical greatly enhance their educational outcomes (Carter-Francique, Hart, & Cheeks, 2015; Carter-Francique, Hart, & Steward, 2013). Resistant capital refers to conscious efforts and resources activated for the purpose of dismantling oppressive systems. The literature on Black males who demonstrate progressive and productive masculinities in an effort to counter negative stereotypes attributed to them illustrates resistant capital in action (Bimper, 2015; Bimper et al., 2012; Cooper, 2017; Martin & Harris, 2006; Martin et al., 2010; Smith, Clark, & Harrison, 2014).

Strategic Responsiveness to Interest Convergence

Beyond the aforementioned CRT tenets, the proposed models are also informed by a CRT sub-theory grounded in research on Black male athletes. I surmise the use of interdisplinary lenses is imperative for understanding the holistic experiences of Black male athletes, but it is equally important to develop and utilize theories grounded in empirical data on this sub-group. The study of Black male athletes dates by the late 19th century with the works of scholars such as Sol White and E. B. Henderson (Henderson, 1939; Wiggins & Miller, 2003). Over the past century, there has been an abundance of research published on Black male athletes, but a scacity of theories rooted in their experiences (Bimper, 2016; Cooper, 2009, 2016a; Cooper & Cooper, 2015b; Hodge et al., 2008). The CRT sub-theory informing the proposed models is strategic responsiveness to interest convergence (SRIC; Cooper & Cooper, 2015b).

Analyzing the experiences of Black male college athletes across different academic performance levels at a Division I HWI, my colleague and I theorized from the data regarding participants' utilization of navigational strategies and resources to overcome the contested environment of a big-time college sport culture and stigmatizing campus climate (Cooper & Cooper, 2015b). From this study, we coined SRIC as a theory to explain counter-hegemonic coping mechanisms activated by Black male athletes. I applied this theory in a more recent study on Black male college athletes who attended a HWI as well as those who attended a HBCU. The application of the theory on these two sub-groups of Black male college athletes and their experiences in different educational, sport, and socio-cultural contexts reflects its transferability (Cooper, 2017).

The three tenets or components of SRIC include: (1) holistic consciousness, (2) internalized empowerment, and (3) engagement in counter-actions (Cooper & Cooper, 2015b). Holistic consciousness refers to an individual or group recognizing an inequitable structural arrangement designed to exploit them. This awareness involves an understanding of multi-level systems as well as critical reflexivity of one's self, group membership, and context. Internalized empowerment refers to the belief that an individual and/or group possess the power to improve their personal and collective outcomes within an inequitable arrangement. Engagement in counter-actions refers to specific action steps or behavioral modifications geared towards maximing individual and collective holistic benefits within an inequitable system while simulateously weakening and deconstructing this oppressive system (Cooper & Cooper, 2015b). In sum, the CRT tenets and sub-theories offer a valuable race-based theoretical foundations for exploring the lived experiences and outcomes of Black males including athletes.

Anti-Deficit Achievement Framework and Progressive and Productive Black Masculinities

Another relevant theory for examining Black male athletes' socialization processes is Harper's (2012) anti-deficit achievement framework. In an effort to disrupt the monolithic narrative of Black male academic underachievement, Harper (2012) developed a theory on Black males who successfully navigate educational and social milieu that has historically disadvantaged them. In contrast to focusing on barriers, deficits, and limitations, the anti-deficit achievement framework centralizes conduits for personal success including expectations, relationships, resources, and supports. This intentional focus on high-performing Black males directly challenges the dominant narrative about this sub-group that deems them as intellectually inferior, academically apathetic, and socially inept in educational and occupational spaces beyond sports and entertainment. Similar to college student development theories, Harper (2012) disaggregates the model into three sequential phases: 1) pre-college socialization and readiness, 2) college achievement, and 3) post-college success. Within these phases there are eight dimensions of influences: (a) familial factors, (b) K-12 forces, (c) out-of-school college prep resources, (d) classroom experiences, (e) out-of-class engagement, (f) enriching educational experiences, (g) graduate school enrollment, and (h) career readiness.

In previous work, I have incorporated the anti-deficit achievement framework in my examination of Black male and female college athletes' educational experiences particularly as it relates to their positive academic, athletic, and social outcomes (Cooper, 2016b, 2017; Cooper & Cooper, 2015a; Cooper, Cooper, & Baker, 2016; Cooper & Hawkins, 2014b). Across each study, pre-college socialization for participants involved a strong emphasis on education and racial and cultural pride in defying negative stereotypes from family members and mentors. For example, when confronted with overt and covert racism at HWIs, Black male college athletes have relied on their positive academic and racial self-efficacy and enacted resistant strategies to challenge misguided beliefs about their intellectual capabilities (i.e., Black dumb jocks)

(Cooper, 2016b, 2017). Participants described how they engaged in a range of intentional actions to demonstrate their academic prowess: (a) performing at a high level on assignments at the beginning of the semester, (b) intentionally asking and answering questions in class throughout the semester, (c) proving their merit in study groups, and (d) meeting with their professors outside of class (Cooper, 2016b, 2017). In another study of Black male and female college athletes at a HBCU, my colleague and I identified how positive identity affirmation from family, professors, coaches, and peers contributed to productive academic behaviors and subsequent college achievement (Cooper & Cooper, 2015a).

Regarding, post-college success, my research indicated how three Black male college athletes who majored in Engineering later earned their degrees and successfully secured employment in their respective areas of Civil and Mechanical Engineering (Cooper, 2016a). In order to counter-deficit laden perspectives and related research on Black male athletes, it is important to incorporate anti-deficit lenses to better understand how, what, when, where, and why individuals within this sub-group are able to navigate spaces designed to marginalized them. Nonetheless, the inclusion of this approach is not intended to promote the problematic notion of exceptionalism among specific Black males, but rather offer diverse perspectives and accounts of their lived experiences and highlight key influences throughout their lifespan that facilitate these outcomes. Since the preponderance of literature and popular discourse on Black males is deficit-based and negative, anti-deficit studies seek to offer more balance through the presentation of counter-stories, counter-perspectives, and positive outcomes.

Furthermore, emerging anti-deficit based research has documented positive masculine behaviors and outcomes exhibited among Black male athletes, which are discussed in greater detail in Chapters 7 and 8 (Bimper et al., 2012; Cooper, 2016a, 2017; Cooper & Cooper, 2015a; Cooper & Hawkins, 2014a; Fuller, Harrison, Bukstein, Martin, Lawrence, & Gadsby, 2016; Harris, Hines, Kelly, Williams, & Bagley, 2014; Harrison, Martin, & Fuller, 2015; Martin & Harris, 2006; Martin, Harrison, & Bukstein, 2010; Smith et al., 2014). The collective findings from these studies echo research of a broader sample of Black males (including mostly non-athletes) who excel academically and socially in the K-20 educational pipeline whereby these young men conceptualize productive manhood in terms of leadership, campus involvement, academic success, and civic engagement (Cuyjet, 2006; Harper, 2012; Harper & Harris, 2012; Howard, 2014; Noguera,

2008; Wood & Palmer, 2014). In connection to racialized gender identity development, Martin and Harris (2006) defined productive masculine conceptions "as feelings, beliefs, and interpretations about masculinities that encourage men to engage in and express positive gender-related behaviors and attitudes" (p. 360). Along the same lines, in her edited text titled, *Progressive Black Masculinities*, Mutua (2006) explored the intersection between progressive Blackness and progressive masculinities. The author defined progressive Black masculinities as "the unique and innovative performances of the masculine self that, on the one hand, personally eschew and actively, ethically stand against social structures of domination, and, on the other, that value, validate, and empower black humanity" (Mutua, 2006, p. 35).

This definition corresponds with Curry's (2017) challenge of theories that view Black males as aspiring patriarchs who seek to resemble domineering White males. Mutua (2006) asserts that Black males who adopt progressive masculinities possess distinct perceptions and ideals of racial, ethnic, gender, class, and religious/spiritual identities that are culturally grounded. In addition, Mutua (2006) also contends that progressive Blackness and progressive masculinities seek to eliminate all forms of domination and oppression including traditional cisheteropatriarchal and classist norms. In other words, in contrast to hegemonic masculinity, which necessitates the subordination of specific groups such as women and non-cisheteronormative men, progressive masculinities reject domination. Thus, the commitment to Black humanity and empowerment coincide with the disruption of hegemonic norms in society founded upon and structured by WRC. More specific to Black male athletes, the models presented later in Chapters 4–8 disrupt hegemonic ascriptions in scholarly literature and popular discourse by providing socio-ecological nuance within each analysis.

Excellence Beyond Athletics Framework

In concert with SRIC (Cooper & Cooper, 2015b) and the Black male athletic identity foreclosure and role engulfment sub-theory presented in Chapter 2, the Excellence Beyond Athletics (EBA) framework is a theoretical framework grounded in research on Black male athletes (Cooper, 2016b). The EBA approach incorporates an anti-deficit framing to highlight critical success factors (CSFs; Cooper, 2009) that contribute to Black male athletes' successful navigation through different societal systems and institutions including (mis)education and sport. The purpose of the EBA framework is to empower, educate, and inspire Black male athletes to maximize their full potential as holistic individuals both within and beyond athletic contexts (Cooper, 2016b). The value added of this approach involves:

> Centralizing holistic development and empowerment of Black male student athletes instead of prioritizing their athletic abilities, the EBA approach enables them to attain a heightened level of consciousness of the various ways this system oppresses them and an enhanced sense of urgency to engage in behaviors that counter afore-mentioned forces. (i.e., SRIC) (Cooper, 2016b, p. 271)

In particular, the EBA framework examines the interplay between conditions, relationships, and expectations facing Black male athletes (Cooper & Cooper, 2015b). Edwards (1984, 2000) highlighted the conditions facing Black male athletes in the U.S. such as an overemphasis on their athletic prowess and under emphasis on academic achievement and career exploration beyond sports from family, schools, community, and mass media. In terms of relationships, Black male athletes have experienced strong sense of belonging and positive identity affirmation in athletic spaces (Cooper, 2017; Harrison, Harrison, & Moore, 2002) whereas in contrast in academic and non-athletic social spaces they feel less welcomed and supported (Benson, 2000; Beamon, 2008; Melendez, 2008). Therefore, understanding these trends provides vital contextual information for formulating and enacting strategies designed to foster their holistic development and positive life outcomes.

The six holistic development principles (HDPs) of the EBA approach include "(a) self-identity awareness, (b) positive social engagement, (c) active mentorship, (d) academic achievement, (e) career aspirations, and (f) balanced time management" (Cooper, 2016b, p. 272). Self-identity awareness centralizes holistic identities and intentionally challenges the athletic identity foreclosure process. In particular, Black male athletes within the EBA framework acknowledge and internalize their distinct positionality within a society that is designed to exploit them based on their race, gender, and presumed physicality and athletic abilities. Hence, self-identity awareness equips Black male athletes with a level of holistic consciousness and cultivates racial and cultural pride in their African and Black cultural heritages as well as enhances their academic, critical thinking, leader, and global citizen identities. Positive social engagement refers to involvement in educationally purposeful and personal development activities beyond athletics. These activities can include community outreach groups, fraternities, religious based organizations, and/

or culturally relevant holistic development (CRHD) support groups. Involvement and connection to organized religion and/or spirituality was identified as a CSF for Black male athletes in my previous work (Cooper, 2009), which is consistent with other works on Black males across the African Diaspora (Boykin, 1986; Cuyjet, 2006; Douglas, 2016; Harper, 2012).

Active mentorship refers to consistent interactions with positive role models and mentors who offer vital psychological, emotional, academic, athletic, professional/career, and social guidance. For example, there are a range of culturally relevant mentor programs that have been established to improve the college and post-college experiences of Black male athletes (Bimper, 2016, 2017; Cooper, Corral, et al., 2018; Collective Uplift, 2018). Academic achievement refers to learning and intellectual growth as opposed to exclusively focusing on traditional markers of attainment such as eligibility, GPA, and/or graduation. These latter aims remain important, but do not fully reflect the overarching purpose of education especially given research that highlights Black students' (including athletes and non-athletes) value of non-cognitive factors in terms of their personal success (Carter-Francique et al., 2013; Sedlacek, 1987). Career aspirations refers to Black male athletes' exposure to and exploration of a range of occupational options beyond sport participation. These options can include sport (e.g., coaching, management, media, teaching, research, training, and ownership) and non-sport (e.g., educator in K-20 system, lawyer, doctor, engineer, counselor, police officer, politician, entrepreneur, scientist, minister, etc.) careers. Balanced time management refers to the enactment of values, priorities, and skills both quantitatively (i.e., time spent on tasks) and qualitatively (i.e., quality of time spent on tasks) in a manner that results in holistic benefits including personal well-being. Therefore, healthy holistic identity development requires adequate time spent on a range of areas including, but not exclusive to, sport skill mastery, personal interests, career exploration, etc. The EBA framework is applicable to the analysis of Black male athletes' development over their lifespan (not just during and immediately after their athletic careers) and thus an integral aspect of the proposed models.

African American Male Theory

The foundational theory that informs the African American male theory (AAMT; Bush & Bush, 2013a, 2013b) is Bronfenbrenner's (1977, 1986) ecology systems of human development theory. In an effort to understand the complexity of human development particularly the interplay between individuals and environments, Bronfenbrenner (1977, 1986) proposed the ecological systems theory. Building on research from various disciplines such as psychology, sociology, biology, and ecology, Bronfenbrenner (1977, 1986) concluded that understanding human behavior and outcomes over a lifespan necessitates an in-depth analysis of one's interactions with their immediate environment as well as with broader social systems—bilateral engagement as opposed to unilateral internalization. An individual's sense of self is influenced by sociocultural norms in which the individual lives. For example, Black males' self-schemata associated with the myth of innate athletic superiority in sports such as basketball, football, and track and field within the U.S. context is due to socio-historical realities outlined in Chapter 1. Conversely, an action by an individual or group/community can also challenge and alter culturally based axioms (i.e., Black athlete activism during the Civil Rights Movement in the U.S.) (Cooper, Macaulay, & Rodriguez, 2017; Edwards, 1969).

The original theory was comprised of four systems including micro, meso, exo, and macro (Bronfenbrenner, 1977). Later, a fifth system, the chronosystem, was introduced (Bronfenbrenner, 1986). According to Bronfenbrenner (1977), the *microsystem* refers to the interactions between a developing person and their immediate milieu in which they exist and fulfill a role. Examples of a microsystem include an individual's home, educational setting, professional workplace, etc. A consistent aspect of each system is the assertion that "factors of place, time, physical features, activity, participant, and role constitute the elements of a setting" (Bronfenbrenner, 1977, p. 514). The next level surrounding the microsystem is the *mesosystem*, which refers to the bidirectional influence of interactions across multiple microsystems on an individual at different developmental points. An example of a mesosystem influence is school policies related to the sanctioning of behavioral norms, which also influence family socialization of youth. For example, a school policy mandating extensive reading for achievement can influence family norms to incorporate more reading time at home to enhance a student's probability of academic success.

The *exosystem* is nested between the mesosystem and macrosystem. The exosystem is comprised of influences across both the meso- and macrosystems that indirectly impact an individual as opposed to having direct contact. State and federal government actions are examples of formal exosystem influences (i.e., *No Child Left Behind Act* (2002)). Examples of informal exosystem influences are interactions between parents or guardians and their respective workplaces, which indirectly impacts a young person's developmental experiences. An example of an informal exosystem influence are racial microaggressions at a parent's workplace that can result in increased stress levels and subsequent instability within their home environment for their children. The *macrosystem* refers to broader social and cultural patterns connected to ideologies and social institutions such as the economy, political entities, legal spaces, educational systems, etc. Several sport sociologists have outlined the influence of dominant ideologies on the structure, purpose, and meaning of sport in the U.S. and its ensuing impact on athletes' experiences through participation (Beyer & Hannah, 2000; Coakley, 2017; Sage, 1998). These ideologies include capitalism, White racism, patriarchy/hegemonic masculinity, heterosexism, American nationalism, ableism, and Christianity. Particularly germane to the proposed models is the impact of systemic racism and capitalism on Black male athletes' lived experiences and outcomes. However, each of the dominant ideologies in the U.S. are relevant to varying extents to all individuals within the society including Black male athletes.

The fifth level, the *chronosystem*, refers to influences and developmental processes on an individual's life over time based on the environment in which they exist (Bronfenbrenner, 1986). The chronosystem accounts for evolutionary patterns in society and developmental changes within a given environment as well as within individuals. Moreover, Bronfenbrenner (1986) distinguished life transitions that are normative and non-normative. Examples of normative transitions include beginning school, advancing through adolescence, entering the workforce and/or college, and other potential life experiences such as marriage, parenthood, and retirement. Non-normative transitions include death, family divisions, relocating, and unpredictable life changes such as illnesses or miniscule life-changing opportunities (i.e., winning the lottery). As it relates to Blacks, I assert this categorization ignores the lived experiences of Blacks in the U.S. (as well as globally) who have been perpetually subjected to inhumane, unjust, unfavorable, and unsafe living conditions. Thus, what Bronfenbrenner (1986) describes as non-normative is indeed normative for groups subjected to oppression. Notwithstanding, the aforementioned systems and the interactions therein assist in explaining human developmental processes.

One of the unique aspects of this book is the incorporation of theories exclusively grounded in research on Black males. With regards to ecological systems, Bush and Bush (2013a, 2013b) proposed the AAMT as a theoretical tool that examines the pre- and post-enslavement experiences of African

American men and boys regarding their psychological, social, cultural, edu-cational, occupational/economic, and spiritual socialization in a U.S. society founded upon racist exploitation. Bush and Bush (2013a) describe the utility of the AAMT:

> … a theoretical framework that can be used to articulate the position and trajectory of African American boys and men in society by drawing on and accounting for pre- and post-enslavement experiences while capturing their spiritual, psychological, social, and educational development and station. (p. 6)

This multi-disciplinary approach draws from ecology (Bronfenbrenner, 1977, 1986) and African philosophy and ontology (Asante, 1990, 2003; Asante & Mazama, 2005; Jackson & Sears, 1992; Mazama, 2001). Bush and Bush (2013a, 2013b) outlined the following six tenets of AAMT:

(1) Ecological systems analyses are most appropriate for analyzing African American boys and men;

(2) African American males possess unique characteristics as a result of their racial and ethnic lineage and gender;

(3) African American boys and men are connected to the legacy of African culture, consciousness, and biology;

(4) African American boys and men are resilient and resistant to oppres-sive forces;

(5) Intersecting oppressions such as racism, classism, and sexism have a significant impact on African American boys and men;

(6) Any support efforts for African American boys and men must be grounded in social justice.

Each of the aforementioned tenets offer useful insights into the ways in which Black male athletes in the U.S. experience societal realities in particular the variability in their resistant responses and subsequent life outcomes (i.e., *cool pose* versus SRIC). Similar to Bronfenbrenner's (1977, 1986) ecological sys-tems theory of human development, Bush and Bush's (2013a, 2013b) AAMT includes the micro-, meso-, exo-, macro-, and chrono-systems. However, each AAMT system is distinct towards the unique experiences of Black males of African descent in the U.S. (see Figure 1 on page 9 of Bush and Bush (2013a)). For example, the *microsystem* is differentiated into an inner and outer microsys-tem. The *inner microsystem* includes the biological composition of the African male personality along with their intersecting identities, personal beliefs, and values. The *outer microsystem* is comprised of family (including nuclear, extended, and surrogate) and community members. The *mesosystem* for Black males includes interactions between multiple microsystems such as educational, sporting, political, economic, religious, and other social institutions. *Exosystem* factors unique to African American males include the prison industrial complex, systemic economic deprivation, K-20 miseducation schooling systems, parental educational and occupational attainment, and access (or lack thereof) to various human resources (i.e., health care).

The AAMT *macrosystem* influences include the dominant ideologies mentioned earlier along with culturally based phenomena such as Hip-Hop, Black Nationalism, and African centered pedagogy (Asante, 1990, 2003; Asante & Mazama, 2005; Jackson & Sears, 1992; Mazama, 2001). Related to Black male athletes, sport ideological hegemony (Hawkins, 1998a), athlete manifest destiny (Coakley, 2017), *Black aesthetic* (George, 1992), *cool pose* (Majors & Billson, 1992), and muscular assimilationism (Henderson, 1939) are relevant macrosystem influences. The AAMT *chronosystem* accounts for socio-historical patterns affecting the Black male experience in the U.S. such as chattel slavery, Black codes, Jim Crow laws and practices, segregation and assimilation, prison industrial complex, and mass incarceration to name a few. In addition to the aforementioned systems, Bush and Bush (2013a) also introduced an AAMT *subsystem* that is located in between the micro- and meso-systems as well as above the chronosystem. These subsystems encompass the influence of supernatural, spiritual, collective will and unconscious, and archetypes (also referred to as the *endosystem*). Throughout the history of African cultures, divine intervention and African ancestry connections have been important for people of African descent including Black males in the U.S.

Within their AAMT, Bush and Bush (2013a) asserted "… it is apparent that social and educational challenges facing this group stem from socially constructed systems rather than any innate biological or cultural deficiencies" (p. 10). Similarly, Franklin and Resnik (1973) explained the variance among Blacks' experiences in the U.S. (both within their own racial group and compared to Whites) with their schematic outline of the relationship between equality of opportunity and equality of outcome. In this framework, the authors delineated five distinct life stages for Blacks in the U.S.: 1) initial outcomes—innate potentialities present at birth in a racist society, 2) pre-work environmental process—exposure to schooling, home life, mass media, hegemonic cultural values, etc., 3) work outcomes—labor force experiences, educational attainment, self-efficacy, ability to pass standardized tests, etc. 4) income generating process—employment and occupations across industries and regions, and 5) post-work outcomes—income distribution (Franklin & Resnik, 1973). Each phase is comprised of a bell curve that positions Blacks at the lower to mid areas on the x-axis of graph and Whites at the mid to high areas (see Figure 13.1 on page 241 in Franklin and Resnik, 1973). This illustration indicates how all Blacks are disadvantaged as a result of systemic racism, but not all Blacks experience the same life outcomes within complex ecological systems. In concert with this perspective, the proposed models acknowledge and examine the interplay between ecological systems and Black male athletes' lived experiences and outcomes in and through sport and (mis)education.

The socio-historical and cultural aspects of AAMT account for systemic forces such as cultural hegemony and racism that have significantly shaped Black males' experiences in the U.S. (Bush & Bush, 2013a, 2013b). For example, the emasculation of Black males from chattel slavery to modern day economic deprivation must be acknowledged and addressed in relation to individual and group outcomes. These conditions influence Black males' relationships (or lack thereof) as well as their psychological, social, educational, and economic experiences and outcomes (Bush & Bush, 2013b). More specific to Black male athletes, ecological systems approaches have been employed to examine their experiences and outcomes at the high school (Harris et al., 2014) and college levels (Cooper, Davis, & Daugherty, 2017; Nwadike, 2017; Oseguera, 2010; Singer, 2015). However, there has yet to be an ecological systems framework specifically for Black male athletes' socialization experiences and outcomes. Thus, the Black male holistic (under)development through sport and (mis)education framework fulfills this gap.

Black Male Holistic (Under)Development Through Sport and (Mis)Education Theory and Socialization Models

Given the complex nature of human existence with multi-layered social systems, it is necessary to acknowledge and examine the heterogeneity among Black male athletes' lived experiences and outcomes. Although, there are edited texts that have examined different sub-groups of Black males in college (Celious & Oyserman, 2001; Cuyjet, 2006; Harper &

Harris, 2010; Harper & Nichols, 2008; Wood & Palmer, 2014), Black male college athletes (Bennett, Hodge, Graham, & Moore, 2015), and Black masculinities more broadly (Bass, 2016; Mutua, 2006), there has yet to be a text that has explored the lifespan socialization experiences of Black male athletes. Much of the extant research (Hawkins, 2010; Leonard & King, 2012; Singer, 2015; Smith, 2009) and mainstream discussion (Boyd, 2003; Rhoden, 2006; Powell, 2008) on Black male athletes has focused on their position within the economically exploitative structure of sport. Scholars in disciplines such as sociology, gender studies, and K-12 urban education have argued the importance of analyzing specific sub-groups with nuance whereby a myriad of factors are taken into account in concert with their respective positioning in a given context (Cazenave, 1984; Curry, 2017; Howard, 2014). These diverse experiences and outcomes are a byproduct of factors such as socioeconomic status, intergenerational wealth or poverty, access to networks and role models in diverse occupational fields, quality of primary and secondary schooling, healthcare resources, sporting opportunities, and familial culture as it relates to sport participation to name a few. In other words, I posit *socialization experiences and outcomes are reflective of the extent to which there is congruence and/or incongruence across ecological systems with regards to messaging, support, resources, internalization (or lack thereof), and behaviors.*

Although, corroborated findings across multiple disciplines is important to acknowledge, it also underscores the need for more in-depth examinations of Black males with diverse backgrounds, experiences, and outcomes. More specifically, I define holistic development as the recognition and healthy nurturance of multiple identities via intentional behaviors that foster positive outcomes for self, family, community, and one's own racial and cultural groups resulting in a more equitable society. *The proposed models focus on the systems that Black males are subjected to and influenced by rather than labeling them directly* (e.g., at-risk, deficient, sport obsessed, academically apathetic, etc.), *which the latter is consistent with dominant paradigms guiding deficit-laden assertions about Black males' developmental processes and outcomes* (Cooper, 2016b; Harper, 2012). The current framework and corresponding models centralize Black male athletes' socialization experiences and builds upon Bush and Bush's (2013a, 2013b) AAMT (see Figure 3.1). The first *subsystem* located above the chronosystem refers to the unknown or undiscovered non-matter (Bush & Bush, 2013a, 2013b). Since its origins and impacts are not fully understood at this time, the primary reference to this subsystem is a recognition of its existence. The *chronosystem* specific to Blacks in the U.S. includes broader socio-historical occurrences such as Ante-Bellum period (early 1800s–1860s), Black Liberation Movement during Reconstruction (1880s–1920s), Harlem Renaissance era (1920s–1930s), Black Integration Movement (1930s–1960s), Civil Rights Movement (1960s), Black Power and Black Feminism Movements (Late 1960s–1980s), and Black Lives Matter (2010s) to name a few (Cooper, Mallery, & Macaulay, forthcoming). During each of these periods, significant political, economic, and cultural shifts influenced the nature and quality of Black male athletes' experiences and outcomes within and beyond sport. For example, the trend of Black athlete activism during the 1960s was shaped by the broader Civil Rights Movement. Similarly, the lack of Black athlete activism from the 1970s through early 2000s was a byproduct of a cultural shift towards colorblind, multicultural, assimilationist, and neoliberal societal norms (Bass, 2002; Cooper et al., 2017; Hartmann, 2000; Edwards, 2000).

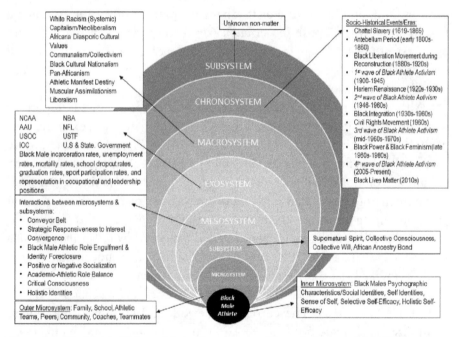

Figure 3.1. Black Male Holistic (Under)Development Through Sport and (Mis)Education Theory.

Source: Adapted from Bush, L. V., & Bush, E. C. (2013a). Introducing African American male theory (AAMT). *Journal of African American Males in Education*, 4(1), p. 9. Copyright 2013 Journal of African American Males in Education

Macrosystem influences facing Black males in the U.S. include dominant ideologies such as White racism, capitalism, and societal structures that
position Blacks as inferior and commodities for White control and pleasure.
This legacy of racism at the macro-system has historical roots as outlined
in Chapter 1 (Curry, 2017; DeGruy, 2005; Du Bois, 1903/2003; Franklin &
Resnik, 1973; Hine et al., 2006; Woodson, 1933/1990). These macro-system
influences infiltrate other ecological systems and contribute to the disproportionate number of Black males participating on White-owned athletic teams
and organizations (Cooper, 2012). Beyond sports, these macro-system influences also explain trends of Blacks' presence in White-controlled federal and
state penitentiaries, special education courses in White-dominated schooling
systems, and underemployment and underrepresentation in schooling spaces
and various occupational fields (Alexander, 2012; Cooper, 2012; Harper,
2012; Howard, 2014; Noguera, 2008).

Formal exosystem influences for athletes in the U.S. include policies and
practices administered by sport governing bodies such as the Amateur Athletic Union (AAU), NCAA, professional sport organizations, U.S. Olympic
Committee (USOC), International Olympic Committee (IOC), and state
and federal governments. Institutional racism is another important exosystem
influence. According to Majors and Billson (1992) institutionalized racism
"refers to the policies and rules, traditional practices, and informal networks
that operate in major social institutions (politics, economics, and education)
to keep minorities "in their place" and out of the mainstream" (p. 24). The
disparate impact of the NCAA's amateurism policies and concurrent NBA and
NFL collective bargaining agreements (CBAs) on Black males' socialization
experiences reflect formal exosystem influences (Cooper, Nwadike, & Macaulay, 2017). Mass media coverage of Black male professional athletes compared
to Black male professionals in occupations beyond sport is yet another formal
exosystem influence (Beamon, 2010; Edwards, 1984, 2000). *Informal exosystem*
influences on Black male athletes and Black youth in general include persistent
unemployment rates of Black adults (including parents, family, and community
members) and federal policies that criminalize Black males at higher rates than
their peers (Alexander, 2012; Curry, 2017; ETS, 2011).

Mesosystem influences are the impact of interactions between various
microsystems (inner and outer) such as family, school, sport teams and organizations, and other social settings (e.g., religious institutions and/or extra-
curricular spaces) on Black male athletes' identity development, experiences,
and outcomes. For Black male athletes, the value of sports and education

within the family structure (*outer microsystem*) affects the nature and quality of relationships with their coaches and teachers who either reinforce or challenge academic and athletic priorities (Beamon, 2010; Beamon & Bell, 2011; May, 2008). For example, families that emphasize sport specialization and performance will often times convey these values to their Black sons and enroll them in sport organizations and athletic-centric schools that reinforce these priorities (Dohrmann, 2010; Rhoden, 2006). Conversely, families that value education over sport will foster conditions, relationships, and expectations that support academic achievement and career exploration beyond sport (Cooper, 2016a, 2017; Gragg & Flowers, 2014; Harrison & Martin, 2012; Martin et al., 2010).

At the *inner microsystem* level, variability exists in terms of agency exhibited by individuals, families, and communities in response to other ecological system influences. As previously mentioned, the dominant narrative of Black male athletes promotes them either as the rags to riches story, the deviant athlete who withered away their opportunity, or the unprepared or ill-equipped athlete who could not navigate academic, athletic, and/or sporting spaces (Beamon, 2008, 2010, 2012; Beamon & Bell, 2011; Edwards, 1984, 2000; Singer & May, 2010). Each of these narratives emphasizes Black male athletes' self-schemata and socialization experiences with families, communities, and mass media that prioritize athletic success. However, the reality is that not all Black male athletes grow up in conditions where education and holistic identity development are devalued nor do all Black males who grow up in environments where athletics are overemphasized at the expense of their academic achievement and career exploration beyond sport avoid athletic role engulfment or identity foreclosure or experience net positive life outcomes. Therefore, diverse microsystems and mesosystems must be differentiated as it pertains to the interplay between ecological systems.

Another *subsystem between the inner and outer microsystems* refers to the spiritual, supernatural, collective will, and unconscious archetype that influence the experiences, beliefs, and values of people within the African Diaspora including Black males (Bush & Bush, 2013a, 2013b). For this subsystem, I posit there are at least two oppositional forces operating at this level. One of the forces operating with this subsystem is akin to DeGruy's (2005) conception of the post-traumatic slave syndrome (PTSS) whereby by Blacks unconsciously inherit counterproductive identities, beliefs, and values due to intergenerational oppression. For example, the uncritical acceptance of racial inequalities and detrimental myths of Blacks is an example of this force at work. For the proposed models, I use the sociological concept of collective memory to refer to a process involving Black male athletes being conditioned to subconsciously accept their own and the Black community's exploitation and oppression without resistance. This collective memory connects to centuries of chattel slavery, colonization, domestic and international terrorism, and multi-layered violence (e.g., spiritually, psychologically, physically, environmentally, economically, etc.). Previous scholars have referenced the dissemination of repressive messaging such as the Willie Lynch letter and the enactment of various horrific practices such as lynching, raping, mutilation, miseducation, malnutrition, etc. and the subsequent impact on the holistic suppression and control of Blacks (Curry, 2017; Du Bois, 1903/2003; DeGruy, 2005; Woodson, 1933/1990).

The second force operating in this system refers positive influences within the subsystem. Similar to Blacks across the globe, numerous Black male athletes attribute their successes in academic and athletic spaces to the presence of divine intervention (Cooper, 2009; Douglas, Ivey, & Bishop, 2015; Gragg & Flowers, 2014). In fact, many attribute their existence and survival to spiritual forces. I posit this positive collective memory and unconscious spiritual force is not only a counteraction against oppressive and evil forces in the world, but also the strongest asset possessed by Blacks across the African Diaspora. As it pertains to African Americans, the connection to their native heritages on the continent of Africa are important in order understand how their spiritual journeys extend beyond their time and physical presence in North America. Asante (2003) refers to this collective conscious as

> ... awareness of our collective history and future, where it has occurred has always been with a deep commitment to Africa itself ... The particular nature of this consciousness expresses our shared commitments, fraternal reactions to assaults on our humanity, collective awareness of our destiny, and respect for our ancestors. (pp. 34–35)

The importance of spiritual connectivity, nourishment, and empowerment cannot be understated. Globally, where Blacks have been suppressed by every measure including having their culture, land, and lives unjustly taken away from them, the spiritual foundation of Blacks and all African people transcends human conceptions of time and space. Thus, any analysis of Black experiences across any context must account for the influence of spirituality.

In sum, the five proposed models expand on previous conceptions of Black male athletes and explain how and why varied outcomes manifest as result of socialization/external and personal/internalization factors. The primary purpose for creating these models is to challenge the notion that Black male athletes are homogenous in terms of their behaviors reflecting a congruency between hegemonic ecological systems. Across these models, I outline the ways in which resistive agency and conditions manifest in different contexts, the interplay between ecological systems, and offer sociological explanations for heterogeneous outcomes. The Black male athlete holistic (under)development models emerged from my previous research on critical success factors (CSFs; Cooper, 2009) and holistic development principles (HDPs; Cooper, 2016b) for Black male athletes' educational and personal growth. Akin to CRT (Bell, 1992; Crenshaw et al., 1995; Ladson-Billings, 1995) and extensions of CRT (Solórzano & Yosso, 2002; Yosso, 2005), the proposed models seek to understand the influence of societal arrangements and offer perspectives that empower this sub-group that has been subjected to oppression, marginalization, and exploitation. In contrast to abstract theorizing, another strength of this theory and embedded models is their grounding in empirical research and personal accounts of Black males' heterogeneous lived experiences. In support of this type of theorizing, Hartmann (2000) cautioned against research that offers singular conclusions:

> Thus, one of the most basic tenets of an approach that treats sport as a site of construction and struggle is the need to guard against the age-old sociological bugaboo of overgeneralization ... The point is that the racial impacts of sport depend upon both the context and conditions within which it is exercised. They cannot be theorized abstractly but must be analyzed concretely. (pp. 241–242)

Building on these frameworks and previous literature, it is important to create models and theories that acknowledge, analyze, and describe conditions while also offering new directions for understandings, programming, and structures. As such, it is important to create and promote frameworks that highlight the reality that Black male athletes are not monolithic. The nature and extent to which Black male athletes experience exploitation and/or empowerment varies based on a range of factors that have been outlined in this chapter. It is my hope that this model will lead to the creation of empowering systems and holistic growth strategies that eliminate athletic role engulfment and identity foreclosure among Black male athletes.

The five models of Black male athlete holistic (under)development through sport and (mis)education include: (a) illusion of singular success model (ISSM), (b) elite athlete lottery model (EALM), (c) transition recovery model (TRM), (d) purposeful participation for expansive personal growth model (P^{2}EPGM), and (e) holistic empowerment model (HEM). Integral to each model is the presence (or lack thereof) of intentional holistic identity cultivation.

Table 3.1. Black Male Holistic (Under)Development Through Sport and (Mis)Education Socialization Models and Lifespan Phases.

Model	Early Youth	Adolescence	Young Adulthood	Adulthood
ISSM	• Negative Sport Socialization • Athletic Identity Centrality Formation • Schooling Fosters Disengagement	• Athletic Manifest Destiny • Conveyor Belt • Muscular Assimilationism • Neoliberalism	• Athletic Role Engulfment and Identity Foreclosure • Academic Neglect	• Extended Post-Athletic Career Identity Disengagement Trauma • Holistic Under-Development
EALM	• Negative or Positive Sport Socialization • Athletic Identity Centrality Formation • Schooling Can Foster Disengagement	• Athletic Manifest Destiny • Conveyor Belt • Muscular Assimilationism • Neoliberalism	• Athletic Role Engulfment • Academic Neglect • Elite College or Professional Sport Involvement	• Professional Sport Careers • Holistic (Under) Development
TRM	• Negative or Positive Sport Socialization • Athletic Identity Centrality Formation • Schooling Can Foster Disengagement	• Athletic Manifest Destiny • Conveyor Belt • Muscular Assimilationism • Neoliberalism • Community Cultural Wealth	• Athletic Role Engulfment and Identity Foreclosure • Academic Neglect or Support • Identity Transition Empowerment	• Personal and Occupational Fulfillment • Holistic Development
P²EPGM	• Positive Sport Socialization • Education Prioritization for Family and Cultural Empowerment	• Academic-Athletic Role Balance • Muscular Assimilationism • Community Cultural Wealth	• Strategic Responsiveness to Interest Convergence • Academic Engagement • Career Exploration	• Personal and Occupational Fulfillment • Holistic Development
HEM	• Positive Sport Socialization • Education Prioritization for Family and Cultural Empowerment	• Strong Racial Identity • Cultural Nationalism/ Counter-Hegemonic Exposure • Community Cultural Wealth	• Critical Consciousness • Internalized Empowerment • Engagement in Counter-Actions • Education for Cultural Uplift	• Direct Resistance Against Oppressive Systems (i.e., activism) • Holistic Development

Unlike previous race-based development models (Cross, 1995), the five models of Black male athlete holistic (under)development involve a multi-stage process whereby an individual can experience identity foreclosure, lower self-efficacy, internalized helplessness, and/or engage in counter-productive actions (see the second sub-section of Chapters 4–8 titled "Socialization Phases of Each Model"). Thus, the models account for the complexity within Black male athletes' socialization processes and demonstrate how life outcomes can and often do evolve over time. Lastly, key factors that contribute to individual and group experiences and outcomes are *exposure, access, support, connectivity/relatability,* and *trust/belief.* The extent to which these factors exist in relation to role models within and beyond sport greatly influence Black male athletes' recognition, internalization, and activation of their holistic abilities and possibilities. In other words, the nature and quality of these interactions determine how Black males encounter and experience a society founded upon and structured by WRC. As the title of the book states, these outcomes can range from exploitation and holistic underdevelopment to empowerment and holistic development. In contrast to dominant paradigms that explain these outcomes by psychological factors alone, the proposed models are ecologically and sociologically grounded to account for a range of factors outside of and within Black male athletes and the influences therein.

Chapter Summary

In this chapter, transdisciplinary theories related to Black male athletes' socialization experiences were presented. CRT in education and sport, CCW, SRIC, anti-deficit achievement framework and progressive and productive Black masculinities, the EBA framework, and AAMT offer multi-faceted perspectives that inform the Black male holistic (under)development through sport and (mis)education theory and models. Previous work has primarily relied on one theory and/or focused on one or two groups of Black male athletes (i.e., those who are academically disengaged or those who excel academically at a high level) whereas the current analysis provides a more nuanced perspective on the complex and heterogeneous experiences and outcomes of Black males athletes.

Note

1. Although I understand and respect the utility of the term "of Color," I personally disagree with its usage on two accounts. One, the use of the term normalizes and privileges Whiteness since White is a color as well. By suggesting "Color" only refers to groups that are non-White makes White exceptional when we should be seeking to use language to challenge racism rather than reiterate it. Similarly, I argue we should not say "White supremacy" as this term privileges the views of the oppressor. Instead, we should call it "Evil actions perpetuated by White systems and agents" or WRC. The second issue with the term "of Color" is the clustering of different racial, ethnic, and cultural groups together without taking into consideration the nuanced nature of their experiences. Even though various groups have been oppressed by Evil actions perpetuated by hegemonic systems, the nature and extent of these unfavorable realities are not the same and thus require distinct attention and analysis. Rather than using of "of Color" I recommend referring to specific groups based on their equity-minded social categorizations, such as their self-defined racial, ethnic, cultural, and various group identity titles (i.e., Blacks of African Descent).

References

Adler, P. A., & Adler, P. (1991). *Backboards and blackboards: College athletics and role engulfment.* New York, NY: Columbia University Press.

Alexander, M. (2012). *The new Jim Crow: Mass incarceration in the age of colorblindness.* New York, NY: The New Press.

Asante, M. K. (1990). *Kemet, Afrocentricity and knowledge.* Trenton, NJ: Africa World Press.

Asante, M. K. (2003). *Afrocentricity: The theory of social change.* Chicago, IL: African American Images.

Asante, M. K., & Mazama, A. (2005). *Encyclopedia of Black studies.* Thousand Oaks, CA: Sage Publications.

Bass, A. (2002). *Not the triumph but the struggle: The 1968 Olympics and the making of the Black athlete.* Minneapolis, MN: University of Minnesota Press.

Bass, L. (2016). *Black mask-ulinity: A framework for Black masculine caring.* New York, NY: Peter Lang.

Beamon, K. K. (2008). "Used goods": Former African American college student-athletes' perception of exploitation by division I universities. *The Journal of Negro Education, 77*(4), 352–364.

Beamon, K. K. (2010). Are sports overemphasized in the socialization process of African American males? A qualitative analysis of former collegiate athletes' perception of sport socialization. *Journal of Black Studies, 41*(2), 281–300.

Beamon, K. (2012). "I'm a baller": Athletic identity foreclosure among African-American former student-athletes. *Journal of African American Studies, 16*(2), 195–208.

Beamon, K. K. & Bell, P. A. (2011). A dream deferred: Narratives of African American male former collegiate athelets' transition out of sports and into the occupational sector. *Journal for the Study of Sport and Athletes in Education, 5*(1), 29–44.

Bell, D. A. (1980). Brown v. Board of Education and the interest-convergence dilemma. *Harvard Law Review, 93*(3), 518–533.

Bell, D. A. (1992). *Faces at the bottom of the well: The permanence of racism.* New York, NY: Basic Books.

Bennett III, R. A., Hodge, S. R., Graham, D. L., & Moore III, J. L. (2015). *Black males and intercollegiate athletics: An exploration of problems and solutions.* Diversity in Higher Education (Vol. 16). Bingley, UK: Emerald Group Publishing.

Benson, K. (2000). Constructing academic inadequacy: African American athletes' stories of schooling. *The Journal of Higher Education, 71*(2), 223–246.

Beyer, J. M., & Hannah, D. R. (2000). The cultural significance of athletics in U.S. higher education. *Journal of Sport Management, 14*(2), 105–132. doi:10.1123/jsm.14.2.105

Bimper, A. Y. (2015). Mentorship of Black student-athletes at a predominately White American university: Critical race theory perspective on student-athlete development. *Sport, Education and Society, 22*(2), 1–19. doi: 10.1080/12573322.2015.1022524.

Bimper, A. Y. (2016). Capital matters: Social sustaining capital and the development of Black student-athletes. *Journal of Intercollegiate Sport, 9*(1), 106–128.

Bimper, A. Y. (2017). Mentorship of Black student-athletes at a predominately White American university: Critical race theory perspective on student-athlete development. *Sport, Education and Society, 22*(2), 175–193.

Bimper, A. Y., Harrison, L., & Clark, L. (2012). Diamonds in the rough: Examining a case of successful Black male student athletes in college sport. *Journal of Black Psychology, 39* (2)1–24.

Boyd, T. (2003). *Young, Black, rich, and famous: The rise of the NBA, the hip-hop invasion and the transformation of American culture.* New York, NY: Doubleday.

Boykin, A. W. (1986). *The school achievement of minority children: New perspectives.* Hillsdale, NJ: Lawrence Erlbaum Associates.

Brewer, B. W., & Petitpas, A. J. (2017). Athletic identity foreclosure. *Current Opinion in Psychology, 16,* 118–122.

Bronfenbrenner, U. (1977). Toward an experiment ecology of human development. The *American Psychologist, 32*(7), 513–531.

Bronfenbrenner, U. (1986). Ecology of the family as a context for human development: Research perspectives. *Developmental Psychology, 22*(6), 723–742.

Bush, L. V., & Bush, E. C. (2013a). Introducing African American male theory (AAMT). *Journal of African American Males in Education, 4*(1), 6–17.

Bush, L. V., & Bush, E. C. (2013b). God bless the child who got his own: Toward a comprehensive theory for African-American boys and men. The Western Journal of Black Studies, 37(1), 1–13.

Carter-Francique, A. R., Hart, A., & Cheeks, G. (2015). Examining the value of social capital and social support for Black student-athletes' academic success. Journal of African American Studies, 19(2), 157–177.

Carter-Francique, A. R., Hart, A., & Steward, A. (2013). Black college athletes' perceptions of academic success and the role of social support. Journal of Intercollegiate Sport, 6(2), 231–246.

Cazenave, N. A. (1984). Race, socioeconomic status, and age: The social context of American masculinity. *Sex Roles, 11*(7–8), 639–656.

Celious, A., & Oyserman, D. (2001). Race from the inside: An emerging heterogeneous race model. *Journal of Social Issues, 57*(1), 149–165.

Children's Defense Fund (2012). Portrait of inequality 2012: Black children in America. Retrieved from https://www.childrensdefense.org/wp-content/uploads/2018/08/portrait-of-inequality-2012.pdf

Coakley, J. (2017). *Sports in society: Issues and controversies* (12th ed.). New York, NY: McGraw-Hill Education.

Collective Uplift (2018). Goals page. Retrieved from http://www.collectiveuplift.com

Cooper, J. N. (2009). *The relationship between the critical success factors and academic and athletic success: A quantitative case study of Black male football student-athletes at a major Division I southeastern institution.* (Unpublished thesis). Chapel Hill, NC: University of North Carolina at Chapel Hill.

Cooper, J. N. (2012). Personal troubles and public issues: A sociological imagination of Black athletes' experiences at predominantly White institutions in the United States. *Sociology Mind, 2*(3), 261–271.

Cooper, J. N. (2016a). "Focus on the bigger picture:" An anti-deficit achievement examination of Black male scholar athletes in science and engineering at a Division I historically White university (HWU). *Whiteness & Education, 1*(2), 109–124.

Cooper, J. N. (2016b). Excellence beyond athletics: Best practices for enhancing Black male student athletes' educational experiences and outcomes. *Equity & Excellence in Education, 49*(3), 267–283.

Cooper, J. N. (2017). Strategic navigation: A comparative study of Black male scholar athletes' experiences at a historically Black college/university (HBCU) and historically White institution (HWI). *International Journal of Qualitative Studies in Education, 31*(4), 235–256. doi: 10.1080/09518398.2017.1379617.

Cooper, J. N., Cavil, J. K., & Cheeks, G. (2014). The state of intercollegiate athletics at historically Black colleges and universities (HBCUs): Past, present, & persistence. *Journal of Issues in Intercollegiate Athletics, 7*, 307–332.

Cooper, J. N., & Cooper, J. E. (2015a). Success in the shadows: (Counter) narratives of achievement from Black scholar athletes at a historically Black college/university (HBCU). *Journal for the Study of Sports and Athletes in Education, 9*(3), 145–171.

Cooper, J. N., & Cooper, J. E. (2015b). "I'm running so you can be happy and I can keep my scholarship:" A comparative study of Black male college athlete' experiences with role conflict. *Journal of Intercollegiate Sport, 8*(2), 131–152.

Cooper, J. N., Cooper, J. E., & Baker, A. R. (2016). An anti-deficit perspective on Black female scholar-athletes' achievement experiences at a Division I historically White instituion (HWI). *Journal for the Study of Sports and Athletes in Education, 10*(2), 109–131.

Cooper, J. N., Corral, M. D., Macaulay, C. D. T., Cooper, M. S., Nwadike, A., & Mallery, Jr., M. (2018). Collective uplift: The impact of a holistic development support program on Black male former college athletes' experiences and outcomes. *International Journal of Qualitative Studies in Education*, DOI: 10.1080/09518398.2018.1522011.

Cooper, J. N., Davis, T. J., & Dougherty, S. (2017). Not so Black and White: A multi-divisional exploratory analysis of male student-athletes' experiences at National Collegiate Athletic Association (NCAA) institutions. *Sociology of Sport Journal, 34* (1), 59–78.

Cooper, J. N., & Hawkins, B. (2014a). An anti-deficit perspective on Black male student athletes' educational experiences at a historically Black college/university. *Race, Ethnicity and Education, 19*(5), 1–30. doi: 10.1080/13613324.2014.946491

Cooper, J. N., & Hawkins, B. (2014b). The transfer effect: A critical race theory examination of Black male transfer student athletes' experiences. *Journal of Intercollegiate Sport, 7*(1), 80–104.

Cooper, J. N., Macaulay, C., & Rodriguez, S. H. (2017). Race and resistance: A typology of African American sport activism. *International Review for the Sociology of Sport*, 1–31. DOI: 10.1177/1012690217718170.

Cooper, J. N., Mallery, M., & Macaulay, C. D. T. (forthcoming). African American sport activism and broader social movements. In D. Brown (Ed.). *Passing the ball: Sports in African American life and culture* (pp. 35–51). Jefferson, NC: McFarland & Company.

Cooper, J. N., Nwadike, A., & Macaulay, C. (2017). A critical race theory analysis of big-time college sports: Implications for culturally responsive and race-conscious sport leadership. *Journal of Issues in Intercollegiate Athletics, 10*, 204–233.

Crenshaw, K. (1989). Demarginalizing the intersection of race and sex: A Black feminist critique of antidiscrimination doctrine, feminist theory and antiracist politics. *University of Chicago Legal Forum*, 1, 139–167.

Crenshaw, K. (1991). Mapping the margins: Intersectionality, identity politics, and violence against women of color. *Stanford Law Review*, 43(6), 1241–1299.

Crenshaw, K., Gotanda, N. T., Peller, G., & Thomas, K. (1995). *Critical race theory: The key writings that formed the movement*. New York, NY: The New Press.

Cross, W. E., Jr. (1995). The psychology of Nigrescence: Revising the Cross model. In J. G. Ponterotto, J. M. Casas, L. A. Suzuki, & C. M. Alexander (Eds.), *Handbook of multicultural counseling* (pp. 93–122). Thousand Oaks, CA: Sage.

Curry, T. J. (2017). *The man-not: Race, class, genre, and the dilemmas of Black manhood*. Philadelphia, PA: Temple University Press.

Cuyjet, M. J. (2006). *African American men in college*. San Francisco, CA: Jossey-Bass.

DeCuir, J. T., & Dixson, A. D. (2004). "So when it comes out, they aren't that surprised that it is there": Using critical race theory as a tool of analysis of race and racism in education. *Educational Researcher*, 33(5), 26–31.

DeGruy, J. (2005). *Posttraumatic slave syndrome: America's legacy of enduring injury & healing*. Milwaukie, OR: Uptone Press.

Delgado, R. (1989). Storytelling for oppositionists and others: A plea for narrative. *Michigan Law Review*, 87(8), 2411–2441.

Delgado, R. (1995). The imperial scholar: Reflections on a review of civil rights literature. In K. W. Crenshaw, N. Gotanda, G. Peller, & K. Thomas (Eds.), *Critical race theory: The key writings that formed the movement* (pp. 46–57). New York, NY: New Press.

Delgado, R., & Stefancic, J. (2001). *Critical race theory: An introduction*. New York, NY: New York University Press.

Delgado Bernal, R. (2002). Critical race theory, Latino critical theory, and critical raced-gendered epistemologies: Recognizing students of Color as holders and creators of knowledge. *Qualitative Inquiry*, 8(1), 105–126.

Dohrmann, G. (2010). *Play their hearts out: A coach, his star recruit, and the youth basketball machine*. New York, NY: Ballantine Books Books.

Donnor J. K. (2005). Towards an interest-convergence in the education of African-American football student athletes in major college sports. *Race, Ethnicity and Education*, 8(1), 45–67.

Douglas, T. (2016). *Border crossing brothas: Black males navigating race, place, and complex space*. New York, NY: Peter Lang.

Douglas, T., Ivey, P., & Bishop, K. (2015). Identity, leadership, and success: A study of Black male student-athletes at the University of Missouri. *National Collegiate Athletic Association (NCAA) Innovations Grant*. [Final Report]. Retrieved from https://www.ncaa.org/sites/default/files/Douglas%2C%20Ivey%2C%20Bishop%2C%20NCAA%20Final%20Report%2C%20Black%20Male%20Student%20Athlete%20Study%2C%201.4.2016%2C%20submitted.pdf

Du Bois, W. E. B. (1903/2003). *The souls of Black folk*. Chicago, IL: A. C. McClurg.

Edwards, H. (1969). *The revolt of the Black athlete*. New York, NY: Free Press.

Edwards, H. (1973). *Sociology of sport.* Homewood, IL: Dorsey Press.

Edwards, H. (1980). *The struggle that must be: An autobiography.* New York, NY: Macmillan Publishing.

Edwards, H. (1984). The Black "dumb jock": An American sports tragedy. *College Board Review, 131,* 8–13.

Edwards, H. (2000). Crisis of black athletes on the eve of the 21st century. *Society, 37*(3), 9–13.

ETS. (2011). *A strong start: Positioning young Black boys for educational success a statistical profile.* Washington, DC: Educational Testing Service.

Fanon, F. (1952/2008). *Black skin, White masks.* New York, NY: Grove Press.

Fanon, F. (1963/2004). *The wretched of the earth.* New York, NY: Grove Press.

Franklin, R. S., & Resnik, S. (1973). *The political economy of racism.* New York, NY: Holt Rinehart and Winston.

Fuller, R. D., Harrison, C. K., Bukstein, S. J., Martin, B. E., Lawrence, S. M., & Gadsby, P. (2016). That smart dude: A qualitative investigation of the African American male scholar-baller identity. *Urban Education,* 1–19. DOI: 10.1177/0042085916668955

George, N. (1992). *Elevating the game: Black men and basketball.* New York, NY: HarperCollins.

Gragg, D., & Flowers, R. D. (2014). Factors that positively affect academic performance of African American football studentathletes. *Journal for the Study of Sports and Athletes in Education, 8*(2), 77–98.

Harper, S. R. (2012). *Black male student success in higher education: A report from the national Black male college achievement study.* Philadelphia, PA: University of Pennsylvania, Center for the Study of Race and Equity in Education.

Harper, S. R., & Harris, F. III (2010). *College men and masculinities: Theory, research, and implications for practice.* San Francisco, CA: Jossey-Bass.

Harper, S. R., & Harris, F. (2012). *Men of Color: A role of policymakers in improving the status of Black male students in U.S. higher education.* Washington, D.C.: The Institute for Higher Education Policy.

Harper, S. R., & Nichols, A. H. (2008). Are they not all the same? Racial heterogeneity among Black male undergraduates. *Journal of College Student Development, 49*(3), 199–214.

Harper, S. R., & Wood, J. L. (2015). *Advancing Black male student success from preschool through Ph.D.* Sterling, VA: Stylus Publishing.

Harris, C. (1993). Whiteness as property. *Harvard Law Review, 106* (8), 1707–1791.

Harris, P. C., Hines, E. M., Kelly, D. D., Williams, D. J., & Bagley, B. (2014). Promoting the academic engagement and success of Black male student-athletes. *The High School Journal, 97*(3), 180–195.

Harrison, C. K., Martin, B. E., & Fuller, R. (2015). "Eagles don't fly with sparrows": Self-determination theory, African American male scholar-athletes and peer group influences on motivation. *The Journal of Negro Education, 84*(1), 80–93.

Harrison, C. K., & Martin, B. (2012). Academic advising, time management and the African American male scholar-athlete. In T. Stoilov (Ed.), *Time management* (pp. 89–106): InTech. Retrieved from http://www.intechopen.com/books/time-management/time-management-academic-advising-and-the-african-american-male-student-athlete

Harrison, L., Jr., Bimper, A. Y., Jr., Smith, M. P., & Logan, A. D. (2017). The mis-education of the African American student-athlete. *Kinesiology Review*, 6(1), 60–69.

Harrison., L. Jr., Harrison, C. K., & Moore, L. N. (2002). African American racial identity and sport. *Sport, Education & Society*, 7(2), 121–133.

Hartmann, D. (2000). Rethinking the relationships between sport and race in American culture: Golden ghettos and contested terrain. *Sociology of Sport Journal*, 17(3), 229–253.

Hawkins, B. (1998a). The dominant images of black men in America: The representation of O. J. Simpson. In G. Sailes (Ed.), *African Americans in sport* (pp. 39–52). New Brunswick, NJ: Transaction Publishers.

Hawkins, B. (1998b). The White supremacy continuum of images for Black men. *Journal of African American Studies*, 3(3), 7–18.

Hawkins, B. (2010). *The new plantation: Black athletes, college sports, and predominantly White NCAA institutions*. New York, NY: Palgrave-MacMillan.

Hawkins, B., Cooper, J. N., Carter-Francique, A. R., & Cavil, J. K. (Eds.) (2015). *The athletic experience at historically Black colleges and universities: Past, present, & persistence*. Lanham, MD: Rowman & Littlefield Press.

Hawkins, B., Carter-Francique, A. R., & Cooper, J. N. (2017). *Critical race theory: Black athletic sporting experiences in the United States*. New York, NY: Palgrave Macmillan.

Henderson, E. B. (1939). *The Negro in sports*. Washington, DC: The Associated Publishers.

Hilliard, A. G., III, (1998). *SBA: The reawakening of the African mind*. Gainesville, FL: Makare Publishing.

Hine, D. C., Hine, W. C., & Harrold, S. (2006). *The African-American odyssey: Since 1965* (Third ed. Vol. Two). Upper Saddle River, NJ: Pearson Prentice Hall.

Hoberman, J. (1997). *Darwin's athletes: How sport has damaged Black America and preserved the myth of race*. Boston, MA: Houghton Mifflin.

Hodge, S. R., Burden, J. W., Jr., Robinson, L. E., & Bennett, R. A., III. (2008). Theorizing on the stereotyping of Black male student-athletes: Issues and implications. *Journal for the Study of Sports and Athletes in Education*, 2(2), 203–226.

Howard, T. C. (2014). *Black male(d): Peril and promise in the education of African American males*. New York, NY: Teachers College Press.

Hylton, K. (2009). *'Race' and sport: Critical race theory*. New York, NY: Routledge.

Jackson, A. P., & Sears, S. J. (1992). Implications of an Africentric worldview in reducing stress for African American women. *Journal of Counseling & Development*, 71(2), 184–190.

Karenga, M. (1978). *Essays on struggle: Position and analysis*. San Diego, CA: Kawaida Publications.

Kendi, I. X. (2017, July 2).The Civil Rights Act was a victory against racism, but racists also won. *Washington Post*. Retrieved from https://www.washingtonpost.com/news/made-by-history/wp/2017/07/02/the-civil-rights-act-was-a-victory-against-racism-but-racists-also-won/?utm_term=.0e2bda534e37

Ladson-Billings, G. (1995). Toward a theory of culturally relevant pedagogy. *American Educational Research Journal*, 32(3), 465–491.

Ladson-Billings, G., & Tate, W. F. (1995). Toward a critical race theory of education. *Teachers College Record*, 97(1), 47–68.

Ladson-Billings, G. (2006). From the achievement gap to the education debt: Understanding achievement in U.S. schools. *Educational Researcher, 35*(7), 3–12.

Lapchick, R., & Balasundaram, B. (2017, June 29). The 2017 racial and gender report card: National Basketball Association. *The Institute for Diversity and Ethics in Sport.* Retrieved from http://nebula.wsimg.com/74491b38503915f2f148062ff076e698?AccessKeyId=DAC3A5 6D8FB782449D2A&disposition=0&alloworigin=1

Lapchick, R., Malveaux, C., Davison, E., & Grant, C. (2016, September 28). The 2016 racial and gender report card: National Football League. *The Institute for Diversity and Ethics in Sport.* Retrieved from http://nebula.wsimg.com/1abf21ec51fd8dafbecfc2e0319a6091?AccessKeyId=DAC3A56D8FB782449D2A&disposition=0&alloworigin=1

Lawrence, C. R., III. (1995). The id, the ego, and equal protection: Reckoning with unconscious racism. In K. Crenshaw, N. Gotanda, G. Peller & K. Thomas (Eds.), *Critical race theory: The key writings that formed the movement* (pp. 253–257). New York, NY: The New Press.

Leonard, D. J., & King, C. R. (2012). *Commodified and criminalized: New racism and African Americans in contemporary sports.* Lanham, MD: Rowman & Littlefield.

Majors, R., & Billson, J. M. (1992). *Cool pose: The dilemmas of Black manhood in America.* New York, NY: Lexington Books.

Martin, B. E., & Harris, F., III. (2006). Examining productive conceptions of masculinities: Lessons learned from academically driven African American male student-athletes. *The Journal of Men's Studies, 14*(3), 359–378.

Martin, B., Harrison, C. K., & Bukstein, S. (2010). "It takes a village" for African American male scholar-athletes: Mentorship by parents, faculty, and coaches. *Journal for the Study of Sports and Athletes in Education, 4*(3), 277–295.

Martin, B. E., Harrison, C. K., Stone, J., & Lawrence, S. M. (2010). Athletic voices and academic victories: African American male student-athlete experiences in the Pac-Ten. *Journal of Sport & Social Issues, 34*(2), 131–153.

Matsuda, M. (1995). Looking to the bottom: Critical legal studies and reparations. In K. Crenshaw, N. Gotanda, G. Peller & K. Thomas (Eds.), *Critical race theory: The key writings that formed the movement.* New York, NY: The New Press.

May, R. A. B. (2008). *Living through the hoop: High school basketball, race, and the American Dream.* New York, NY: New York University Press.

Mazama, A. (2001). The Afrocentric paradigm: Contours and definitions. *Journal of Black Studies, 31*(4), 387–405.

Melendez, M. (2008). Black football players on a predominantly White college campus: Psychosocialand emotional realities of the Black college athlete experience. *Journal of Black Psychology, 34*(4), 423–451.

Mills, C. W. (1959). *The sociological imagination.* New York: Oxford University Press.

Moore, J. L., III, Madison-Colmore, O., & Smith, D. M. (2003). The prove-them-wrong syndrome: Voices from unheard African-American males in engineering disciplines. *The Journal of Men's Studies, 12*(1), 61–73.

Murphy, G. M., Petitpas, A. J., & Brewer, B. W. (1996). Identity foreclosure, athletic identity, and career maturity in intercollegiateathletes. *The Sport Psychologist, 10*(3), 239–246.

Murrell, P. C., Jr. (2002). *African-centered pedagogy: Developing schools of achievement for African American children*. Albany, NY: SUNY Press.

Mutua, A. D. (2006). *Progressive Black masculinities*. New York, NY: Routledge.

Noguera, P. (2008). *The trouble with Black boys … and other reflections on race, equity, and the future of public education*. San Francisco, CA: Jossey-Bass.

Nwadike, A. (2016). *Uncovering the mediating variable between athletic identity and academic performance in revenue-sport student athletes* (Thesis). Athens, GA: University of Georgia.

Nwadike, A. (2017, November 3). *Academically liberating underprepared Black male student-athletes: A theoretical model*. Paper presented at the North American Society for Sociology of Sport conference. Windsor, Canada.

Oseguera, L. (2010). Success despite the image: How African American male student-athletes endure their academic journey amidst negative characterizations. *Journal for the Study of Sports and Athletes in Education, 4*(3), 297–324.

Powell, S. (2008). *Souled out? How Blacks are winning and losing in sports*. Champaign, IL: Human Kinetics.

Rhoden, W. C. (2006). *40 million dollar slaves: The rise, fall, and redemption of the Black athlete*. New York, NY: Crown Publishing Group.

Sage, G. H. (1998). *Power and ideology in American sport: A critical perspective* (2nd ed.). Champaign, IL: Human Kinetics.

Sailes, G. (2010). The African American athlete: social myths and stereotypes. In G. Sailes (Ed.), *Modern Sport and The African American Athlete Experience* (pp. 55–68). San Diego, CA: Cognella.

Schott Foundation for Public Education (2010). Yes we can: The Schott 50 state report on public education and Black males (pp. 144). Cambridge, MA: Schott Foundation for Public Education. Retrieved from http://schottfoundation.org/resources/yes-we-can-schott-50-state-report-public-education-and-black-males

Schott Foundation for Public Education. (2015). Black lives matter: The Schott 50 state report on public education and Black males. In A. Beaudry (Ed.), The Metropolitan Center for Research on Equity and the Transformation of Schools at New York University (pp. 1–68). Retrieved from http://www.blackboysreport.org/2015-black-boys-report.pdf

Sedlacek, W. E. (1987). Black students on White campuses: 20 years of research. *Journal of College Student Personnel, 28*(6), 484–495.

Simons, H. D., Rheenen, D. V., & Covington, M. V. (1999). Academic motivation and the student-athlete. *Journal of College Student Development, 40*(2), 151–161.

Singer, J. N. (2005). Understanding racism through the eyes of AfricanAmerican male student-athletes. *Race, Ethnicity and Education, 8*(4), 365–386.

Singer, J. N. (2009). African American football athletes' perspectives on institutional integrity in college sport. *Research Quarterly for Exercise and Sport, 80*(1), 102–116.

Singer, J. N. (2015). The mis-education of African American male college athletes. In E. Comeaux (Ed.), *Introduction to intercollegiate athletics* (pp. 193–206). Baltimore, MD: Johns Hopkins University Press.

Singer, J. N., & May, R. A. B. (2010). The career trajectory of a Black male high school basketball player: A social reproduction perspective. *International Review for the Sociology of Sport, 46*(3), 299–314.

Smith, E. (2009). *Race, sport and the American dream* (2nd ed.). Durham, NC: Carolina Academic Press.

Smith, M. P., Clark, L. D., Harrison, L., Jr. (2014). The historical hypocrisy of the Black student-athlete. *Race, Gender & Class, 21*(1–2), 220–235.

Solórzano, D. G., & Yosso, T. J. (2002). Critical race methodology: Counter-storytelling as an analytical framework for education research. *Qualitative Inquiry, 8*(1), 23–44.

Steele, C. M. (2010). *Whistling vivaldi: And other clues to how stereotypes affect us (Issues of our time)*. New York, NY: W. W. Norton & Company.

Steele, C. M., & Aronson, J. (1995). Stereotype threat and the intellectual test performance of African Americans. *Journal of Personality and Social Psychology, 69*(5), 797–811.

Sue, D. W., Capodilupo, C. M., Torino, G. C., Bucceri, J. M., Holder, A. M., Nadal, K. L., & Esquilin, M. (2007). Racial microaggressions in everyday life: Implications for clinical practice. *American Psychologist, 62*(4), 271–286.

Taylor, E., Gillborn, D., & Ladson-Billings, G. (2009). *Foundations of critical race theory in education*. New York, NY: Routledge.

Wiggins, D. K., & Miller, P. B. (2003). *The unlevel playing field: A documentary history of the African-American experience in sport*. Urbana, IL: University of Illinois Press.

Wood, J. L., & Palmer, R. T. (2014). *Black men in higher education: A guide to ensuring student success*. New York, NY: Routledge.

Woodson, C. G. (1933/1990). *The mis-education of the Negro*. Trenton, NJ: Africa World Press.

Yosso, T. J. (2005). Whose culture has capital? A critical race theory discussion of community cultural wealth *Race, Ethnicity and Education, 8*(1), 69–91.

· 4 ·

ILLUSION OF SINGULAR
SUCCESS MODEL

Holistic Underdevelopment and Athletic Identity Foreclosure Through Unconscious Exploitation

The sports establishment benefits from the African American athletes' skills and labor by providing the illusion of an opportunity at fame, fortune, and education. However, in the end, the majority of the African American athletes are exploited without any measureable compensation for their service.

—Sellers (2000, p. 135)

Yeah they always defend you, look how they say your name, But if you rupture a tendon I bet them feelings change … Love the game know this coming from a different place … All the cortisone in the world couldn't conceal the pain.

—Wale from *Varsity Blues* song (2011)

The Interplay of Systemic Conditions for the Illusion of Singular Success Model and Black Male Athletes

"*Sometimes I dream that he is me, got to see that's how I dream to be, I dream I move, I dream I groove, like Mike, if I could be like Mike, I want be like Mike, like Mike, if I could be like Mike*" (Gatorade commercial for Michael Jordan in 1992), "*The Answer*" (Reebok nickname and shoe line for Allen Iverson starting in 1997), "*We are all Witnesses*" (Nike campaign for LeBron James touting him as the savior of the Cleveland Cavaliers and the NBA in 2007), and "*Superman*" (label attributed to Shaquille O'Neal in 1997, Dwight Howard in 2008, and Cam Newton in 2011). Each of the aforementioned quotes and labels have been promulgated by the White capitalistic mass media and corporate sponsors to depict Black male athletes as exceptional and superhuman. It is this notion of human exceptionality that harkens back to slavery when selected Black males were chosen to fight for White slave owners and even worse the pathological myth asserting that Blacks were insensitive to pain (i.e., violent brute), which justified their enslavement and the harsh conditions therein (e.g., intense whippings, excruciating labor conditions, lynchings, castrations, and various inhumane actions) (Curry, 2017; Edwards, 1973; Hawkins, 1998a, 1998b; Sailes, 2010; Wiggins, 2014; Wiggins & Miller, 2003). The depiction of Black male athletes in this manner through social stereotypes and cultural tropes is intended to appeal to young impressionable Black males in such a way to mask racist undertones. Furthermore, the preponderance and intensity of these messages are also designed to sustain WRC. More specifically, within this arrangement only a select few Black males are viewed and treated as special and granted economic rewards (albeit economically benefitting White benefactors more – i.e., Michael Jordan, Tiger Woods, and Lebron James generate more revenue for Nike than themselves via their specific endorsements) whereas the collective Black community remains oppressed and subject to insidious pathologies (read: ideological hegemony) (Edwards, 1969, 1973, 1980, 1984, 2000; George, 1992; Harrison, 1998).

The macro-level influence of ideological hegemony and exo-level influence of mass media in the U.S. plays a major part in the sustenance of the illusion of singular success through sport found among Black males (see Figure 4.1). Popular films such as *The Program* (Goldwyn, Henderson, Rothman, & Ward, 1993), *Hoop Dreams* (James & Marx, 1994), *Varsity Blues* (Robbins, Tollin, Laiter, & Wiley, 1999), *Blue Chips* (Friedkin, 1994), *He Got Game* (Lee, 1998), *The Blind Side* (Hancock, 2009), and more recently the Netflix docu-miniseries *Last Chance U* (Whitely & Ridley, 2016), all perpetuate one-dimensional images of Black males as being at-risk youth with family dysfunction and academic deficiencies. Consequently, sport serves as their only pathway for personal fulfillment and upward mobility. Another common aspect of this narrative rooted in WRC is the juxtaposition of the Black community as the culprit of their problems and White coaches, scouts, or families are portrayed as the beacons of hope and uplift (see Hughey (2014) for a detailed discussion of the White savior complex in Hollywood films). Harris (1997) highlighted the prevalence of mass media's impact on popular narratives attributed to Black male athletes:

> The message from most media identifies sport as a way for anyone who has talent and is willing to work hard to improve his or her station in life. Nearly every article written about African American athletes by sports magazines (e.g., Sports Illustrated, Sport, etc.) points to the athletes' rise from the ghetto, drug-infested neighborhoods, etc. as evidence of sport's ability to elevate one's status. And, of course, the obligatory comparison of the athlete who made it to all of his or her friends who did not make it—those with or without athletic talent. (p. 311)

The fact that the NBA and NFL are consistently comprised over 70 percent Black males on any given year and around the clock coverage via networks such as the Entertainment and Sports Programming Network (ESPN) intensifies young Black males' psychological attraction to sport and influences how they view themselves in terms of their race, gender, and athletic status. Hence, minimizing the recognition and actualization of their holistic identities. The multitude of commercialized images of Black male athletes in contrast to positive portrayals of Black males in roles such as chief executive officers (CEOs), engineers, lawyers, politicians, teachers, and doctors reifies the gendered racism embedded in the U.S. society (Coakley, 2017; Edwards, 1984, 2000; Harrison, 1998). These images and messages are damaging for all Black males, but particularly those who grow up in environments with limited economic resources and access to positive same race and gender role models who embody a range of identities and experiences beyond stereotypical portrayals in society; thus, the impact of formal and informal exosystem influences. In a society where multiple barriers prevent Black males from pursuing opportunities for respect, self-affirmation, and economic stability in areas outside of sport and entertainment the cumulative effect results in the illusion of singular success and long-term holistic underdevelopment. These barriers are interconnected across various social institutions including economic, educational, political, healthcare, legal, religion, and sport. Understanding the connection across historical contexts, socially engineered messaging, and broader social patterns is imperative for decoding dominant ideologies and corresponding multi-level socialization influences and processes that greatly impact Black male athletes' experiences and outcomes in and through sport and miseducation.

Relatedly, the ISSM is also marked by a clear lack of intentional cultivation of holistic development (also referred to as holistic underdevelopment). I argue that the normalization of *Blaxploitation through sport* is a major reason why this holistic underdevelopment occurs on a systematic basis. *Blaxploitation through sport* refers to a context where sport participation involves an inequitable economic relationship between two or more stakeholder groups (e.g., owners, organizers, sponsors, institutions, organizations, etc. vs. athletes and their home/native communities) that results in the holistic underdevelopment of Black athletes and negative outcomes for their home/native communities in accordance with the core aims of WRC. For example, the shear fact that the NBA, NFL, and NCAA generate billions of dollars based on the labor of a large number of Black male athletes exist at the same time there is pervasive poverty in predominantly Black communities in the same cities where these teams and universities are located underscores how *Blaxploitation through sport* is institutionalized in the U.S. This arrangement serves as an extension of racially exploitative systems dating back to 17th century chattel slavery (Edwards, 1973; Wiggins, 2014; Wiggins & Miller, 2003). The term *Blaxploitation through sport* seeks to disrupt taken-for-granted notions of sport being a utopic space and highlight specific instances where the purpose/meaning and structure of these activities result in exploitative arrangements and outcomes Edwards (1980) explained the intricate nature of this longitudinal process:

> So over the course of their development, because little is expected of Black athletes intellectually, many eventually come to demand nothing of themselves academically. Therefore, what begins as a childhood dream of achieving the affluence of professional sports stardom is by the end of high school already well along toward becoming a last chance and highly dubious career possibility. The real tragedy is that there is absolutely nothing deficient in these young people's intellectual capabilities. They have simply been victimized by a society and a sports institution that presumes, and therefore tolerates, an almost exclusive relationship between intellectual and athletic excellence—and doubly so for African Americans. (p. 223)

Along the same lines, Hartmann (2000) described this overinvestment as a byproduct of the belief that sports is the most viable option for upward mobility and self-respect, which results in extensive time, energy, and focus being spent on developing one's athletic abilities. The combination of hegemonic mass media influences (macro- and exo-level) along with limited opportunities and resources (macro-, exo-, meso-, and micro-level interactions) for positive Black masculine identity affirmation in society creates a situation where Black males are more likely to perceive sport as their primary pathway to success in life. Unfortunately, in this pursuit of affirmation through sport many Black males internalize maladaptive self-stereotyping, which represents what Harrison (2001) described as the "self-fulfilling prophecy" (p. 104). Applying an ISSM analysis to this phenomenon, I surmise that Black males' affinity towards sports (*inner microsystem internalizations*) is not only a result of a search for positive identity affirmation, but also an intense desire for human dignity that extends beyond mere recognition.

Previous works have argued Black males' attraction to sports is primarily associated with their longing for respect in a society that devalues them (Coakley,

2017; Harrison, 1998). Although, I agree with this deduction, there is also a deeper psychological, sociocultural, and spiritual manifestation occurring within this phenomenon that is connected to the historical dehumanization of Blacks. In a majority of spaces within societies founded upon and structured by WRC Black male existence and expression is suffocated whereas spaces such as sport and entertainment reflect an oxygen release (literally and figuratively) albeit disguised in exploitation. In other words, I contend sport participation is more than just about being cool (Majors & Billson, 1992; George, 1992), but rather an effort to pursue a sense of self that is otherwise elusive in a racially oppressive society. This situation occurs when there is a lack of Afrocentric socialization (Asante, 1990, 2003; Asante & Mazama, 2005; Hilliard, 1998; Jackson & Sears, 1992; Karenga, 1978; Mazama, 2001), culturally sustaining pedagogy (Ladson-Billings, 2006), and adequate resources and protections for the cultivation of progressive and productive Black masculine development (Mutua, 2006). Hence, it is imperative to engage in sociological and ecological analyses of the systems and conditions that contribute to Black male athletes' life experiences and outcomes in and through sport and miseducation (see Figure 4.1).

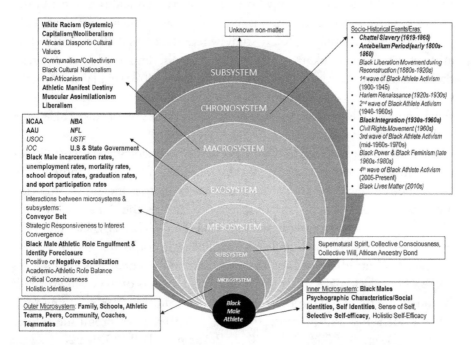

Figure 4.1. Illusion of Singular Success Model (ISSM).

Source: Adapted from Bush, L. V., & Bush, E. C. (2013a). Introducing African American male theory (AAMT). *Journal of African American Males in Education*, 4(1), p. 9. Copyright 2013 Journal of African American Males in Education.

Socialization Phases of the Illusion of Singular Success Model

The early youth phase of the ISSM involves sport exposure to impressionable Black males. Initial attraction to the sport is a result of what Harrison, Harrison, and Moore (2002) refer to as the immersion stage of Nigrescence whereby Black males view their participation in specific sports (e.g., basketball, football, and track and field) as a space where their racial and gender identities are not only affirmed, but amplified. However, in the 21st century, unlike in the pre-assimilation eras (pre-1960s) when Black sport involvement was integrally connected the political, social, and economic plight of the broader Black community, Black male sport involvement in the post-assimilation era (post-1960s) results in a unique form of Black male athletic role engulfment. Not only are Black male athletes highly susceptible to identity foreclosure (Beamon, 2012; Marcia, 1966), but they also are conditioned to view themselves and their accomplishments in neoliberal terms whereby they become psychologically (and often times physically and socially) disconnected from the broader Black community who endure oppressive realities. An illustrative example of this phenomenon is revealed in Brown, Jackson, Brown, Sellers, Keiper, and Manuel's (2003) study where they found Black and White athletes were equally likely to view that racial discrimination is no longer a problem in the U.S. Along the same lines, Rhoden (2006) explained how the Convey or Belt was designed to detach talented Black males from their native Black communities in order to meet the capitalistic desires of powerful Whites seeking to exploit them.

The second phase of the ISSM occurs during adolescence when Black males' athletic promise and skill development begin to receive more intensive exposure and attention. Major purveyors of this increased attention are elite grassroots youth sport organizations such as the Amateur Athletic Union (AAU), Elite Youth Basketball Club League (EBYL), USA Basketball, Pop-Warner Football, and university/college, corporate, and/or private sponsored scouting showcases, tournaments, and events. It is during this phase when Black males are introduced to components of the Conveyor Belt (Rhoden, 2006). Adults in their lives communicate messages affirming their athletic identities and promote the idea that they have promising futures in sport (Beamon, 2008, 2010, 2012; Beamon & Bell, 2002, 2006; 2011; Castine & Roberts, 1974; Johnson & Migliaccio, 2009; Singer & May, 2010). Furthermore at the adolescence phase, their lives and self-identities begin to be fully immersed in activities such as traveling for athletic skill development and exposure. A significant amount of time is dedicated to sport and concurrently the adulation and support for sport has an impact on their focus (or lack thereof) on academics and exploration of identities outside of being an athlete. Validation for their athletic identities include receiving invitations and/or participating in elite camps and having college and/or professional scouts recognize them for their abilities. In addition, it is not uncommon for players, their families, and those affiliated with the scouting circuits to record trainings and performances to create highlight videos and post them on social media and/or share them with scouts.

Although, the minute statistics of earning a college scholarship and securing a professional career are often widely known, at this phase of the ISSM Black males are convinced that they are the exception. The ISSM disregards the statistics cited in Henry Louis Gates' article in a 1991 issue of *Sports Illustrated*, which noted that Blacks were 12 times more likely to be lawyers, 2.5 times more likely to be dentists, and 15 times more likely to be doctors than athletes (Gates, 1991, p. 78). Despite the fact that a version of these statistics are shared among young athletes of all races including Black youth, the more pressing reality that is constantly overlooked when analyzing their inattentiveness to these statistics is their lack of *exposure, access,* and/or *connectivity* to professionals in fields beyond sport. For example, national statistics and research on young Black males in the U.S. reveals the harsh reality facing many of them. This unfortunate reality includes a lack of access to and strong relationships with positive Black male role models (ETS, 2011; Howard, 2014; Noguera, 2008), which is directly connected to systemic racist policies that lead to the widespread unemployment and mass incarceration of Black males (Alexander, 2012). According to an ETS (2011) report, between 1985 and 2000 more than 75% of Black children grew up in highly economically disadvantaged neighborhoods marred by unemployment, poverty, welfare recipients, a dearth of two-parent households, racial segregation, and large number of children below the age of 18. In 2013, the poverty rate for Black children in 2013 was 38% compared to 42.5% for Hispanics, 21.8% for Whites, and 20.6% for Asians (Patten & Krogstad, 2015).

Additional issues connected to systemic racism that have contributed to Black males' holistic underdevelopment is their exposure to underfunded schools with few teachers with subject matter expertise among a myriad of other structural issues. These issues include, but not limited to, a lack of racially and ethnically diverse educator workforce, inadequate academic learning resources, and unsafe and non-conducive school infrastructures for widespread educational growth (ETS, 2011). Thus, Black athletes growing up in lower socioeconomic environments where athletics is the primary access mechanism for affordable post-secondary enrollment are more susceptible to the illusion of singular success and related holistic underdevelopment, exploitation, neglect, isolation, and deprivation. In addition, societal arrangements also contribute to intra-racial social class segregation that physically separates potential Black male adult role models and mentors from middle and upper class backgrounds from the Black male youth in economically disadvantaged neighborhoods (Frazier, 1957; Hine, Hine, & Harrold, 2006). This physical separation is often accompanied by psychological, sociocultural, and political differences as well since the realities under which groups within the same race live vary across socioeconomic and geographical contexts.

Notwithstanding, Black male athletes across various demographic and psychographic backgrounds (e.g., socioeconomic statuses, family educational history, ethnic identities, etc.) are not beyond the reach of the WRC apparatus due to the width and depth of its influence (e.g., psychologically embedded stereotype schemas, gendered racist institutions, policies, and practices, etc.). Even though, Black male youth who grow up in the "socioeconomic middle or upper class"[1] are also susceptible the ISSM, those living in working class/ economically disadvantaged conditions are *particularly vulnerable* to this type of socialization. The latter's decreased likelihood of having access to resources and information that are valued and rewarded in a society founded upon and structured by WRC result in their heightened susceptibility to oppressive forces such as ISSM. In a related vein, Black males who strongly identify with their African Diasporic heritages (e.g., Nigerian, Liberian, Ghanaian, Jamaican, Haitian, Bahamian, Bermudian, etc.) are potentially less likely to be influenced by the ISSM especially if their family's migration to the U.S. was predicated on pursuing a better quality of life via education and occupational attainment unrelated to sport. In other words, Black males who grow up in the U.S. (i.e., African Americans) who have a more acute connection to the vicissitudes of the racist history in this country (also referred to as PTSS—see DeGruy (2005)) are more susceptible to the ISSM than their Black male peers who have life exposure outside of the U.S. The popularity of sport combined with the unique history of the connection between Black masculinity and sport in the U.S. creates a distinctive paradox (as outlined in Chapter 1). This does not mean similar patterns may not be observed in other global contexts, but rather emphasizes the unique circumstances facing Black males in the U.S. as result of chattel slavery and anti-Black misandrist realities (Curry, 2017). Even so, my previous work has revealed that Black males across the African Diaspora who are exposed to gendered racist ideologies, messaging, and conditions prevalent in and beyond the U.S. are not immune to its adverse effects such as PTSS (DeGruy, 2005) and the ISSM (Cooper, 2016b; Cooper & Cooper, 2015b). Collectively, historical, economic, political, social, cultural, and ecological factors influence the nature and extent to which Black males experience distinct socialization processes in and through sport and (mis)education.

Following adolescence, the young adulthood phase of ISSM involves continued immersion into Black male athletic role engulfment. At this phase, Black males are participating in their primary sports and either enrolled in a college (4-year and/or junior college (JUCO)), athletic-centric private or public school, and/or prep school. The athletic scholarships often undergird their access to these educational institutions, which signals to them that they should prioritize athletic performance over academic achievement. In many cases, at this point they have been socialized to meet the bare minimum eligibility standards and receive assistance from academic support staff, tutors, friendly teachers/professors, and coaches in an effort to ensure they remain academically eligible for athletic competition (Beamon, 2008; Benson, 2000; Singer, 2005, 2009; Whitely & Ridley, 2016). However, the culminating impact of academic devaluation throughout their K-20 schooling experiences intensifies their athletic role engulfment and identity foreclosure at this phase (albeit more acute at certain junctures that correspond with a heightened emphasis on sport). In addition, during this phase Black males in the ISSM experience varying levels of athletic success at their respective institutions. Some perform at a high level, which strengthens the viability of the dream of making to the professional level. Others do not perform at a high level and attribute these outcomes to various intrinsic (e.g., lack of effort, motivation, improvement, etc.) and extrinsic factors (e.g., injury, coach, team, system, school, family issues, etc.). The high transfer rates among college athletes in football and men's basketball suggests a primary explanation for unfulfilled expectations or underperformance is coaching and/or the system within the athlete's previous team (Auerbach & Prisbell, 2012). Regardless of sport performance at this phase, Black males in the ISSM continue to possess strong athletic identity centrality as a result of their role engulfment. Consequently, they continue to place more focus, time, and energies towards pursuing a professional sport career.

The fourth phase of the ISSM is adulthood where the unrealized dream of securing a professional sports career fully confronts Black males. Black males who experience the ISSM are a part of the 96.6% of high school basketball athletes who do not make it to NCAA ranks, 93.2% of high school football athletes who do not make it to the NCAA ranks, 98.9% of NCAA men's basketball players who do not matriculate to the NBA, 98.5% of football players who do not matriculate to the NFL, and the large number of Black males across various sports who do not matriculate the professional level domestically or internationally. This dejection results in the post-athletic career disengagement trauma (Edwards, 1984) and accompanied by varying degrees of psychological, social, personal, and professional transition challenges. Previous research on Black male former athletes have highlighted their encounters with depression, identity foreclosure, unemployment, under employment, career dissatisfaction, familial issues, and financial challenges to name a few (Beamon, 2008, 2012; Beamon & Bell, 2011; Northcutt, 2013; Singer, 2009; Singer & May, 2010). This identity crisis is a byproduct of Black male athletes being holistically underdeveloped throughout their lives. Despite the fact that multiple systems and people are responsible for this outcome (see Figure 4.1 for visualization of the confluence of these systems), the miseducation through the ISSM promulgates a neoliberal mentality whereby Black males primary blame themselves for their condition and to a lesser extent they acknowledge the impact of extrinsic factors. The lack of culturally sustaining pedagogy (Ladson-Billings, 2006) with their athletic-centric lives has resulted in limited to no consciousness of systemic factors and processes that greatly shape their life outcomes. Within this chapter, illustrative examples of the ISSM and its damaging effects on Black male athletes' life experiences and outcomes is presented and analyzed.

Evidence of the Illusion of Singular Success Model

In the popular film *Varsity Blues* (Robbins et al., 1999), which is based on H. B. Bissinger's (1990) critically acclaimed book *Friday Night Lights: A Town, A Team, and a Dream*, the character of Boobie Miles, based on the real life of James Miles, Jr. during the early 1980s, reflects the sad and harsh reality of a Black males' immersion in the ISSM. In both the film and book, Boobie's interest in football is motivated by several environmental factors. For example, Boobie experienced significant trauma as a child when his mother exited his life at an early age and subsequently he was subjected to physical abuse from his father's significant other. Consequently, he was sent to foster care and later his Uncle retained custody of him. In addition to these familial challenges, Boobie struggled academically and was labeled with a learning disability. Additional contextual factors worth noting are his working class family's economic challenges, his Uncle's unfulfilled dream of becoming a professional athlete, and a football culture in the state of Texas and in particular in the Odessa community that glorified the high school football team and treated football as a religion. Collectively, these microsystem conditions combined with broader ecological system impacts (e.g., meso-, exo-, macro-, and chrono-) greatly influenced Boobie's lack of access to quality psychological and educational support, which consequently enhanced his desire for positive identity affirmation through football. Although, his attraction to sport was intended to serve as outlet for the internalized pain he experienced in his life outside of football, the story of Boobie's journey in the film concludes when his suffers a torn anterior crucial ligament (ACL) injury. Along with tendon damage to his other leg, his athletic career was permanently derailed.

To an uncritical audience, this film depicts the failure of a Black family to uphold their childrearing responsibilities and a young Black male who had misplaced priorities on athletic fame and success over education. This dominant narrative fits within what Feagin, Vera, and Batur (2000) called the White racial frame whereby systemic inequalities privileging Whites and disadvantaging Blacks in every facet of human existence on multiple levels (macro, exo, meso, and micro) are ignored due to cognitive dissonance and disconfirmation bias. Conversely, when applying the ISSM and a race-conscious ecological systems analysis, the plight of Boobie is emblematic of outcomes in a systemic racist U.S. society that creates structures (economic, political, environmental, educational, and sport) that devalue Black lives and reduces the life chances of Black males from birth (ETS, 2011). The psychological state of Boobie's family is illustrative of many Black families suffering from intergenerational trauma and perpetual economic distress (Curry, 2017; DeGruy, 2005; Woodson, 1933/1990). The factors contributing to Boobie's mother leaving him, the abuse from his father's significant other, and his Uncle's overemphasis on athletics over education were intertwined with ecological systems disadvantaging Blacks. As a result, Blacks like Boobie and his family perpetually suffer from limited access to quality economic and healthcare resources. The lack of adequate mental health concern and support for Boobie's psychological needs from his childhood trauma (i.e., abandonment and abuse) along with an overemphasis on athletic success from coaches, fans, medical doctors, and family with no regards to the long-term impacts of his physical injuries (i.e., opting to bypass surgery to wear a brace with higher risks for further damage) reveal how mesosystem interactions can combine to negatively alter Black males' life outcomes. Educationally, it was and remains a travesty that in any U.S. state a student who is undereducated (often referenced as academically under prepared) is allowed to participate in a varsity sport. This insidious institutional and cultural practice signifies that Black males' educational development is not valued. Thus, Boobie's primary worth in the eyes of the predominantly White football-obsessed community and broader U.S. society, as is the case with too many young Black males, is based on the entertainment spectacle and revenue generation associated with his body; hence, reproducing the American tradition of objectifying and commodifying Black males' bodies at the expense of their holistic well-being.

Another example of a Black male who suffered from the ISSM is Tristian Akeen (T. A.) McLendon who was one of the most decorated high school football players in U.S. history. According to National Federation of State High School Associations (NFHS), McLendon eclipsed the U.S. record for the most single season rushing touchdowns (TDs) in high school football history with 68 TDs (2001) and still ranks among the top 3 career rushing TDs with 170 (1999–2001) (NFHS, 2018). As a heralded freshman at North Carolina (N.C.) State University, he rushed for 1, 100 yards and broke the single season school rushing TD record with 18 TDs (Fox Sports, 2018). Early in the 2002 season, he was touted as a potential Heisman Trophy candidate and at the end of the year he was recognized as the Atlantic Coast Conference (ACC) Rookie of Year. Despite tremendous success at the high school and college levels, McLendon never made it to the NFL, he did not earn his bachelor's degree after leaving college before his senior year, and subsequently experienced a range of personal challenges. Misguided popular labels of McLendon referred to him as an over-rated high school legend from a lower divisional school who later became a college bust who faltered under pressure and did not meet expectations. His high school, Albermarle, was classified as a 1-A school, which is the level for smaller schools in NC and viewed as less competitive in comparison to 4-A which includes larger schools and viewed as the most competitive level. Yet, McLendon's outcomes were not an isolated occurrence nor were they primarily a result of decisions within his internal locus of control. Rather McLendon's personal troubles as a young talented Black male athlete in the U.S. (and more specifically in the Southeastern U.S. where football is prominent) reproduce broader public issues where systemic gendered racism against Black males devalues their holistic well-being and limits their life chances (Cooper, 2012).

In 2013, McLendon participated a poignant interview with WRAL News and told his story (WRAL, 2013). He began the interview telling the interviewer that he would like to be referred to as Tristan, which is his birth name as opposed to the popular T. A. nickname that was used throughout his football career. Similar to the commercialized quotes and nicknames presented at the beginning of this chapter, many Black male athletes adopt names other than their birth names during the ascension of their athletic careers, which creates a level of cognitive dissonance between their holistic selves and the glorified athlete who they became. Subtle messaging such as the lack of reference to one's birth name contributes to Black males' internalization that in order to be valued, revered, and respected in a society founded upon and structured by WRC they must adopt athletic-centric and celebrity-like alter egos. Several White-controlled corporate sponsors such as Nike, Under Armour, and Adidas exploit the use of nicknaming athletes to magnify their exceptional athletic abilities and eccentric personal traits, which are highly valuable in terms of brand marketing. The social affirmation that comes with these labels extends throughout the local community to mass media outlets. Thus, Tristan's intentional preference to his birth name symbolized a reclamation of his core identity (also referred to as his holistic self) that was lost over the course of his celebrated athletic career.

Unlike many Black males who start out specializing in a single sport and participate in organized leagues at an early age, Tristan's initial involvement in sport was informal (WRAL, 2013). He explained how he did not have the opportunity to play Pop-Warner football due to his mother's responsibilities so he spent a fair amount of his free time playing in the neighborhood with friends. As a youth, Tristan, his mother, and brother moved around frequently staying with different people and it was not until they moved to his Aunt's home that he began participating in organized sport. With a bright smile on his face in the video, Tristan recalled earning his first trophy and described how his playful passion for football grew even more. On his Junior Hornets football team, he was the biggest person on the team and began capturing the eyes of coaches in the town. By his eighth grade year (his second year of playing organized football), he averaged four to five TDs per game and garnered the attention of the Albemarle High School head football coach. Upon entering high school, Tristan still primarily played football because he loved the game without any thoughts of earning a college scholarship or even playing in the NFL. However, as his productivity increased on the field, he received attention from major Division I football programs. Similar to Boobie Miles, Tristan grew up in a small town where high school football was one of the centerpieces of the community. The local, state, and national attention he began to receive for his on-the-field accomplishments afforded him and his town unprecedented attention, which psychologically deepened his athletic identity.

After graduating high school in 2001, he enrolled at N.C. State on a full athletic scholarship. He mentioned how earning a college degree was very important to him and he felt he could attain this goal at N.C. State. However, throughout the interview he mentioned several problematic statements indicating his deflated academic identity such as "I wasn't good at school" and "I wasn't a smart guy" (WRAL, 2013). In fact, other than the fact that N.C. State was close to his hometown (Albemarle, NC), he said a major reason he did not consider other prominent Division I football programs in the state was because he did not feel he had the academic abilities to excel there (i.e., Duke University and UNC-Chapel Hill). He described how he did not apply himself as much academically due to the time, physical, and mental demands associated with football. During his time at N.C. State, he suffered numerous injuries to his wrist, shoulder, and legs that resulted in sub-par production after his stellar ACC Rookie of the Year freshman season. After his junior year, he declared for the 2004 NFL Draft and subsequently he went undrafted. He attributed this disappointing outcome to numerous factors such as his injuries, lack of preparation in terms of focus on learning the game of football (i.e., studying film), lack of maturity (i.e., indicated that he was dishonest about his marijuana usage during the NFL Combine interviews), and lack of proper support in navigating the NFL Draft process (i.e., chose an agent based on a relationship with his father versus his own personal assessment). He worked out for a few NFL teams such as the Atlanta Falcons and Green Bay Packers, but never secured a contract. He tried to play in the Arena Football League (AFL), but did not receive extensive playing time.

After the realization that his football glory days were over, he expressed his deflation when he said "I don't have nothing … it is hard to get that adrenaline from anything like scoring a touchdown or making a hard hit … once it's gone it's gone … what else is there to do. I don't know what else to do outside of football … I had to transition from something to nothing" (WRAL, 2013). Tristan's interview underscored the power of the CRT tenet of counter storytelling where Black males tell their own story (DeCuir & Dixson, 2004; Delgado, 1989; Delgado & Stefancic, 2001; Matsuda, 1995; Solórzano & Yosso, 2002). Tristan's outcome after his athletic career reflects the fourth phase of the ISSM for Black males whereby holistic underdevelopment reaches a climax. He was miseducated and mislead by an athletic-centric society founded upon and structured by WRC to believe his greatest asset was his body and football ability. Like thousands of Black males before him, he was conditioned to view himself as only exceptional based on his athletic prowess and once he was no longer a valued athletic asset in the sporting system of WRC his existence was deemed to be futile. The fact that Tristian primarily attributed his challenges and outcomes to factors that were within his control (as opposed to engaging in a broader sociological critique of the antecedents and systems that influenced his life) was very telling. In the U.S., Black males are socialized to view the world in neoliberal terms whereby their individual experiences and outcomes are separated from the historical and contemporary social, cultural, economic, and political conditions facing them and their racial group in a society founded upon and structured by WRC.

Tristan left N.C. State without completing his Sociology major degree requirements and as of the 2013 interview he had yet to earn his degree. The sub-title of the interview indicated he was back living at home with his mother. Before his enrollment, he had college coaches from all across country calling his house phone seeking to recruit him to their institution. Throughout his college tenure, he had coaches who closely monitored his actions to ensure he stayed focus on producing on the football field. However, after his playing days were over, all the coaches and fans who were celebrating him for scoring TDs were nowhere to be found and little support is present to encourage him to complete his degree. This Black male figurative death through sport and concurrent lack of support from previous stakeholders illustrates the harsh reality of the ISSM. Throughout the interview, Tristan offers a somber reflection on his journey and the lessons he learned along the way. He primarily attributed his shortcomings to poor personal decision making and immaturity. Yet, the reality is the ISSM and ecological systems embedded in the U.S. society (see Figure 4.1) failed and continue to fail Black males as a collective group.

The effects of the aforementioned factors extended well beyond high school. As with all forms of trauma, when untreated effectively and monitored consistently, Boobie's life outcomes were exacerbated. Not only did he experience significant transitional challenges after an unfulfilled high school athletic career, but later in 2009 he was arrested for aggravated assault and placed on probation. Shortly thereafter, he violated his parole and was sentenced to a 10 year prison sentence in 2012 (Zaleon, 2015). Similarly, in 2007, McLendon was arrested on drug possession charges and subsequently incarcerated (Huffman, 2007; WRAL, 2013). In contrast to Eurocentric psychological theories that offer deficit-based explanations for Boobie's and McLendon's situations, I argue these scenarios are a byproduct of what I call the athletic-prison industrial complex (A-PIC) or the sport to prison pipeline, which describes the conditions and outcomes of Black male holistic death through societal conditions including sport participation. Although, previous scholars have noted the parallels between the athletic and prison industrial complexes (Hawkins, 2010; Smith, 2009), I posit that there is a direct relationship between the structure of sport and prisons as opposed to them being two parallel institutions. Black males are overrepresented in both environments by design rather than by happenstance as an extension of institutional arrangements grounded in the idea of White racism, which also served as the justification of centuries of chattel slavery, colonization, and imperialism (Du Bois, 1903/2003; Fanon, 1963/2004; Hawkins, 2010). In both settings (sport and prison), White capitalists control and economically benefit from Black males' miseducation, holistic underdevelopment, and labor.

Moreover, in sport and prison, Black males are socialized to unquestionably adhere to orders from largely White authority with little to no regard for their holistic well-being from key stakeholders (e.g., coaches, athletic directors, commissioners, and sport policy makers—politicians, police, legal officers, and wardens representing the state in terms of law enforcement). In both settings, they are conditioned to exercise their anger and energies (mental and physical) against one another versus against the system exploiting them and involvement in both systems often includes levels of physical, psychological, and social isolation from their families and the broader Black community. The dire results for Black males trapped in the ISSM often involves intense long-term mental health issues and trauma including depression, unemployment, career instability, familial challenges, jail, prison, and/or eventual unnatural deaths. There are multiple tragedies associated with this situation and all of them have two things in common: 1) they are a byproduct of systemic racism and concurrent devaluing and neglect of Black well-being and 2) they result in catastrophic acute and intergenerational trauma for Black males, their families, and the broader Black community.

The stories of Boobie Miles and Tristan A. McLendon illustrated the A-PIC whereby the holistic underdevelopment of Black males through sport and miseducation led to their presence in the criminal justice system. However, even when Black male former athletes do not end up in jail or prison, many still suffer from the same "disengagement trauma" that stifles their personal growth and quality of life post-athletic career (Edwards, 1984, p. 9). The effects of this trauma often lead to acute and long-term depression, substance abuse, alcoholism, domestic violence, moodiness, and suicide among a range of other negative psychological and social outcomes (Edwards, 1984). The story of Kevin Ross provides an illustrative example of how the ISSM facilitates detrimental outcomes for Black males both during and after their athletic careers. Kevin Ross grew up the Midwest U.S. in the 1960s and 1970s. As a standout basketball player, he was recruited to play at Creighton University in Omaha, Nebraska. After enrolling at Creighton for four years (1978–1982) and participating on the men's basketball team, he left the university with no degree and functionally illiterate (Donnor, 2005). After leaving Creighton, he attended Westside Prep Elementary School where his mentor, Marva Collins, assisted him with his literacy skills (ESPN, 2002). Three years after graduating from Westside Prep in 1983, he was unable to complete his education at Roosevelt University in Chicago and subsequently he was "unemployed, depressed, and abusing drugs and alcohol" (ESPN, 2002, p. 1).

Shortly thereafter in 1987, Ross's severe depression and alcohol abuse led to a horrific suicide attempt (ESPN, 2002). Thankfully, he survived and was checked into a mental health institution. Twenty years after participating in a multi-million dollar college sport industry and attending an "institution of higher education," at the age of 43, Ross worked as a custodian and part-time substitute teacher at his former junior high school in Kansas City, Kansas (ESPN, 2002). Ross's story is alarming and disheartening, but unfortunately it is not unusual or surprising to those familiar with Black males' plight in a society governed by WRC. His story is representative of the ills associated with the deeply embedded ISSM where Black males are holistically underdeveloped systematically through academic neglect, racial discrimination, social isolation, economic deprivation, and limited access to leadership positions (Cooper, 2012). In 1988, Ross sued Creighton University for educational malpractice, negligent admission, and emotional distress (Donnor, 2005). The suit was settled out of court in 1992 and Ross received $30, 000 even though Creighton admitted to no liability (ESPN, 2002).

Although, a majority of recent public attention has been shifted to the intercollegiate level where situations like Kevin Ross' academic neglect has been documented in critically acclaimed books and exposés (Barker, 2012; Nocera & Strauss, 2016; Smith & Willingham, 2015), the ISSM is a socialization process that is institutionalized at the primary and secondary levels. In particular, athletic-centric public and private high schools and exclusive prep schools serve as farm systems for colleges athletic programs (i.e., diploma mills), where predominantly White-controlled schools recruit talented Black males for the sole purpose of bolstering their athletic reputation and revenue sources (e.g., major shoe apparel sponsorships, donations, etc.) with little to no regard for academic proficiencies. In the Blockbuster documentary titled, *Hoop Dreams* (James & Marx, 1994), the film directors document the teenage lives of star high school basketball players, Arthur Agee and William Gates. Both players hailed from Chicago and possessed NBA aspirations. Similar to several Hollywood films featuring sports stories of Black male athletes, the White savior complex narrative is pervasive (Hughey, 2014) and reinforces the sustainment of the ISSM because native Black communities are portrayed as deficient and destructive as a result of cultural and moral failings rather than the primary victims of WRC and its oppressive forces.

Within the film, both players are scouted by a White male coach from Saint Joseph's High School in a Chicago suburb area of Westchester (James & Marx, 1994). Not unlike other historically White high schools, colleges, and universities with successful basketball programs, St. Joseph's athletic reputation has been predicated on the mining and migration of talented Black male athletes from the predominantly Black and lower socioeconomic communities in urban areas such as the Chicago inner city. In exchange, Black male athletes receive a scholarship to a prestigious private school and access to athletic benefits such as increased exposure and reputable coaching staffs. This arrangement reflects the interest convergence tenet of CRT (Bell, 1980, 1992) whereby the advancement of Black male athletes from economically oppressed neighborhoods who attend these institutions are only granted opportunities when the White schools benefit more from their services. Given the fact that they are provided access to these benefits solely based on their athletic abilities illuminates issues of racial exploitation through sport for White economic gain and institutional prestige at "educational" institutions or rather miseducation schooling sites that devalue the holistic well-being of Black males. In contrast to the dominant racist narrative that suggests all Black males hail from dysfunctional families, both athletes are surrounded by loving family and community members. However, due to the systemic economic deprivation impacting their communities and families, both Agee and Gates are forced to view sports as their primary means to achieve upward mobility. The foundation of ISSM as it relates to Black males involves a high level of economic dependency and limited access to viable alternative upward mobility resources and opportunities.

In addition to the athletic-centric high schools (public and private), prep schools, and JUCOs, unregulated grassroots youth sports is another major space where Black males are exploited via the ISSM. In fact, aside from the NFL and

NBA combines and professional competitions, perhaps there is no other space where the White gaze and homoeroticism towards Black males (Boyd, 2003; Curry, 2017; Oates, 2007) is more pronounced than at elite youth sporting events such as national tournaments and showcases (e.g., AAU, EYBL, US Track and Field National Youth Championships, etc.) and sponsored football camps (e.g., university-sanctioned, apparel company-operated, etc.). At these events, hundreds of White coaches pack gyms, fields, and tracks all across the country to recruit the next Black male or group of Black males who will take their programs to the next level. Hence, the interest convergence tenet of CRT (Bell, 1980, 1992) is in full operation at these events. White coaches and their institutions receive significant economic rewards by securing the services of talented Black male athletes. In exchange, Black males, many of which college attendance would be a significant financial burden if not improbable without the assistance of an athletics scholarship, receive an opportunity to attend a postsecondary institution and gain access to a platform to showcase their skills for professional scouts. From the grassroots youth sports level to the professional ranks, White males control nearly every facet of the business and aspiring Black male athletes are dependent on these systems for economic opportunities (Rhoden, 2006).

A primary example of this phenomenon is evident in the story of Lenny Cooke. In 2001, Lenny Cooke was ranked as the top high school player in the country over future NBA All-Stars Carmelo Anthony, LeBron James, and Amar'e Stoudemire (Araton, 2012). Cooke grew up in public housing in Atlantic City, New Jersey and later in Brooklyn, New York (Shopkorn, Noah, Safdie, & Safdie, 2013). In typical ISSM fashion, he was first noticed during his early high school years when he began playing competitive basketball with the Long Island Panther basketball club (Mayemura & Benezra, 2001). After experiencing a growth spurt and working hard on his game, Cooke's physique resembled a prototypical Division I basketball player and his talent and potential was evident to any basketball expert. In the short documentary titled *Lenny Cooke* (Shopkorn et al., 2013), he retroactively narrates video coverage of his adolescence and ascension to high school basketball stardom. Brief commentary from professional and collegiate scouts, family, and friends is also included in the film. More specifically, the film details Cooke's intense encounter with Black male athletic role engulfment and identity foreclosure. Once Cooke was identified as a top professional and college basketball prospect he was placed on the Conveyor Belt (Rhoden, 2006). In 2001, he was invited to the prestigious Adidas ABCD basketball camp founded by Sonny

Vicarro where he impressed onlookers and outperformed many of his peers. In the same summer, he played at the famous New York City Rucker Park league and shined among several NBA and other professional players such as Stephon Marbury and Ray Allen (Mayemura & Benezra, 2001).

Cooke received attention from nearly every major college basketball coach, numerous NBA agents, and became a national celebrity before he turned 18 (Shopkorn et al., 2013). Intensifying the illusion of singular success through sport for Cooke was the fact that in 2001 Kwame Brown became the first high school player to be the number one pick in the NBA draft. The public frenzy surrounding Cooke made him feel as though academics were not important and he began to intentionally miss classes and his grades suffered as a result. In addition, Cooke and his girlfriend had a son, Anahijae, while he was in high school (Mayemura & Benezra, 2001). After his junior year in high school his mother, Alfreda Hendrix, moved to Emporia, Virginia, and Cooke moved to Old Tappan, New Jersey to live with a former teammates' family. Debbie Bortner, a White middle-age mother of one of Cooke's teammates, took a liking to him and felt that having custody of him would provide him with structure and support for transitioning into the next phase of his life. As previously noted, a common theme in documentaries (full and short) and movies on *Black male athletes is the present of the White savior narrative (see Hoop Dreams* (James & Marx, 1994), *Blue Chips* (Friedkin, 1994), and *The Blind Side* (Hancock, 2009) to name a few).

A major criticism of Cooke throughout the film from scouts, coaches, and Debbie Bortner was his lack of discipline. This White racial framing neglects to acknowledge the systemic factors that contributed to Cooke's upbringing from growing up in an economically disadvantaged neighborhood without his father present consistently throughout his life to the fact that certain upward mobility opportunities were only afforded to him based on his athletic abilities with less attention being paid and support for his academic and personal development. In 2002, a year after his famous summer debut, Cooke turned 19 and he was no longer eligible to compete in high school basketball in New Jersey (Shopkorn et al., 2013). Shortly thereafter he signed with an agent with Immortal Sports, which made him ineligible to participate in college basketball in the U.S. in accordance with NCAA rules. He received $350, 000 for signing with the agency. In the film, a reflective Cooke describes how he did not really love the game of the basketball, but rather played it because he was good at it and saw it as an opportunity to financially assist his family. Cooke poignantly said, "I played because I wanted certain things that my Mom could not provide." Hence, the ISSM is a byproduct of the systemic economic depri-vation facing Black families (Cooper, 2012; ETS, 2011). Since sport is one of the few pathways for upward mobility, glamorized by mass media and sup-ported through institutional norms in secondary and postsecondary schools, it is internalized as the best option for Black males who otherwise would be deemed as deviant and academically unsuited for college level rigor to gain access to these types of institutions.

After going undrafted in the 2002 draft for undisclosed reasons (it was suggested that his lack of discipline, attitude, documented risky lifestyle, immaturity, and not playing basketball during his senior year were among the top reasons), Cooke was understandably dejected. In the summer of 2003, Cooke played in the NBA Summer League with the Boston Celtics, but despite putting forth a good showing teams were still reluctant to sign him. After playing in several lower tiered professional basketball leagues such as the United States Basketball League (USBL) in 2003, Philippines Basketball Association (PBA) in 2003, and Continental Basketball Asso-ciation (CBA) in 2006, he decided to relinquish his dream of playing in the NBA. Following the disheartening 2002 NBA Draft when he went undrafted and throughout his 20s through his late 30s, Cooke experienced psychological and transition challenges common among Black male ath-letes experiencing post-athletic career disengagement trauma including intense bouts with depression, anger, and alcohol usage as a coping mech-anism (Edwards, 1984). Harrison (1998) described the detrimental impact of an over investment in sport for Black males: "This placement of total identity and self-esteem into sports results in despair and hopelessness for many African-American males" (p. 65).

Similar to Tristian A. McLendon, an older more mature Cooke referred to himself as Leonard in his documentary when he was interviewed years after his athletic career concluded. The reference to Leonard was the name his family and close friends knew him by before the stardom. Referring to the basketball world he said "They made me Lenny Cooke and that fucked me up. People that know me called me Leonard" (Shopkorn et al., 2013). As noted earlier, the use of nicknames is one of the subtle ways by which structures within WRC such as the ISSM seek to detach Black males psychologically from their familial and cultural roots. In retrospect, Cooke said in the film he would have chosen to attend St. John's University after high school instead of signing with the Immortal Sports agency (Shopkorn et al., 2013). Cooke's story is symbolic of the ISSM. His journey was comprised of multiple micro-, meso-, exo-, and macro-systems valuing his athletic prowess over educational and personal development. As a result, Whites who controlled the elite sport circuit exploited him and his family. His dependency on this system was a byproduct of systemic economic deprivation, which influenced his personal and family decisions with regards to sport. Furthermore, the creation of an alter ego or persona psychologically disconnected him from his familial origins and true holistic self. Also, consistent with the ISSM was the presence of a White savior narrative and progressive holistic underdevelopment through sport and miseducation.

Some would argue the aforementioned narratives are anecdotal and not grounded in scholarly or empirical research and therefore not worthy of consideration for critical analysis and/or substantive intervention. I vehemently disagree with intellectual elitist claims that disregard lived experiences, outcomes, and realities that are too often overlooked or under investigated in the academy. I argue these stories are real, important, and valid regardless if they are ever researched by a "traditional" academic scholar or covered by a mass media outlet. Notwithstanding, for those critics who dismiss the aforementioned stories as adequate evidence indicating the nature and extent of the ISSM, there is ample scholarly literature that further illustrates the phenomenon of Black male athletes' holistic underdevelopment through sport and miseducation. In addition to persistently graduating at lower rates than their college athlete peers (NCAA, 2017a), quantitative studies on Black male athletes have highlighted the various challenges they face psychosocially and academically while managing the pressures associated with being an athlete. For example, these studies have documented how Black male athletes are:

(a) less likely to have academics emphasized over athletics during their youth socialization experiences (Beamon & Bell, 2006),
(b) more likely to be socialized into sport as a viable career path (Harris, 1994),
(c) experience feelings of having less control over their lives in college compared to their athlete peers (American Institutes for Research, 1989),
(d) difficulty with discussing personal issues with coaches and teammates (American Institutes for Research, 1989),
(e) encounters with racial discrimination and isolation at HWIs (American Institutes for Research, 1989),

(f) more likely to feel treated and viewed as athletes in college as opposed to students compared to their White male athlete peers (Cooper, Davis, & Dougherty, 2017),

(g) male college athletes in high profile sports (football and men's basketball) were more likely to report experiencing less favorable perceptions of campus climate and more likely to feel treated differently because they were athletes than their low-profile (Olympic sports other than football and men's basketball) college athlete peers[2] (Cooper et al., 2017),

(h) more likely to enter college academically underprepared (American Institutes for Research, 1989; Gaston-Gayles, 2004; Harrison, Comeaux, & Plecha, 2006),

(i) experience lower levels of academic motivation and/or engagement compared to their college peers (Cooper et al., 2017; Gaston-Gayles, 2004; Simons, Van Rheenen,& Covington, 1999),

(j) increased athletic identity and/or stereotype threat was found to have an inverse relationship/impact on academic performance (Cooper et al., 2017; Stone, Harrison, & Mottley, 2012),

(k) first generation status is negatively associated with academic performance (Cooper et al., 2017),

(l) Black college athletes (males and females) at HWIs earned lower GPAs than their college athlete peers at HBCUs (American Institutes for Research, 1989; Cooper & Dougherty, 2015),

(m) Black college athletes (males and females) at HWIs report experiencing less positive relationships, lower levels of engagement, and lower levels of satisfaction compared to their peers at HBCUs (American Institutes for Research, 1989; Cooper & Dougherty, 2015),

(n) Black college athletes (males and females) at HWIs reported spending more time on athletics compared to their peers at HBCUs (Cooper & Dougherty, 2015),

(o) more likely to adopt a Failure-Avoider (low measures on approaching success and high measures on failure avoidance) versus Success-Oriented (high measures on approaching success and low measures on failure avoidance) mentality compared to their college athlete peers (Simons et al., 1999),

(p) more likely to be on probation, suspension, and deemed academically ineligible compared to White male college athlete peers although the latter failed more classes (Beamon & Bell, 2006), and

(q) experience lower cognitive gains as measured by writing skills, reading comprehension, and critical thinking compared to their male non-athlete peers and lower reading comprehension and critical thinking scores compared to non-revenue sport athlete peers[3] (Pascarella, Bohr, Nora, & Terenzini, 1995; Pascarella, Truckenmiller, Nora, Terenzini, Edison, & Hagedorn, 1999).

These collective findings ranging over a three-decade time span indicate the prevalence of academic devaluation and athletic prioritization in the miseducation schooling experiences of Black male athletes. The fact that these studies were conducted at different institutions across the U.S. also reiterate the magnitude of this phenomenon, which corresponds with the assertions undergirding the ISSM.

Moreover, a majority of the research that offers more in-depth insight into the conditions facing and lived experiences of Black male athletes who experience the ISSM have been qualitative studies (Beamon, 2008, 2010, 2012; Benson, 2000; Cooper & Cooper, 2015b; Douglas, Ivey, & Bishop, 2015; May, 2008; Singer, 2009; Singer & May, 2010). Similar to the stories presented throughout this chapter, consistent findings across these studies involve Black males' being holistically underserved and subsequently experiencing athletic role engulfment, identity foreclosure, and significant transitional challenges post-athletic career. Since many of these studies were outlined in Chapter 2, I will highlight a select few studies here that were not were not explored in detail earlier. In an ethnographic study of Black male high school basketball players, May (2008) examined how structural inequalities associated with their race and class shaped participants' perceptions, experiences, opportunities (or lack thereof), and life outcomes.

In addition, a majority lived in a neighborhood reflective of oppressed Black communities in the U.S. where violence, poverty, and substance abuse was pervasive (May, 2008). As a result, basketball was not only viewed as a safe haven from negative environmental conditions, but also a perceived pathway for upward mobility. Sport participation provided them with a heightened social status in their community, a level of protection from being recruited to participate in illegal or deviant activities, and access to positive Black male role models in the form of coaches.

These findings mirror historical data on Black males who participated in organized sports in the ante-bellum period whereby outstanding sport performance was accompanied by increased social status and personal perks in a society otherwise deeming them inferior (Wiggins, 2014). Furthermore, this point of attraction is important to note because sport as opposed to traditional schooling, religious, and other sanctioned spaces was the primary place where these Black male participants found solace. Hence, when sport participation is the main source of safety and positive identity affirmation, individuals are more likely to experience negative transitional outcomes once their athletic careers conclude. Regarding contextual influences, May (2008) poignantly reflected on how various socialization agents including himself as an Assistant Coach promoted the elusive myth of meritocracy regarding the dream of securing a college athletic scholarship and professional sport career to the detriment of the participants' personal development outside of sport. From his research findings, May (2008) surmised that "in order for our sociocultural institutions to be maintained and perpetuated such deceptions occur systematically" (p. 3). This assertion corroborates Edwards' (1984) notion that Black males are not innately dumb jocks, but rather a product of an insidious system designed to exploit them via structural constraints and psychological propaganda and deception. May (2008) emphasized how contrary to the some high profile interscholastic athletes, participants in his study were not extraordinarily talented in basketball (in comparison to national competition), but yet they still possessed deeper convictions about their chances of becoming professional athletes. The author asserts how the internalization of this colorblind capitalist ideology without critical examination hinders vulnerable Black males who grow up in economically disadvantaged environments that often prevent them from accessing vital resources for upward mobility.

In the epilogue, it is revealed that one of the main participants in the study later committed suicide (May, 2008). It was noted he had been experiencing severe chest pains among additional stressors prior to his death. Even though, it is cannot be conclusive that his death was a direct result of what scholars have called post-athletic career disengagement trauma (Edwards, 1984), it can be surmised the environmental violence, racial oppression, and economic deprivation he experienced throughout his life resulted in cumulative effects that have been found to contribute to shorter lifespans for Black males in the U.S. particularly those who grow up in poverty (Alexander, 2012; ETS, 2011; Howard, 2014; Noguera, 2008). In another study, a Black male participant from a lower socioeconomic status experienced similar challenges (Messner, 1990). Throughout high school and college, he was close to illiterate and internalized a feel of entitlement through his football prowess, which was reinforced by those around him. Unfortunately, he suffered a career-ending knee injury at 20 and subsequently in a dire position ended up robbing a bank. He ended up serving a life term sentence in prison, which reflects yet another example of the A-PIC in operation as referenced earlier in the chapter. Messner (1990) highlighted how respect and recognition were primary markers of masculinity for the men in his study and sport was the most accessible means to achieve these aims. However, instead of attaining upward mobility, participants in this study experienced intense long-term psychological challenges. Sport provided these men with a sense of social status, self-efficacy, and dignity in the face of disadvantaged life circumstances associated with living in a low-income environment. As such, these studies highlight how the ISSM is intertwined with the reproduction of oppressive dominant ideologies such as WRC and neoliberalism that deceive individuals from disadvantaged groups to believe personal drive will be enough to overcome structural inequalities when in reality the design of the system relies on this uncritical acceptance in order to sustain its functioning. Thus, the myth of meritocracy does not apply to Black males as a collective group and thus individual and group outcomes can only be fully understood when ecological factors are taken into account.

In another research study examining the post-athletic career transition outcomes of African American male former Division I athletes, Beamon and Bell (2011) found participants experienced a range of psychological, social, and occupational challenges. One participant referenced the end of his athletic career being similar to losing a body part. The authors summarized the emergent theme from the participants: "Most describe feeling depressed and reported feeling a loss liken to personal death, the loss of a body part, or the loss of a family member. They grieved and mourned for the loss of a part of them that had been extremely significant throughout most of their lives" (p. 41). In a similar view, a participant from Douglas et al.'s (2015) study described the psychological challenges he faced as a result of the insurmountable pressure associated with pursuing the elusive professional sport dream while attending a Power 5 HWI:

> But then I just get to this place where, and that's the only time I will let myself say I might be depressed just because I do have a sense of hopelessness. But like my sense of control over my day to day life gets so small like I'll just wake up with a pit in my stomach, you know what I mean, nervous so hard you want to smoke just to get that nervousness away. (p. 16)

The convergent findings across numerous studies and stories of Black male athletes who experience post-athletic career disengagement trauma (Edwards, 1984) underscore the real and damaging effects of the ISSM. The inattention to holistic development of Black males in and through sport and miseducation is a matter of life and death (literally and figuratively). For too many, even when their lives are not marred by suicide or other untimely physical deaths, the extended challenges they face in discovering and in some cases reconnecting (or connecting for the first time) with their holistic selves is a figurative death in and of itself and without question taxing journey.

Chapter Summary

Since those who control sport view Black male athletes as dualistic and not holistic (Harrison, 1998), the ISSM persists when this belief is transmitted into the minds of Black males and systems are created to perpetuate this gendered racist belief. Black males who experience the ISSM suffer from what Edwards' (2000) described as the triple tragedy. These tragedies can be summarized as the holistic underdevelopment of Black males to the detriment of themselves, their families, and the broader Black community. One of the core problems with the ISSM is the fact that sport participation for these Black males is a central source of identity, but for those organizing and economically benefitting from the system they view sport as a business. When transactional processes are made and accumulative advantages are acquired for White power holders, Black male athletes whose athletic utility is exhausted are left for dead (figuratively and at times literally). Common experiences across Black males who experience the ISSM include: a) athletic glorification via the exceptionalism label and treatment, b) social adoration from family, teachers, coaches, peers, community, and mass media for athletic prowess, c) detachment from the broader Black community (physical, psychological, and/or social), d) a decline from sport grace, e) self-blame, f) a lack of critical analysis of the ecological systems that contributed to their life experiences and outcomes, and g) lack of intentional support for holistic development (rhetoric vs. systematic structural support). The labeling and recognition of this process and its interworking at a systems level serves as one progressive step in the eventual eradication of it.

Notes

1. Quotations inserted here to indicate the subjective application of class labels over time, culture, and context.
2. This finding was not exclusive to Black males, but since the sample included high profile sports with a sizable representation of Black male participants patterns within these sports (Harper, 2018), that findings can be inferred for Black male college athletes on these football and men's basketball teams.

3. In these studies (Pascarella et al., 1995; Pascarella et al., 1999), race was not indicated, but given that Black males are overrepresented on football and men's basketball teams the findings attributed to this group can be reasonably inferred towards them.

References

Adler, P. A., & Adler, P. (1991). *Backboards and blackboards: College athletics and role engulfment.* New York, NY: Columbia University Press.

Alexander, M. (2012). *The new Jim Crow: Mass incarceration in the age of colorblindness.* New York, NY: The New Press.

American Institutes for Research. (1989). The experiences of Black intercollegiate athletes at NCAA Division I institutions. *Studies in Intercollegiate Athletics.* Palo Alto, CA: Center for the Study of Athletics.

Araton, H. (2012, March 3). Star-to-be who never was. *The New York Times.* Retrieved from http://www.nytimes.com/2012/03/04/sports/basketball/lenny-cooke-star-to-be-who-never-was.html

Asante, M. K. (1990). *Kemet, Afrocentricity and knowledge.* Trenton, NJ: Africa World Press.

Asante, M. K. (2003). *Afrocentricity: The theory of social change.* Chicago, IL: African American Images.

Asante, M. K., & Mazama, A. (2005). *Encyclopedia of Black studies.* Thousand Oaks, CA: Sage Publications.

Auerbach, N., & Prisbell, E. (2012, November 6). College basketball's free agency era. *USA Today.* Retrieved on June 1, 2013 from http://www.usatoday.com/story/sports/ncaab/2012/11/06/ncaa-mens-college-basketball-transfers/1679115/

Barker, J. (2012, December 12). 'Special admissions'bring colleges top athletes, educational challenges. *The Baltimore Sun.* Retrieved from http://articles.baltimoresun.com/2012-12-22/sports/bs-sp-acc-sports-special-admits-20121222_1_athletes-graduation-success-rate-college-courses/2

Beamon, K. K. (2008). "Used goods": Former African American college student-athletes' perception of exploitation by division I universities. *The Journal of Negro Education, 77*(4), 352–364.

Beamon, K. (2010). Are sports overemphasized in the socialization process of African American males?: A qualitative analysis of former collegiate athletes' perception of sport socialization. *Journal of Black Studies, 41*(2), 281–300.

Beamon, K. (2012). "I'm a baller": Athletic identity foreclosure among African-American former student-athletes. *Journal of African American Studies, 16*(2), 195–208.

Beamon, K. K., & Bell, P. A. (2002). "Going pro": The deferential effects of high aspirations for a professional sports career on African-American student athletes and White student athletes. *Race & Society, 5*(2), 179–191.

Beamon, K. K., & Bell, P. A. (2006). Academics versus athletics: An examination of the effects of background and socialization on African-American male student athletes. *The Social Science Journal, 43*(3), 393–403.

Beamon, K., & Bell, P. A. (2011). A dream deferred: Narratives of African American male former collegiate athelets' transition out of sports and into the occupational sector. *Journal for the study of Sport and Athletes in Education, 5*(1), 29–44.

Bell, D. A. (1980). Brown v. Board of Education and the interest convergence dilemma. *Harvard Law Review, 93*(3), 518–533.

Bell, D. A. (1992). *Faces at the bottom of the well: The permanence of racism.* New York, NY: Basic Books.

Benson, K. F. (2000). Constructing academic inadequacy: African American athletes' stories of schooling. *The Journal of Higher Education, 71*(2), 223–246.

Bissinger, H. G. (1990). *Friday night lights: A town, a team, and a dream.* Cambridge, MA: Da Capo Press.

Boyd, T. (2003). *Young, Black, rich, and famous: The rise of the NBA, the hip-hop invasion and the transformation of American culture.* New York, NY: Doubleday.

Brown, T. N., Jackson, J. S., Brown, K. T., Sellers, R. M., Keiper, S., & Manuel, W. J. (2003). "There's no race on the playing field": Perceptions of racial discrimination among White and Black athletes. *Journal of Sport and Social Issues, 27*(2), 162–183.

Castine, S. C., & Roberts, G. C. (1974). Modeling in the socialization process of the black athlete. *International Review for the Sociology of Sport, 9*(3), 59–74.

Coakley, J. (2017). *Sports in society: Issues and controversies* (12th ed.). New York, NY: McGraw-Hill Education.

Cooper, J. N. (2012). Personal troubles and public issues: A sociological imagination of Black athletes' experiences at predominantly White institutions in the United States. *Sociology Mind, 2*(3), 261–271.

Cooper, J. N. (2016b). Excellence beyond athletics: Best practices for enhancing Black male student athletes' educational experiences and outcomes. *Equity & Excellence in Education, 49*(3), 267–283.

Cooper, J. N., & Cooper, J. E. (2015b). "I'm running so you can be happy and I can keep my scholarship": A comparative study of Black male college athletes' experiences with role conflict. *Journal of Intercollegiate Sport, 8*(2), 131–152.

Cooper, J. N., Davis, T. J., & Dougherty, S. (2017). Not so Black and White: A multi-divisional exploratory analysis of male student-athletes' experiences at National Collegiate Athletic Association (NCAA) institutions. *Sociology of Sport Journal, 34* (1), 59–78.

Cooper, J. N., & Dougherty, S. (2015). Does race still matter?: A post bowl championship series (BCS) era examination of student athletes' experiences at a Division I historically Black college/university (HBCU) and predominantly White institution (PWI). *Journal of Issues in Intercollegiate Athletics, 8,* 74–101.

Curry, T. J. (2017). *The man-not: Race, class, genre, and the dilemmas of Black manhood.* Philadelphia, PA: Temple University Press.

DeCuir, J. T., & Dixson, A. D. (2004). "So when it comes out, they aren't that surprised that it is there": Using critical race theory as a tool of analysis of race and racism in education. *Educational Researcher, 33*(5), 26–31.

DeGruy, J. (2005). *Posttraumatic slave syndrome: America's legacy of enduring injury & healing.* Milwaukie, OR: Uptone Press.

Delgado, R. (1989). Storytelling for oppositionists and others: A plea for narrative. *Michigan Law Review, 87*(8), 2411–2441.

Delgado, R., & Stefancic, J. (2001). *Critical race theory: An introduction.* New York, NY: New York University Press.

Donnor J. K. (2005). Towards an interest-convergence in the education of African-American football student athletes in major college sports. *Race, Ethnicity and Education, 8*(1), 45–67.

Douglas, T., Ivey, P., & Bishop, K. (2015). Identity, leadership, and success: A study of Black male student-athletes at the University of Missouri. *National Collegiate Athletic Association (NCAA) Innovations Grant.* [Final Report]. Retrieved from https://www.ncaa.org/sites/default/files/Douglas%2C%20Ivey%2C%20Bishop%2C%20NCAA%20Final%20Report%2C%20Black%20Male%20Student%20Athlete%20Study%2C%201.4.2016%2C%20submitted.pdf

Du Bois, W. E. B. (1903/2003). *The souls of Black folk.* Chicago, IL: A. C. McClurg.

Edwards, H. (1969). *The revolt of the Black athlete.* New York, NY: Free Press.

Edwards, H. (1973). *Sociology of sport.* Homewood, IL: Dorsey Press.

Edwards, H. (1980). *The struggle that must be: An autobiography.* New York, NY: Macmillan Publishing

Edwards, H. (1984). The Black "dumb jock": An American sports tragedy. *College Board Review, 131,* 8–13.

Edwards, H. (2000). Crisis of black athletes on the eve of the 21st century. *Society, 37*(3), 9–13.

ESPN (2002). Outside the Lines: Unable to Read. Transcript of Episode 103 from March 17, 2002. Retrieved from http://www.espn.com/page2/tvlistings/show103transcript.html.

ETS. (2011). *A strong start: Positioning young Black boys for educational success a statistical profile.* Washington, DC: Educational Testing Service.

Fanon, F. (1963/2004). *The wretched of the earth.* New York, NY: Grove Press.

Feagin, J., Vera, H., & Batur, P. (2000). *White racism* (2nd ed.). New York, NY: Routledge.

Fox Sports (2018). T. A. McLendon player stats. Retrieved from https://www.foxsports.com/college-football/ta-mclendon-player-stats

Frazier, E. F. (1957). *Black bourgeoisie.* New York, NY: Free Press.

Friedkin, W. (1994). *Blue chips* [movie]. Paramount Pictures (Distributor).

Gates, H. L. (1991). Delusions of grandeur. Sports Illustrated, August 19. Retrieved from https://www.si.com/vault/1991/08/19/124714/#

Gaston-Gayles, J. L. (2004). Examining academic and athletic motivation among student athletes at a Division I university. *Journal of College Student Development, 45*(1), 75–83.

George, N. (1992). *Elevating the game: Black men and basketball.* New York, NY: HarperCollins.

Goldwyn, S., Jr., Henderson, D., Rothman, T., & Ward, D. S. (1993). *The program* [Film]. United States: Touchstone Pictures, Samuel Goldwyn Company.

Hancock, J. L. (2009). *The blind side* [Film]. United States: Alcon Entertainment.

Harper, S. R. (2018). *Black male student-athletes and racial inequities in NCAA Division I college sports: 2018 edition.* Los Angeles, CA: University of Southern California, Race & Equity Center.

Harris, O. (1994). Race, sport, and social support. *Sociology of Sport Journal, 11*(1), 40–50.

Harris, O. (1997). The role of sport in the Black community. *Sociological Focus, 30*(4), 311–319.

Harrison, C. K., (1998). Themes that thread through society: Racism and athletic manifestation in the African-American community. *Race, Ethnicity and Education, 1*(1), 63–74.

Harrison, C. K., Comeaux, E., & Plecha, M. (2006). Faculty and male football and basketball players on university campuses: An empirical investigation of the 'intellectual' as mentor to the student-athlete. *Research Quarterly for Exercise and Sport, 77*(2), 277–284.

Harrison, L. Jr. (2001). Understanding the influence of stereotypes: Implications for the African American in sport and physical activity. *Quest, 53*(1), 97–114.

Harrison., L. Jr., Harrison, C. K., & Moore, L. N. (2002). African American racial identity and sport. *Sport, Education & Society, 7*(2), 121–133.

Hartmann, D. (2000). Rethinking the relationships between sport and race in American culture: Golden ghettos and contested terrain. *Sociology of Sport Journal, 17*(3), 229–253.

Hawkins, B. (1998a). The dominant images of black men in America: The representation of O. J. Simpson. In G. Sailes (Ed.), *African Americans in sport* (pp. 39–52). New Brunswick, NJ: Transaction Publishers.

Hawkins, B. (1998b). The White supremacy continuum of images for Black men. *Journal of African American men, 3*(3), 7–18.

Hawkins, B. (2010). *The new plantation: Black athletes, college sports, and predominantly White NCAA institutions*. New York, NY: Palgrave Macmillan.

Hilliard, A. G., III, (1998). *SBA: The reawakening of the African mind*. Gainesville, FL: Makare Publishing.

Hine, D. C., Hine, W. C., & Harrold, S. (2006). *The African-American odyssey: Since 1965* (Third ed. Vol. Two). Upper Saddle River, NJ: Pearson Prentice Hall.

Howard, T. C. (2014). *Black male(d): Peril and promise in the education of African American males*. New York, NY: Teachers College Press.

Hughey, M. W. (2014). *The White savior film: Content, critics, and consumption*. Philadelphia, PA: University of Temple Press.

Huffman, D. (2007, September 12). Ex-Pack star McLendon arrested on drug charges. *WRAL Sports Fan*. Retrieved from https://www.wralsportsfan.com/rs/story/1805682/

Jackson, A. P., & Sears, S. J. (1992). Implications of an Africentric worldview in reducing stress for African American women. *Journal of Counseling & Development, 71*(2), 184–190.

James, S., & Marx, F. (1994). *Hoop dreams* [documentary]. Minneapolis, MN: Kartemquin Films.

Johnson, T. S., & Migliaccio, T. A. (2009). The social construction of an athlete: African American boy's experience in sport. *The Western Journal of Black Studies, 33*(2), 98–109.

Karenga, M. (1978). *Essays on struggle: Position and analysis*. San Diego, CA: Kawaida Publications.

Ladson-Billings, G. (2006). From the achievement gap to the education debt: Understanding achievement in U.S. schools. *Educational Researcher, 35*(7), 3–12.

Lee, S. (1998). *He got game* [Film]. United States: Touchstone Pictures, 40 Acres & A Mule Filmworks.

Majors, R., & Billson, J. M. (1992). *Cool pose: The dilemmas of Black manhood in America*. New York, NY: Lexington Books.

Marcia, J. E. (1966). Development and validation of ego-identity status. *Journal of Personality and Social Psychology, 3*(5), 551–558.

Matsuda, M. (1995). Looking to the bottom: Critical legal studies and reparations. In K. Crenshaw, N. Gotanda, G. Peller & K. Thomas (Eds.), *Critical race theory: The key writings that formed the movement* (pp. 63–79). New York, NY: The New Press.

May, R. A. B. (2008). *Living through the hoop: High school basketball, race, and the American Dream.* New York, NY: New York University Press.

Mayemura, M., & Benezra, D. (2001). Cooke makes best move off the court. *ESPN Recruiting.* Retrieved from http://www.espn.com/recruiting/s/cooke.html

Mazama, A. (2001). The Afrocentric paradigm: Contours and definitions. *Journal of Black Studies, 31*(4), 387–405.

Messner, M. (1990). Masculinities and athletic careers: Bonding and status differences. In D. Sabo & M. Messner (Eds.), *Sport, men and the gender order: Critical feminist perspectives* (pp. 97–108). Champaign, IL: Human Kinetics.

Mutua, A. D. (2006). *Progressive Black masculinities.* New York, NY: Routledge.

NCAA (2017). Trends in graduation success rates and federal graduation rates at NCAA Division I institutions. *NCAA.* Retrieved from https://www.ncaa.org/sites/default/files/2017D1RES_Grad_Rate_Trends_FINAL_20171108.pdf

NCAA (2018, April 20). Estimated probability of competing in professional athletics. *NCAA website.* Retrieved from http://www.ncaa.org/about/resources/research/estimated-probability-competing-professional-athletics

NFHS (2018). Record book result. *National Federation of State High School Associations.* Retrieved from https://www.nfhs.org/RecordBook/Record-book-result.aspx?CategoryId=382

Nocera, J., & Strauss, B. (2016). *Indentured: The inside story of the rebellion against the NCAA.* New York, NY: Portfolio/Penguin Random House.

Noguera, P. A. (2008). *The trouble with Black boys … and other reflections on race, equity, and the future of public education.* San Francisco, CA: Jossey-Bass.

Northcutt, K. J. (2013). *The dilemma: Career transition of African American male football players at Division I institutions.* Dissertation. University of Mississippi.

Oates, T. P. (2007). The erotic gaze in the NFL draft. *Communication and Critical/Cultural Studies, 4*(1): 74–90.

Pascarella, E. T., Bohr, L., Nora, A., & Terenzini, P. T. (1995). Intercollegiate athletic participation and freshman-year cognitive outcomes. *The Journal of Higher Education, 66*(4), 369–387.

Pascarella, E. T., Truckenmiller, R., Nora, A., Terenzini, P. T., Edison, M., & Hagedorn, L. S. (1999). Cognitive impacts of intercollegiate athletic participation: Some further evidence. *The Journal of Higher Education, 70*(1), 1–26.

Patten, E., & Krogstad, J. M. (2015, July 14). Black child poverty rate holds steady, even as other groups see declines. *Pew Research Center.* Retrieved from http://www.pewresearch.org/fact-tank/2015/07/14/black-child-poverty-rate-holds-steady-even-as-other-groups-see-declines/

Rhoden, W. C. (2006). *40 million dollar slaves: The rise, fall, and redemption of the Black athlete.* New York, NY: Crown Publishing Group.

Robbins, B., Tollin, M., Laiter T., & Wiley, M. (1999). *Varsity blues* [Film]. Paramount Pictures (Distributor), United States: Tollin/Robbins Productions, MTV Films.

Sailes, G. (2010). The African American athlete: Social myths and stereotypes. In G. Sailes (Ed.), *Modern sport and the African American Athlete Experience* (pp. 55–68). San Diego, CA: Cognella.

Sellers, R. M. (2000). African American student-athletes: Opportunity or exploitation? In D. A. Brooks, R. (Ed.), *Racism in college athletics: The African American athlete's experience* (2nd ed., pp. 133–154). Morgantown, WV: Fitness Information Technology, Inc.

Shopkorn, A., Noah, J., Safdie, J., & Safdie, B. (2013). *Lenny Cooke* [Documentary]. New York, NY: Shopkorn Productions.

Simons, H. D., Van Rheenen, D., & Covington, M. V. (1999). Academic motivation and the student-athlete. *Journal of College Student Development, 40*(2), 151–162.

Singer, J. N. (2005). Understanding racism through the eyes of AfricanAmerican male student-athletes. *Race, Ethnicity and Education, 8*(4), 365–386.

Singer, J. N. (2009). African American football athletes' perspectives on institutional integrity in college sport. *Research Quarterly for Exercise and Sport, 80*(1), 102–116.

Singer, J. N., & May, R. A. B. (2010). The career trajectory of a Black male high school basketball player: A social reproduction perspective. *International Review for the Sociology of Sport, 46*(3), 299—314.

Smith, E. (2009). *Race, sport and the American dream* (2nd ed.). Durham, NC: Carolina Academic Press.

Smith, J. M., & Willingham, M. (2015). *Cheated: The UNC scandal, the education of athletes, and the future of big-time college sports.* Omaha, NE: University of Nebraska Press.

Solórzano, D. G., & Yosso, T. J. (2002). Critical race methodology: Counter-storytelling as an analytical framework for education research. *Qualitative Inquiry, 8*(1), 23–44.

Stone, J., Harrison, C. K., & Mottley, J. (2012). "Don't call me a student-athlete": The effect of identity priming on stereotype threat for academically engaged African American college athletes. *Basic and Applied Social Psychology, 34*(2), 99–106.

Wale (2011). Varsity blues [Recorded by Wale]. On *The Eleven One Eleven Theory* mixtape. Washington, D.C. Every Blue Moon.

Whitely, G., & Ridley, A. (2016). Last chance U [Documentary Series]. *Condé Nast Entertainment.* [Netflix]. https://www.netflix.com/title/80091742

Wiggins, D. K. (2014). 'Black athletes in White men's games': Race, sport and American national pastimes. *The International Journal of the History of Sport, 31*(1–2), 181–202.

Wiggins, D. K., & Miller, P. B. (2003). *The unlevel playing field: A documentary history of the AfricanAmerican experience in sport.* Urbana, IL: University of Illinois Press.

Woodson, C. G. (1933/1990). *The mis-education of the Negro.* Trenton, NJ: Africa World Press.

WRAL (2013). McLendon: I squandered an opportunity. Retrieved online from https://www.wralsportsfan.com/colleges/video/12920770/

Zaleon, A. (2015, October 31). Flashback: Boobie Miles found fame, trouble under Friday Night Lights; his son set course of his own at Irving. *The Dallas Morning News.* Retrieved from https://sportsday.dallasnews.com/high-school/high-schools/2017/07/04/boobie-miles-found-fame-trouble-friday-night-lights-son-sets-course

ELITE ATHLETE LOTTERY MODEL

Holistic (Under)Development and Interest Convergence with Exploitative Systems

> To enslave men successfully and safely it is necessary to keep their minds occupied
> with thoughts and aspirations short of the liberty of which they are deprived. A
> certain degree of attainable good must be kept before them.
> —Douglass (1962 cited in Wiggins & Miller, 2003, p. 16)

The Interplay of Systemic Conditions for the Elite Athletic Lottery Model and Black Male Athletes

Within any system of oppression, there must be exceptions to the rule in order
to maintain hegemonic norms. In other words, as Frederick Douglass (1881,
1962) asserted, distracting an oppressed group via nominal rewards and entertainment is vital for the sustainability of ideological hegemony (also referred
to as normalized inequalities/inequitable arrangements) and more importantly for the minimization of any resistance efforts (i.e., revolts). Although,
Douglass (1881, 1962) was referencing the ante-bellum and post-bellum eras
in the U.S., this same mechanism of racialized social control is evident in
the 21st century with institutions such as sport. In the case of the elite athlete lottery model (EALM), sport is viewed as an institution within a broader

social apparatus designed to maintain the disproportionate power structure that positions Blacks as a collective group as the most inferior, dependent, and vulnerable in the established (socially constructed as opposed to biologically or divinely determined) racial and class hierarchies. The EALM creates pathways for a limited number of Blacks to attain access to monetary gains via salaries, endorsements, and sponsorships while minimizing the collective group's access to wealth, management, and ownership.

The EALM also serves as a means to distract the masses of young Black males to pursue a professional sports career while simultaneously not analyzing the oppressive systems in which they exist (e.g., educationally, politically, economically, culturally, etc.—also referred to as the triple tragedy (Edwards, 2000)). In reality, only 1.6% of all NCAA athletes make it to the professional level including the 74.5% of NBA and 69.7% of NFL players whom are Black (Lapchick & Balasundaram, 2017; Lapchick et al., 2016; NCAA, 2018). In addition, Black males constitute a sizable portion of the U.S. track and field teams and this does not include other professional track and field athletes who are not members of the national team. Although, the representation in sports such as soccer, baseball, etc. are significantly lower than the aforementioned sports, the racial arrangement involving the underrepresentation of in Blacks in ownership, management, and coaching positions compared to their participation rates reinforce the aims of WRC (Coakley, 2017; Wiggins, 2014). Therefore, when examining the heterogeneous socialization experiences and outcomes of Black male athletes it is important to acknowledge there are a small percentage of those who successfully matriculate to the professional ranks either for a long term or short term career. Their lived experiences matter as well and deserve scholarly attention. This analysis is necessary to facilitate a broader sociological and ecological understanding of the systems that contribute to these outcomes as well as the patterns associated with Black males (including athletes) more generally (see Figure 5.1).

In an effort to explain Black males' interest and success in sports, Coakley (2017) offered a sociological hypothesis connecting racial ideologies with psychological processes and behavioral patterns. According to the hypothesis, since the 17th century in the U.S. White power wielders have created conditions based on the Black male innate physicality myth and concurrently limited opportunities for Black males to experience upward mobility and acquire respect in areas outside of sport, entertainment, and imprisonment. The ubiquitous nature of the insidious ideology was used to justify chattel slavery and other forms of Black intensive labor for White economic gains (i.e., *Blaxploitation through sport*). The result of the racist ideology and corresponding societal conditions resulted in Blacks internalizing the notion that their biological and cultural destiny is connected to sport excellence and thus concerted efforts are put forth in this area (Coakley, 2017). Related to biological destiny, numerous Black athletes, notably Michael Johnson, 4-time Olympic Gold medalist (400m in 1996 and 2000; 200m in 1996; 4 × 400 in 1992), have expressed the fallacious belief that they possess genetic predispositions attributed to their race, which enable them to excel in their respective sports (i.e., fast muscle twitch muscles, longer limbs, etc.). It is commonplace for athletes, commentators, and fans alike to solely attribute Black athletes' sporting feats to their "natural gifts," "God given talents," "freakish abilities" to name a few. Yet, an abundance of scientific research has revealed that *race is a social construct* and the complex interplay between various deoxyribonucleic acid (DNA) cells (over millions) and environmental conditions disproves the idea that genetic traits associated with phenotypical features could explain athletic abilities and/or sport performances (Edwards, 1973; Smedley & Smedley, 2005). Culturally, this hypothesis reflects what Ogden and Hilt (2003) described as collective identity through sport whereby activities associated with specific cultures are adopted as a means of self-identity development and the conditions necessary for success in these endeavors are created by the groups involved as opposed to being a result of biological determinism or divine ordination.

Beyond individual internalizations of innate Black athletic genes, mass media and educational spaces (i.e., athletic team racial compositions—see the concept of racial stacking in Loy and Elvogue (1970)) have also contributed to the taken-for-granted acceptance of this myth via stereotype acceptance and reproduction (Harrison, 1998; Harrison, Harrison, & Moore, 2002; Hodge et al., 2008). The result of the accepted biological and cultural destiny among Black athletes combined with socially engineered actions and opportunities is success in sport (Coakley, 2017). This process of *athletic manifest destiny* (Coakley, 2017; Edwards, 2000; Fuller et al., 2016; Harrison, 1998) incorporates various ecological systems (chrono-, macro-, exo-, meso-, and micro-) and helps explain a part of the ISSM and EALM. Otherwise stated, the presence and influence of the athletic manifest destiny on Black males' socialization and achievements in and through sport offers a more nuanced analysis of this phenomenon in contrast to the racist myths and overly simplistic rationales that have been popularized since the late 19th century (i.e., innate athletic superiority myth) (Sailes, 2010; Wiggins & Miller, 2003).

It is also important to note that not all talented Black male athletes are afforded the opportunity to experience long-term success via professional sports. More specifically, the apolitical, neutral, colorblind, and passive Black male athletes are rewarded more handsomely by macro- and exo-system entities with corporate sponsorships and diverse fanfare than their peers who do not acquiesce to this WRC code of behavior (Rhoden, 2006; Hawkins, 1998b). Notable athletes such as Jesse Owens, Joe Louis, Michael Jordan, Magic Johnson, and Tiger Woods fit this label. Each of them were or are extraordinarily talented within their respective sports, but more importantly to the system of WRC they are non-disruptive to the hegemonic social order. It is also not an accident that this type of Black male athlete is often able to successfully transition into commentator or analyst roles upon completion of their careers (e.g., Charles Barkley, Deion Sanders, etc.). In other words, these broader observations of mass media are consistent with research that has highlighted how Black male athletes are socialized to be colorblind and assimilate into White normative cultural standards (Bimper & Harrison, 2011; Brown et al., 2003). In this way, the power structure further reinforces the rewarding of this type of passive assimilation via tangible and intangible benefits.

Along the same lines, Rhoden (2006) explained how the Conveyor Belt rewards and celebrates this type of Black male athlete for numerous reasons. One, they perpetuate the meritocratic ideals promulgated by dominant American ideologies that promote racial assimilation and maintain Whites at the top of the hierarchy (i.e., White Anglo-Saxon middle-class heteronormative cultural norms viewed as the golden standard). In addition to White racism, additional ideologies within this hegemonic context include neoliberalism, patriarchy/sexism, heternormativity, protestant ethic, and capitalism (Beyer & Hannah, 2000; Coakley, 2017; Sage, 1998). These ideologies foster desirable behaviors such as conformity, good citizenship, and achievement motivation (Beyer & Hannah, 2000). The logic/myth goes if these Black males can be "successful" in sports, then all Black males who work hard enough can acquire success in the capitalistic system across all industries. Therefore, current societal patterns can be explained by the fact that Whites simply work harder and possess more intellectual abilities than Blacks. This racist logic blatantly disregards the impact of historical and contemporary atrocities that involve White violence, oppression, and marginalization towards Blacks (e.g., chattel slavery, Jim Crow Laws, Black Codes, separate and unequal, redlining, gentrification, racialized social stratification (also known as WRC), health malpractice, intergenerational theft, lynchings, mass incarceration, and many more) (Alexander, 2012; Curry, 2017; Du Bois, 1903/2003; DeGruy, 2005; ETS, 2011; Franklin, 1947; Franklin & Resnik, 1973; Hine, Hine, & Harrold, 2006; Woodson, 1933/1990).

Another benefit of this arrangement is the illusion of racial harmony and integration. When people see Blacks participating on racially mixed athletic teams, receiving scholarships, and securing professional sport contracts they are less likely to criticize widespread systemic inequalities in education, health-care, the criminal justice system, the economy, and politics. This is precisely how ideological hegemony works. A third benefit of this system for its benefac-tors and protectors involves the quelling of the collective power of the Black community. Essentially, Black male athletes in the EALM and Conveyor Belt (Rhoden, 2006) are socialized into a neoliberal culture that teaches them to prioritize themselves and their family with little to no regard for their native communities or the broader Black community. Rhoden (2006) described the detrimental impact of this socialization when he said: "... the Conveyor Belt, with its breeding of a deep competitive spirit, does not engender camarade-rie and kinship" (p. 183). Furthermore, when talented Black male athletes are extracted from their native communities (Hawkins, 2010; Smith, 2009), the psychological, physical, social, and economic distance from the major-ity of Blacks in the U.S. minimizes the likelihood of establishing a cohesive racial movement akin to the Civil Rights Movement in the 1960s. It was not by accident that after the 1960s, widespread assimilation ensued and spaces such as sports were strategically chosen for this experiment because of its far-reaching propaganda utility and social engineering for subtle ideological diffusion (Bass, 2002; Cooper, Macaulay, & Rodriguez, 2017; Edwards, 1973; Hartmann, 2000).

A fourth benefit of this arrangement is the conditioning of Black depen-dency on White economic benefactors including White-controlled professional sport leagues, corporate sponsors, and educational institutions (Rhoden, 2006). The White savior complex (Hughey, 2014) that is so often depicted in Holly-wood movies actually reflects real life whereby the same inequitable economic arrangement that was instilled during 17th century chattel slavery is sustained in the 21st century via access restrictions to ownership and asset accumulation. This dependency works in tandem with the psychological, physical, social, and economic separation of Black males in the EALM since it creates a level of mistrust between fellow Blacks and a greater level of partnerships with White capitalists (Rhoden, 2006). With the exception of individuals such as LeBron James, many Black male athletes conduct much of their business endeavors with White sport agents, accountants, entrepreneurs, realtors, and other corporate partners while competent Black professionals are overlooked due to the formers' internalized racist belief that Whites inherently provide better services in a society founded upon and structured by WRC. This belief and subsequent actions further reinforce the myth of Black inferiority. Although, these White capitalists may at times have positive intentions, they are less likely to engage in and/or encourage transformative actions that lead to Black racial uplift as a group (discussed in greater detail in Chapter 8). Sport and miseducation schooling are two of the many interconnected social institutions where Black empowerment is intentionally stagnated (e.g., in both spaces there is a lack of Afrocentric curricula, a lack of knowledge of Black prowess and excellence pre-, during, and post-enslavement) (Bush & Bush, 2013a, 2013b). In concert with the CRT tenet of interest convergence, Black progress is primarily permitted when it benefits the White power structure to a greater degree (Bell, 1980, 1992). Thus, sport is a powerful tool in sustaining ideological hegemony in the U.S. (Hawkins, 1998a).

However, simply categorizing all Black male athletes who excel in sports as passive perpetuators of the status quo ignores the various benefits derived from their athletic success (individually and collectively) and also homogenizes their identities and experiences (meso- and micro-system interactions and outcomes). Black males who experience the EALM come from diverse backgrounds. For example, NBA stars such as LeBron James and Kevin Durant grew up in single mother households in low-income predominantly Black communities. Along the same lines, a recent study highlighted how Black male NFL players are more likely to grow up in socioeconomically disadvantaged, densely populated, and predominantly Black communities compared to their White male NFL peers (Allison, Davis, & Barranco, 2016). Whereas, NBA stars like Kobe Bryant, Grant Hill, and Stephen Curry were sons of former professional athletes and they grew up in upper-class households in predominantly White and/or non-Black communities. In essence, even though all of the aforementioned males are Black, they each received different resources and experienced unique paths to their professional sport destinations. The outer microsystem and exosystem factors of family backgrounds, socioeconomic status, and occupational patterns were impactful on their perceptions of and access to sport opportunities. For Black male athletes like James, Durant, and several other Black male athletes who grow up in lower income backgrounds, the Conveyor Belt facilitates their athletic success outcomes since access to broad based exposure is otherwise severely limited in these neighborhoods (Rhoden, 2006). Contrarily, Black male athletes who come from middle and upper-class backgrounds with access to specialized trainings and social capital with individuals who have connections to intercollegiate and professional sport opportunities, these individuals are not as dependent on the Conveyor Belt for their success outcomes in and through sport. Acknowledging and understanding this heterogeneity and the interplay between nuanced ecological systems is a core aim of each socialization model presented in this text.

Additionally, other meso-level characteristics must be taken into account when examining Black male athletes' socialization experiences. These characteristics include family, community, and cultural emphasis on sport and/or education, (mis)educational or schooling experiences, resources associated with sport and non-sport enrichment activities, geographical location to name a few. For example, regarding geography, football is more popular in the South and Midwest compared to the Northeast and Northwest regions of the

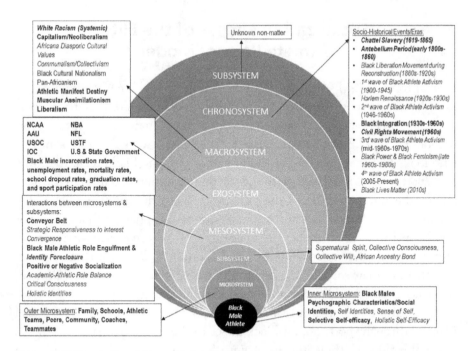

Figure 5.1. Elite Athlete Lottery Model (EALM)

Source: Adapted from Bush, L. V., & Bush, E. C. (2013a). Introducing African American male theory (AAMT). *Journal of African American Males in Education*, 4(1), p. 9. Copyright 2013 Journal of African American Males in Education.

U.S. and certain communities have a rich history of producing talent athletes such as the metro Chicagoland, Miami Dade County, and Washington, District of Columbia (D.C.) and Baltimore areas. Depending on where a Black male grows up influences their sport participation options, experiences, and outcomes. Any analysis of Black male athletes' experiences is strengthened by taking into account socio-structural and cultural factors (Allison, Cooper, Gawrysiak, & Hawkins, 2012; Davis, & Barranco, 2016; Floyd, Shinew, McGuire, & Noe, 1994; Harris, 1994; Harrison, 1998; Harrison, Harrison, & Moore, 2002; Ogden, 2004; Ogden & Hilt, 2003; Ogden & Rose, 2005). Moreover, the professional sport career outcomes (within and beyond sporting contexts) and subsequent retirement experiences of Black male athletes vary as well. Therefore, the EALM outlines the socialization experiences and outcomes Black male athletes who successfully matriculated to the professional level, which includes the 1.2% of NCAA men's basketball and 1.6% of NCAA football players (NCAA, 2018) as well as others who play professionally in leagues outside the U.S. across multiple sports.

Socialization Phases of the Elite Athlete Lottery Model

Similar to the ISSM, the early socialization phase of the EALM involves an introduction to sport. In concert with Harrison et al.'s (2002) assertion, sport participation choices are closely connected to Black males' racial identity formation. In the U.S. where young Black males are more likely to see someone who looks like them on a NBA, NFL, and/or track and field team than in a non-sport occupational role (with the notable exception of music) in the mass media, the internalization of the athletic manifest destiny (Coakley, 2017) occurs at an early age. In many instances during this phase, a Black male has a relationship with an influential male adult of the same race such as their father, uncle, older brother, family friend, mentor, and/or coach who encourages them to view sport as an opportunity to experience personal fulfillment, social acceptance, and racial and masculine affirmation.

In contrast to Harrison et al.'s (2002) model of African American racial identity through sport, not all Black males in the EALM experience a racial encounter prior to their immersion into football, basketball, and track and field. In the former model, the authors stated that similar to Cross' (1995). Nigrescence model, prior to fully immersing one's self in racially and culturally sanctioned activities (i.e., playing sports where Blacks are overrepresented)

African American males experience a racist encounter, which dissuades them from being associated with any activities deemed as "White" or "Eurocentric" (Harrison et al., 2002). Whereas, in the EALM, those who choose to participate in sports outside of football, basketball, and track and field are likely to have exposure to familial, cultural, and/or community environments where access to different sport opportunities was present and supported. For example, in a study with my colleagues, we found that Black male baseball players at HBCUs were heavily influenced to participate in the sport from an early age by their fathers, older brothers, coaches, and a Southeastern regional environment where baseball was popular in the Black community. Irrespective of sport participation choices, the EALM echoes Ogden and Rose's (2005) hypothesis that the outcomes from these decisions involve the following common characteristics: a) affirming self-identity, b) a level of cultural pride manifested at the inner microsystem level (with football, basketball, and track and field as a collective racial group whereas in sports like soccer, tennis, baseball, and hockey serving as a representative of the racial group is internalized), c) public support from family and at times from the broader community, and d) socio-structural support in the form of financial and physical accessibility to participation opportunities.

The adolescence phase of the EALM is characterized by increased competitive sport involvement. At this phase, Black male athletes begin to participate in elite sport organizations such as AAU and school sponsored athletic teams. Some Black males are already recruited to attend athletic-centric public and private schools where they are being groomed to be the next star player at the high school level. Participating in sports and/or training year around is common at this phase. Depending on advice and guidance from their support systems, some Black males will participate in multiple sports to avoid burnout, maintain conditioning, and develop a range of transferable athletic skills. Other Black males will begin to participate in intense single-sport specialization. Consciously or sub-consciously Malcolm Gladwell's (2011) 10, 000 hour rule is enacted whereby Black male athletes in the EALM recognize the need to hone their skills in order to be competitive for the next level. Similar to the ISSM, players, their families, and at times friends, teams, and/or scouting agencies will often record trainings and performances for personal branding purposes (i.e., create YouTube videos). The intensification of their self-identity through sport participation and performance is prevalent at this phase.

Since, the prospects of pursuing a college scholarship and/or turning professional are primary goals and nurtured by support systems, the Conveyor Belt process is fully activated at this phase (Rhoden, 2006). Support and encouragement from family is pivotal since the time required and stakes associated with participation are heightened (Beamon & Bell, 2011; Dohrmann, 2010; Harris, 1994). Participating in high profile national (and some cases international particularly with soccer) tournaments and events is important for all sports with the exception of football. However, in recent years select top high school football teams have competed in inter-state contests and been featured on ESPN (USA Today High School Sports, 2017), but traditionally football teams compete within their respective states. Individual athletes with college and professional prospects are recruited to participate in showcases sponsored by corporate sponsors (i.e., Under Armour All-America Camp). The recruitment process is in full swing during the middle to end of the adolescent phase. Black male athletes in the EALM receive scholarship offers from smaller to mid-major to big-time college athletic programs. It is also not uncommon for sport agents, runners, and others affiliated with corporate sponsors and professional sport teams to begin to communicate directly and indirectly with Black male prospects and their family. Additionally, local high schools and communities begin to benefit off the celebrity status of Black male athletes and the Black male athletic role engulfment process ensues (i.e., the case of LeBron James is discussed later in this chapter).

With the adulation and pressure associated with athletic performance, Black males in the EALM often prioritize their development in their sport over educational achievement. However, it is important to note that academic performance outcomes vary based on family support, educational experiences and resources, personal interests in academics, cognitive development, and values systems (inner and outer microsystems). For example, several Black males in the EALM such as Chris Paul (NBA) and Richard Sherman (NFL) excelled academically throughout their K-12 educational experiences. Others academically perform at a level above or around minimal eligibility standards for college admission, but not at an exemplar level. Notwithstanding, there are other Black males in the EALM such as those admitted to schools via special admissions who are academically underprepared for college and without sport their postsecondary enrollment options to four-year institutions would be limited (Barker, 2012; Cooper & Cooper, 2015b; Hawkins, 2016, & Nwadike, Baker, Brackebusch). The adolescence phase concludes with Black male athletes deciding on which college, prep school, or JUCO to attend. In a select few circumstances, Black male athletes at the end of this phase choose to pursue a professional career either in the U.S. or abroad (i.e., Brandon

Jennings choosing to play in Europe professionally in 2009 after completing his time at national powerhouse prep school Oak Hill Academy in Mouth of Wilson, VA and a year before declaring for the NBA draft).

The young adulthood phase of the EALM involves the college, prep school, JUCO, and/or early professional sport experience. It is at this phase, where the commercialized nature of college sports and high stakes culture at prep schools and JUCOs, when the focus on athletics over academics is a strictly business decision. Domonique Foxworth, former standout defensive cornerback at the University of Maryland, former NFL player, Harvard Business School graduate, and current Sport Commentator, described in the film *Schooled: The Price of College Sports* how athletics took precedence over academics when he was in college: "I knew that it was more important for me to get an interception and score a touchdown for my school than it was to earn an A in class … We had a saying that C's get degrees" (Finkel & Martin, 2013). In the film, the directors interviewed numerous former big-time college athletes including Johnathan Franklin (University of California at Los Angeles (UCLA) football), Arian Foster (University of Tennessee football), and Ed O'Bannon (UCLA basketball). The institutional cultures from the JUCO level to the top-tier Division I programs often create conditions that prioritize eligibility (not the transmission of a well-rounded education, intellectual growth, and personal achievement) and reward Black males for their athletic prowess (Adler & Adler, 1991; Beamon, 2008; Benson, 2000; Cooper & Cooper, 2015b; Singer, 2009; Whitely & Ridley, 2016).

The one-and-done phenomenon in Division I men's basketball illustrates the EALM whereby Black males with draft prospects take advantage of the opportunity to be compensated more equitably for their athletic abilities at the professional level versus having to abide by arbitrary academic standards for athletic eligibility and other disadvantageous rules at the intercollegiate level. This option is prevalent among all sports with the exception of football and baseball. For football and baseball, the process is slightly different since both the NFL and MLB require players be three years removed from high school before becoming draft eligible (with baseball they can be drafted out of high school, but if they enroll in college then it is expected that they are three years removed from high school before being eligible to participate on a major or minor league team). Therefore, many of them play in college anywhere from two to five years (depending on whether they redshirt and/or transfer) before taking their talents to the professional ranks. Prior the late 1990s and early 2000s, most Black male basketball players in the EALM stayed in college at least through their junior year. However, after the late 1990s, more Black male college athletes in the EALM have opted to leave college early to pursue professional opportunities.

The adulthood phase of the EALM involves Black male athletes' professional careers and retirement. The primary differences between those in the EALM and ISSM is based on whether the Black male athlete experienced some level of professional sport experience and corresponding financial gains (albeit temporary). In the ISSM, little to no professional sport career experience is attained. Whereas, in the EALM, Black male athletes experienced short to long term professional sport careers. Professional careers vary in terms of success and personal outcomes. As previously mentioned, the Conveyor Belt (Rhoden, 2006) has already conditioned a vast majority of these Black male athletes to focus on maximizing their athletic abilities and financial wealth accumulation within the acceptable bounds of the WRC society (macro-, exo-, and meso-system interactions). Those who remain apolitical, assimilate, and overtly distance themselves from the broader Black community and social justice efforts are rewarded during and oftentimes after their playing careers with various endorsement, social, and professional opportunities. Rhoden (2006) explained the new reality for these type of Black male athletes:

> The Belt usually carries young Black athletes out of black America and introduces them to a world with very few African Americans, a world of white agents, real estate brokers, ban presidents, trustees, and lawyers. The fact that so many of the athlete's closest advisers are not African means that they're never around black models of leadership ... (p. 193)

Some of these Black male athletes remain financially stable throughout the remainder of their lives due to smart investments and responsible money management. Others experience financial downfalls and subsequently encounter similar post-athletic career disengagement trauma as those who experience the ISSM (both groups are discussed in greater detail later in this chapter). In addition, when examining Black male athletes' socialization experiences and outcomes it is important to view them on a continuum rather than dichotomous over different periods of their lifespan (e.g., varying levels of race-consciousness and engagement with social justice issues, financial prudency at various junctures in their lives, holistic identity awareness and cultivation at different points in their lives, etc.). These types of delineations are important and reflect one of the core aims of these socializations models, which is to acknowledge and examine the heterogeneity of experiences among Black male athletes who experience distinct socialization processes.

Evidence of the Elite Athlete Lottery Model

Two high-profile NBA players who share similar upbringings and trajectories through the EALM are LeBron James and Kevin Durant. In the film, *More Than a Game* (Belman, Mason, Mann, & Perniciaro, 2008), the high school basketball journey of now NBA superstar LeBron James and his former St. Vincent-St. Mary high school teammates is documented. The majority of the coverage highlights LeBron's ascension into superstardom as he became the mostly highly touted high school basketball player in U.S. history. In the documentary titled, *Still KD: Through the Noise* (Burde & Kleiman, 2017), and a Chris Haynes interview titled, *Kevin Durant and Michael Beasley Walk Down Memory Lane* (ESPN, 2018), the life of Kevin Durant is presented and narrated. In the interview, Durant states, "I didn't think I would be in the NBA, I didn't know for sure, but like I didn't plan for anything else since I was like 9" (1:24–1:31; ESPN, 2018). Contrary to popular biological myths that attribute athletic abilities and performance to one's race (Hoberman, 1997), these documentaries illustrate Coakley's (2017) assertion about the power of athletic manifest destiny whereby these two Black males, with notable physical traits, possessed an internalized belief in their ability to excel in their sport and thus engaged in countless hours of hard work on their craft, which resulted in the successful pursuit of long-term professional sport careers.

Prior to the fame that came with being the top ranked high school basketball players in the country, the films provide insight into their humble upbringings. James grew up in Akron, Ohio as an only child with his mother, Gloria James. Due to various circumstances, he and his mother moved around multiple times during his childhood. In the documentary, there is a nostalgic scene where he visits an apartment where he and his mother once lived and he recalled memories when financial difficulties caused them tremendous stress (Belman et al., 2008). Similarly, Durant grew up with his mother, Wanda Durant, and his older brother Tony Durant in Seat Pleasant, Maryland (Prince George's (PG) county) and the Washington, D.C. area. Durant explained how his family moved frequently in the PG county area, which contributed to their family's instability (e.g., socially, financially, etc.) (ESPN, 2018). In both cases, exposure to economic deprivation at an early age had a profound impact on their future sport aspirations. Similar to those who experience the ISSM, a shared reality among these Black male athletes is the fact that sport serves as a safe haven and space where they feel a sense of validation and peace away from the challenging circumstances surrounding their lives (e.g., in some cases short-term or long-term abandonment from or absence of family members, environmental pressures, barriers to healthy life choices and habits, threats to their lives, etc.).

Within their neighborhoods, among the most visible and resonating figures who possess financial security are Black males in the NBA, which reiterates the power of media and reference groups on Black males' identity development through sport (Edwards, 2000; Harrison, 1998; Harrison, Harrison, & Moore, 2002; Powell, 2008; Rhoden, 2006; Singer & May, 2010). As a pre-teen, James participated in organized basketball with local teams such as the Akron Basketball Association (ABA) Shooting Stars AAU team coached by Dru Joyce who served as a father figure and positive role model for him among other male coaches. This AAU team was among the top 12-U AAU basketball teams in the U.S. in the 1997. Durant started playing competitive youth basketball at the Seat Pleasant Activity Center, a local recreation league, and later played on the Prince George Jaguars and D.C. Blue Devils AAU teams where experienced comparable success to James at the state, regional, and national levels (ESPN, 2018). From an early age, both James and Durant displayed exceptional basketball skills and athletic abilities, which served as a primary source of positive identity affirmation for them. As his reputation expanded, LeBron and his teammates were recruited to attend a predominantly White catholic high school, St. Vincent-St. Mary. Originally, LeBron and his teammates were on track to attend a public high school with a larger Black student population, but since the elite private White school had more resources and could provide more exposure they were able to lure James and his teammates. Similar scenarios have been depicted in several Hollywood films such as the critically acclaimed documentary *Hoop Dreams* (James & Marx, 1994). Along the same lines, Durant was recruited to national basketball powerhouse schools such as National Christian Academy (Washington, D.C.), Oak Hill Academy (Mouth of Wilson, Virginia), and Montrose Christian Academy (Rockville, Maryland). Both James's and Durant's recruitment to elite White and athletic-centric private high schools and prep schools officially signified their placement on the Conveyor Belt (Rhoden, 2006).

Rhoden (2006) explained the nature of this process: "the prime raw resource of the sports industry has been black muscle. The work of the industry is to extract those bodies from where they primarily reside—in the black neighborhoods of rural and urban America—put them to work" (p. 174). Hawkins (2010) referenced Black male college athletes who attend HWIs as oscillating migrant laborers, but it is clear from the aforementioned descriptions that the extraction of Black males and concurrent deprivation of the Black community begins well before the postsecondary and professional levels. In other words, Black males in the EALM learned to be oscillating migrant laborers starting in their adolescence in preparation for future college and professional sport careers that will require them to travel to different locations for work. As noted, a core detriment of this arrangement is the physical, social, and psychological separation of these talented Black male athletes away from their native communities. This arrangement often results in the underdevelopment and continued oppression of the Black community whereby talented youth from these environments are extracted and socialized to disconnect themselves from their roots (Edwards, 1984, 2000; Rhoden, 2006).

Black male athletes in the EALM are only expected to give back in nominal ways, but under no circumstances can they engage in efforts to draw attention to or disrupt the broader oppressive conditions impacting their native communities (philanthropy and charity are acceptable since they are not as disruptive as activism and social, political, and economic reconfiguration). For example, Black athletes who are deemed as activists or code word troublemakers and not primarily focused on their sport and assimilating in the system of WRC are swiftly denied opportunities for upward mobility in mainstream sporting structures (i.e., the post-protest expulsion of Colin Kaepernick from the NFL). These tactics enable the status quo racial hierarchy to remain intact (i.e., White privilege vs. Black oppression) while the illusion of meritocracy is strengthened since a select few Blacks are rewarded and experience financial success even though their native communities remain plagued in economically dire conditions. Furthermore, applying a CRT lens to the situation enables us to see interest convergence in action (Bell, 1980, 1992). Both James and Durant were primarily granted an opportunity to earn access to enroll in elite private and prep schools and participate on high profile basketball teams because the former received increased athletic exposure and access high quality facilities while the latter economically and institutionally benefitted off of the players' athletic abilities. There was little to no concern for their academic development beyond eligibility or the well-being of their native communities including the schools they would have attended had they not opted to attend these White private and prep schools.

Relatedly, Black males' perceptions of race and privilege in a society founded upon and structured by WRC develop at an early age. For example, at the 20:03–21:04 mark in the ESPN (2018) interview, Durant and longtime friend and former teammate, Michael Beasley, while reminiscing on their childhood memories joked about how they thought one of their White team-mates was rich for no other reason than he was White and did not live in the same neighborhood as them. After they chuckled, Durant made a point to say that the White teammate was in actuality not from a wealthy back-ground and retrospectively it was revealing to him that they would assume this social class status because of his race. Durant explained how they (Black males from a low-income predominantly Black environment) were socialized to view Whites as privileged and Blacks as poor. This commentary offers vital insight into the ways in which racial stereotyping is internalized among Black youth at an early age (Harrison et al., 2002). The internalized racism and mental association of Whiteness with economic stability and better resources influenced their decisions to attend White private high schools as opposed to the Black high schools near their homes.

Beyond high school, this same psychological schema influenced them to not consider attending a HBCU instead of a HWI; although, in James's case he bypassed college altogether whereas Durant attended the University of Texas at Austin (a HWI) for one year. The macro-level influence of systemic racism (i.e., inequitable schooling structures) in conjunction with chrono- and exo-level patterns of racially segregated housing arrangements and related economic disparities create conditions that convince young impressionable Black males to equate success and mobility with acquiescing to the desires and needs of Whites. In the case of Black male athletes, this appeasement involves performing at a high level athletically in order to gain access to resources and stability otherwise denied to Blacks from their backgrounds (see Figure 5.1). Understanding the permanence of racism (Bell, 1992; Lawrence, 1995) that is embedded in this seemingly innocuous space of sport requires a level of consciousness about how power, privilege, ideologies, and systems operate to sustain the exploitation and oppression of groups such as Blacks in the U.S. in an (in)visible normalized manner.

After James and his teammates enrolled at St. Vincent-St. Mary, they took the basketball program to unprecedented heights including winning three state championships, a USA Today #1 national ranking, playing a national schedule against perennial powerhouse high schools and prep schools includ-ing televised games on ESPN, and securing a lucrative Adidas sponsorship deal for the athletic program (Belman et al., 2008). Similarly, Durant would lead all three schools he attended to impressive seasons against the nation's best teams and national rankings. This arrangement represented a modern example of how systemic racism (Feagin, 2006) manifests whereby the unjust impoverishment of the Black communities where James and Durant grew up was exacerbated by the wealth transfer and unjust enrichment of the elite private White high schools and prep schools. Although, individually James and Durant benefitted, the larger issue is the perpetual neglect and under-development of their native communities (Edwards, 2000). It is very telling how White-controlled professional sport leagues, athletic programs at HWIs, apparel companies, and corporate sponsors are willing to offer thousands to millions of dollars to individual Black athletes to represent their brands, but seldom if ever inclined to financially invest in the communities from whence they come. In essence, they do not mind exploiting Black communities for talent extraction. Yet, they have no interest or concern in uplifting the plight of Blacks as a collective group. The system of WRC does not mind reward-ing a select few Blacks financially so as long as the broader racial hierarchy remains intact (Franklin & Resnik, 1973; Frazier, 1957). Thus, sport serves as a powerful tool in the sustenance of WRC because it creates an illusion of racial harmony and equal opportunity through meritocracy when in reality it is an evolved form of the century old system of Black oppression for the eco-nomic, psychological, political, and social benefits of Whites (Edwards, 1980, 1984, 2000; Hawkins, 2010; Powell, 2008; Rhoden, 2006; Sage, 1998).

Accompanying this interest convergence is the permanence of racism (Bell, 1992; Lawrence, 1995) and Whiteness as property tenets of CRT (Harris, 1993) whereby the racist arrangement of Black laborers and White controlling entities (e.g., HWIs, NBA, NFL, Nike, Under Armour, Adidas, etc.) remains intact and not only goes largely unquestioned by the large numbers of Black male ath-letes and their families, but often times it is supported and defended. These out-comes illustrate the ways in which colorblind neoliberalism is indoctrinated in the minds of oppressed groups (Bonilla-Silva, 2010; DeCuir & Dixson, 2004). The Whiteness as property tenet of CRT explains how elite Whites can benefit from ownership of sport entities including leagues, franchises, and numerous major corporate sponsors largely without any protests on the basis of the racist arrangement (Harris, 1993). Moreover, Black male athletes who sign lucrative endorsement deals with White-owned shoe companies, similar to their profes-sional sport contracts, generate far more wealth for the companies (and team owners) than themselves. Yet, since they are content with their upward mobility and financial standing, disruption to the racist arrangement is quelled.

The economic arrangement between Blacks and elite Whites in the U.S. in general, and Black male athletes and elite Whites controlling major sport orga-nizations and sponsors more specifically, is a foundational reality that cements the interplay between personal troubles among this sub-group and public issues (systemic oppression) facing the broader racial group whether they are acknowledged or not (Cooper, 2012). Malveaux (2000) explicates this subverted racist dynamic in a society founded upon and structured by WRC:

> ... hoopsters become hucksters while the invisible (white) male role as power broker is reinforced. In too many ways the rules and profit of the game reinforce the rules, profit, and history of American life, with iconic gladiators serving as symbols and servants of multinational interests. Blacks who entertain serve as stalkers for white men who measure profits. Neutered black men can join their white colleagues in cha-chinging cash registers but can never unlock the golden handcuffs and the platinum muzzles that limit their ability to generate independent opinions. (pp. 55–56)

Often, Black male athletes who experience success in the EALM are conditioned to either outright ignore systemic inequalities once they have secured their desired financial status or engage in efforts that lead to positive change (i.e., charity), but not transformative disruption for collective sustained empowerment for Blacks as a racial and cultural group (i.e., empowering activism—discussed in greater detail in Chapters 8 and 9).

In 2001, James was invited to the coveted Adidas ABCD Camp where he shined among the nation's top high school basketball players (Shopkorn, Noah, Safdie, & Safdie, 2013). Adidas had already signed former standout high school players and then NBA stars Kobe Bryant and Tracy McGrady to multi-million dollar shoe endorsement deals and LeBron was targeted to be next in line. Similar to other elite high school boys' sport showcases such as the McDonald's All-American game (both James and Durant won MVP honors in this game in 2003 and 2006, respectively), the optics of these events involve a sea of White onlookers including prominent college coaches, professional scouts, sport agents, and corporate sponsors all focused on large numbers of Black male bodies. I argue this obsession with the Black male body is not only tied to economic exploitative motives, but a longstanding gender racist history of homoeroticism via the White gaze that positions Black males as objects for White pleasure and desires (Boyd, 2003; Curry, 2017; Oates, 2007). The intertwinement between this normalized homoeroticism in and through sport and the racial, economic, and social order of the U.S. society underscores the magnitude and layers of oppressive power structures and systems as well as the overt/visible and covert/invisible or less visible nature of WRC in operation.

In 2002, James was placed on the coveted *Sports Illustrated* cover as a junior in high school (Belman et al., 2008; Rhoden, 2006). In 2003, James would be selected as the first pick in the NBA draft and he would go on lead a Hall of Fame worthy NBA career. In 2015, James signed a lifetime endorsement deal with Nike estimated at $1 billion (Knowlton, 2016). He has been listed on Forbes as one of the richest athletes in the world and secured numerous endorsement deals with companies such as Samsung, Upper Deck, Audemar Piquet, Beats by Dre, Intel, Verizon, and Coca-Cola to name a few (Forbes, 2018). In 2007, Durant became the first freshman to win the Naismith College Basketball Player of the Year and John R. Wooden Player of Year awards for his stellar season as a member of the University of Texas Longhorns men's basketball team. Later that year, Durant was the second pick in the 2007 NBA Draft and on the same track as James to being a future Hall of Famer (Burde & Kleiman, 2017). His most recent Nike endorsement deal is estimated at $300 million for 10 years and he has also acquired lucrative endorsement deals with companies such as Beats by Dre, American Family Insurance, BBVA, Sparkling Ice, Panini, and NBA 2K (Forbes, 2017; Manfred, 2014).

In contrast to Lenny Cooke and numerous Black male athletes who experience the ISSM (Chapter 4), the EALM enabled James and Durant to achieve their professional sport goals and secure long-term financial stability for their families. Growing up in single mother households in low-income communities where statistics for Black males' life outcomes are dire (ETS, 2011), it is safe to say James and Durant won the *elite athlete lottery* in a major way. Consistent with previous research, their race and socioeconomic status greatly influenced the meaning they attached to sport and future career aspirations (Eitle & Eitle, 2002; Singer & May, 2010). Sellers (2000) contended that proponents of sport participation often emphasize these stories to justify the status quo. ESPN routinely publicizes and romanticizes these "rags to riches" stories through their programming (e.g., *30 for 30 mini-documentary series*, *SC Features*, etc.). As previously noted, Hollywood films and documentaries such as *The Program* (Goldwyn, Henderson, Rothman, & Ward, 1993), *Hoop Dreams* (James & Marx, 1994), *Varsity Blues* (Robbins, Tollin, Laiter, & Wiley, 1999), *Blue Chips* (Friedkin, 1994), *He Got Game* (Lee, 1998), and *The Blind Side* (Hancock, 2009) also reproduce this narrative as a means to stabilize the internalization of the prevailing racial hierarchy and corresponding social stratification. However, the more somber reality is the outcomes experienced by James and Durant are extremely rare and unfortunately exacerbate the illusion of singular success among Black males discussed in Chapter 4, which results in the perpetuation of systemic holistic underdevelopment of Black males through sport and miseducation or as Edwards' (2000) described as the "triple tragedy" (p. 9). For example, at the 24:43–24:57 mark of the ESPN (2018) interview Durant candidly responds to Chris Haynes' question about what he believes he would be doing at 30 years old if was not a professional basketball player: "Right now, probably living with my Mom … I swear." This response in actuality describes the life outcome of many Black males who experience the ISSM; thus, highlighting the *dangerously* thin line between ISSM and EALM outcomes.

Beyond their contributions on the court, both James and Durant are what I call *leverage capitalists with collectivist inclinations* (LCCIs). LCCIs are individuals who excel in a capitalistic system while engaging in philanthropic and equity minded endeavors (e.g., charities, fundraisers, etc.) that produce positive change for historically disadvantaged groups (i.e., Blacks who live in economically oppressed conditions). In 2018, Durant established the *Kevin Durant Foundation* in Oklahoma City, Oklahoma, which provided $1 million towards those affected by the tornadoes in Oklahoma in 2013. He also funded the establishment of *A Strong & Kind Summer with KD* program for students labeled at-risk and the *Build It and They Will Ball Courts Renovation Initiative*, which provides high quality basketball courts for youth in disadvantaged areas in the U.S. and abroad (Scutari, 2018). Durant also donated $3 million to the University of Texas ($2.5 million for the men's basketball program and $500, 000 to the Center for Sports Leadership and Innovation) and $10 million to the Prince George's Public Schools and College Track to support an after-school program that assists young people from disadvantaged backgrounds in their matriculation to the postsecondary level (Ortiz, 2018). Along the same lines, James established the *LeBron James Family Foundation* (LJFF), which offers a range of programming in the Greater Akon area including the I Promise Elementary and Secondary School, Lab and 330s, St. Vincent-St. Mary School, University of Akron I Promise Unlimited, and Legacy (LJFF, 2018). One of the more notable accomplishments of LJFF is the donation of $41 million to support the college enrollment, attendance, and graduation of 1, 100 young people from Akron who participate in the program. In addition, the LJFF raises funds for numerous national charities including the *Boys & Girls Club of America, Smithsonian National Museum of African American History and Culture Exhibit for Muhammad Ali, After-School All-Stars, The Children's Defense Fund, Gabriel's Angle Foundation*, and *ONEXONE* (Berman, 2017).

James and Durant are not alone in their collectivist inclinations as numerous other Black male EALM athletes engage in similar efforts such as Jalen Rose with the establishment of the Jalen Rose Leadership Academy

(JRLA) charter high school in Detroit, Michigan, Warrick Dunn with his Warrick Dunn Charities (WDC) partnership with Habitat for Humanity, previous Black male winners of the NFL Walter Payton Man of the Year Award, NBA Sportsmanship award, ESPN Sports Humanitarian of the Year award, and countless others who use their platform and resources to impact change in invaluable ways. These humanitarian efforts are important to acknowledge and should be celebrated. Nonetheless, the remaining paradox lies in the fact that the success of these Black males athletes and subsequent charitable efforts fosters the illusion of collective racial progress and reinforces (rather than disrupts and dismantles) WRC. This reinforcement signals that any Black male who works hard and is talented enough can and should experience this level of financial success so as long as they do not overtly challenge the power structures that granted them these privileges that are systemically denied to the critical mass of Blacks in the U.S. society. Yet, the chances of Black males winning the actual lottery are higher than them securing a lucrative professional sports career (Leonard & Reyman, 1988; NCAA, 2018). The ISSM and EALM propaganda and related systems have little interest in the life outcomes of Black male athletes and so when and if they are holistically underdeveloped either during or after their playing careers conclude they are discarded since their economic, political, and psychosocial utility for the system of WRC is no longer valued; therein lies the crux of issue with the ISSM and EALM.

Aside from the proverbial "rags to riches" narratives, the reality is Black males in the EALM are not homogenous. In fact, Dubrow and adams (2012) conducted an in-depth longitudinal content analysis of media artifacts and found that African American males from middle and upper class backgrounds are more likely to be in the NBA than African American and White males from economically disadvantaged backgrounds. This study dispels the racist myth asserting that a majority of Black males in the NBA come from poor socioeconomic backgrounds. Moreover, several Black males in the NBA and NFL grew up with upper class socioeconomic statuses. NBA stars Kobe Bryant, Grant Hill, and Stephen Curry are all sons of former professional athletes and grew up in economically stable households. For these Black male athletes, the emphasis on biological destiny (Coakley, 2017) combined with the resources associated with their family's occupational and socioeconomic backgrounds significantly contributed to their success in sport. Whereas, the cultural destiny (Coakley, 2017) combined with mass media effects and imposing realities such as limited opportunities for upward mobility aside from sport are more likely to be sources of motivation and explanations for the athletic performance of Black males who grow up in economically disadvantaged backgrounds (Eitle & Eitle, 2002; Ogden, 2004; Ogden & Hilt, 2003; Ogden & Rose, 2005; Singer & May, 2010). The Black socio-structural advantage of Black male EALM athletes who grow up in middle and upper class households enable them to meet and/or surpass the 10, 000 hour expert/mastery rule promulgated by Gladwell (2011) without immense concerns for their basic human needs. Whereas, these concerns are prevalent among a large number of Blacks in the U.S. living in economically disadvantaged conditions (ETS, 2011). For the Black male athletes who grow up in the latter conditions like James and Durant, the view of sport as the most viable pathway for upward mobility along with the social and cultural support for participating in basketball creates a circumstance where meeting or surpassing the 10, 000 hour rule (Gladwell, 2011) is *more than just a love for the game, but rather a means for survival and a potential life altering opportunity to improve the intergenerational plight of their families.*

Furthermore, I surmise it is not a coincidence that Black male NFL players are more likely to grow up in predominantly Black and economically disadvantaged backgrounds than their peers (Allison et al., 2016) and 78% of former NFL players file for bankruptcy or experience significant financial challenges two years into retirement (Corben, 2012). In contrast, former NBA players fare noticeably better since 60% of them experience similar fates five years after they retire (Corben, 2012). One may surmise the shorter NFL careers and larger roster sizes explains this difference. However, a critical sociological perspective suggests the accumulative advantages that accompany various types of capital in a society founded upon and structured by WRC (e.g., intergenerational economic advantages, social capital for financial and career mobility and sustainability, access to specialized training, educational resources, etc.) have major impact on Black male athletes' experiences in and through sport and (mis)education. These factors not only influence their life outcomes before and during their athletic careers, but also after retirement. Therefore, Black male EALM athletes have a few definitive things in common: a) race, b) gender, c) strong work ethic, d) subsequent exceptional skill, and e) a keen interest in their respect sports. However, as noted in this chapter, the nature of their journeys, opportunities, and resources are not homogenous and thus aside from the aforementioned commonalities other demographics and psychographics among these individuals can vary considerably. A core aim of the socialization models presented in this book is the call for more nuanced critical analyses of the lived realities of and social factors impacting Black male athletes' socialization processes and outcomes as opposed to the uncritical acceptance of racist stereotypes rooted in ideological hegemony (Hawkins, 1998a; Harrison, 1998; Sailes, 2010). The variation outlined in this chapter reflects this aim.

In addition to not having the same type of upbringing prior to securing a professional sport career, not all Black male EALM athletes experience the same level of financial and personal stability. In fact, more Black male EALM athletes encounter significant challenges during their professional sports careers and in retirement than those who do not. The critically acclaimed *ESPN Films 30 for 30* documentary titled *Broke* detailed the reoccurring financial mismanagement among former professional athletes. Black male former athletes featured in the film were Andre Rison (NFL), Cliff Floyd (MLB), Keith McCants (NFL), and Bart Scott (NFL) to name a few (Corben, 2012). These Black male athletes in the film detailed how they experienced extreme financial difficulties due to a lack of financial literacy, poor money management, and trusting individuals who did not have their best interests in my mind. Their stories were not unlike the several former professional athletes who filed for bankruptcy shortly after their athletic retirement.

In an open letter to his younger self in *The Player's Tribune*, Antoine Walker candidly reflected upon his poor financial decisions over the course of his 16–year NBA career where he earned over $108 million (Walker, 2016). Consistent across all the models presented in this book, I assert that *context always matters*. Walker grew up in Chicago, Illinois in a low-income household with his mother and five siblings. Like many Black male EALM athletes, he did not have the privilege of learning about financial literacy, money management, and wealth building as a youth or young adult compared those who grow up with more economically privileged backgrounds. Consequently, when he won the *elite athlete lottery* he was not equipped with the mentality, skills, and knowledge necessary to effectively manage the responsibilities that come with a $10 million per year contract (not including endorsements). The systemic oppression that has unjustly impoverished Blacks in the U.S. combined with a schooling system that miseducates them produces Black male holistic underdevelopment and the aforementioned outcomes. The economic deprivation not only denies Blacks in working class conditions access to monetary resources and comfort, but also a lack of knowledge (social, navigational, and cultural) regarding how to acquire and manage wealth. It is should also be noted the role of sport agents, a majority of which are White, also play a significant role in the exploitation of several Black male athletes in the EALM. The underrepresentation of Blacks in positions such as sport agents and financial advisors is yet another byproduct of systemic racism and unjust intergenerational impoverishment (Cooper, 2012; Feagin, 2006; Franklin & Resnik, 1973). The controllers of the WRC system do not mind transferring millions of dollars toward young Black males who have been miseducated in the EALM because they realize the aim was to create the *illusion of opportunity*, which strengthens rather than transforms the racial hierarchy status quo. The conditioning of Black male EALM athletes through the Conveyor Belt (Rhoden, 2006) ensures they adopt neoliberal values and focus more on sustained assimilation versus transformative racial uplift. Therefore, it is important for all those concerned with the plight of Black male EALM athletes and those who experience all socialization models to understand the multi-level systems at work and strategically engage in counteractions to acquire more collective sustained racial empowerment.

Beyond financial woes, an even more disturbing reality and outcome associated with Black males' experience in the EALM involves extensive trauma and various forms of holistic death (figurative and literal). This trauma manifests in the form of depression, substance abuse, interpersonal violence, mental health instability, life dissatisfaction, holistic underdevelopment, and/or untimely deaths. Former standout Nebraska running back (1993–1996) and NFL first round draft pick in 1996, Lawrence Phillips, is an example of the tragic outcomes resulting from an oppressive society that celebrates Black males' athletic prowess more than it cares for and addresses their holistic needs. Phillips was considered the best player in the country in 1994 and 1995 when he led the University of Nebraska Cornhuskers football team to back-to-back national championships (Peter, 2015). Throughout his adult life, Phillips was involved in numerous domestic violence, assault, and vandalism incidences where he was criminally charged and convicted. While incarcerated he was accused of murdering his cellmate, Damion Soward (Greenburg, 2016). A deficit-laden perspective common in White mainstream media would explain Phillip's situation as an example of a delinquent Black male who did not take advantage of opportunities and available support systems to make his life situation better. These types of framing blame individuals rather than oppressive environmental conditions that precede and influence behaviors. In contrast, a critical sociological and ecological perspective would argue that the intergenerational trauma and continued oppression of Blacks who grow up in environments like Phillips did in Southern California (West Covina) limit their life chances before they exit their mother's wounds. The Black experience in the U.S. involves varying levels of exposure to systemic racism and post-traumatic slave syndrome (PTSS) and for those living in economically disadvantaged neighborhoods this exposure can be even more intense (DeGruy, 2005; ETS, 2011). Furthermore, these conditions also have particularly damaging effects on Black males due to the prevailing anti-black misandry embedded in societal structures, practices, and beliefs (Curry, 2017).

It has been documented that Phillips experienced a traumatic childhood (Greenburg, 2016). Participation in football did not resolve these issues and potentially exacerbated them. In fact, I would argue that in addition to the environmental conditions, which preceded and greatly influenced his individual behaviors, Phillips encounters with the violent nature of the sport, the hubris and "glorified status" associated with being a high-profile athlete, and lack of adequate attention towards addressing his psychological health needs contributed to his holistic underdevelopment and subsequent downfall (Beamon, 2012, p. 204). On January 13, 2016, Phillips committed suicide (Greenburg, 2016). The post-athletic career disengagement trauma (Edwards, 1984) is not unique to Phillips and countless Black males who experience the ISSM and EALM have had similar outcomes. Sadly, Phillips was not as fortunate as Kevin Ross who was highlighted in Chapter 4. Phillips' suicide, Ross's attempted suicide, and other negative life outcomes associated with the ISSM and EALM are public issues manifesting as personal troubles (Cooper, 2012). Unless we address the former, the latter will inevitably continue.

In addition to the aforementioned stories, there is also scholarly literature that highlights the experiences of Black male former athletes who participated in major Division I athletics and the professional ranks constituting their socialization through the EALM. Common themes across these studies was the experience with holistic underdevelopment via a lack of emphasis on education within athletic-centric sub-cultures, a lack of support for career exploration and interests beyond sport, and an overall inattention to personal needs such as psychological and sociocultural well-being. These studies detailed the significant transitional challenges experienced by these Black males as a result of athletic role engulfment, identity foreclosure, and career under preparedness (Beamon, 2008, 2012; Northcutt, 2013). For example, in Beamon's (2008) study she found that several of her participants referred to their roles in college as "athlete-students," which refers to the tremendous amount of time, energy, and focus they were required to expend on their athletic tasks

(p. 356). Participants also stated how academic eligibility was emphasized over achievement. Ultimately, they felt exploited based on what they were told during their recruitment that they would be provided with a quality education compared to what they actually received (essentially a sub-par educational experience in a professional sports type environment minus the equitable compensation and plus significant restrictions on their agency). The author highlighted how their socialization into sport was reinforced by family, community members, and the mass media before and during their college experiences. Regarding career under preparedness, participants explained how due to the athletic time constraints they were forced to major in areas that did not connect with their career interests (Beamon, 2008).

In another study, Beamon (2012) found that African American male former athletes reported experiencing athletic identity foreclosure starting during their youth and it continued through the conclusion of their college athletic and professional sport careers. Consistent with the EALM socialization phases, participants described how from a young age they internalized messages from society that their race and gender identities were synonymous with being athletes. This echoes her previous work where African American male former Division I athletes expressed how their glorified self was supported and intensified by their family and local community members (Beamon & Bell, 2011). Hence, these studies accentuate the significant impact of the mesosystem influences, which involve the interplay between inner microsystem (i.e., Black males' personality and psyche) and outer microsystem (i.e., community) on Black male identity development. The attachment to their athletic identity was supplanted early in life and deepened as their involvement and success in sport increased. Pertaining to career readiness, the author noted the following observation from her data analysis: "Even after sports participation had ceased, they were either unwilling or ill-equipped to engage in exploratory behavior that is necessary for new self-identities to develop and emerge from foreclosure athletic identities" (Beamon, 2012, p. 201). This lack of holistic identity development including career exploration throughout their lives led to transitional challenges upon athletic retirement. Participants cited encounters with depression and described how their athletic disengagement pain was akin to "a personal death, the loss of a body part, or the loss of a family member" (Beamon, 2012, p. 204). Beamon and Bell (2011) further noted that two participants in their study reported feeling suicidal after their athletic careers concluded. In the aforementioned studies, 20 participants participated at the Division I level and 14 out of the 20 matriculated to the professional level after college thus a majority them fall within the EALM (Beamon, 2008, 2012; Beamon & Bell, 2011).

Along the same lines, Northcutt (2013) interviewed six African American male former Division I and professional football players. Even among this smaller sample size, heterogeneity was present. Four out of the six participants at the time of the study had earned their bachelor's degrees, two had earned doctorates, four grew up in single parent households, and five grew up in low-income environments. Similar to Beamon's (2008, 2012) work, key findings from his study highlighted how intense sport socialization was present at an early age, throughout their college experiences athletics took precedent over academics in the minds of their coaches and athletic support staff, and subsequent career transition difficulties occurred after their respective retirement from sport (Northcutt, 2013). Moreover, consistent with the EALM, football was viewed as a pathway for upward mobility. Based on the fact that five out of the six grew up in lower income environments, participants described how their economic challenges growing up impacted their lives and subsequent motivations to use sport as a tool for upward mobility. The convergent experiences among participants in this study and the EALM stories mentioned earlier in this chapter (James, Durant, and Phillips) underscore the frequency of this reality among Black male athletes. As a result, these realities must seriously be addressed on a systematic level both within and beyond sport with a focus on redressing oppressive conditions at the chrono, macro, exo, meso, and micro levels of society.

Related to career transitions, since all participants were former professional athletes, shifting to another occupation and lifestyle was a challenge on multiple levels (Northcutt, 2013). These transitions included a shift in identity, routines, and financial income. One of the participants (Kendrell) poignantly described how his sport success affected his identity development and career transition: "And I believe, along with the success I had early on, it gave me this false sense of who I was ... You're trying to redefine yourself or find yourself" (pp. 74–75). In essence, the EALM by design is not intended to socialize Black male athletes' holistically. Even though, many experience sustained personal success during and after their athletic careers, far more are less fortunate. Despite the allure and illusion of sports glory, those who care about the holistic well-being of Black male athletes must critically analyze the pros and cons of the EALM on the collective group and the Black community at large. Pursuing the dream of being a professional athlete is not a problem in and of itself, but the broader systemic oppression facing Blacks and the concurrent lack of holistic development, critical consciousness enhancement, and preparation for life beyond sports is indeed a major problem that cannot continue.

Chapter Summary

The power of the ISSM, EALM, and corresponding Conveyor Belt (Rhoden, 2006) is rooted in psychological manipulation and economic exploitation. Since elitist White capitalists control the mass of wealth in society due to systemic racism and unjust enrichment (Feagin, 2006), they are in the position to create conditions that socialize Black males into internalizing ahistorical and colorblind neoliberal values as the ultimate measure of success in life. Instead of measuring success by Black collective empowerment economically, politically, culturally, and socially, Black male EALM athletes are groomed to value themselves and their families. Not only do they not question their own exploitation, but they are also often not engaged in efforts to eliminate the oppression of Blacks in the U.S. and globally through connectivity to broader race-conscious social justice movements (Cooper, Macaulay, & Rodriguez, 2017; Cooper, Mallery, & Macaulay, forthcoming).

In sum, the EALM is characterized by an intense focus on sport glory and maximizing one's athletic ability to benefit the sporting structure embedded within WRC. This process involves multi-level systems, targets talented Black males at a young age, intensifies this targeting through adolescence and adulthood, and maintains differential economic and psychological arrangements to preserve the status quo. As a result, a large number of Black male athletes in the EALM are disconnected from the broader Black community even while experiencing personal advancement. Nonetheless, there is heterogeneity in the experiences and outcomes among Black male athletes in EALM. Some are fortunate enough to experience sustained economic sustainability and lead quality and healthy lives after their professional sport careers. Some become leverage capitalists with collectivist inclinations (LCCIs) and engage in meaningful efforts to improve the plight of the Black community albeit to varying extents. However, too many others experience falls from sport grace and sadly never recover from Black male athletic role engulfment and identity foreclosure and suffer from the extenuating effects of the EALM including figurative and literal holistic deaths.

References

Adler, P. A., & Adler, P. (1991). *Backboards and blackboards: College athletics and role engulfment.* New York, NY: Columbia University Press.

Alexander, M. (2012). *The new Jim Crow: Mass incarceration in the age of colorblindness.* New York, NY: The New Press.

Allison, R., Davis, A., & Barranco, R. (2016). A comparison of hometown socioeconomics and demographics for black and white elite football players in the US. *International Review for the Sociology of Sport, 53*(5), 1–15. doi: 10.1177/1012690216674936.

Barker, J. (2012, December 12). 'Special admissions' bring colleges top athletes, educational challenges. *The Baltimore Sun.* Retrieved from http://articles.baltimoresun.com/2012-12-22/sports/bs-sp-acc-sports-special-admits-20121222_1_athletes-graduation-success-rate-college-courses/2

Bass, A. (2002). *Not the triumph but the struggle: The 1968 Olympics and the making of the Black athlete.* Minneapolis, MN: University of Minnesota Press.

Beamon, K. K. (2008). "Used goods": Former African American college student-athletes' perception of exploitation by division I universities. *The Journal of Negro Education, 77*(4), 352–364.

Beamon, K. (2012). "I'm a baller": Athletic identity foreclosure among African-American former student-athletes. *Journal of African American Studies, 16*(2), 195–208.

Beamon, K. K, & Bell, P. A. (2011). A dream deferred: Narratives of African American male former collegiate atheletts' transition out of sports and into the occupational sector. *Journal for the study of Sport and Athletes in Education, 5*(1), 29–44. Bell, D. A. (1980). Brown v. Board of Education and the interest convergence dilemma. *Harvard Law Review, 93*(3), 518–533.

Bell, D. A. (1992). *Faces at the bottom of the well: The permanence of racism.* New York, NY: Basic Books.

Belman, K., Mason, H., Jr., Mann, K., & Perniciaro, M. (2008). *More than a game.* [Documentary]. Harvey Mason Media. St. V., Spring Hill Entertainment.

Benson, K. F. (2000). Constructing academic inadequacy: African American athletes' stories of schooling. *The Journal of Higher Education, 71*(2), 223–246.

Berman, N. (2017). Lebron James: Five humongous charitable donations. *Money Inc.* Retrieved from http://moneyinc.com/lebron-james-five-humongous-charitable-donations/

Beyer, J. M., & Hannah, D. R. (2000). The cultural significance of athletics in U.S. higher education. *Journal of Sport Management, 14*(2), 105–132. doi:10.1123/jsm.14.2.105

Bimper, A. Y., Jr., & Harrison, L., Jr. (2011). Meet me at the crossroads: African American athletic and racial identity. *Quest, 63*(3), 275–288.

Bonilla-Silva, E. (2010). *Racism without racists: Color-blind racism and the persistence of racial inequality in the United States* (3rd ed.). Lanham, MD: Rowman & Littlefield.

Boyd, T. (2003). *Young, Black, rich, and famous: The rise of the NBA, the hip-hop invasion and the transformation of American culture.* New York, NY: Doubleday.

Brown, T. N., Jackson, J. S., Brown, K. T., Sellers, R. M., Keiper, S., & Manuel, W. J. (2003). "There's no race on the playing field": Perceptions of racial discrimination among White and Black athletes. *Journal of Sport and Social Issues, 27*(2), 162–183.

Burde, D., & Kleiman, R. (2017). *Still KD: Through the noise.* [Mini-documentary]. Brandon Loper Film. Avocados and Coconuts Productions.

Bush, L. V., & Bush, E. C. (2013a). Introducing African American male theory (AAMT). *Journal of African American Males in Education,* 4(1), 6–17.

Bush, L. V., & Bush, E. C. (2013b). God bless the child who got his own: Toward a comprehensive theory for African-American boys and men. The Western Journal of Black Studies, 37(1), 1–13.

Coakley, J. (2017). *Sports in society: Issues and controversies* (12th ed.). New York, NY: McGraw-Hill Education.

Cooper, J. N. (2012). Personal troubles and public issues: A sociological imagination of Black athletes' experiences at predominantly White institutions in the United States. *Sociology Mind,* 2(3), 261–271.

Cooper, J. N., & Cooper, J. E. (2015b). "I'm running so you can be happy and I can keep my scholarship": A comparative study of Black male college athletes' experiences with role conflict. *Journal of Intercollegiate Sport,* 8(2), 131–152.

Cooper, J. N., Gawrysiak, J., & Hawkins, B. (2012). Racial perceptions of baseball at historically Black colleges and universities. *Journal of Sport and Social Issues,* 37(2), 196–221.

Cooper, J. N., Macaulay, C., & Rodriguez, S. H. (2017). Race and resistance: A typology of African American sport activism. *International Review for the Sociology of Sport,* 1–31. doi: 10.1177/1012690217718170.

Cooper, J. N., Mallery, M., & Macaulay, C. D. T. (forthcoming). African American sport activism and broader social movements. In D. Brown (Ed.). *Passing the ball: Sports in African American life and culture* (pp. 35–51). Jefferson, NC: McFarland & Company.

Corben, B. (2012). *Broke.* [Documentary]. ESPN Films (Distributor). Invincible Pictures: Rakontur.

Cross, W. E., Jr. (1995). The psychology of Nigrescence: Revising the Cross model. In J. G. Ponterotto, J. M. Casas, L. A. Suzuki, & C. M. Alexander (Eds.), *Handbook of multicultural counseling* (pp. 93–122). Thousand Oaks, CA: Sage.

Curry, T. J. (2017). *The man-not: Race, class, genre, and the dilemmas of Black manhood.* Philadelphia, PA: Temple University Press.

DeCuir, J. T., & Dixson, A. D. (2004). "So when it comes out, they aren't that surprised that it is there": Using critical race theory as a tool of analysis of race and racism in education. *Educational Researcher,* 33(5), 26–31.

DeGruy, J. (2005). *Post-traumatic slave syndrome: America's legacy of enduring injury & healing.* Milwaukie, OR: Uptone Press.

Dohrmann, G. (2010). *Play their hearts out: A coach, his star recruit, and the youth basketball machine.* New York, NY: Ballantine Books.

Douglass, F. (1881). *Life and times of Frederick Douglass: His early life as a slave, his escape from bondage, and his complete history to the present time.* Hartford, CT: Park Publishing.

Douglass, F. (1962). Holiday times. In F. Douglass, *Life and Times of Frederick Douglass: His Early Life as a Slave, His Escape from Bondage, and His Complete History,* (pp. 145–148). New York, NY: Collier Books.

Du Bois, W. E. B. (1903/2003). *The souls of Black folk.* Chicago, IL: A. C. McClurg.

Dubrow, J. K., & adams, j. (2012). Hoop inequalities: Race, class and family structure background and the odds of playing in the National Basketball Association. *International Review for the Sociology of Sport, 47*(1), 43–59.

Edwards, H. (1973). *Sociology of sport.* Homewood, IL: Dorsey Press.

Edwards, H. (1980). *The struggle that must be: An autobiography.* New York, NY: Macmillan Publishing Co., Inc.

Edwards, H. (1984). The Black "dumb jock": An American sports tragedy. *College Board Review, 131,* 8–13.

Edwards, H. (2000). Crisis of black athletes on the eve of the 21st century. *Society, 37*(3), 9–13.

Eitle, T. M., & Eitle, D. J. (2002). Race, cultural capital, and the educational effects of participation in sports. *Sociology of Education, 75*(2), 123–146.

ESPN (2018). Kevin Durant and Michael Beasley walk down memory lane in exclusive sit-down interview. *ESPN News.* Retrieved from https://www.youtube.com/watch?v=pxRV0hZbA7M

ETS. (2011). *A strong start: Positioning young Black boys for educational success a statistical profile.* Washington, DC: Educational Testing Service.

Feagin, J. (2006). *Systemic racism: A theory of oppression.* New York, NY: Routledge.

Finkel, R., & Martin, T. (2013, October 16). *Schooled: The price of college sports.* [Documentary]. Strand Releasing (Distributor), United States: Makuhari Media.

Floyd, M. F., Shinew, K. J., McGuire, F. A., & Noe, F. P. (1994). Race, class, and leisure activity preferences: Marginality and ethnicity revisited. *Journal of Leisure Research, 26*(2), 158–173.

Forbes (2017). *Forbes Profile Kevin Durant.* Retrieved from https://www.forbes.com/profile/kevin-durant/

Forbes (2018). The world's 100 highest-paid athletes. Retrieved from https://www.forbes.com/pictures/mli45lleg/4-lebron-james-6/#49c908ae16a8

Franklin, J. H. (1947). *From slavery to freedom: A history of Negro Americans.* New York, NY: Knopf.

Franklin, R. S., & Resnik, S. (1973). *The political economy of racism.* New York, NY: Holt Rinehart and Winston.

Frazier, E. F. (1957). *Black bourgeoisie.* New York, NY: Free Press.

Friedkin, W. (1994). *Blue chips* [movie]. Paramount Pictures (Distributor).

Fuller, R. D., Harrison, C. K., Bukstein, S. J., Martin, B. E., Lawrence, S. M., & Gadsby, P. (2016). That smart dude: A qualitative investigation of the African American male scholar-baller identity. *Urban Education,* 1–19. DOI: 10.1177/0042085916668955

Gladwell, M. (2011). *Outliers: A story of success.* New York, NY: Back Bay Books.

Goldwyn, S., Jr., Henderson, D., Rothman, T., & Ward, D. S. (1993). *The program* [Film]. United States: Touchstone Pictures, Samuel Goldwyn Company.

Greenburg, R. (2016). *Running for his life: The Lawrence Phillips Story.* [Documentary]. Showtime.

Hancock, J. L. (2009). *The blind side* [Film]. United States: Alcon Entertainment. Harris, C. (1993). Whiteness as property. *Harvard Law Review, 106*(8), 1707–1791.

Harris, O. (1994). Race, sport, and social support. *Sociology of Sport Journal, 11*(1), 40–50.

Harrison, C. K., (1998). Themes that thread through society: Racism and athletic manifestation in the African-American community. *Race, Ethnicity and Education, 1*(1), 63–74.

Harrison, L. (2001). Understanding the influence of stereotypes: Implications for the African American in sport and physical activity. *Quest, 53*(1), 97–114.

Harrison., L. Jr., Harrison, C. K., & Moore, L. N. (2002). African American racial identity and sport. *Sport, Education & Society, 7*(2), 121–133.

Hartmann, D. (2000). Rethinking the relationships between sport and race in American culture: Golden ghettos and contested terrain. *Sociology of Sport Journal, 17*(3), 229–253.

Hawkins, B. (1998a). The dominant images of black men in America: The representation of O. J. Simpson. In G. Sailes (Ed.), *African Americans in sport* (pp. 39–52). New Brunswick, NJ: Transaction Publishers.

Hawkins, B. (1998b). The White supremacy continuum of images for Black men. *Journal of African American men, 3*(3), 7–18.

Hawkins, B. (2010). *The new plantation: Black athletes, college sports, and predominantly White NCAA institutions.* New York, NY: Palgrave-Macmillan.

Hine, D. C., Hine, W. C., & Harrold, S. (2006). *The African-American odyssey: Since 1965* (Third ed. Vol. Two). Upper Saddle River, NJ: Pearson Prentice Hall.

Hoberman, J. (1997). *Darwin's athletes: How sport has damaged Black America and preserved the myth of race.* Boston, MA: Houghton Mifflin.

Hodge, S. R., Burden, J. W., Jr., Robinson, L. E., & Bennett, R. A., III. (2008). Theorizing on the stereotyping of Black male student-athletes: Issues and implications. *Journal for the Study of Sports and Athletes in Education, 2*(2), 203–226.

Hughey, M. W. (2014). *The White savior film: Content, critics, and consumption.* Philadelphia, PA: Temple University Press.

James, S., & Marx, F. (1994). *Hoop dreams* [documentary]. Minneapolis, MN: Kartemquin Films.

Knowlton, E. (2016, May 17). LeBron James' business partner confirms lifetime deal with Nike is worth over $1 billion. *Business Insider.* Retrieved from http://www.businessinsider.com/lebron-james-nike-deal-exceeds-1-billion-maverick-carter-says-2016-5

Lapchick, R., & Balasundaram, B. (2017, June 29). The 2017 racial and gender report card: National Basketball Association. *The Institute for Diversity and Ethics in Sport.* Retrieved from http://nebula.wsimg.com/74491b38503915f2f148062ff076e698?AccessKeyId=DAC3A56D8FB782449D2A&disposition=0&alloworigin=1

Lapchick, R., Malveaux, C., Davison, E., & Grant, C. (2016, September 28). The 2016 racial and gender report card: National Football League. *The Institute for Diversity and Ethics in Sport.* Retrieved from http://nebula.wsimg.com/1abf21ec51fd8dafbecfc2e0319a6091?AccessKeyId=DAC3A56D8FB782449D2A&disposition=0&alloworigin=1

Lawrence, C. R., III. (1995). The id, the ego, and equal protection: Reckoning with unconscious racism. In K. Crenshaw, N. Gotanda, G. Peller & K. Thomas (Eds.), *Critical race theory: The key writings that formed the movement* (pp. 253–257). New York, NY: The New Press.

Lee, S. (1998). *He got game* [Film]. United States: Touchstone Pictures, 40 Acres and A Mule Filmworks.

Leonard, W. M., II, & Reyman, J. E. (1988). The odds of attaining professional athlete status: Refining the computations. *Sociology of Sport Journal*, 5(2), 162–169.

LJFF (2018). The LeBron James family foundation [Website]. Retrieved from http://lebron-jamesfamilyfoundation.org/

Loy, J. W., & Elvogue, J. F. (1970). Racial segregation in American sport. *International Review for the Sociology of Sport*, 5(1), 5–24.

Malveaux, J. (2000). Gladiators, gazelles, and groupies: Basketball love and loathing. In T. Boyd & K. L. Shropshire (Eds.), *Basketball Jones: America above the rim* (pp. 51–58). New York, NY: New York University Press.

Manfred, T. (2014, September 4). Kevin Durant's monster Nike deal is a huge win for Jay Z. *Business Insider*. Retrieved from http://www.businessinsider.com/kevin-durant-nike-jay-z-roc-nation-2014-9

NCAA (2018). Estimated probability of competing in professional athletics. NCAA. Retrieved from http://www.ncaa.org/about/resources/research/estimated-probability-competing-professional-athletics

Northcutt, K. J. (2013). *The dilemma: Career transition of African American male football players at Division I institutions*. Dissertation: University of Mississippi.

Nwadike, A. C., Baker, A. R., Brackebusch, V. B., & Hawkins, B. J. (2016). Institutional Racism in the NCAA and the racial implications of the "2.3 or take a knee" legislation. *Marquette Sports Law Review*, 26(2), 523–543.

Oates, T. P. (2007). The erotic gaze in the NFL draft. *Communication and Critical/Cultural Studies*, 4(1): 74–90.

Ogden, D. C. (2004). The welcome theory: An approach to studying AfricanAmerican youth interest and involvement in baseball. *Nine: A Journal of Baseball History and Culture*, 12(2), 114–122.

Ogden, D. C., & Hilt, M. L. (2003). Collective identity and basketball: An explanation for the decreasing number of African-Americans on America's baseball diamonds. *Journal of Leisure Research*, 35(2), 213–227.

Ogden, D. C., & Rose, R. A. (2005). Using Giddens's structuration theory to examine the waning participation of African Americans in baseball. *Journal of Black Studies*, 35(4), 225–245.

Ortiz, J. (2018, February 25). Kevin Durant donates $10 million to Prince George's Co. students. *WTOP*. Retrieved from https://wtop.com/prince-georges-county/2018/02/kevin-durant-donates-10-million-students-prince-georges-co/

Peter, J. (2015, June 2). The terrifying prison letters from ex-Nebraska star Lawrence Phillips. *USA Today*. Retrieved from https://ftw.usatoday.com/2015/06/ex-nfl-running-back-lawrence-phillips-sends-terrifying-letters-from-jail-this-place-is-a-jungle

Powell, S. (2008). *Souled out? How Blacks are winning and losing in sports*. Champaign, IL: Human Kinetics.

Rhoden, W. C. (2006). *40 million dollar slaves: The rise, fall, and redemption of the Black athlete*. New York, NY: Crown Publishing Group.

Robbins, B., Tollin, M., Laiter T., & Wiley, M. (1999). *Varsity blues* [Film]. Paramount Pictures (Distributor), United States: MTV Films, Tollin/Robbins Productions.

Sage, G. H. (1998). *Power and ideology in American sport* (2nd ed.). Champaign, IL: Human Kinetics.

Sailes, G. (2010). The African American athlete: Social myths and stereotypes. In G. Sailes (Ed.), *Modern sport and the African American athlete experience* (pp. 55–68). San Diego, CA: Cognella.

Scutari, M. (2018). The servant: Keep a close eye on NBA superstar Kevin Durant's philanthropy. *Inside Philanthropy*. Retrieved from https://www.insidephilanthropy.com/home/2018/2/1/kevin-durant-philanthropy

Sellers, R. M. (2000). African American student-athletes: Opportunity or exploitation? In D. A. Brooks, R. (Ed.), *Racism in college athletics: The African American athlete's experience* (2nd ed., pp. 133–154). Morgantown, WV: Fitness Information Technology, Inc.

Shopkorn, A., Noah, J., Safdie, J., & Safdie, B. (2013). *Lenny Cooke* [Documentary]. New York, NY: Shopkorn Productions.

Singer, J. N. (2009). African American football athletes' perspectives on institutional integrity in college sport. *Research Quarterly for Exercise and Sport, 80*(1), 102–116.

Singer, J. N., & May, R. A. B. (2010). The career trajectory of a Black male high school basketball player: A social reproduction perspective. *International Review for the Sociology of Sport, 46*(3), 299–314.

Smedley, A., & Smedley, B. D. (2005). Race as biology is fiction, racism as a social problem is real: Anthropological and historical perspectives on the social construction of race. *American Psychologist, 60*(1), 16–26.

Smith, E. (2009). *Race, sport and the American dream* (2nd ed.). Durham, NC: Carolina Academic Press.

USA Today High School Sports (2017, June 28). ESPN reveals blockbuster football schedule for GEICO high school kickoff. Retrieved from http://usatodayhss.com/2017/espn-reveals-blockbuster-football-schedule-for-geico-high-school-kickoff

Walker, A. (2016, June 28). Letter to my younger self. *The Player's Tribune*. Retrieved from https://www.theplayerstribune.com/en-us/articles/2016-6-28-antoine-walker-nba-letter-to-my-younger-self

Whitely, G., & Ridley, A. (2016). Last chance U [Documentary Series]. *Condé Nast Entertainment*. [Netflix]. https://www.netflix.com/title/80091742

Wiggins, D. K. (2014). 'Black athlete in White men's games': Race, sport and American national pastimes. *The International Journal of the History of Sport, 31*(1–2), 181–202.

Wiggins, D. K., & Miller, P. B. (2003). *The unlevel playing field: A documentary history of the African-American experience in sport*. Urbana, IL: University of Illinois Press.

Woodson, C. G. (1933/1990). *The mis-education of the Negro*. Trenton, NJ: Africa World Press.

· 6 ·

TRANSITION RECOVERY MODEL

From Holistic Underdevelopment and Unconscious Exploitation to Holistic Development and Conscious Empowerment

> As a people, we have responsibility to learn about the realities of black sports involvement—its liabilities as well as its opportunities—and to teach our children to deal with these realities intelligently and constructively.
> —Edwards (1984, p. 13)

The Interplay of Systemic Conditions of the Transition Recovery Model and Black Male Athletes

"I came from nothing," "Sport is my sanctuary," "Sport is the only thing I am good at," and *"Sport is all I know"* are common phrases internalized by Black male athletes. Each of these quotes suggest sport affords them distinctive affirmation and personal growth opportunities. Positive feelings and outcomes associated with sport participation are not inherently problematic. However, a critical sociological analysis of the aforementioned statements would highlight how these statements say more about the nature of Black males' realities outside sport than it does within it. For example, the *"I come from nothing"* phrase reinforces a deficit narrative rooted in WRC and neoliberal ideologies that suggest all the issues in Black communities are a byproduct of cultural and moral decay rather than systemic oppression (Majors & Billson, 1992). It also reflects the lack of awareness and internalization among these Black male

athletes about the greatness within their racial, ethnic, and cultural lineages throughout history (pre-, during, and post-enslavement) across the African Diaspora (Bush & Bush, 2013a, 2013b). Furthermore, the notion that Black males in these communities have not been exposed to positive same race and gender role models also assumes there are few, if any, people who currently live in these communities who engage in positive behaviors worth imitating. This gross generalization serves as a tool of ideological hegemony in order to sustain WRC because it unquestionably devalues Black community cultural wealth (CCW; Yosso, 2005). According to Yosso (2005) CCW is "an array of knowledge, skills, abilities, and contacts possessed and utilized by Communities of Color to survive and resist macro and micro-forms of oppression" (p. 77). The misguided socialization that teaches Blacks to view themselves and their communities as inferior illustrates what Woodson (1933/1990) coined in the title of his book as the "miseducation of the Negro." Related to sport, young Black male athletes are not only miseducated to view sport as the primary means to acquire dignity, respect, positive identity affirmation, and upward mobility, but also they are often exposed to environments where this view is validated. Thus, Black male athletes' perceptions and behaviors are a direct result of the systems in which they exist and their respective interactions with them.

Referring back to Kevin Durant's comments during his interview with Chris Haynes from Chapter 5, he described how he, Michael Beasley, and their peers who grew up in the PG county and D.C. areas had internalized racist beliefs about their own predominantly Black communities as well as of the Whites who lived outside of their community (ESPN, 2018). In particular, both Durant and Beasley referenced how they had few role models in their neighborhoods who looked like them who exhibited positive behaviors and possibilities for them aside from sport. Durant referenced a few Black male role models including his former coach and director of the Seat Pleasant Activity Center, Taras "Stink" Brown, but even with him the primary connection was through sport. In essence, *their perception was their reality and their reality was their perception.* Unfortunately, these racist beliefs were not unfounded. Systemic gentrification and environmental violence that has plagued the Black community for decades creates conditions that economically deprive them of access to high quality resources such as employment opportunities, healthy and affordable food options, and livable housing (ETS, 2011). As a result, too often Black males and their families are underserved and miseducated whereby the disruption of the Black community through mass incarceration, racist schooling systems, and economic neglect intersect to meet the needs and desires of the benefactors of WRC while concomitantly oppressing the collective well-being of Blacks (Alexander, 2012; Bush & Bush, 2013a, 2013b; Howard, 2014; Noguera, 2008).

In concert with environmental conditions undermining the optimal functioning of the Black community, a primary strategy of the miseducation curricula is to convince Blacks there is no value in their own communities, which for Black male athletes this erroneous notion fosters their athletic role engulfment and misplaced trust in White opportunists (e.g., athletic-centric capitalist college coaches, exploitative sport agents, etc.) (Corben, 2012). Several critical scholars have offered counter perspectives to reframe the ways in which Black communities are viewed. For example, Yosso (2005) offered the CCW framework as way to describe the various forms of capital communities of Color utilize to navigate an oppressive U.S. society. The six types of CCW capital include *aspirational, navigational, social, linguistic, familial,* and *resistant.* Black male athletes who persevere and experience positive life outcomes through traditional and non-traditional educational means including those in the transition recovery model (TRM) exhibit aspirational capital (see Figure 6.1). Their success outcomes occur in spite of a society that dehumanizes, criminalizes, hypersexualizes, and demonizes them (Curry, 2017; Howard, 2014; Noguera, 2008). Black male athletes in the U.S. are conditioned and miseducated to view aspirational capital as only valid when pursuing sport goals despite the minute probabilities of them earning a college athletic scholarship and securing a career at the professional level. Hence, I argue the creation and reproduction of the athletic manifest destiny process among Black males (Coakley, 2017), although at times yielding positive outcomes for select athletes (i.e., EALM benefactors), is a tool of a gendered racist society that seeks to limit the focus and self-efficacy of them on sport performance while concurrently undervaluing of their holistic prowess.

In addition, in a neoliberal U.S. society, Black males are also socialized to view their goal attainment through mental and physical exertion in *individualistic* and *meritocratic* terms. When they succeed, it is because of their own hard work and thus if more Blacks engage in similar efforts then they would achieve similar success. This fallacious assertion ignores the impact of systemic inequalities and the inherent stratification associated with capitalist cultures whereby only a limited number of individuals from oppressed groups are allowed to acquire certain levels of economic success. Isolated incidents of economic attainment is allowed among Blacks who assimilate and do not threaten the core of WRC. Whereas, the collective economic empowerment of Blacks as racial group in a society founded upon and structured by WRC is apocalyptic and forbidden at all costs; hence, the long history of overt and covert policies, practices, and promotion of unfounded myths intended to suppress equal opportunities for Blacks while privileging Whiteness. In other words, racism and other forms of oppression do not prove innate inferiority, but rather justify socially constructed hierarchies. In concert with Edwards' (2000) assertions, I contend it is by design that a racist capitalist system benefits when Black males as a collective group have a myopic transmission of aspirational capital towards sport and entertainment, but not in areas such as education, business, politics, science, technology, engineering, law, architecture, health, social work, and humanities.

Related to linguistic capital (Yosso, 2005), it has been widely noted how the intersection between Black music genres such as Hip-Hop and Jazz and sport have utilized language as a powerful tool for cultural empowerment and expression (Boyd, 2003; George, 1992; Leonard & King, 2012). More recently, scholars have called for the adoption of Hip-Hop pedagogies to reflect culturally sustaining educational practices as well as to serve as vital forms of counter storytelling to challenge White Euro-centric beliefs (Emdin & Lee, 2012; Love, 2014). Within the U.S. culturally bias tests such as the Scholastic Aptitude Test (SAT) and American College Test (ACT) marginalize the native languages and perspectives of Blacks (along with Latinx, Indigenous Peoples/ Native Americans, and Asians) by utilizing White Anglo-Saxon middle class cultural norms as the benchmark for intelligence (Sellers, 2000). These racist metrics and accompanying schooling practices disenfranchise thousands of Black male athletes who do not meet traditional admission standards to HWIs from accessing potential educational and athletic opportunities (Cooper, 2012; Nwadike, Baker, Brackebusch, & Hawkins, 2016; Sellers, 2000; Singer & Willingham, 2015). Similar racist origins undergirded the intelligence quotient (I.Q.) tests, White-Eurocentric cognitive metrics, and various educational barriers facing Blacks throughout U.S. history (e.g., anti-literacy laws, *Plessy v. Ferguson* (1896), etc.) (Anderson, 1988; Howard, 2014; Noguera, 2008; Woodson, 1933/1990)). Consequently, these assessments have had a disparate impact on Black male academic achievement and reinforce the myth of White intellectual superiority (Schott Foundation for Public Education, 2010).

Within a society founded upon and structured by WRC, family ties among Blacks are viewed and treated as personal liabilities for Black males as opposed to being valued as sources of knowledge, wisdom, expertise, and positive support. Racist films such as *Hoop Dreams* (James & Marx, 1994), *Varsity Blues* (Robbins, Tollin, Laiter, &Wiley, 1999), *Blue Chips* (Friedkin, 1994), *The Blind Side* (Hancock, 2009), and *Running for his life: The Lawrence Phillips Story* (Greenburg, 2016) along with mainstream media coverage of Black male athletes (i.e., *ESPN 30 for 30* mini-documentaries, *ESPN SC Special Features*, *Last Chance U* mini-docuseries, etc.) all propagate stereotypical assertions about Black families in general and particularly those connected to Black male athletes. The degradation and stigmatization of Black families has been promulgated for centuries dating back to the early 17th century via White-controlled institutions (Woodson, 1933/1990). This miseducation continued through the mid-20th century with the widely publicized policy shaping Moynihan Report in the 1960s into the latter 20th and early 21st century with publication of scholarly work (i.e., *the cool pose*) and public discourses grounded in pathological myths attributed to Black males.

Modern day political propaganda in the 21st century put forth by conservative and Alt-Right groups perpetuate racist beliefs about the "dysfunctional" Black family and specifically the inept Black male who as a result of his nature (as opposed to systemic forces grounded in gender racism and oppression) is unsuited for success in mainstream society with the exception of a few areas (i.e., sports and entertainment which conform to the White racist psyche regarding Blacks' abilities). Thus, justifying Black males' marginalization, incarceration, and extermination (Alexander, 2012; Curry, 2017). More specific to Black male athletes, the athletic industrial complex (AIC; Hawkins, 2010; Smith, 2009), Conveyor Belt (Rhoden, 2006), and athletic seasoning complex (ASC; Howard, 2014) are designed to disassociate Black male athletes from their native families and cultures and adopt a more colorblind capitalist orientation whereby they prioritize relationships with White stakeholders (also referred to as colonizers—see Hawkins (2010)). This disassociation is not only from biological family members (i.e., nuclear and extended), but also from fictive kinships in the Black community that have historically served as conscious raising entities and protective forces against outside threats (Douglas, 2016).

Along the same lines as familial capital, under the influence of the AIC (Hawkins, 2010; Smith, 2009), Conveyor Belt (Rhoden, 2006), and ASC (Howard, 2014), Black male athletes are conditioned to pursue strong relationships or social capital with influential Whites in sport and corporate entities. These relationships can yield significant financial rewards. Conversely,

Black male athletes are only expected to value relationships within their own race when it serves the interests of influential Whites (i.e., recruiting a team-mate to enroll in the same university such as the case with the Michigan Fab 5 in the early 1990s) (Rhoden, 2006). Nonetheless, there are numerous Black male athletes including those who experience the TRM who engage in resistance efforts against WRC by strategically utilizing their familial and social capital within their race to maintain a sense of self and challenge racist labels placed upon them, their families, and their communities. This type of capital is prevalent in the form of constellation mentoring or the presence of multiple mentors who fulfill distinct developmental purposes for the men-tee(s) (Kelly & Dixon, 2014).

In concert with the aims of Yosso's (2005) CCW, Douglas and Peck (2013) posited that community based pedagogies were valuable sources of empowerment and education for Black males. More specifically, they chal-lenged the taken-for-granted notion that traditional schooling sites are the primary purveyors of true education for Black students across the African Diaspora. The authors argued that with African cultural systems, educa-tive spaces transcend physical school buildings and extend to familial, reli-gious, athletic, musical, art, and other social spaces in the Black community. Within their study, they focused on the role of Black churches and barber-shops as culturally sanctioned spaces for Black males' personal development (Douglas & Peck, 2013). Notwithstanding the positive benefits of these spaces, they can also often times simultaneously foster negative outcomes. Douglas and Peck (2013) acknowledged the complex nature of these com-munity based pedagogical spaces when they noted: "… animating pedagogy in these venues, may, in fact, provide debilitating instruction that is devoid of necessary counternarrative to destructive, mainstream discourses of peo-ple of African descent" (p. 69). However, the often overlooked aspect of these spaces is that they do indeed serve as productive educational spaces for personal development and community uplift. The authors emphasized the importance of these spaces: "… within Black communities … traditional schooling experiences alone are not sufficient for preparing and, in effect, educating Black people for life, resiliency, and service" (Douglas & Peck, 2013, p. 70).

Regarding navigational capital (Yosso, 2005), unlike their White peers in the U.S., Blacks have historically and in modern times had to acquire a level of cultural sophistication (i.e., code switching) for their survival and navigation in and through marginalizing spaces. Furthermore, when Black male athletes are recruited to historically White private high schools, prep schools, JUCOs, and four-year colleges and universities, unfortunately they have been forced to rely on academic staff that often place them on eligibility plans in order to reach the end goal of graduation (Beamon, 2008; Benson, 2000; Cooper & Cooper, 2015; Fountain & Finley, 2009; Singer, 2005). This type of detrimental navigation is a byproduct of miseducation and schooling. Whereas, the navigational capital that Yosso (2005) described in her article refers to connections with advocates and allies who assist Black male athletes in actualizing their holistic development both while they are in school and after graduation (Bimper, 2016, 2017; Cooper, Corral, et al., 2018; Kelly & Dixon, 2014).

Perhaps the most suppressed form of CCW among Black male athletes is resistant capital (Yosso, 2005). As previously noted, Black male athletes who activate resistant capital in mainstream sporting systems are ostracized and disposed (Cooper, Macaulay, & Rodriguez, 2017; Edwards, 1969, 1980; Rhoden, 2006). Mahmoud Abdul-Rauf (formerly Christopher Jackson's) exile from the NBA after the 1995–1996 season when he refused to stand for the National Anthem as an act of protest against U.S. militarism, imperialism, islamophobia, and capitalism is a prime example of the responses from dominant sporting structures towards resistant capital. The compounded effect of macrosystem level racist ideologies, exosystem and mesosystem levels of racist policy enforcement, and microsystem level outcomes experienced by Black male athletes who engage in resistant capital illustrates the importance of ecological systems analyses. Despite insurmountable odds, Black male athletes throughout history have utilized their resistant capital as a means of disrupting the WRC status quo both within and beyond sport (Cooper, Macaulay, & Rodriguez, 2017; Cooper, Mallery, & Macaulay, forthcoming; Edwards, 1969, 1980, 2016; Wiggins, 2000). Connecting the concepts of CCW framework (Yosso, 2005), community-based pedagogies (Douglas & Peck, 2013), and ecological systems (Bush & Bush, 2013a, 2013b) with Black male athletes' lived experiences in and through sport and (mis)education is a necessary foundation for understanding the TRM. Similar to educational efforts during the antebellum and Reconstruction eras designed to dismantle the institution of Black African enslavement (e.g., spiritually, mentally, physically, politically, and economically) (Woodson, 1933/1990), the TRM serves as an emancipatory tool that enables Black male athletes to move from being holistically underdeveloped, exploited, and miseducated to holistically developed, empowered, and educated.

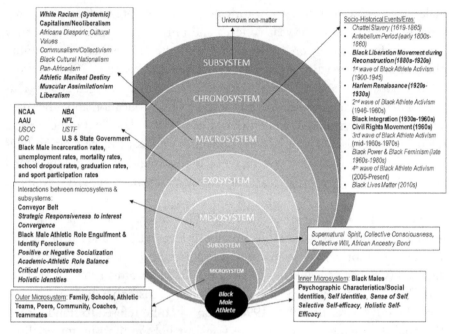

Figure 6.1. Transition Recovery Model (TRM).

Source: Adapted from Bush, L. V., & Bush, E. C. (2013a). Introducing African American male theory (AAMT). *Journal of African American Males in Education*, 4(1), p. 9. Copyright 2013 Journal of African American Males in Education

Socialization Phases of the Transition Recovery Model

Similar to the early phase of those who experience the ISSM and EALM, Black male athletes in the TRM perceive sport participation as an activity to affirm their racial and masculine identities due to various societal, community, and familial messaging. In particular, the influence of mesosystem intersections between community, family, and young Black males has a significant impact on their sport participation choices and subsequent identity attachment. Black males at this phase participate in informal and formal sporting opportunities based on family resources and geographical location. As they approach pre-adolescence, they join more competitive leagues, teams, and organizations as the importance of skill development heightens as they approach middle/junior high and high school. Educationally, at this phase Black males' engagement varies from low to high engagement based on family emphasis on academic achievement and learning, schooling contexts, access to academic enrichment supports, personal interests in school, and other related demographic and psychographic characteristics of the individual, family, community, and setting.

During the adolescence phase, Black male athletes in the TRM participate on school-sponsored teams. For sports like football and track and field, these teams are important spaces for demonstrating their skill sets among their peers. For basketball, soccer, tennis, and baseball, in addition to school sponsored teams, participation in community-based and/or privately funded organizations becomes important because several scouting services begin ranking players at this phase. Although, I argue any rankings prior to high school are premature and misleading, the proliferation of scouting services and the value attached to them has been well documented (Dohrmann, 2010). In addition, similar to the ISSM and EALM at this phase, the increased use of multi-media platforms such as YouTube to create highlight videos for enhanced exposure is commonplace. As Black males in the TRM progress towards high school, they continue to participate on school sanctioned teams and many will participate in non-school sanctioned showcases to attract the attention of college recruiters. Attending summer team camps and receiving recruiting correspondence is expected at this phase. Essentially, the progressive phases from early youth to adolescence are similar to the ISSM and EALM models.

At the young adulthood phase, this is where the distinction between the ISSM and EALM models become more apparent. The difference between the ISSM and TRM at this point lies in the timing and internalization of the reduced salience of athletic identity centrality and subsequent holistic identity transition and cultivation outcomes. For those in the ISSM, they experience an extended period of post-athletic career disengagement trauma (Edwards, 1984). An extended period is defined as a calendar year or longer. As previously stated, disengagement symptoms can include, but not limited, to identity crisis/loss of sense of self, depression, moodiness/irritability, career uncertainty and dissatisfaction, interpersonal challenges, unhealthy weight gain or weight loss, poor dieting, unhealthy competitive mindset transference, substance abuse, and/or related mental, physical, and spiritual health issues. Typically, upon retirement from competitive sport, all athletes experience some level of disengagement nostalgia, but the Black male athletic role engulfment process can be more acute due to socio-historical, ecological, racial, and gender factors.

Moreover, those who are considered *early adapters to transition*[1] in the TRM experience positive identity shifts and reduced post-athletic career disengagement trauma within a year or less. Early adapters to transition leverage CCW and accessible resources (e.g., significant others, mentors, family, culturally responsive support groups, etc.) to facilitate their positive transition out of sport participation. Those who experience transition after a year are considered *progressive adapters to transition*. Individuals who are progressive adapters to transition can include those who previously experienced the ISSM and EALM. The previously mentioned symptoms associated with post-athletic career disengagement trauma are more intense for progressive adapters compared to the early adapters due to the length of time between retirement and positive identity detachment from strong athletic identity centrality. For both early and progressive adapters, the identification of alternative career paths, social engagement, and identity affirming activities prior to and during sport participation facilitates positive transitional processes (i.e., exposure to the Excellence Beyond Athletics (EBA) framework (Cooper, 2016b) or similar supports)".

After retirement, *identity transition empowerment* (ITE) is facilitated through engagement in alternatives such as participation in recreational and/or competitive physical activities or sports, non-sport interest exploration (i.e., travel), spiritual growth, involvement in meaningful relationships (dyad or large groups), mentoring, community service, and reconnecting with past interests to name a few. ITE occurs when an athlete "… redirects and amplifies their energies and focus on their educational attainment and personal development beyond athletics" (Cooper, 2016a, p. 118). Within this definition, athletics refers to involvement in formal competitive youth, interscholastic, intercollegiate, and/or professional sports. Therefore, involvement in competitive or non-competitive recreational sport is not included. In addition, former athletes' transition into training, coaching, administration, and/or related roles within sporting spaces is also viewed as post-athletic participation career involvement. Furthermore, at this point the difference between the Black males who experience the EALM versus the TRM is that the former still possesses legitimate prospects to matriculate to the next level whereas the chances for the latter have diminished due to various reasons such as injury, lack of scholarship opportunity, reduced playing time, unsuccessful attempt to secure a professional contract, retirement, etc. (Cooper, 2016a, 2016b; Cooper & Cooper, 2015).

At adulthood phase, early adapters have fully experienced ITE (Cooper, 2016a). It is important to note that many Black male athletes who initially were in the ISSM and EALM eventually shift to the TRM; hence, the value of analyzing Black male athletes' life experiences longitudinally as opposed to only during their athletic careers or immediately thereafter. The progressive adapters experience full immersion in ITE although it typically occurs later than the early adapters. The end result of the TRM involves a comprehensive and authentic reflection on one's previous involvement in sport, the broader systems that influenced their participation experiences, and most importantly the manifestation of their healthy multi-faceted identities and an overall positive quality of life (e.g., positive relationships, career satisfaction and growth, etc.). The more time away from the initial retirement the more holistic perspective is gained by Black male athletes who experience the TRM because they experience more life where their prior involvement in competitive athletics in pursuit of a professional career is no longer the central source of their identity or purpose. Many former athletes write memoirs, autobiographies, or pursue roles where they can share their stories with younger athletes. Throughout this chapter, I offer illustrative examples of early and progressive adapters who experience ITE within the TRM.

Evidence of the Transition Recovery Model

There are countless Black males who have experienced the TRM. Unfortunately, these stories receive far less media coverage and scholarly recognition because attention to these realities would magnify the deep problems associated with seemingly positive societal practices and arrangements related to sport participation and (mis)educational schooling institutions. For example, research on Black male former athletes' reflections on their experiences in and through White-controlled sport organizations such as the NCAA and U.S. professional sport leagues reveals scathing critiques of how they experienced exploitation, disenfranchisement, and holistic underdevelopment. (Beamon, 2008, 2010, 2012; Beamon & Bell, 2002; Cooper, Corral, et al., 2018; Singer, 2005, 2009). Therefore, the amplification of these counter narratives/counter stories illustrates the damaging short-term and long-term effects of systems that overemphasize sport performance and undervalue Black male athletes' holistic development. It is worth noting there are select times when individual institutions or entities like the NCAA strategically recognize Black males who have experienced the TRM albeit for their own agendas (i.e., brand impression management), which creates the problematic illusion that the system is not flawed and produces more positive outcomes than negative (see Southall and Nagel (2010) and Southall and Staurowsky (2013) for a detailed critical analysis of the institutional logics associated with the NCAA collegiate model). Nonetheless, I argue these efforts emanate from inequitable interest convergence (Bell, 1980, 1992) and White racial framing (Feagin, Vera, & Batur, 2000) designed to benefit the WRC status quo. The aforementioned interplay is discussed in greater detail throughout this chapter.

One highly visible example of a Black male athlete who experienced the EALM and subsequently shifted into the TRM is Vince Young. As one of the most decorated college football players in the U.S., Young's accolades in sport are well documented. These accomplishments include being the star quarterback on the 2006 National Champion University of Texas Longhorns football team, a 2005 Heisman Trophy Candidate, a 2005 All-American, and the third overall NFL draft pick in 2006. Raised by his mother and grandmother in Houston, Texas, Young faced common pressures for Black males growing up in economically disadvantaged neighborhoods throughout his childhood (OWN, 2015). One major challenge Young encountered was the absence of his biological father's physical and emotional presence during his early childhood, which had a profound impact on him. His father like many Black males in the U.S. ended up in the prison industrial complex (PIC; Alexander, 2012). Thus, the systemic pattern of disproportionately incarcerating Black males who are fathers results in immeasurable harm to their families particularly their children as well as the broader Black community. Often times, Black males are drawn to sport more so than other activities because it is in these spaces where they are able to access adult males who can serve as surrogate or kin-like father figures to them. The aforementioned analysis underscores the interplay between various ecological systems (chrono, macro, meso, exo, and micro) in a society founded upon and structured by WRC and their subsequent impact on Black male athletes' life experiences within and beyond sport.

In an exclusive interview with the OWN (2015) network *In Deep Shift* with Jonas Elrod series, Young described how growing up as the only male in his household made him grow up fast. This desire to fulfill an adult masculine role as a young person specifically as a Black male can prevent a child from experiencing healthy developmental processes. As opposed to being able to psychologically and socially mature at a pace deemed as normal by child psychologists, Black males subjected to what Bronfenbrenner (1977) described as non-normative circumstances such as trauma via environmental stressors can result in significant maladjustment from childhood through adulthood if not adequately treated. The impact of an absent father in the lives of young Black males cannot be overstated even though the nature and extent of the impact varies by person and situation. Often times for young Black males whose fathers are not physically present in their lives, they seek out masculine validation and support in culturally sanctioned spaces such as sports (Messner, 1990).

In addition to growing up in an economically disadvantaged neighborhood without his father, Young also experienced a traumatic life threatening accident during his youth where he was hit by car resulting in a ruptured appendix (OWN, 2015). Unfortunately, mass media outlets only acknowledge this type of background information when seeking to promote the Black male "rags to riches" story whereas when they experience a fall from grace these factors are seldom referenced as important antecedents for subsequent life outcomes. In other words, I argue that contextual factors are not only important to acknowledge, but also these realities should be understood with an optimal level of empathy (or at least sympathy) and cultural sensitivity. Too often Black males including athletes are subjected to the harsh realities of anti-Black misandrist societies (Curry, 2017) and rather than analyzing ecological factors that influence their life outcomes simplistic (and erroneous) pathological and deficit based explanations are purported and widely accepted in concert with ideological hegemonic norms. For example, they are often bombarded with deficit-based commentary characterizing them, their families, and the Black community as the primary culprits for any and all of their adverse life circumstances. In an effort to challenge this dominant ideology, I analyze the lives of Black male athletes such as Young within a broader ecological and sociological apparatus and with an optimal level of empathy, sympathy, and cultural sensitivity.

More specifically, this type of analysis allows for a more expansive understanding of what Curry (2017) calls Black male vulnerability, which is too often omitted from popular discourse and scholarly inquiry due to deeply embedded gender racism portraying Black males as either sub or super human. In Young's case, due to his exceptional athletic prowess, during his athletic career he was portrayed as superhuman. In this sense, being super human means that personal empathy and broader sociological understandings are not warranted. This type of treatment is consistent with racist ideologies that dehumanize Black males and does not deem the tragedies in their lives worth addressing beyond sensationalism. Therefore, the description of Young's background presented here is not intended to perpetuate Black male pathologies, but rather for the purpose of critically examining the societal conditions that contribute to the manifestation of observed patterns among Black males. In the face of adversity, like many Black males in the U.S., Young accessed and leveraged vital forms of CCW including aspirational capital and familial capital (Yosso, 2005). Aspirational capital was demonstrated in his immense desire to improve the plight of his family by utilizing his unique skill set to earn a college scholarship, a degree, and become a professional football player. However, the most powerful source of strength for Young was his familial capital particularly with his mother and grandmother who instilled in him a strong foundation of faith and core values that enabled him to overcome his early life challenges (OWN, 2015). Additionally, the presence and support of his siblings, extended family, and kinship in his local community also played a pivotal role in his development, perseverance, and success.

As a high school quarterback in Texas, Young earned state and national recognition for his performances. Over the course of his high school career, he threw for nearly 13, 000 yards as a three year starter (Texas Sports, 2018). In 2002, he enrolled at the University of Texas (UT) on a full athletic scholarship. His most decorated season was in 2005 during his junior year when he earned All-American honors and starred in arguably the greatest college football game in U.S. history in the 2006 Rose Bowl in Pasadena, California. In a title-bout style game, Young led the Longhorns by throwing for over 260 yards and rushing for another 200 yards including 3 TDs. In one of the most miraculous plays in U.S. sports history, Young rushed for a game-winning TD in the whining seconds to secure the Longhorns 41–38 victory over the highly favored University of Southern California Trojans. He completed his college career as one of the most accomplished quarterbacks in UT history and his jersey was retired in 2008 (Texas Sports, 2018). Following this season, Young entered the NFL Draft and was selected third overall by the Tennessee Titans (Johnson, 2018). Young experienced early success in the league by earning Offensive Rookie of the Year in 2006. However, his career was marred with injuries, issues with his head coach, and unfulfilled expectations. By 2012, he was no longer in the NFL.

As the case with many Black quarterbacks in the NFL, Young faced racist stereotypes about his intellectual and technical abilities to play the position as an elite pocket passer versus his "natural" athletic abilities to run (Eitzen & Sanford, 1975; Loy & Elvogue, 1970; Sailes, 2010). Despite, his decorated performances at the highest level of college football as a starting quarterback, Young's abilities were questioned based on his race and the longstanding racist stereotypes attributed to Black male quarterbacks. During this same time, coupled with on-the-field challenges, Young began to experience psychological and personal issues off the field. In 2008, after suffering a medial collateral ligament (MCL) strain, it was reported by his head coach from conversations with Young's therapist that he reportedly referenced having suicidal thoughts multiple times (ESPN, 2013). In 2010, he was charged for assault at a Dallas Nightclub. Aside from frustrations with his experiences with the business culture of the NFL, Young cited family issues as the reason why he considered retirement after his rookie season. In 2013, Young was no longer in the NFL and $2 million in debt (Associated Press, 2013). Young's personal troubles were connected to public issues that impact thousands of Black males who grow up the impact of Black males who grow up with in a society that limits the life chances for Black males and subjects them to intergenerational economic deprivation (e.g., lack of financial literacy, wealth acquisition, etc.), untreated trauma (e.g., psychological, social, etc.), and overall structural conditions that devalue Black humanity/self-worth.

At this point, Young's story is synonymous with many Black male athletes who experience the ISSM and those who have negative life outcomes as a result of experiencing the harsh realities (as opposed to the glamorized aspects) of the EALM. Despite the fact that mass media outlets focus on Young's challenges and unfulfilled expectations, emblematic of Black male athletes in the TRM his story did not end with him in financial debt, athletic dejection, and personal turmoil. Leveraging his familial, social, aspirational, and navigational capital (Yosso, 2005), Young earned his bachelor's degree in Education from UT in 2013. He currently owns a real estate agency and volunteers with the Neighborhood Longhorns Program, which is a program that assists youth in Austin, Texas from economically disadvantaged neighborhoods with academic and social support (Johnson, 2018). The presence and utilization of vital forms of CCW enabled him to experience ITE as a progressive adapter. Contrast to dominant ideologies that position Blacks as a perpetually and innately regressive group, Black males (athletes and non-athletes) who experience ITE embody the essence of Black resiliency, resolve, and excellence throughout human history including pre- and post-enslavement in the U.S. (Bush & Bush, 2013a, 2013b). As opposed to theories such promulgating the ISSM (e.g., social reproduction theory, athletic role engulfment, athletic manifest destiny), a comprehensive analysis of the heterogeneous experiences of Black male athletes reveals their active resistance and ability to counter stereotypical expectations of them to experience ITE.

Another standout Black male athlete who exemplifies the TRM is Marcus Lattimore. Lattimore was a heralded football star from Duncan, South Carolina. Growing up in a small town in Southeastern Conference (SEC) football country where the sport is comparable to a religion and success in this arena means one will be revered for ages (CSRI, 2018). In the Southeastern U.S., football is a rite of passage for many males across racial groups, but it also has a unique purpose for Black males who have found this space to be one of the few areas where they are celebrated and coveted by Whites. The popularity and economic vitality of high school, college, and professional football in the South along with the primary laborers being Black males eerily resembles the pre-Civil War racial, economic, political, and sociocultural arrangements in the U.S. (Hawkins, 2010; Rhoden, 2006). Hence, the collective memory in this region for Black males (as well as White onlookers) perpetuates a normalcy of the racist (albeit subtle to the common spectator) entertainment spectacle and concurrent interest convergence (Hawkins, Carter-Francique, & 2017).

Before proceeding with Lattimore's story, it is important to discuss the socio-historical context that precedes and informs the environment he and other Black males in the U.S. encounter. Understanding this context allows for a more comprehensive lens for analyzing their lived experiences. In 1850, there were an estimated 3.2 million African Americans enslaved in the U.S., including 872, 924 males, a majority of which were living in the South (Alexander, 2012; DuVernay, Barish, & Averick, 2016; U.S. Census, 2018). Similar demographic trends remain evident in the early 21st century whereby according to the 2010 U.S. Census data, 55% of the African American population in the U.S. were located in the South (Rastogi, Johnson, Hoeffel, & Drewery, 2011). After the *Emancipation Proclamation of 1865*, the passage of the 13th, 14th, and 15th amendments, and the Reconstruction era (1865–1877), the latter part of the 19th and early part of the 20th century was filled with White backlash in response to the abolishment of slavery (Hine, Hine, & Harrold, 2006). In Southern states where slavery was not only a way of life, but the primary source of economic sustainability, Whites in these areas viewed and treated Blacks with particular disdain. Public lynchings were commonplace and indicative of the vitriol Whites had towards Blacks (Wells-Barnett, 1892, 1997). Consequently, HWIs and their athletic programs excluded Blacks during this period. In fact aside from HBCUs, the limited number of Blacks who were granted access postsecondary education were located in the Northeast, Midwestern, and Western regions of the U.S. (e.g., Rutgers, Cornell, Ohio State, and UCLA to name a few) (Wiggins, 2000).

As noted in Chapter 1, it was not until after Jackie Robinson famously broke the color barrier in MLB in 1947 when Blacks were allowed to participate in mainstream sports in the U.S. across all levels (Wiggins, 2000). At the college level, White-controlled athletic governing bodies such as the National Association for Intercollegiate Athletics (NAIA) and the NCAA did not allow HBCUs as members until 1953 and 1965, respectively (Cooper, Cavil, & Cheeks, 2014; Hodge, Collins, & Bennett, 2013). However, Black athletes were not recruited in mass until after the 1970s. A watershed moment that led to this shift occurred in 1970. During this year, in a season opener between the University of Southern California Trojans whom had Black and White players versus the all-White legendary Alabama Crimson Tide led by

Paul "Bear" Bryant, Sam "Bam" Cunningham (a Black male) rushed for 135 yards and scored two TDs as the underdog Trojans defeated the Crimson Tide 42–21 (Cooper, Cavil, & Cheeks, 2014; Hodge, Collins, & Bennett, 2013). After this victory, Coach Bryant publicly acknowledged the need to recruit talented Black athletes, which signified a psychological and cultural shift from the post-Reconstruction racial exclusion era to the post-Civil Rights racial assimilation era. In fact, the SEC was the last major intercollegiate athletic conference to allow Blacks to participate on athletic teams in 1967 (Wiggins, 2000). Therefore, Whites in the South similar to their predecessors viewed Blacks as commodities for economic exploitation and only deemed them to be acceptable in their presence so as long as they were in a subservient role (i.e., White controlling coaches, administrators, and financially contributing fans such as alumni *overseeing* Black athletic labor). Hence, the reference to athletic spaces such as football fields particularly in the South as *the new plantation* that reproduce the same racial hierarchies and power arrangements as the 17th through late 19th centuries in Confederate states (Hawkins, 2010).

Replacing the economic production associated with cotton, tobacco, sugar, and other cash crops, athletic entertainment (along with mass incarceration – as outlined in Chapters 1 and 2), became one of the South's new revenue generating sources where Black male bodies continued to serve as a central labor force. Given this economic arrangement, for Black males in the South, the use of their physical prowess to fulfill the desires of economically and politically powerful Whites (in terms of ownership of land and monetary resources) constituted a rite of passage into Black manhood where they could financially provide for their families since Black ownership was significantly limited. This psychological deduction is akin to Henderson's (1939) philosophy of muscular assimilationism, which was prevalent in the Black community during the early 20th century. A cursory overview of the geographical backgrounds of NFL players in conjunction with a general knowledge of racial migration patterns in the U.S. reveals the deeply embedded nature of this racist arrangement (Allison, Davis, & Barranco, 2016). As such, contextual factors such as geography, history, and culture greatly shape Black males' identity development (e.g., racial, masculine, etc.) and sport participation choices, experiences, and outcomes.

Fast forward to Lattimore's story, he was considered one of the best football players in the U.S. from 2008–2010 and earned national recognition (CSRI, 2018). He was recruited by the nation's top football programs and decided to attend his home state school, the University of South Carolina, which is a member of the heralded SEC. During his freshman season, he eclipsed school records with 1, 197 rushing yards, 17 rushing TDs, and 19 total TDs (Aschoff, 2016). However, mid-way through his sophomore campaign in 2011, he suffered ACL and MCL injuries including torn knee ligaments in his left knee. The following year, he experienced another leg injury, which was diagnosed as a dislocated right knee with nerve damage (Aschoff, 2016). After this second knee injury with nerve damage, the doctors said there was high likelihood he would never be able to walk comfortably on two legs again. He was drafted in the fourth round of the 2013 NFL draft to the San Francisco 49ers and had a one year stint with them. However, he was unable to return to previous form and subsequently retired before completing his second season. Following these injuries along with the passing of his grandparents, he experienced depressive symptoms consistent with human encounters with non-normative life circumstances (Aschoff, 2016; Brofenbrenner, 1977). However, as previously mentioned, Black males are a distinct population in the U.S. and encounter "non-normative" circumstances on a consistent basis given their positionality within a society founded upon and structured by WRC. More specifically, Black male athletes who experience athletic role engulfment are particularly vulnerable to the intense long-term effects of post-athletic career disengagement trauma in concert with other normative and non-normative transitional challenges facing them in a gendered racist society.

During a discussion panel at the *2018 College Sport Research Institute* conference, Lattimore candidly discussed his athletic career and retirement experiences (CSRI, 2018). Regarding his athletic career as a Black male college athlete at a HWI in the South, he described the difficulties he and his teammates faced trying to balance academic and personal responsibilities while managing the intense pressures and time commitments associated with being a major Division I football player in one of the premier football conferences in the country. Like many college athletes, he explained how he was encouraged to enroll in a major that was convenient for maintaining eligibility and fitting within the pre-established athletic schedule as opposed to pursuing a major that was in alignment with his personal interests. This practice of academic clustering or majoring in eligibility has been cited in the literature and illustrates the academic exploitation of Black male college athletes (Beamon, 2008; Cooper & Cooper, 2015; Fountain & Finley, 2009; Oseguera, 2010). This academic exploitation involves the needs of White institutions and athletic departments being placed above the academic interests and educational needs of Black male college athletes who are persistently overrepresented in the highest revenue generating sports of football and basketball, yet more likely to be academically clustered, graduate a lower rates than their peers, and less likely to be satisfied with their college experiences compared to their White counterparts (Cooper, 2012; Cooper, Davis, & Dougherty, 2017; Fountain & Finley, 2009). In conjunction with being academically clustered, Lattimore also felt he could not fully explore his holistic identity while competing because the stakes for him to perform well athletically were all consuming. Therein lies the exploitative nature of the current structure of big-time college sports for Black males (Cooper, Nwadike, & Macaulay, 2017).

Despite these obstacles, similar to Young, Lattimore was a progressive adapter and later experienced ITE. In 2016, he graduated from the University of South Carolina with a degree in Public Health. Using his reputation, familial capital, social capital, and what I call *spiritual capital*,[2] he persevered and experienced ITE (Cooper, 2017). In addition to earning his bachelor's degree, he started his own foundation called *The Marcus Lattimore Foundation*. This foundation financially assists high school athletes with major injury rehabilitation as well as it includes a college and life development component. He operates his own youth football camps, organizes outreach for the underserved in the local community, and currently works as Director of Player Development for his alma mater's football team and serves as an Assistant Coach for the Heathwood Hall high school football team (Aschoff, 2016). As with all athletes, he experienced some level of post-athletic career disengagement trauma (Edwards, 1984), but considering his previous level of stardom conventional wisdom would expect him to experience an extensive identity crisis. In true progressive adapter form, Lattimore explained the fullness of his ITE:

> Life is a little bit more enjoyable now because of what I've been through ... I wouldn't change a thing that happened—put those knee injuries back in my life. I'm such a better person, overall. I'm wiser and I'm grateful for every single day that I get out of bed and I can walk, and I can run if I want to. The little things, they matter a little bit more than they did in the past ... I'm thankful for those knee injuries. They really saved me and now I feel like I can do anything. Every time I go speak, every time I'm able to stand in front of a crowd, I heal personally. (Aschoff, 2016, p. 1)

At the CSRI (2018) panel, Lattimore attributed his resolve and holistic perspective to his faith. Spirituality is a major component of Black and African Diasporic cultures (Boykin, 1986; Constantine et al., 2003; Douglas, 2016; Douglas & Peck, 2013) and previous research has documented its salience among Black male athletes (Cooper, 2009; Douglas, Ivey, & Bishop, 2015; Gragg & Flowers, 2014). In concert with Yosso's (2005) conception of CCW,

Black males in the TRM leverage vital social and familial capital to overcome difficult circumstances in a society designed to holistically under develop and exploit them. In contrast to popular notions that stigmatize Black male athletes' families as liabilities, the magnification of these counter-stories offers a more accurate and nuance depiction of the role Black communal systems fulfill as life lines for Black male athletes. In addition, Lattimore's spiritual and aspirational capital are an inspiration to all who know his story. He epitomized the essence of his character and the promise that undergirds the TRM when he said: "There's always light on the other side of the tunnel. I'm living proof of it". (Aschoff, 2016, p.1)

If you can recall the stories of Lenny Cooke and Kevin Ross from Chapter 4, their journeys did not end with the ISSM. Based on the extent and length of their post-athletic career disengagement trauma (Edwards, 1984), there stories were illustrative of the ISSM. However, as progressive adapters both of them experienced ITE later in their adult life. In 2014, Cooke married his longtime significant other, Anita Solomon, and he is currently coaching high school basketball and touring the country as a motivational speaker and sharing his documentary. Similar to Lattimore, in true TRM fashion, Cooke is using his story and platform to empower other young Black males to avoid the pitfalls he experienced. Ross became literate thanks to the help of his mentor Marva Collins (Cohn, 2006). He later sued Creighton University in 1990 for breach of contract and the university settled with him for $30, 000. This seminal case provided a precedent for college athletes to use the legal system to hold exploitative institutions of higher education accountable for creating conducive learning environments for educational attainment as opposed to normalizing academic fraud, exploitation, and malpractice (Davis, 1992; Donnor, 2005; Sellers, 2000; Smith & Willingham, 2015). Thus, ITE not only facilitates personal development, but also stimulates action among Black male athletes to challenge and alter the systems they experienced.

This counter-action is a core aspect of strategic responsiveness to interest convergence (SRIC), which is a tool utilized to cultivate empowerment and consciousness among Black male college athletes (this concept is explored in greater detailed in Chapter 7). In addition, Ross became a father of three children. Like Lattimore and Cooke, he became a motivational speaker and shares his poignant story across the country (Cohn, 2006). From the film *Hoop Dreams* (James & Marx, 1994), Arthur Agee established a foundation to support the education of inner city youth and created a sportswear line and William Gates became a senior pastor at a community center (Singer & May,

2010). As such those who experience the negative outcomes of the ISSM and at times the EALM, *always* have the possibility of evolving to the TRM so as long as they are physically alive (i.e., early adapters and progressive adapters). However, as noted in Chapter 1, the tragedy is too many of them experience holistic death figuratively and literally before reaching their ITE. Thus, promoting the stories of Black male athletes in the TRM serves as an emancipatory tool to break the cycle of exploitation and holistic underdevelopment through the systematic production of Black male athletic role engulfment, identity foreclosure, and holistic suppression/suffocation and death.

Along with the lack of attention to the stories of Black males who experience the TRM in mass media there is also a conspicuous omission of these narratives in scholarly literature. However, there is an emerging body of literature that has highlighted Black male former athletes who have experienced successful transitional outcomes. For example, Sellers (2000) documented the story of Dr. Thomas LaVeist who was a former football player at the University of Maryland Eastern Shore (UMES). LaVeist grew up in a low-income neighborhood in Brooklyn, New York where the odds were stacked against him to experience upward mobility. During his youth and adolescence, LaVeist possessed strong academic prowess, but due to various circumstances he performed below his abilities. Hence, his early exposure to environmental stressors resulted in his holistic underdevelopment via athletic role engulfment and academic role abandonment. His breakthrough occurred after he was granted an athletic scholarship to UMES. During his tenure in college, LaVeist excelled academically and later went on to earn a doctorate in medical sociology. As a professor in the Johns Hopkins University School of Public Health, he published impactful research and inspired hundreds of students. LaVeist's story is an example of the TRM because he initially focused on athletics more than academics, but due to the influence of socialization factors (i.e., influential family and mentors—CCW (Yosso, 2005)) and the educational opportunity to attend UMES he was able to successfully pursue positive life outcomes during and after college (Sellers, 2000).

Along the same lines, in Northcutt's (2013) qualitative study of African American male former Division I and NFL football players, four out of the six participants earned their bachelor's degrees and two of the participants earned doctorates. All six participants reported having a strong athletic identity in college and experiencing challenges balancing their holistic needs while fulfilling their responsibilities as Division I football players. As previously mentioned, the system of sports in a neoliberal capitalist society is designed for Black males to maximize their athletic skills while there is little to no concern for their personal development beyond sports. This miseducation is exacerbated at the college level as documented in Chapter 2. The participants' experiences with intense athletic role conflict signified one of the many consequences of these types of athletic-centric cultures and corresponding socialization processes. As a result, five out of the six participants cited experiencing post-athletic career disengagement trauma. One of the participants was an early adapter to ITE and the other five were progressive adapters. At the time of the study, the following educational and occupational information was recorded: a) Tre—Assistant Director of Championships for the SEC, b) Brad—earned his master's degree in Gifted Education and doctorate in Health Education and Wellness Promotion and worked with a private foundation focused on education, c) Eddie—became an entrepreneur and started a foundation that raises money for lupus research called Quick Start, d) Kolby —worked as an Assistant Football Coach (Running Backs) at Western Kentucky University, e) Tommy—earned his master's degree in Adult Education and doctorate in Educational Foundations, Leadership, and Technology and worked in Student-Athlete Support Services at the Auburn University, and f) Kendrell—became an entrepreneur and real estate agent (Northcutt, 2013).

Another example of the TRM in scholarly research is reflective in a one of my recent studies conducted with my colleagues where we examined the college and post-college life experiences of the founders and initial members of a culturally relevant holistic development program (CRHD) program grounded in the Excellence Beyond Athletics (EBA) framework (Cooper, 2016b) called Collective Uplift (CU). Along with a group of Black male college athletes at the University of Connecticut (UConn), I co-founded CU during the Fall 2014 semester (Cooper et al., 2017; Collective Uplift, 2018). The purpose of CU is to empower, educate, support, and inspire Black athletes to maximize their full potential as holistic individuals both within and beyond athletic contexts (Collective Uplift, 2018). From our initial study with participants involved in the group, findings revealed nine recent CU alumni (five of which were founding members) earned their bachelor's degrees within five years of their initial enrollment in college. Additional findings regarding their post-graduation outcomes indicated the following outcomes as of 2018: a) Niner[3] (Psychology BA) is enrolled in a School Counseling master's program, b) John Albert Reyes (Sociology BA) played three years in the NFL and currently finishing his second year in a Sport Management master's program, c) Juice (Political Science BA) earned his master's degree in Special Education and working as Primary and Secondary Educator, d) Sean (Economics BA) is a Financial Advisor and works for Merrill Lynch (Bank of America), e) Geremy Christian (Sociology BA) works as a Juvenile

Detention Center and Law Enforcement Officer, f) Justice Vance (Communications BA) earned his master's degree in Public Administration, founded his own marketing and branding company, started a chapter of CU at Old Dominion University in 2016, a proud member of Omega Psi Phi Fraternity Incorporated, and currently interning with a Division I athletics department in their Student Athlete Leadership Office, g) Vessel (Urban Youth Development and Health BA) earned his master's degree in Special Education and currently working as a Christian Ministry Leader, h) Hillary (Communications BA) is currently playing in the NFL, and i) Clinton (Business Management BS) earned his real estate license and working as a realtor while continuing to pursue an NFL career (Cooper et al., 2017). All of the participants in both Northcutt's (2013) and our study (Cooper et al., 2018) were subjected to sport and miseducation schooling conditions that fostered Black male athletic role engulfment and identity foreclosure. Yet, due to their access to and activation of vital CCW (Yosso, 2005), they were able to overcome these obstacles via the TRM and experience ITE and positive life outcomes after their athletic careers concluded.

Chapter Summary

This chapter highlighted the conditions that facilitate the socialization processes of Black male athletes who experience the TRM. As noted, Black male athletes who experience the ISSM and EALM can and often do successfully overcome post-athletic career disengagement trauma, identity crisis, identity foreclosure, career under preparation, and holistic underdevelopment. The transmission and activation of CCW, EBA framework, and related sources of support enable Black male athletes to acquire an authentic perspective on their sporting and (mis)educational experiences after their athletic careers conclude and more importantly they experience ITE. The lack of attention in mainstream media and academic literature on Black male athletes who experience the TRM illustrates the continued gendered racism imposed upon this group in covert and overt ways in order to sustain the perpetual oppression of Blacks in the U.S. via systems that holistically underserve and under develop them. This chapter offered a few of the countless stories of Black male athletes who defy the odds and experience holistic development in a society founded upon and structured by WRC. Consistent with the legacy of African people across the world including the Black liberation struggle and resistance efforts in the U.S., Black males who experience the TRM reflect the resiliency, resolve, redemption, and unbreakable spirit of this group.

Notes

1. The use of affirmative and non-deficit oriented terms to describe Black males is consistent with my previous work and underscores my philosophical underpinnings with Afrocentric and Black collectivist orientations whereby Blackness inherently contains infinite positive potential for growth especially in the face of unfavorable conditions (Cooper, 2009, 2016; Cooper & Cooper, 2015).
2. Spiritual capital refers to the possession of faith and connection to a Higher Being/Entity and/or forces beyond the observable world that enable a person to experience immeasurable fulfillment, sense of purpose, and ability to overcome challenging life circumstances. Spiritual capital is often nurtured through exposure and involvement to religious scriptures and/or institutions or groups (e.g., churches, mosques, synagogues, temples, etc.).
3. These names are pseudonyms selected by the participants to preserve their anonymity.

References

Alexander, M. (2012). *The new Jim Crow: Mass incarceration in the age of colorblindness*. New York, NY: The New Press.

Allison, R., Davis, A., & Barranco, R. (2016). A comparison of hometown socioeconomics and demographics for black and white elite football players in the US. *International Review for the Sociology of Sport, 53*(5), 1–15. DOI: 10.1177/1012690216674936.

Anderson, J. D. (1988). *The education of Blacks in the South: 1860–1935*. Chapel Hill, NC: The University of North Carolina Press.

Aschoff, E. (2016, May 17). The rise, and fall, and rise again of Marcus Lattimore. *ESPN*. Retrieved from http://www.espn.com/college-football/story/_/id/15528475/former-south-carolina-gamecocks-rb-marcus-lattimore-finds-new-life-happiness-knee-injuries

Associated Press. (2013, February 12). Ex-adviser: Vince Young needed loan for $300, 000 party. *USA Today*. Retrieved from https://www.usatoday.com/story/sports/nfl/2013/02/12/vince-young-lockout-party-ronnie-peoples/1913655/

Beamon, K. K. (2008). "Used goods": Former African American college student-athletes' perception of exploitation by division I universities. *The Journal of Negro Education, 77*(4), 352–364.

Beamon, K. K. (2010). Are sports overemphasized in the socialization process of African American males? A qualitative analysis of former collegiate athletes' perception of sport socialization. *Journal of Black Studies, 41*(2), 281–300.

Beamon, K. (2012). "I'm a baller": Athletic identity foreclosure among African American former student-athletes. *Journal of African American Studies, 16*(2), 195–208.

Beamon, K., & Bell, P. A. (2002). "Going pro": The deferential effects of high aspirations for a professional sports career on African-American student athletes and White student athletes. *Race & Society, 5*(2), 179–191.

Bell, D. A. (1980). Brown v. Board of Education and the interest convergence dilemma. *Harvard Law Review, 93*(3), 518–533.

Bell, D. A. (1992). *Faces at the bottom of the well: The permanence of racism.* New York, NY: Basic Books.

Benson, K. F. (2000). Constructing academic inadequacy: African American athletes' stories of schooling. *The Journal of Higher Education, 71*(2), 223–246.

Bimper, A. Y. (2016). Capital matters: Social sustaining capital and the development of Black student-athletes. *Journal of Intercollegiate Sport, 9*(1), 106–128.

Bimper, A. Y. (2017). Mentorship of Black student-athletes at a predominately White American university: Critical race theory perspective on student-athlete development. *Sport, Education and Society, 22*(2), 175–193.

Boyd, T. (2003). *Young, Black, rich, and famous: The rise of the NBA, the hip-hop invasion and the transformation of American culture.* New York, NY: Doubleday.

Boykin, A. W. (1986). *The school achievement of minority children: New perspectives.* Hillsdale, NJ: Lawrence Erlbaum Associates.

Bronfenbrenner, U. (1977). Toward an experimental ecology of human development. *American Psychologist, 32*(7), 513–531.

Bush, L. V., & Bush, E. C. (2013a). Introducing African American male theory (AAMT). *Journal of African American Males in Education, 4*(1), 6–17.

Bush, L. V., & Bush, E. C. (2013b). God bless the child who got his own: Toward a comprehensive theory for African-American boys and men. The Western Journal of Black Studies, 37(1), 1–13.

Coakley, J. (2017). *Sports in society: Issues and controversies* (12th ed.). New York, NY: McGraw-Hill Education.

Cohn, L. (2006, December 10). Humiliation to triumph: A student-athlete's odyssey. *The Press Democrat.* Retrieved from http://www.pressdemocrat.com/news/2120248-181/humiliation-to-triumph-a-student-athletes

Collective Uplift (2018). *Goals page.* Retrieved from http://www.collectiveuplift.com

Constantine, M. G., Gainor, K. A., Ahluwalia, M. K., & Berkel, L. A. (2003). Independent and interdependent self-construals, individualism, collectivism, and harmony control in African Americans. *Journal of Black Psychology, 29*(1), 87–101.

Cooper, J. N. (2009). *The relationship between the critical success factors and academic and athletic success: A quantitative case study of Black male football student-athletes at a major Division I southeastern institution.* (Unpublished thesis). Chapel Hill, NC: University of North Carolina at Chapel Hill.

Cooper, J. N. (2012). Personal troubles and public issues: A sociological imagination of Black athletes' experiences at predominantly White institutions in the United States. *Sociology Mind, 2*(3), 261–271.

Cooper, J. N. (2016a). "Focus on the bigger picture:" An anti-deficit achievement examination of Black male scholar athletes in science and engineering at a Division I historically White university (HWU). *Whiteness & Education, 1*(2), 109–124.

Cooper, J. N. (2016b). Excellence beyond athletics: Best practices for enhancing Black male student athletes' educational experiences and outcomes. *Equity & Excellence in Education, 49*(3), 267–283.

Cooper, J. N. (2017). Strategic navigation: A comparative study of Black male scholar athletes' experiences at a Historically Black college/university (HBCU) and Historically White university (HWU). *International Journal of Qualitative Studies in Education, 31*(4), 235–256. doi: 10.1080/09518398.2017.1379617.

Cooper, J. N., Cavil, J. K., & Cheeks, G. (2014). The state of intercollegiate athletics at historically Black colleges and universities (HBCUs): Past, present, & persistence. *Journal of Issues in Intercollegiate Athletics, 7*, 307–332.

Cooper, J. N., & Cooper, J. E. (2015). "I'm running so you can be happy and I can keep my scholarship": A comparative study of Black male college athletes'experiences with role conflict. *Journal of Intercollegiate Sport, 8*(2), 131–152.

Cooper, J. N., Corral, M. D., Macaulay, C. D. T., Cooper, M. S., Nwadike, A., & Mallery, Jr., M. (2018). Collective uplift: The impact of a holistic development support program on Black male former college athletes' experiences and outcomes. *International Journal of Qualitative Studies in Education*, DOI: 10.1080/09518398.2018.1522011.

Cooper, J. N., Davis, T. J., & Dougherty, S. (2017). Not so Black and White: A multi-divisional exploratory analysis of male student-athletes' experiences at National Collegiate Athletic Association (NCAA) institutions. *Sociology of Sport Journal, 34*(1), 59–78.

Cooper, J. N., Macaulay, C., & Rodriguez, S. H. (2017). Race and resistance: A typology of African American sport activism. *International Review for the Sociology of Sport*, 1–31. doi: 10.1177/1012690217718170.

Cooper, J. N., Mallery, M., & Macaulay, C. D. T. (forthcoming). African American sport activism and broader social movements. In D. Brown (Ed.). *Passing the ball: Sports in African American life and culture* (pp. 35–51). Jefferson, NC: McFarland & Company.

Cooper, J. N., Nwadike, A., & Macaulay, C. (2017). A critical race theory analysis of big-time college sports: Implications for culturally responsive and race-conscious sport leadership. *Journal of Issues in Intercollegiate Athletics, 10*, 204–233.

Corben, B. (2012). *Broke.* [Documentary]. ESPN Films (Distributor). Invincible Pictures: Rakontur.

CSRI (2018, April 13). Athlete career transitions: Where do go from here? *College Sport Research Institute.* Columbia, South Carolina.

Curry, T. J. (2017). *The man-not: Race, class, genre, and the dilemmas of Black manhood.* Philadelphia, PA: Temple University Press.

Davis, T. (1992). Examining educational malpractice jurisprudence: Should a cause of action be created for student-athletes? *Denver University Law Review, 69*, 57–96.

Dohrmann, G. (2010). *Play their hearts out: A coach, his star recruit, and the youth basketball machine.* New York, NY: Ballatine Books.

Donnor J. K. (2005). Towards an interest-convergence in the education of African-American football student athletes in major college sports. *Race, Ethnicity and Education, 8*(1), 45–67.

Douglas, T. (2016). *Border crossing brothas: Black males navigating race, place, and complex space.* New York, NY: Peter Lang.

Douglas, T., Ivey, P., & Bishop, K. (2015). Identity, leadership, and success: A study of Black male student-athletes at the University of Missouri. *National Collegiate Athletic Association (NCAA) Innovations Grant.* [Final Report]. Retrieved from https://www.ncaa.org/sites/default/files/Douglas%2C%20Ivey%2C%20Bishop%2C%20NCAA%20

Final%20Report%2C%20Black%20Male%20Student%20Athlete%20Study%2C%20
1.4.2016%2C%20submitted.pdf

Douglas, T. M., & Peck, C. (2013). Education by any means necessary: Peoples of African descent and community-based pedagogical spaces. *Educational Studies*, 49(1), 67–91.

DuVernay, A., Barish, H., & Averick, S. (2016). *13th*. [Documentary]. Forward Movement. United States: Kandoo Films.

Edwards, H. (1969). *The revolt of the Black athlete*. New York, NY: Free Press.

Edwards, H. (1980). *The struggle that must be: An autobiography*. New York, NY: Macmillan Publishing.

Edwards, H. (1984). The Black "dumb jock": An American sports tragedy. *College Board Review, 131*, 8–13.

Edwards, H. (2000). Crisis of black athletes on the eve of the 21st century. *Society*, 37, 9–13.

Edwards, H. (2016). *The fourth wave: Black athlete protests in the second decade of the 21st century*. Keynote address at the North American Society for the Sociology of Sport (NASSS) conference in Tampa Bay, Florida.

Eitzen, D. S., & Sanford, D. C. (1975). The segregation of blacks by playing position in football: Accident or design? *Social Science Quarterly*, 55(4), 948–959.

Emdin, C., & Lee, O. (2012). Hip-hop, the "Obama Effect," and urban science education. *Teachers College Record, 114* (2), 1–24.

ESPN (2013). Fisher reached out to police because therapist said Young mentioned suicide. Retrieved from http://www.espn.com/nfl/news/story?id=3584636

ESPN (2018). Kevin Durant and Michael Beasley walk down memory lane in exclusive sit-down interview. *ESPN News*. Retrieved from https://www.youtube.com/watch?v= pxRV0hZbA7M

ETS. (2011). *A strong start: Positioning young Black boys for educational success a statistical profile*. Washington, DC: Educational Testing Service.

Feagin, J., Vera, H., & Batur, P. (2000). *White racism* (2nd ed.). New York, NY: Routledge.

Fountain, J. J., & Finley, P. S. (2009). Academic majors of upperclassmen football players in the Atlantic Coast Conference: An analysis of academic clustering comparing White and Minority players. *Journal of Issues in Intercollegiate Athletics*, 2, 1–13.

Friedkin, W. (1994). *Blue chips* [movie]. Paramount Pictures (Distributor).

George, N. (1992). *Elevating the game: Black men and basketball*. New York, NY: HarperCollins.

Gragg, D., & Flowers, R. D. (2014). Factors that positively affect academic performance of African American football studentathletes. *Journal for the Study of Sports and Athletes in Education*, 8(2), 77–98.

Greenburg, R. (2016). *Running for his life: The Lawrence Phillips Story*. [Documentary]. Showtime.

Hancock, J. L. (2009). *The blind side* [Film]. United States: Alcon Entertainment. Left Tackle Pictures. Netter Productions.

Hawkins, B. (2010). *The new plantation: Black athletes, college sports, and predominantly White NCAA institutions*. New York, NY: Palgrave MacMillan.

Hawkins, B., Carter-Francique, A. R., & Cooper, J. N. (2017). *Critical race theory: Black athletic sporting experiences in the United States*. New York, NY: Palgrave Macmillan.

Henderson, E. B. (1939). *The Negro in sports*. Washington, DC: The Associated Publishers.

Hine, D. C., Hine, W. C., & Harrold, S. (2006). *The African-American odyssey: Since 1965* (Third ed. Vol. Two). Upper Saddle River, NJ: Pearson Prentice Hall.

Hodge, S. R., Collins, F. G., & Bennett, R. A., III, (2013). The journey of the Black athlete on the HBCU playing field. In D. Brooks & R. Althouse (Eds.), *Racism in college athletics* (pp. 105–134). Morgantown, WV: Fitness Information Technology.

Howard, T. C. (2014). *Black male(d): Peril and promise in the education of African American males.* New York, NY: Teachers College Press.

James, S., & Marx, F. (1994). *Hoop dreams* [documentary]. Minneapolis, MN: Kartemquin Films.

Johnson, M. (2018, January 24). Vince Young remembers the Titans. *ESPN's The Undefeated.* Retrieved from https://theundefeated.com/features/black-quarterback-vince-young-remembers-the-titans/

Kelly, D. D., & Dixon, M. A. (2014). Successfully navigating life transitions among African American male student-athletes: A review and examination of constellation mentoring as a promising strategy. *Journal of Sport Management, 28*(5), 498–514.

Leonard, D. J., & King, C. R. (2012). *Commodified and criminalized: New racism and African Americans in contemporary sports.* Lanham, MD: Rowman & Littlefield.

Love, B. L. (2014). Urban storytelling: How storyboarding, moviemaking, and hip-hop-based education can promote students' critical voice. *The English Journal, 103*(5), 53–58.

Loy, J. W., & Elvogue, J. F. (1970). Racial segregation in American sport. *International Review for the Sociology of Sport, 5*(1), 5–24.

Majors, R., & Billson, J. M. (1992). *Cool pose: The dilemmas of Black manhood in America.* New York, NY: Lexington Books.

Messner, M. (1990). Masculinities and athletic careers: Bonding and status differences. In D. Sabo & M. Messner (Eds.), *Sport, men, and the gender order: Critical feminist perspectives* (pp. 97–108). Champaign, IL: Human Kinetics.

Noguera, P. A. (2008). *The trouble with Black boys … and other reflections on race, equity, and the future of public education.* San Francisco, CA: Jossey-Bass.

Northcutt, K. J. (2013). *The dilemma: Career transition of African American male football players at Division I institutions.* Dissertation. University of Mississippi.

Nwadike, A. C. Baker, A. R., Brackebusch, V. B., & Hawkins, B. J. (2016). Institutional Racism in the NCAA and the racial implications of the "2.3 or take a knee" legislation. *Marquette Sports Law Review, 26*(2), 523–543.

Oseguera, L. (2010). Success despite the image: How African American male student-athletes endure their academic journey amidst negative characterizations. *Journal for the Study of Sports and athletes in Education, 4*(3), 297–324.

OWN (2015). In deep shift with Jonas Elrod. OWN website. Retrieved from http://www.oprah.com/own-indeepshift/does-vince-young-want-to-get-back-into-the-nfl-video *Plessy v. Ferguson*, 163 U.S. 537 (1896).

Rastogi, S., Johnson, T. D., Hoeffel, E. M., & Drewery, M. P., Jr. (2011). *The Black population: 2010 census briefs.* U.S. Census website. Retrieved from https://www.census.gov/prod/cen2010/briefs/c2010br-06.pdf

Rhoden, W. C. (2006). *40 million dollar slaves: The rise, fall, and redemption of the Black athlete.* New York, NY: Crown Publishing Group.

Robbins, B., Tollin, M., Laiter T., & Wiley, M. (1999). *Varsity blues* [Film].. Paramount Pictures (Distributor), United States: Tollin/Robbins Productions, MTV Films.

Sailes, G. (2010). The African American athlete: Social myths and stereotypes. In G. Sailes (Ed.), *Modern sport and the African American Athlete Experience* (pp. 55–68). San Diego, CA: Cognella.

Schott Foundation for Public Education (2010). *Yes we can: The Schott 50 state report on public education and Black males* (pp. 1–38). Cambridge, MA: Schott Foundation for Public Education.

Sellers, R. M. (2000). African American student-athletes: Opportunity or exploitation? In D. A. Brooks, R. (Ed.), *Racism in college athletics: The African American athlete's experience* (2nd ed., pp. 133–154). Morgantown, WV: Fitness Information Technology, Inc.

Singer, J. N. (2005). Understanding racism through the eyes of AfricanAmerican male student athletes. *Race, Ethnicity and Education, 8*(4), 365–386.

Singer, J. N. (2009). African American football athletes' perspectives on institutional integrity in college sport. *Research Quarterly for Exercise and Sport, 80*(1), 102–116.

Singer, J. N., & May, R. A. B. (2010). The career trajectory of a Black male high school basketball player: A social reproduction perspective. *International Review for the Sociology of Sport, 46*(3), 299–314.

Smith, E. (2009). *Race, sport and the American dream* (2nd ed.). Durham, NC: Carolina Academic Press.

Smith, J. M., & Willingham, M. (2015). *Cheated: The UNC scandal, the education of athletes, and the future of big-time college sports*. Omaha, NE: University of Nebraska Press.

Southall, R., & Nagel, M. S. (2010). Institutional logics theory: Examining big-time college sport. In E. Smith (Ed.), *Sociology of sport and social theory* (pp. 67–79). Champaign, IL: Human Kinetics.

Southall, R. M., & Staurowsky, E. J. (2013). Cheering on the collegiate model: Creating, disseminating, and imbedding the NCAA's redefinition of amateurism. *Journal of Sport and Social Issues, 37*(4), 403–429.

Texas Sports (2018). Vince Young profile. University of Texas Sports website. Retrieved from https://texassports.com/roster.aspx?rp_id=5058

U.S. Census (2018). Comparative table of population: Table I—Population of the United States Decennially from 1790 to 1850. Retrieved from https://www2.census.gov/library/publications/decennial/1850/1850a/1850a-02.pdf

Wells-Barnett, I. B. (1892/ 1997). *Southern horrors: Lynch law in and all its phases*. In Royster, J. J. (Ed.), Southern horrors and other writings: The anti-lynching campaign of Ida B. Wells, 1892–1900 (pp. 49–72). Boston, MA: Bedford Books.

Wiggins, D. K. (2000). Critical events affecting racism in athletics. In D. Brooks, & R. Althouse (Eds.), *Racism in college athletics: The African American athlete's experience* (2nd ed., pp. 15–36). Morgantown, WV: Fitness Information Technology.

Woodson, C. G. (1933/1990). *The mis-education of the Negro*. Trenton, NJ: Africa World Press.

Yosso, T. J. (2005). Whose culture has capital? A critical race theory discussion of community cultural wealth. *Race, Ethnicity and Education, 8*(1), 69–91.

PURPOSEFUL PARTICIPATION FOR EXPANSIVE PERSONAL GROWTH MODEL

Holistic Development Through Conscious Navigation of Exploitative Systems

> So, when I see statistics that *we* all think *we* can play the game, I know the commentators don't really know *us* … No, lots of us are not obsessed, don't regret that we never made it, but still have a Jones for the game.
>
> —Shropshire (2000, p. xviii)

The Interplay of Systemic Conditions for the Purposeful Participation for Expansive Personal Growth Model and Black Male Athletes

Since the mid-20th century, the *Black dumb jock* myth has been attributed to Black males who were recruited to attend HWIs for their athletic prowess (Edwards, 1984). This pejorative label reflects how the macro-level dominant ideologies of WRC manifest themselves in exosystem level structures and policies, and trickles down to mesosystem interactions and microsystem internalized beliefs and normalized behaviors (see Figure 7.1). In fact, these same racist assertions were disseminated in the late 19th and early 20th century against standout Black athletes within and outside of higher education. Black male college athletes such as Jesse Owens and non-college athletes such as Jack Johnson were labeled as intellectually deficient, yet assumed to possess biological traits that enabled them to excel in their respective sports (Harris,

2000; Sailes, 2010). Fallacious theories such as the *mandingo, survival of the fittest, genetic, psychological mismatch,* and *dumb jock myth* were widely accepted as fact (Sailes, 2010).

More specifically, both the mandingo and survival of the fittest theories attributed African American sport performance during the early 20th century to conditions associated with chattel slavery and the transatlantic slave trade. The mandingo theory posited that since physicality was valued in slavery, White oppressors would force Blacks to selectively procreate based on their physique and thus muscular genes were transmitted intergenerationally. The myth purported that the same skills that made a productive slave would also translate into coveted athletic abilities and prowess. In 1988, Jimmy "The Greek" Snyder, a popular CBS sports broadcaster, infamously promoted this idea on air when he said Blacks' success in sports was due to selective breeding during slavery and Whites were better suited to be coaches and managers (Sailes, 2010; Solomon, 1988). Although, selective breeding was prevalent during chattel slavery (DeGruy, 2005), the idea that one's race and physical abilities would innately determine their intellectual and athletic capacities reinforced racist pseudo-science beliefs such as Social Darwinism. In other words, these socially constructed ideas were created with the intent of systematizing oppressive racial hierarchies rather than being grounded in any objective scientific facts. Snyder was subsequently fired due to nationwide backlash, but the ideas he expressed were not uncommon and in actuality they were often internalized by people of all races who have been exposed to racist ideological hegemony (Hawkins, 1998a; Sage, 1998; Sage & Eitzen, 2013; Sailes, 2010).

Along the same lines, the survival of the fittest theory posits that during the middle passage (also known as the transatlantic slave trade) only the strongest Black Africans survived and consequently these individuals were deemed as "physically superior beings compared to those who perished" (Sailes, 2010, p. 63). The dichotomous belief that Blacks were simultaneously sub- (intellectually inept) and super-human (physically gifted) reflects the socially constructed and malleable (and in my estimation whimsical and arbitrary) nature of ideological assertions designed to justify the racist and inhumane actions of exploitative Whites. To further illustrate this hypocrisy, as noted in Chapter 1, prior to the early 20th century Blacks were considered both inferior intellectually *and* physically and viewed as animals who must be tamed, which justified their enslavement. After the international victories of Major Taylor in cycling from 1898–1910, Isaac Murphy in horseracing from 1882–1884, Jack Johnson in the boxing ring in 1909 and 1910, and Jesse Owens in the 1936 Olympics, the idea of innate athletic inferiority was morphed into physical superiority and intellectual inferiority, which still maintained the status of quo Whites who believed they were predestined to oversee and control the minds and bodies of Blacks as well as other racialized/oppressed groups (Harris, 2000; Wiggins, 2014; Wiggins & Miller, 2003).

The genetic theory asserted that African American sport performance was not explained by environmental and socio-structural conditions combined with personal effort and time spent on skill development, but rather a result of hereditary predispositions. For examples, Sailes (2010) referenced how the genetic theory was promoted in sports media to explain how African Americans' success in sports such as football, basketball, and track and field sprinting events occurred because they supposedly possessed "... more white fast twitch muscle fibers and whites had more slow twitch muscle fibers" (Sailes, 2010, p. 63). Even though, talented Black male athletes such as Paul Robeson (Rutgers University), Jerome "Brud" Holland (Cornell University), and Fritz Pollard (Cornell University) had attended prestigious HWIs in the early 20th century and excelled both academically and athletically, the racist beliefs that Blacks were innately intellectually inferior had already been deeply embedded in the White American psyche (Smith, Clark, & Harrison, 2014). In the same vein as Snyder's endorsement of the mandingo theory, advocates of the psychological theory suggest that Blacks' innate intellectual abilities make them unfit to uphold leadership positions in sport. In 1987, Al Campanis, then Vice President of the Los Angeles Dodgers, in a nationally televised interview on American Broadcasting Company (ABC) news stated how he felt Blacks' lacked the necessities to fulfill leadership positions in baseball (ABC News, 2012; Sailes, 2010). Modern day evidence of the acceptance of this belief is presence in the perpetual underrepresentation of Blacks in leadership positions in sports across the intercollegiate and professional levels (TIDES, 2018).

In a related vein, another popular racist assertion against Blacks is the dumb jock theory, which suggests Black athletes' lack the cognitive aptitude to excel in academic spaces while possessing the athletic prowess to compete in their respective sports (Sailes, 2010). Widely cited evidence to affirm this insidious stereotype are statistics that reveal Blacks are more likely to enter college less academically prepared, more likely to have lower SAT and ACT scores, and less likely to graduate college after being granted access to a "quality educational opportunity" (or rather more accurately described as a racist and oppressive schooling space) compared to their White peers (Cooper, 2012; Edwards, 1984; Harris, 2000; Sailes, 2010; Sellers, 2000). Consequently, the NCAA has implemented several *de facto* colorblind racist policies such as Propositions 48, 16, and 42 in an effort to increase the academic readiness of entering first-year college athletes (Cooper, Nwadike, & Macaulay, 2017). Using the test scores of culturally bias standardized assessments such as the SAT and ACT (in conjunction with high school GPAs) without taking into account widespread racial and socioeconomic inequities in the U.S. society including in the K-12 schooling system underscores the NCAA's misguided, yet well-intentioned efforts to improve academic outcomes for college athletes. As a result, these colorblind racist policies have had a disparate impact on Black male prospective college athletes (Cooper, 2012; Cooper et al., 2017; Davis, 1992; Sellers, 2000).

During the time when these legislations were being implemented in the 1980s and 1990s, several critics including notable Black head coaches such John Thompson II (Georgetown University) and John Chaney (Temple University) criticized these policies for being racist and denying young Black males who without an athletic scholarship would otherwise not have an opportunity to attend college (Davis, 1992; Sellers, 2000). These well-meaning coaches were thinking about the personal ethic of care they showed their Black male athletes upon enrollment into the university, as opposed to their White peers who may not have had the same intentions or culturally competency to provide the same support, to ensure that they were supported throughout their time at their respective institutions (e.g., educationally, socio-culturally, etc.). However, my colleagues and I have noted in previous work that removal of access discrimination does not eliminate treatment discrimination after enrollment (Cooper et al., 2017). In fact, the use of special admission standards discussed in Chapter 2 and the NCAA's low academic initial eligibility standards (especially compared to admissions standards for the general student population at these institutions) combined with questionable academic major trends (i.e., clustering) and a general lack of adequate culturally relevant academic supports at these institutions creates conditions to affirm rather challenge the label of the *"Black dumb jock"* (Cooper et al., 2017; Davis, 1992; Edwards, 1984). Hence, Sellers (2000) asserted that the mind of Black male athletes were being (and continue to be) devalued and underdeveloped by NCAA member institutions while their bodies are being exploited and harnessed for White economic gains.

Despite the prevalence of the aforementioned theories and related unfavorable societal conditions, an often overlooked reality is there are numerous Black males who defy the odds to attain positive life outcomes. For example, according to the most recent Schott Foundation for Public Education (2015) report, the estimated national graduation rate for Black males was 59% in 2012–2013. Even though, this number does not constitute optimal success by any means, it does reveal that over half of the Black males assessed in this report graduated from high school, which is a starkly different narrative from the mainstream negative commentary associated with this sub-group (i.e., Black males as academic failures). According to the Pew Research Center, in 2012, there were 1.7 million Blacks between the ages of 18–24 enrolled in college, which accounted for *14% of the total student enrollment in college between the ages of 18–24* (Krogstad & Fry, 2014). According to a Brookings report, *17.2% of Black men between the ages of 25–35 had bachelor's degrees* (Reeves & Guyot, 2017). More specific to athletes, at the Division I level, the graduation success rate (GSR) for African American males was 72% (NCAA, 2017a). Among the power 5 conferences, Harper (2018) documented the graduation rates for *Black males overall and Black male college athletes was 60.1% and 55.2%*, respectively. Bear in mind, Blacks constitute roughly *13% of the U.S. population* and Black males specifically account for roughly 6.2% (U.S. Census Bureau, 2017a). Although, these percentages are not necessary analogous, the point in highlighting these statistics is not to dismiss the dire conditions and realities facing Black males in the U.S or to ignore the concurrent problematic nature of these trends (both independently and in comparison to their peers), but rather to shift the perspective and shed light on the fact that there are a plethora of Black males including athletes who are navigating a system that was not designed for them to succeed.

In a related vein, using national data from his study of 219 Black male high academic achievers in college, Harper (2010, 2012) introduced the anti-deficit achievement framework in an effort to alter the negative stereotypes associated with Black males' academic propensities. In a report of his study and findings, Harper (2012) offered the following explanation for the purpose of this framework:

> The framework inverts questions that are commonly asked about educational disadvantage, underrepresentation, insufficient preparation, academic underperformance, disengagement, and Black male student attrition … to better understand how Black undergraduate men successfully navigate their way to and through higher education and onward to reward post-college options. (p. 8)

The reframing of the statistics presented in the previous paragraph reflect an anti-deficit lens on Black males' outcomes in the K-20 U.S. schooling system.

Within the anti-deficit achievement framework, there are three distinctive pipeline points including pre-college socialization and readiness, college achievement, and post-college success (Harper, 2012). In the pre-college socialization and readiness pipeline, key dimensions include familial factors, K-12 school forces, and out-of-college prep resources. In the college achievement pipeline, classroom experiences, out-of-class engagement, and enriching educational experiences are outlined as key areas of influence. For the post-college success pipeline, graduate school enrollment and career readiness are explored. In concert with college student development frameworks (Pascarella & Terenzini, 2005), this model accounts for personal, social, and environmental factors between early childhood through adulthood.

Thus, the infusion of the anti-deficit achievement framework (Harper, 2010, 2012) in the examination of Black male athletes' experiences and outcomes offers a more expansive understanding of this sub-group and the conditions and influences that facilitate their holistic development in and through sport and education. For example, Hodge, Burden, Robinson, and Bennett (2008) asserted that Black youth and their parents should have a stronger balance between academics and athletics. This assertion not only echoes previous scholars (Beamon & Bell, 2011), but also reinforces a stereotypic notion that does not account for various historical and ecological factors that influence observed educational outcomes and sport participation patterns. This belief also ignores the numerous Black males and their families who balance academics and athletics. However, these individuals and groups receive far less media attention and until recently they were largely ignored in scholarly literature (Cooper & Cooper, 2015a, 2015b; Cooper, 2017; Fuller et al., 2016; Harrison & Martin, 2012; Martin & Harris, 2006). In addition, previous research has highlighted how race and class influence sport participation patterns and the meaning attached to it (Eitle & Eitle, 2002; Singer & May, 2010). Hodge, Burden, Robinson, and Bennett (2008) also highlighted the prevalence of self-stereotyping among Black male athletes. Yet, in my work, I have researched Black males at HWIs and HBCUs who participate in sports beyond football, basketball, and track and field and found insightful findings that challenge common stereotypes attributed to Black male athletes. In one study, my colleague and I found that Black college athletes across multiple sports at a Division I HWI reported lower levels of athletic identity compared to their White college athlete peers, which underscores the value of examining those who participate in sports within *and* beyond football and basketball (Cooper & Dougherty, 2015).

Later in this chapter, I will highlight the academic success stories of Black male athletes in sports such as soccer, track and field, cross country, football, and basketball. In other words, *not all Black male athletes are obsessed with pursuing professional sport careers, not all of them participate in football and basketball, not all of them are underperforming academically*, and *not all of them experience holistic underdevelopment through sport and miseducation* (e.g., academic attrition, Black male athletic role engulfment and identity foreclosure, career under preparedness and dissatisfaction, etc.). Many of them view sport as a means for personal development via participation, transferable skill acquisition, scholarship/financial assistance for accessing higher education, cultural exposure, and networking. The models presented in this text, including the purposeful participation for expansive personal growth model (P²EPGM) discussed in this chapter, explore the impact of ecological factors on Black male athletes' holistic development through sport and (mis)education over their lifespans.

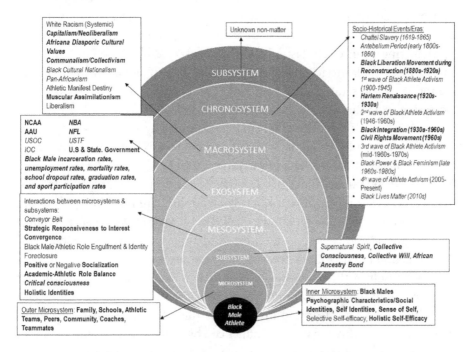

Figure 7.1. Purposeful Participation for Expansive Personal Growth Model (P²EPGM).

Source: Adapted from Bush, L. V., & Bush, E. C. (2013a). Introducing African American male theory (AAMT). *Journal of African American Males in Education*, 4(1), p. 9. Copyright 2013 Journal of African American Males in Education.

Socialization Phases for the Purposeful Participation for Expansive Personal Growth Model

The early phase of the P²EPGM involves informal involvement in sport participation. In contrast to the previous models (ISSM, EALM, and TRM), Black males in this model from an early age are encouraged to view education as the ultimate aim and sport participation as means to an end as opposed to an end in itself. This initial socialization serves as an instillation of protective measures against the Black male athletic role engulfment outcomes experienced by those in the ISSM, some in the EALM, and many in the TRM. Eitle and Eitle (2002) found that Black males who had access to cultural classes and household resources were less likely to participate in basketball and football. This finding suggests when Black males are provided with positive developmental opportunities aside from sport they are less likely to view sport participation as their only source of identity affirmation and path for upward mobility (i.e., the athletic manifest destiny allure associated with the NBA and NFL). More specifically, findings indicated that Black males with low cultural capital living in a two-parent household have a 26% likelihood of participating in interscholastic basketball and 52% likelihood of participating in interscholastic football; whereas, for Black males with high cultural capital with the same parent household composition, the likelihood of participation in interscholastic basketball and football declines to 3% and 30%, respectively (Eitle & Eitle, 2002). These findings juxtaposed with previous works that found Black families overemphasize sport (Beamon & Bell, 2002, 2006; Beamon, 2010; Harris, 1994; Johnson & Migliaccio, 2009; Singer & May, 2010) add nuanced insights into the diversity within this group. In other words, these findings highlight how Black families are not homogenous and the meaning attached to sport varies based on a range of factors such as familial background and values, community, geography, and access to various forms of capital and resources.

As a result of the early socialization balance of academics and athletics, Black males in the adolescent phase continue to exert equal if not more focus on achievement and learning in school as they do with sporting activities. The competitive drive to excel is influenced by factors such as family, community, role models (direct and indirect/reference), teachers, mentors, and exposure to people who have accomplished great things outside of sport including those who are physically alive as well as those who are deceased (i.e., Paul Robeson as a role model for a Black male athlete in the 21st century). During this period, similar to the early phase, Black males are continuing to be exposed to positive role models from a broad range of professions. Parental/guardian decisions about school enrollments are often predicated on academics and athletics as opposed to only the latter. Black males in this phase participate with their peers in the ISSM, EALM, and TRM, but the focus on excelling in the sport does not supersede performing well above minimal eligibility standards. In other words, Black males who experience the P²EPGM are socialized to possess an Excellence Beyond Athletics (EBA) mentality and approach towards sport participation (Cooper, 2016b). Positive affirmation for academic and athletic achievements from multiple stakeholder groups is reinforced at this phase.

At the young adulthood phase, unlike Black males in the ISSM, EALM, and TRM, the college decision is heavily based on academic and non-sport career interests versus prioritizing athletic reasons such as the opportunity to play at the professional level, reputation of the sport team, etc. Even though, Black males in the P²EPGM also attend colleges and universities with strong athletic programs, these individuals possess a keen focus on majoring in an area of their interest and finding a way to ensure their high academic standards and performance are maintained as much as possible while adjusting to the more intense athletic schedules and conditions at the intercollegiate level. Black males in the P²EPGM are less likely to acquiesce with academic clustering trends and often have the support of family members in this resistance. Black males in this model also value meaningful engagement and development opportunities both within and outside of athletic circles. The P²EPGM reflects Coakley's (2012) assertion about positive socialization experiences through sport:

> … sport participation is associated with positive socialization experiences when it, expands or diversifies a person's identities, relationships, and experiences, especially beyond the sporting contexts. Conversely, sport participation is associated with negative socialization experiences when it constricts or limits a person's identities, relationships, and experiences. (p. 184)

In the P²EPGM, Black males' positive socialization heightens their attentiveness to networking for future career opportunities and connecting with individuals on campus (e.g., non-athlete peers, athlete peers, faculty, staff, and administrators) and off campus (e.g., alumni, professionals in fields of interest, professional organizations, cultural organizations, etc.). Graduation is an imperative within this model, so even if professional aspirations are available, earning their bachelor's before or shortly after exhausting or relinquishing their college athletic eligibility is prioritized.

At the adulthood phase, Black males in the P²EPGM by virtue of their positive socialization and subsequent corresponding actions avoid Black male athletic role engulfment, identity foreclosure, and career under preparedness. However, their holistic nurturance does not prevent them from experiencing any challenges particularly those associated with post-athletic career disengagement trauma, but similar to the early adapters in the TRM in Chapter 6 these Black males manage the shifting of their identities, roles, and statuses more smoothly than their peers in the ISSM and many in the EALM. As such, the outcome of the P²EPGM includes holistic sense of self, career satisfaction and growth, and intentional engagement in mentoring and supporting the next generation to experience similar success.

Evidence of the Purposeful Participation for Expansive Personal Growth Model

Two compelling examples of the P²EPGM are two Black males who earned the internationally renowned Rhodes Scholarship, Myron Rolle and Caylin Moore. Rolle and Moore had two different journeys to the same destination and therefore serve as great examples of the heterogeneity among Black male athletes who experience positive success outcomes in education and sport. Rolle was born in Houston, Texas and spent a portion of his childhood in the Bahamas before moving permanently to Galloway Township, New Jersey (Elfman, 2009). Rolle was the youngest of five boys. Within their middle class household, education was paramount and sports were ancillary. Rolle explained the difference between the rewards he received from academic achievement and athletic performance:

> When I was younger, I'd get straight A's in school and my parents would get me two pizza pies from my favorite Italian restaurant in New Jersey. If I scored a touchdown or 20 points in a basketball game, hit two runs in baseball, they'd give me a pat on the back and say, "Good job." The reward was different. At that point, I realized how significant it was for me to do well in school and how much it meant to them (Ettman, 2009 p. 1).

The familial capital (Yosso, 2005) associated with academics versus athletics facilitated academic-athletic role balance and positive socialization for Rolle. After elementary school, Rolle attended prestigious middle and high schools, the Hun School in Princeton, New Jersey and Peddie School in Highstown, New Jersey, where he excelled academically and participated in a range of co-curricular activities including sport, music, journalism, and arts. These realities offer an alternative perspective of Black male athletes compared to previous literature, which has highlighted how Black families overemphasize athletics over academics (Beamon & Bell, 2002, 2006; Beamon, 2010; Harris, 1994; Johnson & Migliaccio, 2009; Singer & May, 2010). In addition, having access to this type of educational environment provided Rolle with vital cultural, social, and navigational capital to add to his familial and aspirational capital, which primed him for success later in life (Yosso, 2005). During his youth, Rolle read Dr. Ben Carson's book, *Gifted Hands,* and it left an indelible impression on the young scholar and sparked his interest in the field of medicine (Howard, 2017). As previously noted, Black males at a young age are highly impressionable by socialization agents who they have direct contact such as family, but also those who they have indirect contact such as reference groups. Thus, the power and value of exposing Black males to positive same race and same gender role models in person, print, and/or through oral communication cannot be understated.

After graduating high school, he enrolled at Florida State University (FSU) based on their academic reputation first and secondly because of their athletic tradition (Elfman, 2009). This balanced assessment of college selection is consistent with previous research on Black male scholar athletes who excel in college (Cooper, 2016a, 2017; Harrison & Martin, 2012; Martin & Harris, 2006; Martin, Harrison, Stone, & Lawrence, 2010). As an undergraduate at FSU, he completed his bachelor's degree in Exercise Science with a concentration on Pre-Med in two and half years with a 3.75 cumulative GPA (Thompson, 2018). In 2010, Rolle was drafted in the sixth round by the Tennessee Titans (Associated Press, 2010). He played two seasons in the NFL, one with the Titans and the second year with the Pittsburgh Steelers. He then enrolled in the FSU College of Medicine. In an interview with Cable News Network (CNN) contributor Dr. Sanjay Gupta, Rolle recalled the day he was notified that he was selected to be a Rhodes Scholar (Howard, 2017). He described the day he was informed about his acceptance for the Rhodes Scholarship in Birmingham, Alabama just a few hours after his interview. Immediately after being notified, he flew to Maryland where his FSU football team was competing against the University of Maryland Terrapins. He arrived in the second quarter and was able to play in the rest of the game in a 37–3 Seminole victory (Howard, 2017). This scenario epitomizes academic-athletic role balance and the Black male scholar athlete mentality. In response to an interview question from CNN's Dr. Sanjay Gupta, Rolle explained the parallels between his approach towards football and brain surgery: "I felt the same rush, the same intensity in both atmospheres. You have to prepare.

You have to strategize. You have to communicate. The same elements go into it. I pray. I listen to music. I try to get myself ready to go. And uh, it's exciting. It's super thrilling." (Howard, 2017; 2:00–2:24). The cognitive and physical transference of skill sets and mentalities from sports to education along with strong self-efficacy in both spaces for Black males in the P²EPGM stands in stark contrast those who experience the ISSM, who often lack access to the vital forms of capital to navigate oppressive spaces.

After completing his undergraduate degree in 2008, Rolle earned his master's degree in Medical Anthropology from Oxford University in 2010, earned his Medical degree from FSU College of Medicine in 2017, and currently completing his residency in neurosurgery at Harvard Medical School in Boston, Massachusetts. As a brain surgeon, Rolle plans to examine the most effective ways to treat head trauma such as concussions, which was inspired by his experiences as a former football player (Howard, 2017). In addition, he has a passion for redressing global health issues and plans to start a health clinic in his ancestral homeland of the Bahamas (Elfman, 2009). Rolle utilizes his passion for helping people in his medical background as a neurosurgeon as well as well as his establishment of philanthropic public health foundations and his role as an ambassador for the *Clinton Global Initiative* for combating sexual violence in East Africa (Thompson, 2018). Rolle's ascension to the Rhodes Scholarship may be unique (as very few Black males have achieved this feat), but his academic-athletic role balance and Black male scholar mentality is one of many examples throughout the U.S. and world both historically and in contemporary times. Thus, spotlighting stories like Rolle effectively disrupt the taken-for-granted myths attributed to Black male athletes outlined earlier in this chapter.

Another example of a compelling Black male scholar athlete who beat the odds of a society founded upon and grounded in WRC is Caylin Moore. At the 2018 *Black Student Athlete Summit* at the University of Texas at Austin, Caylin Moore delivered a powerful motivational speech detailing his life journey (Moore, 2018). The story of Caylin Moore began in Hollywood, California where he was born. He grew up with his parents, Louis (father) and Calynn (mother), and two siblings, Mi (older sister) and Chase (brother) in Moreno Valley, California during his early childhood before they moved to Compton, California (Rittenberg, 2016). His father was psychologically abusive to his mother and physically abusive to Caylin (Rittenberg, 2016). Subsequently, his parents' marriage dissolved. His father later was incarcerated for murder. Hence, Moore's early childhood experiences and family situation was integrally connected to the systemic forces of WRC including the prison industrial complex (PIC) that encapsulates far too many Black fathers (Alexander, 2012; Bush & Bush, 2013a, 2013b; ETS, 2011).

While raising Moore, his mother worked full-time while earning her law degree and master's degrees in Clinical Psychology and Theory (Rittenberg, 2016). Despite financial and personal challenges, Moore's mother emphasized and role modeled the importance of education to her children, which highlights how the P^2EPGM is present across all socioeconomic statuses and not just among Black families from middle and upper class backgrounds and/or those who have a history of educational attainment in their immediate family lineage. Her faith, perseverance, and role modeling in the form of familial capital (Yosso, 2005) had a profound impact on Moore and his siblings and equipped them with the necessary tools to overcome dire life circumstances, which reflects the legacy of resiliency exhibited by Blacks across the African Diaspora both within and beyond the U.S. (Akbar, 1982; Asante, 1990, 2003; Asante & Mazama, 2005; Boykin, 1986; Hine, Hine, & Harrold, 2006; Karenga, 1978;). Growing up in Compton in an economically disadvantaged neighborhood challenges were in abundance. One obstacle was hunger due to a lack of food at times. Similar to his father's immersion in the PIC, the food insecurity he experienced as a youth is emblematic of broader societal trends among Black families. According to a national report, Nord, Colemann, Jensen, Andrews, and Carlson (2010) found that 35% of Black children were food insecure compared to 17% of White children (ETS, 2011). In his speech, Moore recollected times when his mother would not have enough money to feed him and his siblings so he would do push-ups to offset the pain he felt from being hungry (Moore, 2018). He and his siblings shared a room growing up and at times they did not have hot water (Rittenberg, 2016). As previously noted, the poverty rate for Black children in the U.S. is 36% versus 12% for White children (ETS, 2011). These are just a few of the traumatic challenges Moore had to ensure as a youth.

During his youth, Moore took a liking to football because it provided him an outlet to express his anger and aggression due to his life circumstances. Similar to Trisitan A. McLendon from Chapter 4, LeBron James and Kevin Durant from Chapter 5, and many other Black males who grow up in similar conditions, sport serves as a release and escape from the harsh realities at home and in the neighborhood. As a standout student *and* athlete in high school, Moore was recruited to attend an all-male Catholic school called Verbum Dei High School in Los Angeles, California. He continued to excel academically and athletically. Similar to Rolle, Moore's access to quality secondary education enabled him to acquire vital cultural, social, and navigational capital for matriculating through the U.S. schooling system (Yosso, 2005). In addition to his own intellect and work ethic/aspirational capital (Yosso, 2005), Moore's opportunity to attend an academically reputable secondary school is often inaccessible to many Black males in the U.S. even those who have similar intellect and work ethics. As a result of his academic success in high school, Moore applied to several schools including six Ivy League schools (Rittenberg, 2016).

After exploring his options, Moore enrolled at Marist College in 2013 because it was the most financially prudent option and afforded him the chance to play Division I college football (Rittenberg, 2016). Shortly thereafter, he earned a Fulbright Scholarship. Through this scholarship, he had the opportunity to study at the University of Bristol in England with a research focus on the transatlantic slave trade. After returning to Marist, he suffered a back injury that derailed his playing career temporarily. He transferred to another school and since he was no longer on an athletic scholarship he worked as a janitor to cover his financial needs (Moore, 2018). His aspirational capital (Yosso, 2005) kept him focused on pursuing his dreams of being a Division I college football player and attending Harvard University (Moore, 2018). In his speech, Moore tells a story while he was working as a janitor, a student walked by and said he missed a spot on the floor. After looking on the floor, Moore was puzzled as he had been sweeping meticulously. The student went on to spit on the floor and said to Moore that is the spot he missed. A subsequent conversation ensued where Moore told the student to go to the cafeteria, grab his plate of food, and meet him back at the same spot where he spat. Moore told him that he wanted him to place his food on the floor on the same spot where he spat because the spot would be so clean that anyone could eat off it. He said this response and mentality was inspired by the following quote he read from Dr. Martin Luther King, Jr.:

> If a man is called to be a street sweeper, he should sweep streets even as a Michelangelo painted, or Beethoven composed music or Shakespeare wrote poetry. He should sweep streets so well that all the hosts of heaven and earth will pause to say, 'Here lived a great street sweeper who did his job well. (King (1967) cited by King Center, 2013, p. 1)

Moore took this quote to heart and even to this day he motivates himself with the phrase "*but I missed a spot*" in reference to the statement the student made that day. After working his body back to playing form, he transferred again to Texas Christian University (TCU). While at TCU, Moore continued to excel at a high level academically and he created a program and student organization called TCU SPARK (Strong Players Are Reaching Kids).

He attributed his success to his mother's love, discipline, work ethic, support, and emphasis on his educational attainment, which reflects the impact of familial, aspirational, and navigational capital for Blacks who endure and overcome significant life challenges (Yosso, 2005). Contrary to dominant narratives that suggest Black families particularly those who live in low income environments overemphasize sport (Eitle & Eitle, 2002), the impact of familial and aspirational capital on Moore's success both on and off the field serve as powerful counter-narratives. Interestingly, while in high school in 2008, Moore admired Myron Rolle (Rittenberg, 2016). In 2017, Moore did the improbable to most and the expected for him (and those who believe in the unlimited potential of Black males and the spirit therein), when he was selected as one of the 2017 Rhodes Scholars at Oxford University in England. As of 2018, he is currently studying Latin American Studies as a graduate student and will soon begin his PhD work. During his speech he told the story of how he pursued the prestigious scholarship. He said he wore suit and for multiple consecutive days while he visited different offices on campus inquiring about scholarship opportunities (Moore, 2018). He said his script was "My name is Caylin Moore. I am Black male from the inner city. Do you have any scholarships that I can apply for?" After being turned away numerous times, he was eventually able to retrieve information about potential scholarships and the Rhodes Scholar was one of them. After applying and advancing to the interviews portion of the process, Moore explained how during his interview he did not shy away from his personal background, but rather embraced it and demonstrated to the interviewers that everything in life is not based where you come from, but how you live and maximize your potential and resources regardless of your plight. This approach epitomizes Moore's possession and activation of his aspirational and resistant capital (Yosso, 2005). As a result of this candid humility, the Rhodes Scholars interviewers were impressed with his authenticity, knowledge, intellect, and drive and subsequently he was awarded as one of the accepted candidates for the 2017 class (Moore, 2018). As such, Rolle and Moore had very different paths to the Rhodes Scholarship, but the few important things they did have in common was that they were both Black males with an abundance of community cultural wealth (CCW; Yosso, 2005) who were committed to fulfilling their goals no matter what.

It is important to contextualize the experiences and outcomes of Black male athletes in the 21st century such as Rolle and Moore. This contextualization has been documented in scholarly literature on Black male scholar athletes. Contrary to the ubiquitous dumb jock stereotype, historically Black male athletes dating back to the early 20th century, similar to the non-athlete Black male counterparts, valued education and viewed it as a pathway to success. Smith, Clark, and Harrison (2014) described this reality:

> Interestingly, in the late 1800s and early 1900s, Blacks were poorer but did not see athletics as an opportunity for upward mobility, and Blacks were not always over-represented in professional and collegiate sports. There was a ubiquitous belief that Blacks were athletically inferior. (p. 228)

The authors went on to highlight several Black male scholar athletes who personified the P²EPGM in the latter 19th and early 20th century. Due to widespread racial discrimination (formally and informally via Jim Crow norms and Black Codes – see Hine, Hine, and Harrold (2006) for an extensive coverage of this era) during that period, there were only a limited number of Black males who able to have their total college expenses covered by athletic scholarships and thus they had to find other ways to cover their financial needs. As such, these Black males often secured financial support for their academic as well as their athletic prowess (Smith et al., 2014). Standout Black male scholar athletes such as Paul Robeson (Rutgers University and Columbia University) (he discussed in greater detail in Chapter 8), William Henry Lewis (Virginia Normal and Industrial School, Amherst College, and Harvard University), William Tecumseh Sherman Jackson (Amherst College), Duke Slater (University of Iowa), and Jerome "Brud" Holland (Cornell University and University of Pennsylvania) all demystified the pervasive stereotype of Black intellectual inferiority during the latter 19th and early 20th century (Smith et al., 2014; Wiggins & Miller, 2003). William Henry Lewis studied at Virginia Normal College (an HBCU) and Amherst College. He played football at Amherst and he was one of the first Blacks to integrate an athletic team at a HWI in 1888. Later he enrolled at Harvard Law School and played on the football team for two years. He was the first Black to be selected to the All-American team in 1892. Among his many accomplishments, Lewis authored a book titled *A Primer of College Football* in 1896, became the fourth Black student to graduate from Harvard Law School, and served as the first Black assistant attorney general in 1911 (Smith et al., 2014).

Duke Slater was an All-American football player at the University of Iowa in the early 1900s and became the first Black to be elected into the College Football Hall of Fame in 1951 (Smith et al., 2014). He was the only Black in the NFL between 1927 and 1929 and earned Pro Bowl honors both years. He later pursued a successful career in law and politics and became the first Black member of the Chicago Superior Court as a model and mentor in 1960. Jerome "Brud" Holland attended Cornell University where he was one of five Blacks to be selected as a member of the Sphinx Honors Society and he was a two-time All-American in late 1930s. After earning bachelor's degree, he would then earn his master's degree from Cornell University and doctorate from the University of Pennsylvania. Later, he taught Sociology and Physical Education at Lincoln University and served as President at Delaware State University from 1953–1959 and Hampton Institute from 1960–1970. Both schools are HBCUs. He then served as an Ambassador to Sweden for President Richard Nixon in 1970–1972 and became the first Black board member of the New York Stock Exchange in 1972 and served in this capacity until 1980. After his death in 1985, his posthumously received the Presidential Medal of Honor (Smith et al., 2014).

Meredith Gourdine earned his bachelor's degree in Engineering from Cornell University. He also ran track and field and competed in the long jump and various short distance dash events in late 1940s and early 1950s (Smith et al., 2014). In 1952, Gourdine earned a silver medal in the Olympics in Helsinki for the long jump. Later, he would serve as a Navy Officer and earned a doctorate in Engineering in 1960 from California Institute of Technology. His illustrious career resulted in his induction into the Hall of Fame of Engineering and Science in Dayton, Ohio. Fritz Pollard graduated from Brown University with a bachelor's degree in Chemistry in the early 1900s. He is also known for being the first Black to win the famous Walter Camp All-American recognition in 1916. He was a player-coach with the Akron Pros in the early 1920s and he was the first Black coach in the NFL. Later in 1954, he was inducted into the 1954 College Hall of Fame. He also was an avid Civil Rights activist throughout his adult life (Smith et al., 2014). Applying a socio-historical lens, the aforementioned accomplishments mirrored progressive efforts made by the broader Black community in concert with social movements such as the Black Liberation movement during Reconstruction (1880s–1920s), Harlem Renaissance (1920s–1930s), and Black Integration (1930s–1960s) (see Figure 7.1). The documentation and awareness of the rich legacy of Black excellence in and through sport and education is a vital emancipatory tool that challenges dominant ideologies via counter narratives, magnifies the utilization of CCW, and reflects a commitment to social justice in a society founded upon and structured by WRC (DeCuir & Dixson, 2004; Delgado, 1989; Delgado & Stefancic, 2001; Delgado Bernal, 2002; Matsuda, 1995; Solórzano & Yosso, 2002; Yosso, 2005).

In addition to this historical data, in recent years more research has highlighted the academic prowess of Black male scholar athletes at both the secondary and postsecondary levels. In a qualitative study of Black male high school athletes, Harris, Hines, Kelly, Williams, and Bagley (2014) found that consistent positive messaging and cultural competence across the various support systems including parents, teachers, coaches, advisors, and peers were beneficial for enhancing participants' academic engagement and performance. The authors conceptualized these outcomes as a byproduct of a "team approach" to cultivating Black male student achievement and athletic success (Harris et al., 2014, p. 188). Similar findings have been noted at the postsecondary level. Common themes across studies of Black male scholar athletes in college include:

(a) the importance of familial support (biological, extended, and kinship),
(b) access, activation, and utilization of different types of CCW (Yosso, 2005),
(c) the cultivation of strong academic self-efficacies and pre-college socialization emphasis on education from an early age (e.g., verbal, non-verbal, enrichment opportunities, discipline for time spent on task, consequences for underperformance, rewards for achievement, etc.),
(d) exposure to positive same race role models directly (e.g., their biological and/or surrogate fathers, additional personal mentors, etc.) and/or indirectly (i.e., reference group role models),
(e) positive racial and ethnic identity instilled by family (including nuclear, extended, and kinship),
(f) positive relationships with teachers and peers in alignment with personal goals beyond athletics,
(g) positive adjustments to a lack of encouragement from coaches for academic achievement beyond eligibility and concern for personal well-being aside from athletic performance,
(h) strategically accessing and leveraging supports (including culturally relevant spaces) on campus for academic achievement, individual growth beyond athletics, mental and physical health stability, and cultural affirmation,
(i) adopting productive coping mechanisms for dealing with covert and overt racism;
(j) the embodiment of productive masculine identities, and

(k) engagement in productive and self-care exploratory activities beyond
sports including, but not limited to, religious organizations, spiritu-
ality enhancing spaces, social and professional organizations such as
fraternities, cultural groups, etc. (Bimper , Harrison, & Clark, 2012;
Cooper & Cooper, 2015b;Cooper, 2016a, 2016b, 2017; Douglas, Ivey,
& Bishop, 2015; Gragg & Flowers, 2014; Harrison & Martin, 2012;
Martin & Harris, 2006; Martin, Harrison, Stone, & Lawrence, 2010;
Oseguera, 2010).

In a study of Black male scholar athletes in Science and Engineering at a
Division I HWI, I found participants possessed strong role balance (student
and athlete roles) prior to college enrollment (Cooper, 2016a). This academic-
athletic role balance was instilled in them at an early age from their families
and amplified by their intrinsic interest in excelling academically. Two of the
participants who majored in Mechanical Engineering were soccer players and
one participant was a double major in Civil Engineering and Physics and a
track and field athlete. The two participants who were Mechanical Engineering majors had fathers who were Engineers. As a result, they were exposed to
navigational, cultural, familial, and social capital (Yosso, 2005) related to the
field throughout their lifespans. While in college, these two participants were
involved in the National Society for Black Engineers (NSBE), which further
enhanced their capital acquisition in preparation for successful careers in the
field upon graduation. This type identity balance and congruent behavior
echoed research from Harper's (2012) national anti-deficit achievement study
on Black males at HWIs who excelled in the classroom as well as engaged in
educationally purposeful activities outside of class.

The participant who was a double major in Civil Engineering and Physics and a track and field athlete grew up in a working class inner-city environment with his mother who did not have the opportunity to experience
attending college (Cooper, 2016a). Yet, similar to Moore's mother, despite not
having an abundance of resources that are celebrated in a neoliberal culture,
she instilled in him the value of educational attainment and held him to high
academic expectations throughout his life. Hence, her familial, resistant, and
aspirational capital was transmitted to him (Yosso, 2005). The presence of
Black male scholar athletes from different socioeconomic, geographic, family,
and ethnic backgrounds in this study (the latter is discussed in greater detail
later in this chapter) underscores the heterogeneity among those who experience positive socialization outcomes. At a young age, parents, mentors, and

influential adults instilled in them that they were capable of success beyond athletics and cultivated environments that reflected this belief. Each participant cited how their parents would refer to them as "smart" and set strict academic expectations for them that exceeded the standards conveyed on their athletic teams (Cooper, 2016a, p. 117). In addition, their parents made sure they were enrolled in academically rigorous courses starting from primary school through college. The combination of said factors resulted in Black male athletes in the P²EPGM being less susceptible to athletic role engulfment compared to their peers who do not experience such socialization.

Black male athletes in the P²EPGM also leverage their holistic identities in order to achieve success both within and beyond athletic spaces. These holistic identities include their gender, religious, spiritual, and racial identities. Martin and Harris (2006) and Harrison, Martin, and Fuller (2015) highlighted the perspectives of African American male scholar athletes in their respective studies. In both studies, participants expressed how many of their same race and gender peers, including teammates and Black males who are non-athletes, possessed different motivations and conceptions of success and masculinity compared to their own. According to the participants, their peers focused more on materialism, hypersexuality, and anti-intellectual endeavors, which reiterates previous research that found Black males are vulnerable to internalizing the dominant ideologies put forth in the U.S. society including WRC and neoliberalism (Majors & Billson, 1992; Singer & May, 2010). The authors did not explore the extent to which these factors were influenced by pre-college socialization factors, but previous literature suggests socialization including access and connectedness to positive same race and gender role models and growth opportunities beyond sport can reduce the likelihood of this type of internalization (Cooper, Corral, et al., 2018; Cuyjet, 2006; Gragg & Flowers, 2014; Howard, 2014; Martin & Harris, 2006).

Moreover, several studies have documented how Black male college athletes at HWIs adopt productive coping strategies to manage the covert and overt racism they encounter in these environments. For example, Gragg and Flowers (2014) found that spirituality and participation in Pan-Hellenic fraternities contributed to African American male football college athletes' academic success. In one of my recent studies, similar to their counterparts at HWIs, I found that Black male scholar athletes at HBCUs attributed their achievement outcomes in college to familial emphasis on education (familial capital) and positive relationships with their professors (navigational, cultural, and social capital) (Cooper, 2017). However, unlike their peers at

HWIs, Black male college athletes at HBCUs benefit from the racial and cultural environment at these institutional types as well as express a stronger
sense of belonging on campus based on their race whereas their peers at HWIs
felt more accepted primarily because of their athletic status (Cooper, 2017).
In other words, Black male scholar athletes at HBCUs are accepted because
of their race regardless of their athletic status whereas their peers at HWIs are
welcomed primarily because of their athletic status and in spite of their race,
which consistent with previous literature (Brown , Jackson, Brown, Sellers,
Keiper, & Manuel, 2003; Cooper, 2013; Cooper & Dougherty, 2015; Steinfeldt, Reed, & Steinfeldt, 2010).

Another aspect of Black male athletes' sporting and educational experiences that has been overlooked in scholarly literature is their ethnic backgrounds and family migration patterns. For example, as outlined in Chapter 1,
Black/African American males who are born and grow up in the U.S. are
exposed to a culture where mass media inundates them with a monolithic
image of Black male athletes (or as Brown (2016) described Blathlete –
referring the conflation of their racial, gender, and athletic identities), glo-
rifies sport participation, promotes sport consumption at high levels, and the
macro-system forces shape society in such a way that position Black males
as intellectually inferior and as a physically exploitable commodity (Cooper,
2012; Edwards, 1973, 1980, 1984, 2000). In addition, Black/African American males in the U.S. are more likely be impacted by what DeGruy (2005)
describes as the post traumatic slave syndrome (PTSS), which has distinct
effects on Black African Americans who have ancestral connection to U.S.
chattel slavery and Jim Crow.

In contrast, Black males of African descent who are born in countries
outside of the U.S. (e.g., Nigeria, Ghana, South Africa, Liberia, Ethiopia,
Jamaica, Haiti, Dominican Republic, Bahamas, Trinidad and Tobago, Brasil,
etc.) and migrate to the U.S. are less likely to view sport participation as
a means of upward mobility in the same way as native born Black/African
American males in the U.S. – at least in terms of the most popular North
American sports. Since soccer is popular internationally, I surmise similar
trends may be observed in countries where this sport is impressed upon Black
males in ways akin to how football and basketball are emphasized to Black
males in the U.S. In many cases, families of African descent, like immigrants
of non-African ethnic groups, migrate to the U.S. primarily for better educational and economic opportunities irrespective of sport and this message
is transmitted to their children who become first- and/or second-generation

Americans. For example, according to a recent American Community Survey, Americans who were born in Sub-Saharan African and Caribbean countries attain higher educational and occupational levels as well as experience lower poverty levels compared to native U.S. born African Americans (Ogunwole, Battle, & Cohen, 2017; U.S. Census Bureau, 2017b). This trend is not by happenstance and not only disproves the Black innate intellectual inferiority myth, but also highlights the distinct impact of anti-Black systemic racism within the U.S. and the psychological, economic, and sociocultural influences therein (Alexander, 2012; Curry, 2017; DeGruy, 2005; Du Bois, 1903/2003; Hine, Hine, & Harrold, 2006; Woodson, 1933/1990).

An illustrative example of a Black athlete with close family lineage to a country outside of the U.S. is Emeka Ofafor. Okafor was born in Houston, Texas, but his parents and family are Nigerian. Okafor experienced the P^{2}EPGM and EALM whereby he earned an Honors bachelor's degree in Finance with a 3.8 cumulative GPA in three years from UConn. During his final year in school, he led UConn to the 2004 NCAA National Championship and later he was the second overall pick in the 2004 NBA draft by the Charlotte Bobcats (now the Hornets) (Latack, 2003). Growing up with a father, Pius Okafor, who had a military background and immigrated to the U.S. to provide better life for his family. Okafor's father had a profound impact on his development. Similar to Moore's mother and the participants in my study (Cooper, 2017), Emeka's father role modeled to him the importance of education by doing it himself. Okafor's father earned his bachelor's and master's degrees in Business Administration and later his doctorate in Pharmacy while also being a Certified Public Accountant (Latack, 2003, p. 1). His father was quoted describing the value of education over sport in Nigeria when he said: "Where I'm from, if you're good at sports but not educated, you're nothing," (Latack, 2003, p. 1). It also worth noting that Houston has among the highest concentration of Nigerians in the U.S. and this African sub-group is among the most educated ethnic groups in the U.S. According to a recent U.S. Census Bureau (2017b) report, 61% of Nigerians ancestry 25 or older have bachelor's degree or higher compared to 28.5% for the U.S. average overall. Therefore, as previous scholars have noted taking into account the diversity of ethnicity, nationality, geographical, sociocultural, and family educational backgrounds of Black male athletes' is vital to understanding their lived experiences and outcomes. In addition, examining their family's migration experiences and related cultural nuances fosters more expansive perspectives on how and why they perceive and experience sport and (mis)education in similar and different ways.

In my own work, I have identified a connection between African Diasporic lineage, migration/immigration backgrounds, and Black athletes' (male and female) perceptions of education and sport (Cooper, 2016a, 2016b, 2017; Cooper & Cooper, 2015b). In a study of Black male college athletes who excelled academically, three of the five participants were either first- or second-generation Americans with close family ties to countries across the African Diaspora including Liberia, Jamaica, or Trinidad (Cooper & Cooper, 2015b). Each participant explained how their families emphasized academic achievement as a coveted cultural value particularly given that the circumstances surrounding their parents' migration to the U.S. It is important to note that the internalized cultural value of education is prevalent in the history of Black/African Americans in general (Du Bois, 1903/2003; Hine et al., 2006) and Black/African American athletes in particular (Smith et al., 2014) even though this fact is often times omitted from popular discourse. Despite the fact that the topic of disaggregating the lived experiences of Blacks in the U.S. across the African Diaspora has been explored extensively in fields such as higher education and Africana studies (Asante, 1990, 2003; Asante & Mazama, 2005; Carruthers, 1999; Douglas, 2016; George Mwangi, 2014; George Mwangi & English, 2017; George Mwangi & Fries-Britt, 2015; Hilliard, 1998), it remains conspicuously omitted from the scholarly literature on Black athletes in the U.S. where a majority of the research has focused on the experiences of a smaller group of Black African American male athletes (Beamon, 2008, 2012; Beamon & Bell, 2006; Harrison, Martin, & Fuller, 2015; Harrison & Martin, 2012; Harrison, Bimper, Smith, & Logan, 2017; Harrison, Harrison, & Moore, 2002; Harrison, Sailes, Rotich, & Bimper, 2011; Sailes, 2010; Singer, 2005, 2009, 2015).

As such, there is a need for more nuanced explorations of Black male socialization patterns within and beyond sport. The socialization models presented in this text including the P²EPGM extend the literature towards this aim. Related to socialization experiences, I contend that once Black males across the African Diaspora are immersed into the U.S. culture, particularly if they arrive at a younger age, they are highly susceptible to similar effects experienced by native born Black/African Americans who are suffer from exposure to WRC in the U.S. The mass media coverage of U.S. sport is uniquely pronounced and deeply rooted in neoliberalism (Coakley, 2017; Sage, 1998). Thus, native born Black/African Americans are more vulnerable to the ISSM than their same race different ethnicity peers who do not grow up in the same geographical and cultural environment (i.e., U.S. versus Bahamas or Nigeria) due to varying levels of exposure to the hegemonic culture of WRC in the U.S. Hence, it is important to acknowledge and disaggregate Black males based on their ethnic backgrounds and migration legacies as it relates to their experiences and outcomes in and through sport and (mis)education.

Chapter Summary

Despite the dominant gendered racist narrative that stereotypes all Black male athletes as dumb jocks, the reality is there is a long rich legacy of their excellence in areas within and beyond athletics. Early and consistent socialization centered on the importance and value of education along with the sustainment of balanced holistic identities are key characteristics of the P²EPGM (i.e., formal or informal socialization via a EBA type framework). For Black males in this model, sports are viewed as a means to an end rather than an end in of themselves. Black male scholar athletes such as Paul Robeson, William Henry Lewis, William Tecumseh Sherman Jackson, Duke Slater, Meredith Gourdine and Jerome "Brud" Holland overcame intense racial discrimination during the late 19th to mid-20th century to attain their career goals within and beyond sport. Modern day Black male scholar athletes such as Myron Rolle (2009 Rhodes Scholar), Caylin Moore (2017 Rhodes Scholar), and Emeka Okafor (2004 UConn Honors Graduate) continue to uphold this banner of exemplar achievement. Rolle epitomized the mindset and outcome of immersion into and through the P²EPGM when he said: "I'm glad that I walked into my purpose. I'm glad I walked into something that was a smooth transition from football" (Howard, 2017, p. 1). In concert with the African proverb, "it takes a village to raise a child," Black male athletes in the P²EPGM are equipped with vital community cultural wealth (CCW) to avoid athletic role engulfment and experience post-athletic career identity transition empowerment (ITE), personal fulfillment, and holistic development.

References

ABC News (2012). *1987: Baseball manager's racist remarks*. Retrieved from https://abcnews. go.com/Nightline/video/1987-baseball-managers-racist-remarks-16086569

Akbar, N. (1982). *Miseducation to education*. Jersey City, NJ: New Mind Productions.

Alexander, M. (2012). *The new Jim Crow: Mass incarceration in the age of colorblindness*. New York, NY: The New Press.

Asante, M. K. (1990). *Kemet, Afrocentricity and knowledge*. Trenton, NJ: Africa World Press.

Asante, M. K. (2003). *Afrocentricity: The theory of social change*. Chicago, IL: African American Images.

Asante, M. K., & Mazama, A. (2005). *Encyclopedia of Black studies*. Thousand Oaks, CA: Sage Publications.

Associated Press (2010, April 25). Titans take Rolle with 207th pick. *ESPN*. Retrieved from http://www.espn.com/nfl/draft10/news/story?id=5132897

Beamon, K. K. (2008). "Used goods": Former African American college student-athletes' perception of exploitation by division I universities. *The Journal of Negro Education, 77*(4), 352–364.

Beamon, K. (2010). Are sports overemphasized in the socialization process of African American males? A qualitative analysis of former collegiate athletes' perception of sport socialization. *Journal of Black Studies, 41*(2), 281–300.

Beamon, K. (2012). "I'm a baller": Athletic identity foreclosure among African American former student-athletes. *Journal of African American Studies, 16*(2), 195–208.

Beamon, K., & Bell, P. A. (2002). "Going pro": The deferential effects of high aspirations for a professional sports career on African-American student athletes and White student athletes. *Race & Society, 5*(2), 179–191.

Beamon, K., & Bell, P. A. (2006). Academics versus athletics: An examination of the effects of background and socialization on African-American male student athletes. *The Social Science Journal, 43*(3), 393–403.

Beamon, K.K, & Bell, P. A. (2011). A dream deferred: Narratives of African American male former collegiate athelets' transition out of sports and into the occupational sector. *Journal for the study of Sport and Athletes in Education, 5*(1), 29–44.

Bimper, A. Y., Harrison, L., & Clark, L. (2012). Diamonds in the rough: Examining a case of successful Black male student athletes in college sport. *Journal of Black Psychology, 39*(2), 1–24.

Boykin, A. W. (1986). *The school achievement of minority children: New perspectives*. Hillsdale, NJ: Lawrence Erlbaum Associates.

Brown, D. (2016, November 4). *Blathlete: Black-identity development among Black male student-athletes*. Paper presentation at the North American Society for the Sociology of Sport (NASSS) conference in Tampa, Florida.

Brown, T. N., Jackson, J. S., Brown, K. T., Sellers, R. M., Keiper, S., & Manuel, W. J. (2003). "There's no race on the playing field": Perceptions of racial discrimination among White and Black athletes. *Journal of Sport and Social Issues, 27*(2), 162–183.

Bush, L. V., & Bush, E. C. (2013a). Introducing African American male theory (AAMT). *Journal of African American Males in Education, 4*(1), 6–17.

Bush, L. V., & Bush, E. C. (2013b). God bless the child who got his own: Toward a comprehensive theory for African-American boys and men. The Western Journal of Black Studies, 37(1), 1–13.

Carruthers, J. H. (1999). *Intellectual warfare*. Chicago, IL: Third World Press.

Coakley, J. (2012). Youth sports: What counts as "positive development"?. In R. J. Schinke and S. J. Hanrahan, *Sport for Development, Peace, and Social Justice* (pp. 181–192). Morgantown, WV: Fitness Information Technology.

Coakley, J. (2017). *Sports in society: Issues and controversies* (12th ed.). New York, NY: McGraw-Hill Education.

Cooper, J. N. (2012). Personal troubles and public issues: A sociological imagination of Black athletes' experiences at predominantly White institutions in the United States. *Sociology Mind, 2*(3), 261–271.

Cooper, J. N. (2013). A culture of collective uplift: The influence of a historically Black college/university on Black male student athletes' experiences. *Journal of Issues in Intercollegiate Athletics, 6*, 306–331.

Cooper, J. N. (2016a). "Focus on the bigger picture:" An anti-deficit achievement examination of Black male scholar athletes in science and engineering at a Division I historically White university (HWU). *Whiteness & Education, 1*(2), 109–124.

Cooper, J. N. (2016b). Excellence beyond athletics: Best practices for enhancing Black male student athletes' educational experiences and outcomes. *Equity & Excellence in Education, 49*(3), 267–283.

Cooper, J. N. (2017). Strategic navigation: A comparative study of Black male scholar athletes' experiences at a Historically Black college/university (HBCU) and Historically White university (HWU). *International Journal of Qualitative Studies in Education, 31*(4), 235–256 doi: 10.1080/09518398.2017.1379617.

Cooper, J. N., & Cooper, J. E. (2015a). Success in the shadows: (Counter) narratives of achievement from Black scholar athletes at a historically Black college/university (HBCU). *Journal for the Study of Sports and Athletes in Education, 9*(3), 145–171.

Cooper, J. N., & Cooper, J. E. (2015b). "I'm running so you can be happy and I can keep my scholarship": A comparative study of Black male college athletes' experiences with role conflict. *Journal of Intercollegiate Sport, 8*(2), 131–152.

Cooper, J. N., Corral, M. D., Macaulay, C. D. T., Cooper, M. S., Nwadike, A., & Mallery, Jr., M. (2018). Collective uplift: The impact of a holistic development support program on Black male former college athletes' experiences and outcomes. *International Journal of Qualitative Studies in Education*, DOI: 10.1080/09518398.2018.1522011.

Cooper, J. N., & Dougherty, S. (2015). Does race still matter? A post bowl championship series (BCS) era examination of student athletes' experiences at a Division I historically Black college/university (HBCU) and predominantly White institution (PWI). *Journal of Issues in Intercollegiate Athletics, 8*, 74–101.

Cooper, J. N., Nwadike, A., & Macaulay, C. (2017). A critical race theory analysis of big-time college sports: Implications for culturally responsive and race-conscious sport leadership. *Journal of Issues in Intercollegiate Athletics, 10*, 204–233.

Curry, T. J. (2017). *The man-not: Race, class, genre, and the dilemmas of Black manhood.* Philadelphia, PA: Temple University Press.

Cuyjet, M. J. (2006). *African American men in college.* San Francisco, CA: Jossey-Bass.

Davis, T. (1992). Examining educational malpractice jurisprudence: Should a cause of action be created for student-athletes? *Denver University Law Review, 69*, 57–96.

DeCuir, J. T., & Dixson, A. D. (2004). "So when it comes out, they aren't that surprised that it is there": Using critical race theory as a tool of analysis of race and racism in education. *Educational Researcher, 33*(5), 26–31.

DeGruy, J. (2005). *Posttraumatic slave syndrome: America's legacy of enduring injury & healing.* Milwaukie, OR: Uptone Press.

Delgado, R. (1989). Storytelling for oppositionists and others: A plea for narrative. *Michigan Law Review, 87*(8), 2411–2441.

Delgado, R., & Stefancic, J. (2001). *Critical race theory: An introduction.* New York, NY: New York University Press.

Delgado Bernal, R. (2002). Critical race theory, Latino critical theory, and critical raced-gendered epistemologies: Recognizing students of Color as holders and creators of knowledge. *Qualitative Inquiry, 8*(1), 105–126.

Douglas, T. (2016). *Border crossing brothas: Black males navigating race, place, and complex space.* New York, NY: Peter Lang.

Douglas, T., Ivey, P., & Bishop, K. (2015). Identity, leadership, and success: A study of Black male student-athletes at the University of Missouri. *National Collegiate Athletic Association (NCAA) Innovations Grant.* [Final Report]. Retrieved from https://www.ncaa.org/sites/default/files/Douglas%2C%20Ivey%2C%20Bishop%2C%20NCAA%20Final%20Report%2C%20Black%20Male%20Student%20Athlete%20Study%2C%201.4.2016%2C%20submitted.pdf

Du Bois, W. E. B. (1903/2003). *The souls of Black folk.* Chicago, IL: A. C. McClurg.

Edwards, H. (1973). *Sociology of sport.* Homewood, IL: Dorsey Press.

Edwards, H. (1980). *The struggle that must be: An autobiography.* New York, NY: Macmillan Publishing Co., Inc.

Edwards, H. (1984). The Black "dumb jock": An American sports tragedy. *College Board Review, 131,* 8–13.

Edwards, H. (2000). Crisis of black athletes on the eve of the 21st century. *Society, 37*(3), 9–13.

Elfman, L. (2009). "Putting education first" Rhodes scholar says parents rewarded achievements in the classroom over football field. *Diverse Issues in Higher Education.* Retrieved from http://diverseeducation.com/article/12131/

Eitle, T. M., & Eitle, D. J. (2002). Race, cultural capital, and the educational effects of participation in sports. *Sociology of Education, 75*(2), 123–146.

Ettman, L. (2009, January 5). 'Putting education first' Rhodes scholar says parents rewarded achievements in the classroom over football field. *Diverse Issues in Higher Education.* Retrieved from https://diverseeducation.com/article/12131/

ETS. (2011). *A strong start: Positioning young Black boys for educational success a statistical profile.* Washington, DC: Educational Testing Service.

Fuller, R. D., Harrison, C. K., Bukstein, S. J., Martin, B. E., Lawrence, S. M., & Gadsby, P. (2016). That smart dude: A qualitative investigation of the African American male scholar-baller identity. *Urban Education,* 1–19. DOI: 10.1177/0042085916668955

George Mwangi, C. A., & English, S. (2017). Being black (and) immigrant students: When race, ethnicity, and nativity collide. *International Journal of Multicultural Education, 19*(2), 100–130.

George Mwangi, C. A. (2014). Complicating Blackness: Black immigrants & racial positioning in U.S. higher education. *Journal of Critical Thought and Praxis, 3*(2), 1–27.

George Mwangi, C. A., & Fries-Britt, S. (2015). Black within Black: The perceptions of Black immigrant collegians and their U.S. college experience. *About Campus, 20*(2), 16–23.

Gragg, D., & Flowers, R. D. (2014). Factors that positively affect academic performance of African American football student-athletes. *Journal for the Study of Sports and Athletes in Education, 8*(2), 77–98.

Harper, S. R. (2010). An anti-deficit achievement framework for research on students of color in STEM. *New Directions for Institutional Research, 2010* (148), 63–74.

Harper, S. R. (2012). *Black male student success in higher education: A report from the national Black male college achievement study.* Philadelphia, PA: University of Pennsylvania, Center for the Study of Race and Equity in Education.

Harper, S. R. (2018). *Black male student-athletes and racial inequities in NCAA Division I college sports: 2018 edition.* Los Angeles, CA: University of Southern California, Race and Equity Center.

Harris, O. (1994). Race, sport, and social support. *Sociology of Sport Journal, 11*(1), 40–50.

Harris, S. M. (1995). Psychosocial development and Black male masculinity: Implications for counseling and economically disadvantaged African American male adolescents. *Journal of Counseling and Development, 73*(3), 279–287.

Harris, O. (2000). African American predominance in sport. In D. Brooks & R. Althouse (Eds.), *Racism in college athletics: The African Amerian athlete's experience* (2nd ed., pp. 37–52). Morgantown, WV: Fitness Information Technology.

Harris, P. C., Hines, E. M., Kelly, D. D., Williams, D. J., & Bagley, B. (2014). Promoting the academic engagement and success of Black male student-athletes. *The High School Journal, 97*(3), 180–195.

Harrison, C. K., Martin, B. E., & Fuller, R. (2015). "Eagles don't fly with sparrows": Self-determination theory, African American male scholar-athletes and peer group influences on motivation. *The Journal of Negro Education, 84*(1), 80–93.

Harrison, C. K., & Martin, B. (2012). Academic advising, time management and the African American male scholar-athlete. In T. Stoilov (Ed.), *Time management* (pp. 89–106): InTech. Retrieved from http://www.intechopen.com/books/time-management/time-management-academic-advising-and-the-african-american-male-student-athlete

Harrison, L., Jr., Bimper, A. Y., Jr., Smith, M. P., & Logan, A. D. (2017). The mis-education of the African American student-athlete. *Kinesiology Review, 6*, 60–69.

Harrison., L. Jr., Harrison, C. K., & Moore, L. N. (2002). African American racial identity and sport. *Sport, Education & Society, 7*(2), 121–133.

Harrison, L. Jr., Sailes, G., Rotich, W. K., & Bimper, A. Y. Jr. (2011). Living the dream or awakening from the nightmare: Race and athletic identity. *Race, Ethnicity and Education, 14*(1), 91–103.

Hawkins, B. (1998a). The dominant images of black men in America: The representation of O. J. Simpson. In G. Sailes (Ed.), *African Americans in sport* (pp. 39–52). New Brunswick, NJ: Transaction Publishers.

Hilliard, A. G., III, (1998). SBA: *The reawakening of the African mind.* Gainesville, FL: Makare Publishing.

Hine, D. C., Hine, W. C., & Harrold, S. (2006). *The African-American odyssey: Since 1965* (Third ed. Vol. Two). Upper Saddle River, NJ: Pearson Prentice Hall.

Hodge, S. R., Burden, J. W., Jr., Robinson, L. E., & Bennett, R. A., III. (2008). Theorizing on the stereotyping of Black male student-athletes: Issues and implications. *Journal for the Study of Sports and Athletes in Education, 2*(2), 203–226.

Howard, T. C. (2014). *Black male(d): Peril and promise in the education of African American males.* New York, NY: Teachers College Press.

Howard, J. (2017, May 22). Myron Rolle's journey from NFL to neurosurgery. *CNN*. Retrieved from https://www.cnn.com/2017/05/19/health/myron-rolle-nfl-medical-school-profile/index.html

Johnson, T. S., & Migliaccio, T. A. (2009). The social construction of an athlete: African American boy's experience in sport. *The Western Journal of Black Studies, 33*(2), 98–109.

Karenga, M. (1978). *Essays on struggle: Position and analysis.* San Diego, CA: Kawaida Publications.

King, M. L. Jr. (1967, October 26). *What is your life's blueprint speech.* Philadelphia, PA: Barratt Junior High School.

King Center, (2013, April 9). MLK Quote of the week: "All labor that uplifts humanity has dignity and importance and should be undertaken with painstaking excellence." Quote from Dr. Martin Luther King, Jr. speech "What is Your Life's Blueprint" on October 26, 1967 at Barratt High School in Philadelphia, PA. King Center website. Retrieved from http://www.thekingcenter.org/blog/mlk-quote-week-all-labor-uplifts-humanity-has-dignity-and-importance-and-should-be-undertaken

Krogstad, J. M., & Fry, R. (2014, April 24). More Hispanics, Blacks enrolling in college, but lag in bachelor's degrees. *Pew Research Center*. Retrieved from http://www.pewresearch.org/fact-tank/2014/04/24/more-hispanics-blacks-enrolling-in-college-but-lag-in-bachelors-degrees/

Latack, A. (2003, February 5). Double major. *ESPN*. Retrieved from http://www.espn.com/magazine/vol6no04okafor.html

Majors, R., & Billson, J. M. (1992). *Cool pose: The dilemmas of Black manhood in America.* New York, NY: Lexington Books.

Martin, B. E., & Harris, F., III. (2006). Examining productive conceptions of masculinities: Lessons learned from academically driven African American male student-athletes. *The Journal of Men's Studies, 14*(3), 359–378.

Martin, B. E., Harrison, C. K., Stone, J., & Lawrence, S. M. (2010). Athletic voices and academic victories: African American male student-athlete experiences in the Pac-Ten. *Journal of Sport & Social Issues, 34*(2), 131–153.

Matsuda, M. (1995). Looking to the bottom: Critical legal studies and reparations. In K. Crenshaw, N. T. Gotanda, G. Peller & K. Thomas (Eds.), *Critical race theory: The key writings that formed the movement* (pp. 63–79). New York, NY: The New Press.

Moore, C. (2018, January 17). Caylin Moore speech. *The Power of Race in College Athletics: 2018 Black Student Athlete Summit* at the University of Texas at Austin. Retrieved from https://www.youtube.com/watch?v=NF1ASdrVPQU&t=24s

Nord, M., Coleman-Jensen, A., Andrews, M., & Carlson, S. (2010, November). Household food security in the United States. *United States Department of Agriculture, Economic Research Report (ERR) Number 108*. [Economic Research Service]. Retrieved from https://www.hsdl.org/?view&did=12980

Ogunwole, S. U., Battle, K. R., & Cohen, D. T. (2017). Characteristics of selected Sub-Saharan African and Caribbean Ancestry Groups in the United States: 2008–2012. *American Community Survey Reports, ACS-34*. Retrieved from https://www.census.gov/content/dam/Census/library/publications/2017/acs/acs-34.pdf

Oseguera, L. (2010). Success despite the image: How African American male student-athletes endure their academic journey amidst negative characterizations. *Journal for the Study of Sports and athletes in Education*, 4(3), 297–324.

Pascarella, E. T., & Terenzini, P. T. (2005). *How college affects students: A third decade of research.* San Francisco, CA: Jossey-Bass.

Reeves, R. V., & Guyot, K. (2017, December 4). Black women are earning more college degrees, but that alone won't close race gaps. Brookings. Retrieved from https://www.brookings.edu/blog/social-mobility-memos/2017/12/04/black-women-are-earning-more-college-degrees-but-that-alone-wont-close-race-gaps/

Rittenberg, A. (2016, December 29). The remarkable story of TCU's Rhodes scholar, Caylin Moore. *ESPN*. Retrieved from http://www.espn.com/college-football/story/_/id/18358380/the-remarkable-story-tcu-rhodes-scholar-caylin-moore

Sage, G. H. (1998). *Power and ideology in American sport* (2nd ed.). Champaign, IL: Human Kinetics.

Sage, G. H., & Eitzen, D. S. (2013). *Sociology of North American sport.* New York, NY: Oxford University Press.

Sailes, G. (2010). The African American athlete: Social myths and stereotypes. In G. Sailes (Ed.), *Modern sport and the African American athlete experience* (pp. 55–68). San Diego, CA: Cognella.

Schott Foundation for Public Education. (2015). Black lives matter: The Schott 50 state report on public education and Black males. In A. Beaudry (Ed.), *The Metropolitan Center for Research on Equity and the Transformation of Schools at New York University*. Retrieved from http://www.blackboysreport.org/2015-black-boys-report.pdf

Sellers, R. M. (2000). African American student-athletes: Opportunity or exploitation? In D. A. Brooks, R. (Ed.), *Racism in college athletics: The African American athlete's experience* (2nd ed., pp. 133–154). Morgantown, WV: Fitness Information Technology, Inc.

Shropshire, K. (2000). Shaka's revenge: Not all Black men can jump. In T. Boyd and K. Shropshire (Eds.), *America Above the Rim: Basketball Jones* (p. xiii-xviii). New York, NY: New York University Press.

Singer, J. N. (2005). Understanding racism through the eyes of AfricanAmerican male student athletes. *Race, Ethnicity and Education*, 8(4), 365–386.

Singer, J. N. (2009). African American football athletes' perspectives on institutional integrity in college sport. *Research Quarterly for Exercise and Sport*, 80(1), 102–116.

Singer, J. N. (2015). The mis-education of African American male college athletes. In E. Comeaux (Ed.), *Introduction to intercollegiate athletics* (pp. 193–206). Baltimore, MD: Johns Hopkins University Press.

Singer, J. N., & May, R. A. B. (2010). The career trajectory of a Black male high school basketball player: A social reproduction perspective. *International Review for the Sociology of Sport*, 46(3), 299–314.

Smith, M. P., Clark, L. D., & Harrison, L., Jr. (2014). The historical hypocrisy of the Black student-athlete. *Race, Gender & Class*, 21(1–2), 220–235.

Solomon, G. (1988, January 17). "Jimmy the Greek" fired by CBS for his remarks. *The Washington Post*. Retrieved from https://www.washingtonpost.com/archive/politics/1988/01/17/jimmy-the-greek-fired-by-cbs-for-his-remarks/27536e46-3031-40c2-bb2b-f912ec518f80/?utm_term=.c5f3a2aef5c5

Solórzano, D., & Yosso, T. (2002). Critical race methodology: Counter-storytelling as an analytical framework for education research. *Qualitative Inquiry*, 8(1), 23–44.

Steinfeldt, J. A., Reed, C., & Steinfeldt, M. C. (2010). Racial and athletic identity of African American football players at historically Black colleges and universities and predominantly White institutions. *Journal of Black Psychology*, 36(1), 3—24.

Thompson, W. (2018). The burden of being Myron Rolle. *ESPN OTL*. Retrieved from http://www.espn.com/espn/eticket/story?page=100218/myronrolle

TIDES. (2018). The racial and gender report card. *The Institute for Diversity and Ethics in Sport website*. Retrieved from http://www.tidesport.org/reports.html

U.S. Census Bureau (2017a). Population estimates. Retrieved from https://www.census.gov/quickfacts/fact/table/US/PST045217

U.S. Census Bureau (2017b, June 28). Selected Sub-Saharan African and Caribbean ancestry groups making their mark: Nigerians outpace U.S. educational and occupational levels. Retrieved from https://www.census.gov/newsroom/press-releases/2017/cb17-108-subsaharan.html

Wiggins, D. K. (2014). 'Black athletes in White men's games': Race, sport and American national pastimes. *The International Journal of the History of Sport*, 31(1–2), 181–202.

Wiggins, D. K., & Miller, P. B. (2003). *The unlevel playing field: A documentary history of the African-American experience in sport*. Urbana, IL: University of Illinois Press.

Woodson, C. G. (1933/1990). *The mis-education of the Negro*. Trenton, NJ: Africa World Press.

Yosso, T. J. (2005). Whose culture has capital? A critical race theory discussion of community cultural wealth. *Race, Ethnicity and Education*, 8(1), 69–91.

· 8 ·

HOLISTIC EMPOWERMENT MODEL

Conscious Resistance Against Exploitation

What is called for is not a black retreat from sport but reflection upon the black situation in sport followed by a collective and coordinated offensive aimed ... at aiding student athletes currently vulnerable to academic victimization and athletic exploitation ... and at eliminating or neutralizing the social and institutionalized forces responsible for the systematic creation and accommodation of the black "dumb jock."

—Edwards (1984, p. 10)

The Interplay Between Systemic Conditions for the Holistic Empowerment Model and Black Male Athletes

On August 26, 2016, Colin Kaepernick generated widespread media attention for his peaceful protest when he sat down during the playing of the National Anthem before an NFL preseason game between the San Francisco 49ers and Green Bay Packers. Two days after the game, Kaepernick addressed reporters explaining why he chose not to stand for this nationalistic ritual (KTVU, 2016). In his explanation, he articulated how his gesture signified his solidarity with people in the U.S. who have been and continue to be oppressed particularly those who have unjustly suffered from police brutality,[1] a grossly flawed criminal (in)justice system, perpetual abuses and neglect towards people from economically disadvantaged backgrounds, military veterans being underserved, and a general lack of fairness (Kaepernick, 2018). Even though, the magnification of Kaepernick's actions before the third preseason game were viewed as controversial, he had performed the same gesture during the first two preseason games of the 2016–2017 season with little attention being paid to him. After receiving significant public backlash from this demonstration, Kaepernick had a conversation with former NFL player and U.S. Army Green Beret, Nate Boyer, and subsequently decided to change his protest from sitting to kneeling in an effort to ensure those involved in and supportive of the military did not misinterpret his actions as disrespecting their sacrifices and efforts. The first game Kaepernick kneeled as a protest was September 1, 2016 before the San Francisco 49ers versus San Diego Chargers preseason game. As a professional athlete, who just two years prior signed a $126 million contract, Kaepernick knew his actions would jeopardize his future in the NFL (Gaines, 2017). However, in the face of adversity, he chose *courage and integrity over comfort and conformity. This choice personifies holistic empowerment.*

In order to understand the concept of holistic empowerment, it is important to first examine the history and contexts by which Black male athletes have leveraged their platforms in and through sport to engage in broader social justice efforts on behalf of the Black community (Edwards, 1969, 1980, 2016). From a socio-historical perspective, Kaepernick's symbolic activism did not occur in isolation, but rather it served as an extension of disruptive actions within the broader Black Lives Matter (BLM) movement beginning in 2013 (Cooper, Mallery, & Macaulay, forthcoming). In previous work, my colleagues and I offered the following definition of activism:

> ... engagement in intentional actions that challenge a clearly defined opposition and disrupt hegemonic systems perpetuating oppression, injustice, and inequity while simultaneously promoting empowerment among those historically oppressed, fairness/equity, human dignity, and demands for a shift in power relations in concert with broader social justice movements. (Cooper, Macaulay, & Rodriguez, 2017, pp. 4–5)

Throughout history, Black male athletes have challenged oppressive forces within and beyond sport (Edwards, 1969, 1980, 2016; Hartmann, 2000; Wiggins, 2014; Wiggins & Miller, 2003). Dating back to the late 19th and early 20th century, similar to their Black counterparts outside of sport, Black male athletes have faced outright exclusion, nominal inclusion accompanied by staunch White resistance, racial discrimination, limited access to leadership positions, and economic exploitation (Cooper, 2012).

In the U.S., the prevailing macrosystem is comprised of dominant ideologies such as White racism, capitalism, neoliberalism, and ideological hegemony (see Figure 8.1) (Beyer & Hannah, 2000; Coakley, 2017; Hawkins, 1998a; Sage, 1998). The following state actions enacted these ideologies through legalized oppression: (a) chattel slavery until the passage of the 13th amendment in 1865, (b) unequal citizenship rights based on race until the *Civil Rights Act of 1866*, (c) unequal protection under the law and lack of due process until the passage of the 14th amendment in 1868, (d) unequal access to educational institutions prior to the *Brown v. Board of Education of Topeka* (1954), (e) racial discrimination in public accommodations (e.g., commercialized entities, schools, parks, hospitals, etc.) and labor (e.g., hiring, retention, promotion, firings, job referrals, etc.) until the *Civil Rights Act of 1964*, (f) exclusion from voting until the *Voting Rights Act of 1965* (initially granted via the 15th Amendment in 1870, but due to racist policies such as poll taxes, literacy tests, and verification records among other tactics prevented the full implementation of this law), and (g) housing discrimination until the *Civil Rights Act of 1968* (also referred to as the Fair Housing Act) to name a few (Hine, Hine, & Harrold, 2006). The aforementioned laws were a progressive legal step, but as history has revealed the manifestation of equity, fairness, equality, and justice relies on enforcement and accountability. In concert with the macrosystem, the chronosystem has been comprised of disruption, dysfunction, and destruction of the Black family and community as reflective in trends such as the decreasing number of Black nuclear families, the geographical and psychosocial separation of Black communities (e.g., gentrification, redlining, etc.), and the murder of Black social justice leaders and agitators who challenged WRC (Bell, 1992; Curry, 2017; Hine, Hine, & Harrold, 2006).

Along the same lines, the exosystem for Blacks over the centuries has included systemic unemployment, political disenfranchisement, criminalization via surveillance and incarceration, limited access to quality healthcare, exposure to substandard housing and environments, a lack of protection from imposed state and citizen violence, abuse, and assault, disparate educational attainment, and underrepresentation of Blacks in leadership positions in sport (e.g., ownership, management/administration, and coaching), and *Blaxploitation through sport* to name a few (Bush & Bush, 2013a, 2013b; Brooks & Althouse, 2000; Cooper, 2012; Edwards, 1969, 1973, 1980, 1984, 2000, 2016; ETS, 2011; TIDES, 2018). The mesosystem and microsystem involve interactions

grounded in and an internalization of racist myths, among Black males themselves and those in direct relationship and/or connection to them, such as the
innate athletic superiority and intellectual inferiority myth (Edwards, 1984,
2000; Sailes, 2010), athletic manifest destiny (Coakley, 2017), and Black male
criminality (Alexander, 2012; Curry, 2017; Howard, 2014; Noguera, 2008).

In response to these harsh conditions, Blacks in the U.S. have created and
activated protective counter strategies to ensure their survival and uplift (see
Figure 8.1). These responses have manifested in the forms of spirituality, religion, Afrocentric and Black empowerment philosophies and related politically
driven social movements (e.g., Black Nationalism, Pan-Africanism, Black Exis-
tentialism, Black Feminism, Black Power, Civil Rights Movement, Black Lives
Matter, etc.), music and art (i.e., Harlem Renaissance), economics/businesses
(e.g., Black Wall Street, Black Harlem, etc.), educational institutions, (i.e.,
HBCUs and Black primary and secondary schools), military (e.g., revolts, Black
Power, Deacons for Defense and Justice), and sports (e.g., HBCU athletics, Har-
lem Rens, Negro Leagues, etc.) (Cooper, Macaulay, & Rodriguez, 2017; Cooper,
Mallery, & Macaulay, forthcoming; Edwards, 1980, 2016; Hine et al., 2006).
More specifically during each era, Black athletes (both female and male) have
engaged in emancipatory efforts using their platforms in and through sport.
During the early 1900s through the 1940s, through the efforts of Black male
athletes such as Jack Johnson, Paul Robeson, Fritz Pollard, Moses Fleetwood
Walker, Bud Fowler, Joe Louis, E. B. Henderson, and Rube Foster *enhanced
legitimacy* for the race was pursued in sport, social, educational, business, and
political sectors (Edwards, 2016). These efforts coincided with the Black Liberation Movement through Reconstruction (1880s–1920s) led by leaders such
as W. E. B. Du Bois, Booker T. Washington, Ida B. Wells-Barnett, Anna Julia
Cooper, and Marcus Mosiah Garvey to name a few (Cooper, Mallery, & Macaulay, forthcoming; Smith, 1994; Stewart, 1996). Hence, holistic empowerment
in sport is inextricably connected to the Black struggle in society more broadly.

From the mid-1940s to the early 1960s, Black athlete activism shifted
towards a focus on *acquiring political access and diversity* (Edwards, 2016). This
aim is reflective of the Black Integration Movement (1930s–1960s) that preceded the Civil Rights Movement in the 1960s. During this era, the Congress
for Racial Equality (CORE) was established in 1942 and Southern Christian Leadership Conference (SCLC) in 1957 (Cooper, Mallery, & Macaulay,
forthcoming; Smith, 1994; Stewart, 1996). Along the same lines, when Jackie
Robinson broke the color barrier in MLB in 1947, it was a major victory for
Blacks at the time who believed this change would result in racial integration

and equality for Blacks in all facets of society (Cooper, Macaulay, & Rodriguez, 2017). In fact, seven years later, the landmark *Brown v. Board of Education of Topeka* (1954) decision legally desegregated public schools in the U.S., which extended the momentum for equality through integration. In 1953, the NAIA desegregated by allowing HBCUs to become member institutions. Shortly thereafter, led by Hall of Fame Coach John B. McLendon Tennessee Agricultural and Industrial (A&I) State College (now Tennessee State University), an HBCU, won three straight NAIA championships (1957–1959), which demonstrated the possibilities for Black excellence in racially integrated spaces when granted the opportunity to compete on a leveled playing field with Whites (Cooper, Cavil, & Cheeks, 2014).

The era where Black athlete activism was at its peak occurred in the 1960s when the movement agenda centered on *demanding dignity and respect* (Edwards, 2016). In conjunction with the Civil Rights Movement, the use of sit-ins and peaceful protests were also utilized in sporting spaces reflecting the reach and coordination of Black collectivism. The 1967 *Ali Summit* with Muhammad Ali, Jim Brown, Bill Russell, and Kareem Abdul-Jabbar, the famous 1968 Olympic protest in Mexico City, Mexico led by Tommie Smith and John Carlos, the successful Olympic Project for Human Rights (OPHR) boycott of the New York Athletic Club (NYAC) national indoor track and field meet led by Dr. Harry Edwards, and numerous boycotts at HWIs across the U.S. highlighted the heightened Black consciousness among athletes in this era (Cooper, Macaulay, & Rodriguez, 2017; Edwards, 1969, 1980; Harris, 2000; Hartmann, 2000; Wiggins, 2000). One glaring example of this amplified socio-political consciousness and engagement among Black male athletes occurred on October 17, 1969 when 14 football players at the University of Wyoming were dismissed from the team for protesting overt racist practices condoned by their upcoming opponent, Brigham Young University (BYU) (White, 2014). Led by Earl Lee and Jerry Berry, 14 Black male football players (John Griffin, Willie Hysaw, Don Meadows, Ivie Moore, Tony Gibson, Joe Williams, Mel Hamilton, Jim Issac, Tony Magee, Ted Williams, Lionel Grimes, and Ron Hill) notified their head coach, Lloyd Eaton, that they were planning to wear Black armbands to signify their protest against the Church of Jesus Christ of Latter-Day Saints (LDS; also referred to as Mormons) who at the time had a policy that banned Black males from entering the priesthood. Their symbolic activism (Cooper, Macaulay, & Rodriguez, 2017) received national attention and subsequently led to the desegregation of the BYU football team in 1969 and the LDS priesthood in 1978 (White,

2014). Furthermore, the publication of important texts such as *The Revolt of the Black Athlete* (Edwards, 1969) and the autobiography of Bill Russell, *Go Up for Glory* (Russell & McSweeney, 1966), as a form of scholarly activism commanded dignity and respect from a racist society that subjugated Blacks' intellectual contributions in general and Black athletes more specifically (Cooper, Macaulay, & Rodriguez, 2017). Collectively, the high visibility of Black athlete activism fulfilled a pivotal role in the attainment of racial progress in the Civil Rights era.

According to Edwards (2016), the 1970s–2005 was a period of Black athlete activism *stagnation*. For Blacks in the U.S., there was growing sentiment that the legal victories of the Civil Rights era would result in racial justice and equal opportunities. This misguided assumption underestimated the breadth, depth, and malleability of WRC. Strategies implemented by White power holders included the use of symbolic advances without any substantive change to previously established hierarchies (Bass, 2002). From 2005 to the present day, the Black athlete activism movement has prioritized *securing and transferring power through economic and technological capital* (Edwards, 2016). For example, a class action lawsuit led by Ed O'Bannon, as a form of legal activism, successfully altered exploitative NCAA policies that enabled the organization and its member institutions to unjustly profit off the image and likeness of current and former men's basketball college athletes without compensating them (Cooper, Macaulay, & Rodriguez, 2017; Nocera & Strauss, 2016). Regarding technological power, LeBron James and his Miami Heat teammates participated in a social media campaign titled #WeAreTrayvonMartin to draw attention to the unjust killing of Trayvon Martin and the subsequent not guilty verdict of George Zimmerman in 2012. This use of social media activism connected to the foundational strength of the surging BLM movement in the early 2010s (Cooper, Macaulay, & Rodriguez, 2017).

In sum, during the pre-assimilation era (before the 1960s), Black existence was largely predicated on racial solidarity due to legalized racial segregation. The aforementioned conditions enabled Blacks across various socioeconomic and educational backgrounds to live and socialize in close proximity to one another, which fostered collectivist efforts. However, in the post-assimilation era (after 1960s), previous synergistic efforts have been stifled by WRC and its evolutionary tactics. In particular, in the past race was the primary unifier for Blacks across socioeconomic statuses, political affiliations, gender groups, educational backgrounds, religions, and geographical locations. This galvanization was and remains necessary for sustained social movements. More specific to Black male athlete activism, contrary to the aims of the Conveyor Belt (Rhoden, 2006), these individuals understood their sport participation, accomplishments, and social status did not supersede or negate their connection to the broader Black community and African Diaspora. Otherwise stated, they possessed a level of critical consciousness about macro-, exo-, meso-, and micro-level oppressions imposed upon Black people in WRC and actively resisted these structures, policies, practices, and beliefs.

Moreover, the HEM involves *the intentional cultivation of critical consciousness of oppressive structures, internalized empowerment to change present and future realities, and consistent engagement in counter-actions against ideological hegemonic structures, policies, and practices.*[2] Beyond philanthropic efforts (i.e., charities), Black male athletes in the HEM utilize their agency to engage in concerted efforts to address social injustices and oppressions impacting the Black community. HEM outcomes do not necessarily involve activism, but rather an awareness and intentional use of one's platforms, including in and through sport, to draw attention and direct efforts towards redressing social inequalities, inequities, injustices, and issues impacting the broader Black community. Mutua (2006) explained the significance of this type of identity development with her explanation of progressive Black masculinities:

> As such, combining both progressive blackness and progressive masculine practice, progressive black masculinities are men who take an active and ethical stance against all systems of domination and who act personally and in concert with others in activities against racism, sexism, homophobia and heterosexism, class and economic exploitation, imperialism, and other systems of oppression that limit the human potential of black masculine self and others ... Progressive blackness therefore is this intervention. It is the ethical and active participation in antiracist struggles from the standpoint of black identity and black communities' well-being. (pp. 7–8)

The critical consciousness developed through the HEM inherently involves the embodiment of progressive Black masculinities. This intentional cultivation and internalization is akin to Stevenson's (1994) concept of racial socialization whereby Black youth are educated on the historical, political, social, cultural, economic, and psychological impact of race and racism in society across ecological systems (e.g., chrono, macro, exo, mes, micro, and sub etc.). In a society founded upon and structured by WRC, Blacks are exposed to conditions that foster their holistic underdevelopment and counterproductive masculinities. Particularly germane to Black male athletes are the notions that racism does not exist because their athletic status takes precedence; as males it is expected that they reinforce oppressive heteronormativity and toxic masculinity (also prevalent in mainstream—not be confused with the origins of the culture, lifestyle, and genre—Hip-Hop music which has a longstanding relationship with Black sport culture—see Boyd (2003), Boyd and Shropshire (2000), George (1992), and Leonard and King (2012) for extended analyses on this topic); and ignore broader inequalities in society in order to ensure individual mobility and comfort in spite of the perpetual marginalization of Black people as a collective (Edwards, 1969, 1980, 2000; Hawkins, 1998a, 1998b; Powell, 2008; Rhoden, 2006). The HEM is emblematic of the legacy of resistance against oppressive forces exhibited by Blacks throughout the U.S. and world history. As Edwards (1980) postulated in the title of his autobiography, the HEM exemplifies *the struggle that must be.*

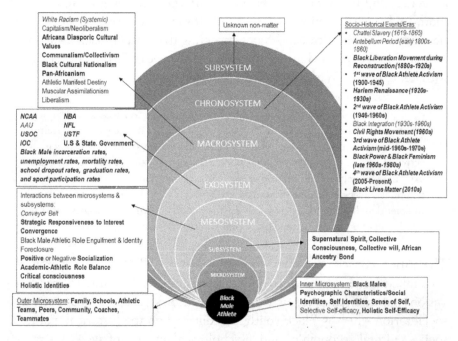

Figure 8.1. Holistic Empowerment Model (HEM).

Source: Adapted from Bush, L. V., & Bush, E. C. (2013a). Introducing African American male theory (AAMT). *Journal of African American Males in Education*, 4(1), p. 9. Copyright 2013 Journal of African American Males in Education.

Socialization Phases of the Holistic Empowerment Model

In the early phase of the HEM, Black male athletes are introduced to sport as a healthy outlet for positive social interaction and character development. Similar to the P²EPGM, Black male athletes in the HEM are socialized to view sports as a means to an end and not an end in of itself. Sport is one of multiple avenues that can lead to personal growth, economic stability, and overall quality of life and satisfaction. Another common early phase socialization experience shared by those in the P²EPGM and HEM is the strong emphasis on educational attainment. Education is viewed as the most important priority in terms of fulfilling one's purposes in life. In contrast to previous models, the HEM involves encounters with conditions, people, and/or information that produces emergent critical consciousness at this early phase. Along the same lines as Harrison, Harrison, and Moore's (2002) application of Cross's (1995) encounter phase in their African American racial identity through sport participation model, Black male athletes in the HEM acquire an intensified level of racial consciousness as a result of encountering a White oppressive force (e.g., poverty, overt racist actions, denied access to equitable education, etc.). However, differences in the HEM and Harrison et al.'s (2002) model is the lack of a pre-encounter phase and the fact that the development of racial consciousness at this phase is not exclusively manifested in sport participation choices. Within their model (Harrison et al., 2002), the pre-counter stage involves race neutral or anti-Black views prior to an encounter whereas the HEM begins and ends with strong positive Black racial identification, which is fostered by family, local community, mentors, role models, and/or race-centric reference groups. Additionally, Harrison et al.'s (2002) model focuses on how racial identity development influences sport participation exclusively while the HEM includes the nurturance of critical consciousness for Black males' navigation through a society founded upon and structured by WRC. Thus, this consciousness is cultivated for survival and thriving in spaces within and beyond sport such as miseducation schooling settings.

During the adolescence phase, Black males in the HEM participate in competitive sports like their peers in the ISSM, EALM, TRM, and P²EPGM. The perception of using sport to fulfill personal, family, and community goals is present at this stage. Since sports has a unique place in the Black community dating back to the mid-1800s, the collective memory regarding the positive benefits of excelling in sport remains salient in the HEM for Black male identity development. However, this interest in sport does not extend to the point of athletic role engulfment as with the ISSM, EALM, and TRM. Consciousness remains present, but due to increased attention and exposure to mass media images of Black male athletes there is not a high level of resistance to the status quo at this point. In other words, Black male athletes and their families are not overtly avoiding participation in White-controlled sporting spaces. Yet, the awareness of the racial and power dynamics is present at this phase. The HEM produces awareness of exploitative tools of WRC through sport such as the Conveyor Belt (Rhoden, 2006) and the flaws in the schooling process embedded in the K-20 miseducation schooling system (Bush & Bush, 2013a, 2013b). This awareness results in tactful approaches regarding how to avoid succumbing to these systems, which occurs with Black male athletic role engulfment, identity foreclosure, and holistic literal and figurative death in the ISSM, EALM, and early phases of the TRM.

The emphasis of Black sport participation being connected to broader racial and cultural goals at the young adulthood phase is akin to the immersion-emersion phase of Harrison et al.'s (2002) model. The adoption of symbols of Afrocentric cultural values and styles is present in both the HEM and Harrison et al.'s (2002) model. Within their model, this stage involves racial segregation, but in the HEM this phase involves more strategic interactions with Whites. For example, at this phase Black males do not hold disdain for Whites individually, but rather begin to understand and have aversion for Whiteness as a system and ideology (Asante, 1990, 2003; Feagin, 2006; Feagin, Vera, & Batur, 2000; Woodson, 1933/1990). In other words, this phase is characterized by Black self-love without dislike of individual Whites, but rather a contempt for WRC. Another difference at this phase is sport participation choices are not self-segregated in the HEM as they are with Harrison et al.'s (2002) model. Some Black male athletes in the HEM will explicitly choose to participate in sports where they are racially in the numerical minority in order to disprove negative stereotypes attributed to their race. For those who participate in sports where Blacks are overrepresented, there is a level of racial and cultural pride exhibited in performing at a high level whereby sport victories against predominantly White teams are viewed symbolic feats for the race.

A third difference at this phase of the HEM and Harrison et al.'s (2002) model is the transference of racial and cultural pride and focus on sport towards excelling in educational spaces. Black males in the HEM understand that improving the plight of Blacks as a collective inherently involves demystifying the "dumb jock" label (Edwards, 1984). Thus, both education and sport are viewed as emancipatory and empowerment tools for Black collective progress when utilized strategically as opposed to inherently being liberating (e.g., schooling, *Blaxploitation through sport*, athletic role engulfment, post-athletic career disengagement trauma, etc. all have negative effects on the health of the Blacks as a collective). Conquering the schooling process (Bush & Bush, 2013a, 2013b) and mastering transformative and revolutionary education is pursued throughout this phase (Edwards, 1980, 2016). Beyond joining organizations and political groups (Harrison et al., 2002), Black males in the HEM actively pursue opportunities to engage in activist actions while being keenly aware of the potential consequences. The rewards associated with racial resistance against oppression outweigh neoliberal and capitalistic aims and penalties.

In the adulthood phase, Black male athletes in the HEM continue to pursue activism and other actions against WRC in a myriad of ways. In previous work, my colleagues and I outlined a typology of African American sport activism with the following categories:

(a) symbolic (i.e., protests),
(b) scholarly (i.e., academic contributions),
(c) sports-based (i.e., leveraged influence to alter rules within a sport, league, or organization),
(d) grassroots (i.e., organization and mobilization efforts at a local level),
(e) economic (i.e., intentional financial enrichment of the Black community and concurrent divestment from sources of WRC),
(f) media (i.e., the use of multi-media platforms to generate social change),
(g) political (i.e., direct involvement in and confrontation with governmental/state entities),
(h) legal (i.e., the use of the judicial system to change laws, procedures, and enforcements for more equity, equality, and justice),
(i) music and art (i.e., hegemonic disruption via cultural expression), and
(j) military (i.e., direct or indirect involvement or support of counter-hegemonic armed actions)
(Cooper, Macaulay, & Rodriguez, 2017; Cooper, Mallery, & Macaulay, forthcoming)

At this phase, Black males in the HEM are pursuing multiple ways to disrupt, reduce, and eliminate the structure of WRC. In addition to the aforementioned types of activism, pioneering (i.e, Jack Johnson becoming the first Black heavyweight boxing champion in 1910), advocacy (i.e., the *Ali Summit* in 1967), and agency (i.e., the wearing of Afros during the 1960s to signify allegiance with the Black Power movement and to exude Black self-love in a society where White phenotypical features are deemed as superior) are strategically pursued as well.

In summary, when Black male athletes' are socialized into viewing themselves as holistic individuals who possess a range of skills, abilities, and knowledge, then they are less likely to be exploited by the athletic industrial complex (AIC; Hawkins, 2010; Smith, 2009). In addition, Black male athletes who are cultivated to understand their role within the broader Black struggle experience holistic consciousness, internalized empowerment, and engagement in counter-actions throughout their lifespan (Cooper, 2016). At an early age, they are exposed to the realities and detrimental effects of the Conveyor Belt system (Rhoden, 2006) and its connection to the broader apparatus of White oppressive forces against Black collective progress. Throughout their lives, Black male athletes in the HEM are intentionally taught and understand how to challenge WRC.

Evidence of the Holistic Empowerment Model

A prominent pillar of the HEM is the life and legacy of Paul Robeson. Robeson was the son of William and Maria Robeson (Robeson, 1958/1988). His father was formerly enslaved and during his teenage years he was able to evade slavery to pursue a career as a minister when he became a free man (Edwards, 1980; Robeson, 1958/1988). At an early age, Robeson was instilled with values of strong racial pride and commitment to improving the plight of Black people through his actions. The lesson he was taught as a youth and later embody as a *holistically empowered agent of change* was "... the conviction that personal integrity was inseparable from the quest for maximum human fulfillment; that its very essence was a relentless struggle for the highest and richest development of one's full potential" (Edwards, 1980, p. 207). Equipped with this critical race-conscious mindset, Robeson noticed how he was always revered for his athletic prowess from his youth through young adulthood particularly when he attended the racially "integrated" (rather assimilated) Somerville High School in Somerville, New Jersey (Edwards, 1980; Robeson, 1958/1988). Despite being labeled as a Black dumb jock, Robeson defied stereotypes by excelling academically and being actively involved in co-curricular activities such as dramatic theater (Robeson, 1958/1988).

After high school, Robeson enrolled at Rutgers University, as the fifth African American student in school history and the only one enrolled in 1915, where he experienced tremendous success both in the classroom and on the football field (Edwards, 1980; Robeson, 1958/1988; Smith, 1994). During his time at Rutgers, he earned Phi Beta Kappa scholar status, a two-time Walter Camp All-American, and became an international star for his acting, oratory, and musical performances (Edwards, 1980; Robeson, 1958/1988). However, this success did not come without a cost. The pervasive racism confronting him from teachers, coaches, teammates, classmates, fans, and opposing teams took a toll on him physically and mentally. Similar treatment continued after he left Rutgers during his professional career as an actor and singer. It has been noted that Black male athletes who disrupt the WRC status quo inevitably face backlash in a multitude of ways (Cooper, Macaulay, & Rodriguez, 2017; Edwards, 1980). From 1919–1923, he simultaneously was enrolled in Columbia Law School and played professional football. He retired from football in 1922 and earned his law degree from Columbia University one year later (Robeson, 1958/1988; Smith, 1994).

At the peak of his acting career, he starred in Shakespeare's famous play, *Othello*, in London and was the first Black actor to fulfill this role (Stewart, 1996). Later in 1937, he was the lead role in the film, *The Emperor Jones*, written by White play writer Eugene O'Neill and the film was considered a symbolic representation of the Harlem Renaissance era because of its compelling depiction of African Americans (Stewart, 1996). In the face of insurmountable obstacles, his spirit was grounded in his belief that his success represented the broader Black community and if change was going to come in society he had to endure and overcome these challenges. This approach is symbolic of those who experience the HEM. Similar to Black male athletes who come after him, Robeson's academic and athletic success was co-opted as the White power structure highlighted it to promote the false liberalist notion that the U.S. was racially progressive and a true meritocratic society. This messaging was particularly prevalent during the World War I (1914–1918) and Cold War eras (early 1940s–early 1990s) where the ideological war between U.S. capitalism and Russian communism intensified militarily, politically, economically, and psychologically (Edwards, 1980; Robeson, 1958/1988).

During the latter part of his life, Robeson was outspoken on human rights issues. He was a public supporter of anti-lynching laws and protested against institutions (e.g., sport, education, etc.) that engaged in racial discrimination (Edwards, 1980; Robeson, 1958/1988). He also was politically active with the Progressive Party, Council of African Affairs, National Negro Congress (NNC), Congress of Industrial Organizations (CIO) labor movement, and an anti-U.S. capitalist Black militant movement that garnered the support of Communist and Third World countries (Smith, 1994). Consistent with the history of powerful Black activists, Robeson was ostracized and his reputation was smeared by the U.S. government. His passport was revoked during the 1950s for views that were deemed as a treasonous against the U.S. (Smith, 1994). Consequently, numerous accomplishments were removed from historical records even at his alma mater Rutgers University (Edwards, 1980). Robeson epitomized the HEM through his political activism, race-conscious advocacy, and excellence and resilience in education, sport, drama, music, and politics. His legacy would inspire future generations of holistically empowered Black male athletes.

Another exemplar of the HEM, within the same Black legacy of excellence exhibited by Robeson, is Dr. Harry Edwards. Growing up in East Saint Louis, Illinois in a working class Black family with his parents and seven siblings, Edwards encountered the acute realities of poverty at an early age (Edwards, 1980). His father was an ex-gang member turned military and his mother worked as a domestic worker and sold food and clothing items to supplant their income. His early childhood experiences involved exposure to violence in the neighborhood, food insecurity, and parental neglect. As noted earlier, his early childhood experiences are reflective of a critical mass of young Black males in the U.S. who suffer from living in a gendered racist society that devalues them at a minimum and dehumanizes and exterminates them at a maximum (Alexander, 2012; Curry, 2017; ETS, 2011). In his autobiography, he described the conditions of his family and environment during his formative years:

> ... we were, for a least a short time, part of the respectable, working Black lower class. But, toward the end, what was left of the Edwards family—namely the children, alone much of the time, malnourished most of the time, and desperately in need of love and supervision all of the time—had descended through even the Black underclass and into the ranks of what can only be termed the "underfooting." (Edwards, 1980, p. 3)

These conditions had a palatable impact of Edwards's identity development and how he understood the world in which he lived. Hence, this environment, which is a direct result of WRC, and its vicious effects on the vast majority of the Black community (ETS, 2011) served as Edwards's intense and extended encounter with oppressive realities and forces (Cross, 1995; Harrison et al., 2002). This insidious system not only created the conditions that subjected his family to inhumane conditions, but ultimately resulted in the dissolution of his parents' marriage. Although, both parents loved him and his siblings, the weight of poverty and regressive impacts on his father's psychological state were a heavy burden on his mother and so she ended up leaving. WRC and its tools seek to interact with Black males in four ways: (a) to exploit, (b) to weaken, (c) to control, and (d) to destroy them psychologically, spiritually, politically, economically, sexually, and physically. once the use to WRC ceases. Edwards' father, like too many Black males in the U.S., suffered from all four of these detrimental aims.

A major influencer who intentionally cultivated critical consciousness and a true education towards Edwards was his grandmother. When reflecting on her life lessons, he said: "... I began to appreciate fully the importance of what my grandmother meant ... Not all education occurs in the classrooms, and graduated is not synonymous with educated" (Edwards, 1980, p. 8). This familial, cultural, and resistant capital (Yosso, 2005) would serve as seeds in Edwards' activist formation that would fertilize over time. From an early age Edwards developed a love for learning and education (Edwards, 1980). He described how despite growing up in impoverished conditions, education was valued by his parents and teachers (familial and aspirational capital) (Yosso, 2005). His socialization communicated that education was the great equalizer and the means by which Blacks could achieve human dignity. Attending all-Black schools in the 1950s, his teachers frequently shared and discussed the importance of Black history. As previously stated, in the pre-assimilation era (before 1960s), possessing a keen knowledge of Black history was integral in Black segregated educational spaces. Even at the primary level at Dunbar Elementary School, he learned about Blacks being lynched and the plunder they had endured in the U.S. as a result of WRC and its agents. Edwards began junior high school at Hughes-Quinn in East Saint Louis, Illinois in 1954, the same year as the landmark *Brown v. Board of Education of Topeka* (1954) case was decided. Admittedly, the three years of junior high school were difficult for him. During this time, Edwards began getting involved in organized sports with support from his father, teachers, and peers. Sport participation was viewed as a vital space for character development and life skills. His father was an avid fan of Jackson Robinson, Joe Louis, and Jesse Owens because they served as Black heroes who advanced the race towards human dignity and equality through their sporting accomplishments (Edwards, 1980).

For high school, Edwards attended newly integrated (or assimilated) East Side High School in East St. Louis, Illinois (Edwards, 1980). Black athletes at his school were enrolled in college prep courses with the assumption that they could possibly earn an athletic scholarship. In fact that was the expectation for Black males at the school who had any chance of going to college. For those who were non-athletes, they were tracked into vocational courses. These mesosystem influences reinforced the macrosystem ideology of innate Black intellectual inferiority and athletic superiority. Even though, Edwards had a love for learning, his grades in junior and senior high school were mediocre. The disruptive environment at the junior high school prohibited his learning. In high school, he encountered White people directly and the message communicated to him and his peers was that education was not for them and they should focus on sports. Consistent with Black sport participation in the early 20th century, this involvement served as a means to humanize Black males to Whites who did not see much worth in them beyond their athletic prowess. Compared to the outcomes of their Black peers who were not athletes, Edwards (1980) referred to the Black athletes as "fortunate" (p. 89). This internalization harkens back to Black athletes in the mid-19th century who received preferential treatment when they exhibited their athletic abilities for the desires of controlling Whites in a society founded upon and structured by WRC (Wiggins, 2014). Edwards was a three sport athlete participating in football, basketball, and track and field (Edwards, 1980).

After graduating high school, he moved to Fresno, California to live with his grandmother and extended family who enrolled him at a local JUCO (Fresno City College). After a series of challenges, Edwards rediscovered his love for learning when reading and studying for a history exam. He became infuriated with the White narratives that seemed to romanticize colonization and slavery. By his accord, he explained this epiphany: "The more I read, the more excited I became. I soon found out that there was a message, a story, somebody's point of view implicit in every book I had been assigned in the course. *I had learned to read critically*" (Edwards, 1980, p. 105). This transformation back to empowerment underscores the power of transmitting knowledge about Blacks' historical experiences in oppressive spaces and the ways in which they challenge these systems. On that exam, he earned the highest grade in the class (93 out of 100). His teacher complimented him on his effort and this gesture made Edwards feel affirmed and valued as a thinker and as a person as opposed to being deemed as a deviant and just an athlete. He earned a B+ cumulative GPA, which was a significant improvement from his high school grades (Edwards, 1980).

In 1960, he accepted an athletic scholarship to San Jose College (SJC; now San Jose State University (SJSU)) where he competed in track and field.

He was also very interested in the School of Social Work at SJC. Initially, the school wanted him to major in Physical Education since that was the major where athletes were clustered for eligibility purposes, but Edwards resisted and negotiated a way to pursue the Social Work major. While in school, he was recruited to play on the basketball team and he agreed. Although, he excelled academically and athletically, socially the environment on campus and surrounding community was challenging because of pervasive racism. Due to a conflict with his track and field coach regarding a racial issue with how one of his teammates was being treated, he was dismissed from the team. Since his grades were above eligibility standards and he continued to play basketball and retained his scholarship. Nonetheless, after this incident, he focused more on academics (Edwards, 1980).

In addition to his course Social Work courses, he also enrolled in "Race Relations, Sociological Theory, Social Problems, Methodology, Social Institutions, and Contemporary Movements" (Edwards, 1980, p. 127). While at SJC, he attended events such as Louis Lomax's speech on the Negro Revolt. Due to his outstanding academic performance in his Sociology classes, one of his professors recommended him for the Woodrow Wilson Fellowship and subsequently he enrolled at Cornell University. He had received materials from the San Diego Chargers and Minnesota Vikings inquiring about his interest in their teams, but he was intent on going to graduate school, which disappointed his father. His father's personal dream was to be a professional athlete (boxer), but because of life circumstances he was not able to live out his dream (Edwards, 1980).

At Cornell, his intellectual prowess continued to grow. The surrounding events in the U.S. during 1964 greatly influenced his political consciousness. He went to New York City to hear Malcolm X speak several times who he had been fond of since listening to him as an adolescent on the radio. Malcolm X was so impressionable upon Edwards that he wrote his master's thesis on the Black Muslim family, which led to his extensive research on Black political and social movements in the U.S. Listening to Malcolm X had changed Edwards' worldview of himself and Black people globally. He described this invigorating experience: "But more than merely stimulating new ideas for me, Malcolm X incited, inflamed, and legitimized a passion to *act* upon deeply felt convictions" (p. 145). Edwards (1980) explained how he felt deprived from his primary schooling years through college because he was not exposed to the writings of Blacks in this way nor to the extent that he had been during his master's and doctoral programs. He expressed how reading the works of Edward (E.) Franklin Frazier, W. E. B. Du Bois, Richard Wright, Langston Hughes, Claude McKay, James Baldwin, and Ralph Ellison lead him to this poignant conclusion: "I discovered myself!" (Edwards, 1980, p. 147). This quote illustrates the outcome of holistic consciousness and internalized empowerment associated with the HEM. In 1966, he completed his master's degree and successfully published his first manuscript titled, "A Comparative Analysis of Black Muslim and Lower-Class Negro Christian Family Relationships" in the *Journal of Marriage and the Family* (Edwards, 1980, p. 150).

After graduating he took a hiatus from Cornell (Edwards, 1980). During this year, he worked as a researcher for the Santa Clara County Economic Opportunity Commission (SCCEOC) and taught two courses as a half time instructor at SJSU from 1967–1970. Along with Ken Noel, a master's student in Sociology at the time and former distance runner, they met with SJSU administration with a list of grievances regarding the racial campus climate. With no success, Edwards organized a Rally on Racism that included a public declaration of nine demands in front of a crowd of 700 including the President and Dean of Students in the Fall of 1967. The primary threat communicated in the speech was the disruption of the opening season football game. Edwards (1980) explained their rationale: "We knew exactly what we were doing and why. We knew that sports were the only area on campus where Blacks could exercise any political leverage—and there *only* if we were organized" (p. 161). Edwards' knowledge and use of various forms of activism (political, symbolic, grassroots—organizational/mobilization, scholarly, and sports-based) underscored his sophisticated understanding of how hegemonic systems and how to attack them (Cooper, Macaulay, & Rodriguez, 2017; Cooper, Mallery, & Macaulay, forthcoming).

Prior to the rally, Edwards had joined the Black Panther Party, but disassociated shortly after a meeting with law enforcement that implied infiltration within the organization (Edwards, 1980). Later, Edwards would find out that their efforts were being monitored by the Federal Bureau of Investigation (FBI). The game versus University of Texas at El Paso was cancelled and the SJSU administration agreed to meet their demands. This symbolic activist victory garnered the attention of then governor, Ronald Reagan. In the Fall of 1967, in concert with his student Tommie Smith and other notable Black male athletes including Lee Evans, Jerry Proctor, John Carlos, and Lew Alcindor (now Kareem Abdul-Jabbar) among others, they organized the Olympic Project for Human Rights (OPHR), whose primary aim was to organize a boycott of the 1968 Olympics in Mexico City, Mexico to draw attention towards and address racial inequalities and injustices in the U.S. They had a Black Youth Conference in Los Angeles, California on November 22, 1967. They eventually gained the support of standout Black male athletes Jesse Owens, Roy Campanella, Don Newcomb, "Deacon" Dan Toliver, Jackie Robinson, and Bill Russell (Edwards, 1980, p. 180). Prominent Civil Rights leaders including Dr. Martin Luther King, Jr., Floyd McKissick, and H. Rap Brown also offered their support of the boycott (Edwards, 1980).

In the months leading up to the Olympics, the OPHR successfully organized a boycott of the NYAC national indoor track and field meet (Edwards, 1980). At the time, the NYAC was a private organization that reserved membership for Whites only. Through coordinated efforts with the Student Non-Violent Coordinating Committee (SNCC), Columbia University Black Law Student Association, H. Rap Brown, Marshall Brown, and local Black community-based groups in Harlem, they organized a boycott with 20, 000 people outside of Madison Square Garden in New York, New York the day of the event. As a result of this successful effort, between the Fall of 1967 and Spring of 1968, Edwards "received over two hundred written or phone death threats" (Edwards, 1980, p. 193). The next focus was on pressuring the President of the International Olympic Committee (IOC) and previous chairman of the United States Olympic Committee (USOC), Avery Brundage, whom was a known racist to resign his post. The plans for the collective Black athlete boycott and protest of the Olympic games dissolved due to a range of issues not the least being a lack of consensus on how and what to do. Notwithstanding, Tommie Smith and John Carlos staged their successful protest on October 16, 1968. Edwards (1980) described the significance of this symbolic activism:

> Their protest demonstration symbolized the courage, commitment, and growing political sophistication of an entire generation of young Black people ... Smith and Carlos were banished for having committed the ultimate Black transgression in a white supremacist society: They dared to become visible, to stand up for the dignity of Black people, to protest from an international platform the racist inhumanity of American society. (pp. 203–204)

Similar to their predecessors and successors in the Black struggle, Smith and Carlos chose *courage and integrity over comfort and conformity*. Edwards went on to earn his doctorate at Cornell University in 1968. He published a book titled *The Revolt of the Black Athlete* in 1969 and published 19 single authored or co-authored manuscript publications while in school. In 1973, inspired by studying previous Black male scholar activist athletes like Paul Robeson,

Edwards published the seminal textbook titled, *Sociology of Sport*. It is considered the first comprehensive systematic analysis of sport in the U.S. and he is widely recognized as the founder of the field of Sport Sociology (Edwards, 1980). Edwards' legacy changed U.S. history and his life through the HEM serves as a beacon of excellence for those committed to the Black struggle.

Muhammad Ali (formerly Cassius Clay) is yet another Black male activist athlete who experienced the HEM. Born in Louisville, Kentucky on January 17, 1942, Cassius Marcellus Clay grew up with humble beginnings and later became one of the most popular sports figures of the 20th century and global icon over the course of his 74 years of life (Ali & Durham, 1975). As a teenager, Clay's boxing career began to ascend. In 1959 and 1960, he won the Golden Gloves Championship in Chicago, Illinois. In 1960, on the international stage he earned a gold medal in the Olympics in Rome. Within the broader society, the racist unrest was mounting. Despite the passage of *Brown v. Board of Education of Topeka* (1954), there was still widespread racism in nearly every facet of society. Blacks were being brutally beaten without penalty. Particularly, in the South, racism through violent acts of the state as well as private citizens such as the Ku Klux Klan was rampant. The horrific murder of Emmett Till on August 28, 1955 greatly impacted Clay's psyche on racial injustice in the U.S. particularly since he and Till were the same age. On September 15, 1963, the bombing of the 16th street Baptist Church in Birmingham, Alabama resulted in the deaths of four Black girls, Addie Mae Collins, Denise McNair, Carole Robertson, and Cynthia Wesley. Irrespective of Clay's success in the ring, he felt compelled to do more to raise awareness and spark action against the injustices being imposed upon Black people in the U.S. (Ali & Durham, 1975).

On February 25, 1964, Clay defeated Sonny Liston to earn the world heavyweight boxing title. Shortly thereafter, Ali joined the Nation of Islam and changed his name from Cassius Clay to Muhammad Ali, which the Arabic translation means "worthy of praise" (Stewart, 1996, p. 359). This transformation was a major turning point in U.S. history. The Nation of Islam was considered a threat to the U.S. social order because it was comprised of an organized group of Blacks who were unapologetic with challenging WRC and oppression against Blacks in the U.S. and racialized groups internationally. Ali's involvement in the group reflected the broader shift in the Black community towards Black Nationalism. In contrast to the non-violent and integrationist tenor of mainstream Civil Rights leaders such as Dr. Martin Luther King, Jr., the Nation of Islam endorsed a stronger self-defense by any means necessary including violence and a racial separatist approach. Ali's frank tone and unabashed confidence demanded recognition and reflected the type of courageous and bold leadership exhibited by his mentor Malcolm X (Ali & Durham, 1975).

On April 28, 1967, Ali publicly expressed his refusal to the Army draft issued by the federal government citing his religious beliefs and anti-war sentiments (Stewart, 1996). Subsequently, he was sentenced to five-years in jail, which he appealed. During this time, his heavyweight title and boxing licensed were revoked. On June 28, 1970, Ali's five-year jail sentence was successfully appealed and the decision was reversed (Ali & Durham, 1975). Ali's political and legal activism was emblematic of his resolve to fight for his rights, beliefs, and values (Cooper, Mallery, & Macaulay, forthcoming). On March 8, 1971, Ali fought Joe Frazier in a fight touted as the "Fight of the Century" at Madison Square Garden in New York, New York. The event was the first multimillion dollar boxing match between two Black boxers and generated over $20 million in revenue with 20, 000 fans in attendance and 1.3 million viewers worldwide; Frazier won the 15-round classic fight (Smith, 1994; Stewart, 1996). Over the next several years, Ali fought multiple high-profile fights against George Foreman ("The Rumble in the Jungle" on October 30, 1974) and a third fight against Joe Frazier on September 30, 1975 in the Philippines in the famous "Thrilla in Manilla" to name a few. Aside from the sporting spectacle of each match, these fights were highly politicized whereby the opponents of Ali, particularly George Foreman, were positioned as representing America's physical weapons to symbolically defeat what Ali represented, *Black revolutionary empowerment*. Ali's commitment to challenging WRC throughout his adult life reflect the core aspects of the HEM.

Aside from historical analyses of Black male athletes' activism throughout the 20th century, [3] there are limited empirical studies that have examined their perceptions of and engagement in activist actions. In a qualitative case study of Black male undergraduate and graduate students' perceptions of race and athlete activism, Agyemang, Singer, and DeLorme (2010) found participants believed race and racism were still major social issues in society in the 21st century and expressed familiarity with notable Black athlete activism of previous generations. Participants also noted how athletes in the post-Civil Rights era were less likely to engage in activism due to concerns about potential backlash regarding their athletic prospects and future professional sport career and financial opportunities. One participant echoed Rhoden's (2006) sentiments that Black athletes in the 21st century are more entitled and thus disconnected from the issues their predecessors fought to address. All six participants in their study reiterated the importance of Black athletes using their platforms to speak out about social issues impacting society (Agyemang et al., 2010).

Related to the cultivation of critical consciousness among Black athletes, there is also a growing body of research that has highlighted the influence of culturally relevant and race-conscious mentoring programs at HWIs on Black male athletes' heightened socio-political consciousness and self-advocacy. For example, Bimper (2015) examined how Black college athletes (11 of the 15 participants were male) involved in a culturally relevant and responsive mentoring program developed a critical understanding of race and racism as well as the benefits acquired through this exposure and involvement. Using CRT, the author found the mentor-mentee relationship increased partici- pants' awareness of Whiteness and how racism manifests itself in subtle ways in racialized spaces such as HWIs. Another theme from this study revealed how the mentor-mentee relationship cultivated self-advocacy among the par- ticipants. One of the men's basketball participants, Terrence, expressed the benefits of the program for him: "The more that I've become, I guess you would say, conscious about black issues like employment, education, poverty, and like what it takes for our people [blacks] to be successful today, then I've just learned how to speak for myself" (Bimper, 2015, pp. 187–188). Similar to Edwards (1969, 1980) work with the OPHR, education is the first step of activism followed by organization and targeted action. Participants in Bim- per's (2015) study greatly benefitted from being in a structured program with a race-conscious framework undergirding its mission and goals.

Along the same lines, with my own work with the culturally relevant holistic development (CRHD) support program at UConn called Collective Uplift (CU), we utilize the strategic responsiveness to interest convergence (SRIC; Cooper & Cooper, 2015) and excellence beyond athletics (EBA; Coo- per, 2016) frameworks as our guiding principles (Collective Uplift, 2018). For SRIC, we focus on cultivating holistic consciousness, building internalized empowerment, and inspiring engagement in counter-actions against WRC and its mechanisms. Awareness of injustices is important as noted in Agyemang et al.'s (2010) study, but we posit this recognition alone is not sufficient. It must be followed by a belief that one possesses the ability to change existing realities and take action to enact improvements as an individual responsi- bility for a collective goal. Similarly, the EBA framework centralizes holistic identity development (also referred to as holistic excellence), which includes socio-political and civic identities and the understanding that every Black person's life, thoughts, choices, and behaviors are integrally connected to the broader Black struggle in the U.S. and globally (Cooper, 2016; Edwards, 1980, 2016). In a recent study of seven CU alumni, my colleagues and I found Black male college athletes who participated in the organization acquired internalized empowerment through collaborative programming with other Black and African centric campus organizations on campus as well as through the weekly meeting topics on social justice issues, Black history, and strategies for facilitating change (e.g., activism, advocacy, agency, etc.) in society (Cooper, Corral, et al., 2018). Additionally, networking sessions with Black role models across different occupational fields also fostered a sense of confidence in participants' belief that they could create the change they seek in the world. Through critical thinking/problem solving and self-reflexivity exercises, participants learned how to devise their own blueprints for racial and cultural uplift both over the short-term and long-term.

Chapter Summary

The development of critical consciousness of the historical, social, political, economic, and cultural implications of racism has informed and continues to influence societal arrangements, psychological schemas, social behaviors, and individual and group outcomes. More specifically, the HEM requires young Black males from an early age to be taught and internalize critical consciousness so they are equipped to navigate, resist, disrupt, and transform WRC including the detrimental social institutions of sport and miseducation. Furthermore, Black athleticism, fame, and glory does not disrupt the social order, but rather it is a necessary part of an apparatus of social control grounded in WRC. In contrast, a *Black holistically empowered agent of change* who participates in sports serves as a major threat to the hegemonic social order because of the visibility of their platform. As a result, the HEM through sport and education cultivates progressive Black masculinities (Mutua, 2006) that foster this engagement in counter-action (Cooper, 2016).

Consequently, *holistically empowered agents of change* who disrupt the WRC status are targeted, stifled, and eliminated at all costs. The personal transgressions experienced by Black activist athletes such as Paul Robeson, Dr. Harry Edwards, Muhammad Ali, Tommie Smith, John Carlos, and more recently Colin Kaepernick underscore the extent to which Whites controlling the dominant oppressive systems are willing to go to blunt the progress of these individuals and the ideas and collective movements they represent. In response, each of these courageous individuals utilized a range of activist approaches (symbolic, scholarly, grassroots, sports-based, economic, political, legal, media, music, art, and military) and coalesced with like-minded organizations to persist in their goals towards Black collective liberation and empowerment. In the spirit of counter-actions and resistance, scholars have also highlighted how culturally responsive and race-based approaches are necessary to integrate in traditional miseducation schooling spaces as a means to disrupt the status quo and create formal and informal pathways for Black athletes to acquire critical consciousness, internalized empowerment, and engagement in counter-actions (Bimper, 2015, 2016; Cooper, 2016; Cooper, Corral, et al., 2018; Singer, 2005, 2015). In other words, holistic empowerment addresses what Harrison (1998) described as assisting young Black males to move beyond viewing racism on the interpersonal level to understanding it on structural and institutional levels. In sum, the HEM promotes Black excellence and collectivism, which is foundational to the legacy and spirit of African people globally.

Notes

1. Examples of high profile cases involving unarmed Blacks being killed are Trayvon Martin, Michael Brown, Rekia Boyd, Alton Sterling, Jordan Davis, Tamir Rice, Eric Gardner, Renisha McBride, and Aiyana Jones, to name a few, and the subsequent lack of convictions of the agents of WRC and/or officers who took their lives.
2. This definition of HEM is a modification of the concept of strategic responsiveness to interest convergence (SRIC; Cooper & Cooper, 2015). My colleague and I posited SRIC involves the following three conditions: "(1) an individual must recognize an inequitable structural arrangement that is designed to exploit them, (2) an individual must internalize or believe they possess the power to alter their personal outcome within this arrangement, and (3) an individual must actively engage in behaviors to counter the inequitable arrangement in such a way to maximize the holistic benefits for themselves" (Cooper & Cooper, 2015; p. 147).
3. A majority of previous work on Black athlete activism has been historical in nature (see Bass (2002), Edwards (1969), Harris (2000), Hartmann (1996, 2000), Wiggins (2000, 2014), and Wiggins and Miller (2003) for extensive reviews).

References

Agyemang, K., Singer, J. N., & DeLorme, J. (2010). An exploratory study of Black male college athletes' perceptions of race and athlete activism. *International Review for the Sociology of Sport, 45*(4), 419–435.

Alexander, M. (2012). *The new Jim Crow: Mass incarceration in the age of colorblindness.* New York, NY: The New Press.

Ali, M., & Durham, R. (1975). *The Greatest: My own story.* New York, NY: Ballantine Books.

Asante, M. K. (1990). *Kemet, Afrocentricity and knowledge.* Trenton, NJ: Africa World Press.

Asante, M. K. (2003). *Afrocentricity: The theory of social change.* Chicago, IL: African American Images.

Bass, A. (2002). *Not the triumph but the struggle: The 1968 Olympics and the making of the Black athlete.* Minneapolis, MN: University of Minnesota Press.

Bell, D. A. (1992). *Faces at the bottom of the well: The permanence of racism.* New York, NY: Basic Books.

Beyer, J. M., & Hannah, D. R. (2000). The cultural significance of athletics in US higher education. *Journal of Sport Management, 14*(2), 105–132. doi:10.1123/jsm.14.2.105

Bimper, A. Y. (2015). Mentorship of Black student-athletes at a predominately White American university: Critical race theory perspective on student-athlete development. *Sport, Education and Society, 22*(2), 175–193. doi: 10.1080/12573322.2015.1022524.

Bimper, A. Y. (2016). Capital matters: Social sustaining capital and the development of Black student-athletes. *Journal of Intercollegiate Sport, 9,* 106–128.

Boyd, T. (2003). *Young, Black, rich, and famous: The rise of the NBA, the hip-hop invasion, and the transformation of American culture.* New York, NY: Doubleday.

Boyd, T., & Shropshire, K. L. (2000). *Basketball Jones: America above the rim.* New York, NY: New York University Press.

Brooks, D., & Althouse, R. (2000). *Racism in college athletics: The African American athlete's experience* (2nd ed.). Morgantown, WV: Fitness Information Technology.

Brown v. Board of Education of Topeka, 347 U.S. 483 (1954).

Bush, L. V., & Bush, E. C. (2013a). Introducing African American male theory (AAMT). *Journal of African American Males in Education, 4*(1), 6–17.

Bush, L. V., & Bush, E. C. (2013b). God bless the child who got his own: Toward a comprehensive theory for African-American boys and men. The Western Journal of Black Studies, 37(1), 1–14.

Coakley, J. (2017). *Sports in society: Issues and controversies* (12th ed.). New York, NY: McGraw-Hill Education.

Collective Uplift (2018). Goals page. Retrieved from http://www.collectiveuplift.com

Cooper, J. N. (2012). Personal troubles and public issues: A sociological imagination of Black athletes' experiences at predominantly White institutions in the United States. *Sociology Mind, 2*(3), 261–271.

Cooper, J. N. (2016). Excellence beyond athletics: Best practices for enhancing Black male student athletes' educational experiences and outcomes. *Equity & Excellence in Education, 49*(3), 267–283.

Cooper, J. N., Cavil, J. K., & Cheeks, G. (2014). The state of intercollegiate athletics at historically Black colleges and universities (HBCUs): Past, present, & persistence. *Journal of Issues in Intercollegiate Athletics, 7,* 307–332.

Cooper, J. N., & Cooper, J. E. (2015). "I'm running so you can be happy and I can keep my scholarship": A comparative examination of Black male college athletes' experiences with role conflict. *Journal of Intercollegiate Sport, 8,* 131–152.

Cooper, J. N., Corral, M. D., Macaulay, C. D. T., Cooper, M. S., Nwadike, A., & Mallery, Jr., M. (2018). Collective uplift: The impact of a holistic development support program on Black male former college athletes' experiences and outcomes. *International Journal of Qualitative Studies in Education*, DOI: 10.1080/09518398.2018.1522011.

Cooper, J. N., Macaulay, C., & Rodriguez, S. H. (2017). Race and resistance: A typology of African American sport activism. *International Review for the Sociology of Sport*, 1–31. doi: 10.1177/1012690217718170.

Cooper, J. N., Mallery, M., & Macaulay, C. D. T. (forthcoming). African American sport activism and broader social movements. In D. Brown (Ed.). *Passing the ball: Sports in African American life and culture* (p. 35–51). Jefferson, NC: McFarland & Company.

Cross, W. E., Jr. (1995). The psychology of Nigrescence: Revising the Cross model. In J. G. Ponterotto, J. M. Casas, L. A. Suzuki, & C. M. Alexander (Eds.), *Handbook of multicultural counseling*. Thousand Oaks, CA: Sage.

Curry, T. J. (2017). *The man-not: Race, class, genre, and the dilemmas of Black manhood*. Philadelphia, PA: Temple University Press.

Edwards, H. (1969). *The revolt of the Black athlete*. New York, NY: Free Press.

Edwards, H. (1973). *Sociology of sport*. Homewood, IL: Dorsey Press.

Edwards, H. (1980). *The struggle that must be: An autobiography*. New York, NY: Macmillan Publishing.

Edwards, H. (1984). The Black "dumb jock": An American sports tragedy. *College Board Review*, *131*, 8–13.

Edwards, H. (2000). Crisis of black athletes on the eve of the 21st century. *Society, 37*, 9–13.

Edwards, H. (2016). *The fourth wave: Black athlete protests in the second decade of the 21st century*. Keynote address at the North American Society for the Sociology of Sport (NASSS) conference in Tampa Bay, Florida.

ETS. (2011). *A strong start: Positioning young Black boys for educational success—a statistical profile*. Washington, DC: Educational Testing Service.

Feagin, J. (2006). *Systemic racism: A theory of oppression*. New York, NY: Routledge.

Feagin, J., Vera, H., & Batur, P. (2000). *White racism* (2nd ed.). New York, NY: Routledge.

Gaines, C. (2016). The highest-paid public employee in 39 US states is either a football or men's basketball coach. *Business Insider*. Retrieved from http://www.businessinsider.com/us-states-highest-paid-public-employee-college-coach-2016-9

Gaines, C. (2017, September 10). Colin Kaepernick received less than one-third of his 'record' $126 million contract. *Business Insider*. Retrieved from https://www.businessinsider.com/colin-kaepernick-record-49ers-contract-2017-8

George, N. (1992). *Elevating the game: Black men and basketball*. New York, NY: HarperCollins.

Harris, O. (2000). African American predominance in sport. In D. Brooks & R. Althouse (Eds.), *Racism in college athletics: The African Amerian athlete's experience* (2nd ed., pp. 37–52). Morgantown, WV: Fitness Information Technology.

Harrison, C. K. (1998). Themes that thread through society: Racism and athletic manifestation in the African-American community. *Race, Ethnicity and Education, 1*, 63–74.

Harrison., L. Jr., Harrison, C. K., & Moore, L. N. (2002). African American racial identity and sport. *Sport, Education & Society, 7*(2), 121–133.

Hartmann, D. (1996). *Race, culture, and the revolt of the Black athlete: The 1968 Olympic protests and their aftermath*. Chicago, IL: The University of Chicago Press.

Hartmann, D. (2000). Rethinking the relationship between sport and race in American culture: Golden ghettos and contested terrain. *Sociology of Sport Journal, 17*(3), 229–253.

Hawkins, B. (1998a). The dominant images of black men in America: The representation of O. J. Simpson. In G. Sailes (Ed.), *African Americans in sport* (pp. 39–52). New Brunswick, NJ: Transaction Publishers.

Hawkins, B. (1998b). The White supremacy continuum of images for Black men. *Journal of African American Studies, 3*(3), 7–18.

Hawkins, B. (2010). *The new plantation: Black athletes, college sports, and predominantly White NCAA institutions*. New York, NY: Palgrave-MacMillan.

Hine, D. C., Hine, W. C., & Harrold, S. (2006). *The African-American odyssey: Since 1965* (3rd ed. Vol. 2). Upper Saddle River, NJ: Pearson Prentice Hall.

Howard, T. C. (2014). *Black male(d): Peril and promise in the education of African American males*: New York, NY: Teachers College Press.

Kaepernick, C. (2018). Colin Kapernick website. Retrieved from https://kaepernick7.com/

KTVU (2016). Colin Kaepernick on decision to sit during anthem. Retrieved from http://www.ktvu.com/news/196750346-video

Leonard, D. J., & King, C. R. (2012). *Commodified and criminalized: New racism and African Americans in contemporary sports*. Lanham, MD: Rowan & Littlefield.

Mutua, A. D. (2006). *Progressive Black masculinities*. New York, NY: Routledge.

Nocera, J., & Strauss, B. (2016). *Indentured: The inside story of the rebellion against the NCAA*. New York, NY: Portfolio/Penguin Random House.

Noguera, P. (2008). *The trouble with Black boys … and other reflections on race, equity, and the future of public education*. San Francisco, CA: Jossey-Bass.

Powell, S. (2008). *Souled out? How Blacks are winning and losing in sports*. Champaign, IL: Human Kinetics.

Rhoden, W. C. (2006). *40 million dollar slaves: The rise, fall, and redemption of the Black athlete*. New York, NY: Crown Publishing Group.

Robeson, P. (1958/1988). *Here I stand*. Boston, MA: Beacon Press.

Russell, B., & McSweeney, W. (1966). *Go up for glory*. Berkley, CA: Berkely Publishing.

Sage, G. H. (1998). *Power and ideology in American sport* (2nd ed.). Champaign, IL: Human Kinetics.

Sailes, G. (2010). The African American athlete: social myths and stereotypes. In G. Sailes (Ed.), *Modern Sport and the African American Athlete Experience* (pp. 55–68). San Diego, CA: Cognella.

Singer, J. N. (2005). Understanding racism through the eyes of African-American male student athletes. *Race, Ethnicity and Education, 8*(4), 365–386.

Singer, J. N. (2015). The miseducation of African American male college athletes. In E. Comeaux (Ed.), *Introduction to intercollegiate athletics* (pp. 193–206). Baltimore, MD: Johns Hopkins University Press.

Smith, E. (2009). *Race, sport and the American dream* (2nd ed.). Durham, NC: Carolina Academic Press.

Smith, J. C. (1994). *Black firsts: 2, 000 years of extraordinary achievement*. Detroit, MI: Visible Ink Press.

Stevenson, H. C. (1994). Racial socialization in African American families: The art of balancing intolerance and survival. *The Family Journal: Counseling and Therapy for Couples and Families, 2*(3), 190–198.

Stewart, J. C. (1996). *1001 things everyone should know about African American history*. New York, NY: Doubleday Dell Publishing.

TIDES. (2018). The racial and gender report card. *The Institute for Diversity and Ethics in Sport*. Retrieved from http://www.tidesport.org/reports.html

White, P. (2014, November 8). The Black 14: Race, politics, religion and Wyoming Football. *WyoHistory.org*. Retrieved from https://www.wyohistory.org/encyclopedia/black-14-race-politics-religion-and-wyoming-football

Wiggins, D. K. (2000). Critical events affecting racism in athletics. In D. Brooks, & R. Althouse (Eds.), *Racism in college athletics: The African American athlete's experience* (2nd ed., pp. 15–36). Morgantown, WV: Fitness Information Technology.

Wiggins, D. K. (2014). "Black athlete in White men's games": Race, sport and American national pastimes. *The International Journal of the History of Sport, 31*(1–2), 181–202.

Wiggins, D. K., & Miller, P. (2003). *The unlevel playing field: A documentary history of the African-American experience in sport*. Urbana, IL: University of Illinois Press.

Woodson, C. G. (1933/1990). *The mis-education of the Negro*. Trenton, NJ: Africa World Press.

Yosso, T. J. (2005). Whose culture has capital? A critical race theory discussion of community cultural wealth *Race, Ethnicity and Education, 8*(1), 69–91.

SUSTAINED EMPOWERMENT

The Unbreakable Legacy Continues

... our circumstances in sports are bound up with and deeply rooted in the broader Black experience in America. And so as long as these circumstances—commensurate with developments in society at large—are dynamic and ever evolving, our struggle in sports must be perpetual and *there can be no final victories*.
— Edwards (1988, p. 140)

Dream dreams that are so big, so unrealistic, so unimaginable, so unfathomable, that without divine intervention they are destined to fail. You have to dream dreams too big.

— Caylin Moore speech on Wednesday, January 17, 2018 at the 2018 Black Student Athlete Summit

The King will reply, *'Truly I tell you, whatever you did for one of the least of these brothers and sisters of mine, you did for me.'*
— Matthew 25:40 (NIV) (Bible, 2011, pp. 1639–1640)

Transformative Sustained Empowerment: A Blueprint for Positive Change Moving Forward

The challenges facing Black males in the U.S. and the broader Black community are alarming and require serious attention, commitment, and systemic changes. Based on nearly every social wellness index, Black males are routinely

among the most disadvantaged and impacted. From disproportionate exposure to impoverished conditions to school suspension, expulsion, and attrition rates to penalization through the criminal (in)justice system to economic
oppression to psychological and physical health issues to low life expectancy
rates, Black males' suffering in a society founded upon and structured by WRC
is undeniable (Alexander, 2012; ETS, 2011). As critical race theory (CRT)
pioneer, Derrick Bell (1992) poignantly proclaimed in the title of his book,
Blacks are indeed the "faces at the bottom of the well." Since WRC positions
White males as the most privileged, Black males in contrast are viewed as
being among the most powerful threats to this hegemonic social order (Curry,
2017). Thus, the pattern of life outcomes among Black males reflects conditions that have been created to sustain their suppression, marginalization, and
disempowerment. As such, every aspect of society must be critically examined to determine the extent to which it either enhances or exacerbates the
plight of Black males. The social institutions of sport and (mis)education
are of particular importance due to their distinct influences on Black males'
holistic (under)development. Within this chapter, I offer multi-level recommendations for creating and sustaining positive holistic development (also
referred to as holistic excellence) for Black males' involved in sport and the
collective empowerment of the Black community at large.

Throughout this book, I have outlined the heterogeneity of Black male
athletes' socialization experiences and outcomes in and through sport and
(mis)education. In concert with this aim, I argue Black male athletes' experiences and outcomes are not deterministic, monolithic, or generalizable, but
rather complex, diverse, and contingent upon a range of factors not the least
of which is the interplay between ecological systems and individual processes.
In contrast to popular assertions, Black males' successes as well as their short-
comings are not primarily based on their own agency with no regard for the
impact of socio-structural, environmental, and other contextual factors. From
a critical sociological perspective, I contend that systems influence *patterns*
and within all systems *exceptions* are present. However, *exceptions to the rule
do not make the rule itself.* Too often when Black male athletes are discussed,
exceptions to the rule are highlighted as examples to reinforce the colorblind
racist myth of meritocracy and suggest inequities are not structural, but rather
behavioral and cultural. These deficit-based hegemonic claims ignore the
reality that the likelihood of success outcomes for any individual or group
is largely based on their access (or a lack thereof) to various forms of valued
capital, treatment based upon stereotypes associated with their intersecting

identities, and their ability (and willingness or not) to assimilate (or strategically navigate and/or resist) in and through systems rooted in dominant ideologies (i.e., social group hierarchies) within a given context. The *patterns* associated with Black males' experiences in and through sport and (mis)education in the U.S. (i.e., lower graduation rates compared to their peers) underscore the intent and aim of these systems (i.e., racist society).

Furthermore, when Black males are holistically underserved and underdeveloped in a society founded upon and structured by WRC, the system is not broken, but rather it is operating exactly within its purpose; hence, the parallels between the economic racial arrangements during chattel slavery in the early 17th century through the modern day U.S. society in the early 21st century when this book is being written (Bell, 1980, 1992; Woodson, 1933/1990). The extent to which Black male athletes experience academic neglect and attrition, athletic identity foreclosure, career under preparedness and dissatisfaction, financial illiteracy and mismanagement, economic deprivation, racial discrimination, social isolation, extensive psychological trauma, and preventable deaths is related to their involvement in sporting and miseducation systems designed to perpetuate said outcomes in conspicuous and subtle ways. This phenomenon reflects the potency of these interconnected structures. It is also worth noting the aforementioned outcomes mirror the challenges facing Blacks in the broader U.S. and globally particularly in neocolonial spaces and thus illustrate how *personal troubles* are indeed *public issues* (Cooper, 2012). As a result, the recommendations in this chapter are designed to address detrimental *patterns* experienced (not primarily caused) by Black male athletes.

The cyclical relationship between ideologies, societal arrangements, policies, practices, and lived experiences and outcomes signifies that any effort seeking to alter these disconcerting trends must involve a multi-level and multi-faceted approach. The ecological models presented in this text highlight how the reproduction and resistance of specific ideologies (consciously and unconsciously) results in varied outcomes in and through sport and (mis)education. More specifically, the outcomes are not simply a byproduct of reproduction or resistance by one individual (i.e., Black male athletes themselves), but rather a convergence of multiple influences.[1] Therefore, the aims of the proposed recommendations in this chapter seek to *deconstruct current systems* that perpetuate the holistic underdevelopment of Black male athletes and *establish new systems* that will result in their continuous holistic development and sustained empowerment (also referred to as holistic excellence) for the Black community at large. In contrast to Maslow's (1943) hierarchy of needs, which is rooted in

Euro-centric cultural values whereby self-actualization is the pinnacle of success, the *transformative sustained empowerment* (TSE) blueprint for Black males prioritizes collective racial and cultural love, uplift, sustainability, positivity, and power as the ultimate goal. In conjunction with Afrocentric cultural values, worldviews, and philosophies (Asante, 1990, 2003; Carruthers, 1999; Hilliard, 1998; Karenga, 1978), the mission of this blueprint is to educate, empower, nurture, protect, embrace, and celebrate Black males' holistic identities in order to facilitate the fulfillment of their multiple divine purposes in connection with Black African collective uplift. The TSE blueprint includes the following goals:

Goal #1:   To cultivate holistic identity development (also referred to as holistic excellence) among Black males within and beyond sport and education as a part of the larger Black African collective uplift.

Goal #2:   To increase critical consciousness of oppressive systems in a society designed to under develop, exploit, miseducate, control, divide, and destroy Black males and the broader Black community.

Goal #3:   To ignite internalized empowerment and commitment to eliminate oppressive systems and realities facing Blacks in general and Black males involved in sport in particular.

Goal #4:   To create sustainable systems rooted in Afrocentric worldviews within and beyond sport and education including structures, institutions, policies, and practices created, controlled, and led by Blacks that result in perpetual empowerment for the collective group intra- and inter-nationally.

Hence, the TSE blueprint seeks to transform personal troubles into personal triumphs and public issues into public progress. Within this chapter, I outline recommendations for the following groups/entities: (a) Black male holistic individuals, families, and communities, (b) primary (mis)education and youth sport organizations, (c) interscholastic (mis)education and sport organizations, (d) postsecondary (mis)education and intercollegiate sport organizations, and (e) the broader society.

Recommendations for Black Male Holistic Individuals, Families, and Communities

The socialization of Black male holistic individuals begins at birth and thus in order to effectively redress negative trends associated with this group it is imperative to highlight areas of improvement within their microsystems including families and communities. The conditions and impacts prevalent in miseducation schooling and sporting spaces are a microcosm of broader societal inequities (ETS, 2011). Thus, identifying and challenging chrono-, macro-, and exo-system issues is imperative to cultivate within the meso-, micro-, and sub-system settings as well as vice versa in a concurrent manner. As such, one recommendation is to adopt, promote, and ingrain positive Black empowerment in the household at an early age to equip young Black males to counteract oppressive ideologies and systems they will encounter throughout their lives. For example, parents/guardians, family and community members, must communicate that WRC is a system of interlocking oppressive ideologies that influence every facet of society. Using the figures presented in this text can aid is the transmission of this information. It is also necessary to accompany this recognition with the study of the history of African people by Black Africans themselves. Several Afrocentric works such as Karenga (1978), Asante (1990, 2003), Hilliard (1998), Diop (1974), and Williams (1974/1987) are recommendations for integrative education and socialization from youth through adulthood. Almanacs and historical artifacts that document the lived experiences including achievements of Black Africans serve as vital emancipatory tools in an oppressive society. Young Black males must understand from whence they came and know that their legacy did not begin or end with slavery, but rather these unfortunate periods were only a part of their collective journeys and revealed the divine spirit within their people who survived and thrived in spite of these atrocities. By centering this socialization process on Afrocentric worldviews, Black males from an early age will understand how their existence and well-being is inextricably connected to the African Diaspora and thus inherently requires them to directly challenge WRC, neoliberalism, and related oppressive ideologies and systems.

In the spirit of community, a key to the success of any thriving group with collectivist ideals involves information and resource sharing. One of the major problems facing many Black families and communities living in a neoliberal society is the lack of seamless transmission of different types of capital for collective progress instead of success for an individual or among a select few. Yosso (2005) described in her community cultural wealth (CCW) framework how Blacks and various groups overcoming intersecting oppressions navigate unfavorable conditions by leveraging aspirational, navigational, social, linguistic, familial, and resistant capital. The aforementioned capital have contributed to the survival and uplift of Blacks in the U.S. Nonetheless, the forces of WRC have also suppressed the dissemination and activation of these resources as well as other vital forms of capital such as economic, political, and property (Bell, 1980, 1992; Crenshaw, Gotanda, Peller, & Thomas, 1995; Harris, 1993). Therefore, at the mesosystem and microsystem levels, there must be a concerted effort to transmit CCW and various forms of capital in all spaces including in sport environments. For example, typically at sporting events there are a number of families and groups present for the purpose of social bonding and athletic entertainment. However, I assert that these spaces offer a valuable opportunity for information sharing and community uplift. Sporting spaces such as practices and competitions must be viewed as educational and communal spaces for addressing social problems impacting the collective as opposed to only serving as outlets for entertainment and leisure. In other words, we should evaluate every facet of the Black community based on its effectiveness in redressing pressing issues affecting the community such as safety, economic needs, environmental improvement, relationship building, counter-actions against systemic racism, and resolving intra-racial and intra-cultural schisms limiting collective progress to name a few. Intentionally incorporating CCW as a framework embedded in these spaces is recommended. Disseminating and reimagining how these sporting spaces can socialize Black male holistic individuals into becoming *active agents of positive change* (AAPC) is a powerful shift away from the detrimental status quo, which seeks to detach them from identifying with the plight of the broader Black community as well as limit their social responsibility beyond traditional charitable giving and community service efforts.[2]

Another recommendation is to replace the current language used to describe individuals who participate in athletics/sports. In order to redress the unhealthy centralization of one's athletic identity, I propose using the terms "holistic individuals (HI)," "holistic sport participant (HSP)" or "holistic athlete (HA)." In this way, Black males from an early age will self-identify as holistic individuals who participate in sports rather than an athlete with an engulfed identity. Initial resistance to this proposal is inevitable, but I argue that Black culture, particularly through music and sports, have redefined and popularized several terms and labels that were not widely accepted at their inception. The proposal of HI, HSP, and HA are mere recommendations that align with other endearing labels that have been used throughout the Black community such as "fam," "brothers," "kings," and "active agents of positive change." This recommendation underscores the importance and value of utilizing linguistic capital (Yosso, 2005) as a form of resistance against hegemonic forces. Language thus serves as a weapon to disrupt and destroy ideas rooted in WRC and concurrently empower Black collectivist perspectives and

Afrocentric worldviews. Beyond the terms listed here, I also recommend additional community driven ideas for language shifts be adopted. Furthermore, I recommend we refer to all Black youth as gifted and talented. If this language was normalized, then it would communicate to them and to the world that they are uniquely created and destined to accomplish special feats in life. This messaging is in direct contrast to current deficit labels (e.g., at-risk, remedial, deficient, etc.) and dehumanizing terms (e.g., freak, beast, monster, etc.) imposed upon them that devalue their holistic potential and humanity. The primary heuristic aim with these recommendations is to create a cognitive shift in the minds of Black males to view sport as a space of self-expression and *a part of who they are versus their whole identity and sense of self-worth* (see Armstrong and Jennings's (2018) work for an in-depth exploration of this topic). I believe the titles internalized by an individual or group greatly influence their conceptions about what is possible and expected of them and thus by promoting empowering self-definitions we disrupt one of the tools of WRC, which is the power to label or otherwise stated to decide who and what we are.

Relatedly, one fact we know from the literature is Black males are highly influenced by the messaging they receive about the celebrity allure of being a professional athlete (Harrison, 1998; Hodge, Burden, Robinson, & Bennett, 2008). In order to counter the influence of the media in a society founded upon and structured by WRC, Black males must be saturated with positive messages of Blacks being successful in areas beyond sport participation. This messaging must come in a myriad of ways. For example, as a part of practices, families and communities can intentionally expose Black males to community members, former residents, and Blacks (both living and deceased) who have contributed positively to society in a diverse range of occupations. Both Stewart (1996) and Smith (1994) are useful resources for these efforts. Akin to the expectation for athletes to memorize plays and training techniques, it would be a new norm for them to learn about great Blacks who utilized their platform in sport to support social justice efforts (e.g., Paul Robeson, Harry Edwards, Muhammad Ali, Arthur Ashe, Bill Russell, Wilma Rudolph, Althea Gibson, Wyomia Tyus, Tine Sloan Green, etc.). In addition, HSPs and their families could also learn about influential Blacks who were not involved in sport (e.g., Marcus Garvey, Martin Luther King, Jr., Malcolm X, Stokely Carmichael (Kwame Ture), Huey P. Newton, Bobby Seale, Eldridge Cleaver, Robert F. Williams, Medgar Evers, Charles Hamilton, Patrice Lumumba, Kwame Nkrumah, Fannie Lou Hamer, Ida B. Wells-Barnett, Shirley Chisholm, etc.). Learning strategies can include flashcards, art, music, inquiry-based techniques, and collaborative learning environments. Black males should not have to wait until they enroll in college and have the option of taking an Africana Studies or African American studies course to learn this vital information that can transform their identity development in infinitely positive ways. Although, it would be ideal for this content to be embedded in K-12 curriculum, given the lack of representation in leadership positions in education at the federal and state levels this change on a systematic level is unlikely at the current time. Nonetheless, it should be pursued and in the meantime promoted in the homes and local communities outside of traditional schooling spaces. The adoption of these practices would reflect an effort to expand sporting spaces from simply being entertainment and leisure to spaces of cultural knowledge transmission and holistic empowerment.

In addition, partnerships with community organizations including local religious groups, institutions, businesses, schools, etc. could be established and/or strengthened so young Black males can no longer say they have not been exposed to positive role models across a range of professions and backgrounds within as well as beyond their own communities. These partnerships could serve as a means of constellation mentoring (Kelly & Dixon, 2014). In conjunction with coordinating in-person and virtual/digital interactions with positive role models and mentors, it is recommended that the dissemination of this information about various career paths between organizations and families become commonplace (i.e., Black Community Career Network). Exposing Black males to a range of career options early in life beyond professional sport must be intentional and consistent. Ensuring Black males' familiarity and connection with resources beyond sport is as intense and impressionable (if not more) as those related to sports is critical for cultivating their holistic development. Every young Black male HSP should be able to name, know, and appreciate Black male professionals in their community who do not participate in sport in a manner comparable to how they can name professional athletes, music artists, and other celebrities.

Moreover, utilizing media platforms that appeal to young Black males to expose them to positive Black male role models should also be prominent at all athletic activities such as practices, games, tournaments, etc. Regarding social media, each family and community organization could spotlight the events when a diverse range of professionals interact with Black youth and key insights gained from these interactions could be documented and shared among the collective. Currently, corporate sponsors are pervasive at youth sporting events. I propose similar investments and effort be placed in promoting positive Black male role models as well as programs and resources at these events such as financial literacy workshops, healthcare services, scholarship opportunities, HBCUs, trade schools, etc. for young Black males to consistently be exposed to a wider range of possibilities for their future. Cohesive communities require key elements such as membership, influence (sense of mattering), integration and fulfillment of needs, and shared emotional connection (McMillan & Chavis, 1986). Many community youth sporting events demonstrate all four features on a regular basis. Beyond sport, religious organizations, schools, and multi-purpose community centers are other spaces where personal and group bonds are established and strengthened. As such, I propose that using the sense of community framework (McMillan & Chavis, 1986), more coordinated community programming centered on the TRM, P²EPGM, and HEM could serve as a means for enhancing holistic development among Black males. For example, using athletic events such as tournaments and games to promote community wellness efforts would strengthened the connection between sport participation and broader social goals. HBCU classic events are a prime example of where this type of empowerment has historically and continues to be intentionally integrated in and for the Black community (Cooper, Cavil, & Cheeks, 2014). At these events, all seven principles of Kwanzaa are on display (*umoja* (unity), *kujichagulia* (self-determination), *ujima* (collective work and responsibility), *ujamaa* (cooperative economics), *nia* (purpose), *kuumba* (creativity), and *imani* (faith) (Karenga, 1978). The presence of numerous Black vendors, community groups, and professional organizations reflect the power of Black collectivism.

Using these HBCU athletic events as blueprints and extant leverage points, future programming could involve working with similar groups to promote racial and cultural uplift within Black communities across all levels of sport. As my research has noted, when Black males experience these type of environments as college athletes they recognize they are a part of legacy much bigger than sports (Cooper, 2013; Cooper & Cooper, 2015). Multiplying these occurrences on similar and different scales through the strategic use of sport in Black communities is a game changing idea that should be established and normalized. Identifying current Black institutions and building stronger connections centered on common collective values could enhance Black male HSPs' developmental outcomes. In addition to local and intra-national efforts, using an Afrocentric worldview (Asante, 1990, 2003; Diop, 1974; Hilliard, 1998; Karenga, 1978; Williams, 1974/1987), these partnerships could also involve institutions, organizations, and groups across the African

Diaspora globally (see Cavil (2018) for an example of a partnership between Texas Southern University (TSU; an HBCU), The Heritage Group (Black owned company), and institutions and businesses across the Virgin Islands and Caribbean region). As a result, the implementation of these strategies will brand athletic events as sanctioned *holistic development spaces* (HDS) whereby indicating to everyone that intentional community building and culturally empowering efforts are taking place. This branding could include a HDS logo similar to the logos for current programming with organizations such as the Young Men's Christian Association (YMCA), AAU, and apparel companies.

In addition, similar to the Black Panther Party Ten Point Program Plan (Newton & Seale, 1967), communities are encouraged to draft a list of specific expectations centered on holistic development for all youth. These concerted efforts can be coordinated across various traditional educational spaces and community-based pedagogical spaces (Douglas, 2016). Ensuring all members of the community are clear about collective racial and cultural goals has been integral to the success of previous Black social justice movements dating back to the early 17th century in the U.S. and throughout history globally (Cooper, Mallery, & Macaulay, forthcoming). Success could also be assessed based on these collectivist efforts including the frequency, length, nature, and quality of career exposure engagement, community uplift/we-reach,[3] holistic identity activities, identification and connection with role models and mentors within and beyond sport, and various other positive developmental measures. For example, using a holistic development curricula such as the Excellence Beyond Athletics (EBA; Cooper, 2016b) and CU frameworks (Collective Uplift, 2018) as benchmarks for success are recommended for consideration.

The dissemination and critical discussions regarding the five socialization models presented in this text (ISSM, EALM, TRM, P²EPGM, and HEM) is another recommendation for cultivating Black male holistic development within families and communities. Viewing films such as *The Lenny Cooke* documentary (Shopkorn, Noah, Safdie, & Safdie, 2013) and similar films listed in Chapter 4 can serve as discussion points for families and communities to analyze the ways in which conditions within these environments and certain values and behaviors are either fostering and/or inhibiting the processes and outcomes of each model. This practice cultivates critical consciousness, internalized empowerment, and engagement in counter-actions for the individual Black males as well as the collective Black community (Cooper, 2016b; Cooper & Cooper, 2015).

Recommendations for Primary (Mis)Education Levels and Youth Sport Organizations

In order for Black male holistic development to manifest more expansively, primary (mis)education schooling and youth sports must transform from places that focus on reproducing dominant U.S. ideologies and values such as capitalism, meritocracy, and neoliberalism (Beyer & Hannah, 2000; Coakley, 2017; Sage, 1998) to spaces where Black males learn how to recognize and respond to ideological hegemonic forces in a society designed to marginalize them. By employing the five socialization models offered in this text, I assert that we can achieve this goal. Several primary schools including public, private, all-male, Charter, and Afrocentric Independent currently engage in this work (Howard, 2014; Noguera, 2008). However, there is a lack of focus on the ways in which sport can be used as a transformational outlet for Black males to challenge (e.g., TRM, P²EPGM, and HEM) as opposed to reinforce (e.g., ISSM and EALM without collectivist inclinations) dominant U.S. ideals, which oppress Blacks as a collective group. Ladson-Billings (1995) posited that culturally relevant pedagogy (CRP) is an emancipatory tool for Blacks in traditional schooling spaces and I agree. However, I also suggest sporting environments must also incorporate this type of education. A major reason why Black males are susceptible to insidious systems such as the Conveyor Belt (Rhoden, 2006), athletic industrial complex (AIC; Hawkins, 2010; Smith, 2009), athletic seasoning complex (ASC; Howard, 2014), and prison industrial complex (PIC; Hawkins, 2010; Smith, 2009) is because they are often isolated from the spaces where this type of learning and cultivation takes place. With the exception of the 1960s and different acute points in the pre-assimilation era (prior to 1960), Blacks including athletes have experienced limited collective consciousness and subsequently have engaged in less than optimal counter-efforts against WRC.

As such, educational spaces including sport could introduce Black male holistic individuals at an early age to different types of sport activism (symbolic, scholarly, sports-based, grassroots, economic, media, political, legal, music and art, and military) as well as the contextual histories therein (Cooper, Macaulay, & Rodriguez, 2017; Cooper, Mallery, & Macaulay, forthcoming). It is imperative for Black males to learn at an early age about the different ways in which activism, advocacy, and agency have been, continue to be, and can be enacted on the individual and group level to address social inequities and uplift the Black community. This awareness will increase the likelihood of their future engagement in these efforts. If the memorization of certain music lyrics and television show commentary is feasible, then so too can the content regarding Afrocentric and Black empowerment within and beyond sport.

The socialization at the youth sport level also serves as a pivotal launch point for reframing how sport is viewed within the larger Black community. Youth sport organizations can adopt the EBA (Cooper, 2016b) and CU frameworks (Collective Uplift, 2018) as models for developing Black males holistically. The EBA model involves the cultivation of the following six holistic development principles (HDPs): (a) self-identity awareness, (b) positive social engagement, (c) active mentorship, (d) academic achievement, (e) career aspirations, and (d) balanced time management (Cooper, 2016b). Primary educational institutions and youth sport organizations should implement specific activities focused on developing these HDPs. One activity outlined in my previous work involves having a young person write down all of their identities, positive perceptions of each of identity from their own view as well as from the view of others, and specific ways in which they can enhance the healthy development of each identity (Cooper, 2016b). For positive social engagement, building and strengthening partnerships with race-based community and professional organizations is recommended. For example, organizations such as the 100 Black Youth Project, Black Lives Matter (BLM), NAACP, Urban League, Pan-Hellenic, Pan-African organizations, etc. could be recruited to disseminate vital CCW (Yosso, 2005). Although, each of these organizations have different approaches towards reaching certain aims, these varying strategies underscore the heterogeneity within the Black community and when leveraged appropriately can yield tremendous benefits for the collective. Moreover, access/exposure and connectedness to role models across a range of fields is likely to expand an individual's conceptualization of what is possible particularly among Black youth who must face the visceral effects of WRC. Individuals exposed to and connected with same race and gender role models in a range of fields are more likely to see themselves in these expansive roles. Conversely, if they only have *access to and/or connectedness to* a limited set of same race and gender role models such as high-profile Black athletes, then they are more likely to engage in social learning and imitation in these areas.

Beyond promoting role models in fields outside of sport, I posit there must be structured programs and a shift in institutional and cultural practices that normalize meaningful engagement with Black male youth and these professionals. Formal and informal mentoring programs with the constellation mentoring framework (the establishment of relationships with multiple mentors as opposed to the traditional dyad structure) could be integrated in all primary and secondary educational and youth sporting spaces (Kelly & Dixon, 2014). Leaders should organize specific community uplift and we-reach activities to foster positive social engagement as well as relationships with secondary and postsecondary organizations and athletic teams. Establishing these connections at an early age would socialize these young Black males to value giving back to their native communities via racial uplift and the importance of relationship building and holistic development. Another recommendation for increasing positive social engagement and active mentorship is to hire more Black males in teaching, administration, and coaching positions. Using an equity-minded framework (Bensimon, 2004), teacher preparation programs and other gateways for these positions should reframe their criteria for who and what would constitute an effective educator, role model, and mentor for young Black males. Without redressing the disproportionate number of Black males in education at the leadership level compared to their representation in the student population, collective progress will remain limited. Notwithstanding, building on the community-based pedagogies paradigm (Douglas, 2016) would also be useful to expand current understandings how, when, where, who, and why education takes place.

Related to academic achievement, primary and secondary educational institutions and youth sport organizations could use innovative strategies to enhance intellectual gains by merging and/or coordinating activities across different areas. Currently, many summer sports camps are void of educational enrichment and vice versa. I propose merging these types of programming and incentivizing academic progress via sporting opportunities. In order for this approach to be effective, organizers must adopt an equity mindset versus an equality mindset. Curriculum should introduce all Black males to a myriad of career opportunities including those that require a four-year degree and those that do not. I concur that we need to enroll and support more Black males through college graduation across various institutional types, but also believe traditional postsecondary education is not the best path for every Black male to experience holistic development. Areas such as literacy and basic mathematics should be paramount in terms of attention and support. No Black male should be participating in sports until their literacy and basic math skills are at an acceptable grade level. By allowing any student, but particularly Black males to participate in sport when their basic literacy and mathematic skills are lacking is nothing short of academic neglect and exploitation. Additionally, more specific cognitive areas in sciences, social studies, etc. should be assessed with an equity minded with the understanding that everyone will not achieve at the same level based on specified metrics, but *everyone is gifted and worthy of high quality investment in preparation for their futures*. Therefore, I recommend early and frequent exposure to programming that does not limit their potential, but rather nurture interests in a multitude of areas.

Along the same lines, for career aspirations, primary and secondary education and youth sport organizations could also promote narratives, stories, and images of Black male athletes who excelled in areas beyond sport. As previously mentioned, the works of Stewart (1996) and Smith (1994) are useful sources as well as the recent works focusing on Black male scholar athletes by Smith, Clark and Harrison, (2014). Currently, society and the media bombards Black males from youth to adulthood with images of Black male athletic success and one of the results have been the detrimental internalization of athletic manifest destiny (Coakley, 2017). In order to reverse this trend, more counter-efforts must be pursued to socialize Black males into positive holistic identities so that it is a new normal for *all Black males to see people who look like them being successful in areas beyond sport participation and internalized that they too can accomplish similar feats with the proper leveraging of resources* such as CCW (Yosso, 2005). The mentorship programs referenced earlier could also help cultivate enrichment opportunities for learning about different career paths and explaining how certain skills translate into effective career mobility.

All Black male holistic individuals involved in sport should be required to write up and research contingency plans for after high school, college, and professional retirement. This activity should involve on-going discussions with various community stakeholders and by the time the student reaches the end of their high school careers they should have a list of at least five viable career pursuits based on this socialization. Related to balanced time management, educators could utilize calendar frameworks to assist Black males with understanding how time spent on specific tasks can enhance skill competency and self-efficacy. Specifically, Gladwell's (2011) concept of 10, 000 hours for expertise can be infused and adapted to assist Black males with recognizing and critically reflecting on how much time is spent on certain activities versus others. This type of activity could serve as a cognitive-switch (Armstrong & Jennings, 2018) whereby Black males learn that skill development in any area is less about genetic predispositions and more about time, focus, interest, energy, and persistence on specific tasks (as well as socio-structural factors, expectations, conditions, and relationships). Therefore, Black males from an early age would dismiss all stereotypic assertions that suggest their abilities are primarily based on racist myths (i.e., genetic theory and other theories outlined at the beginning of Chapter 7) (Sailes, 2010).

In a related vein, the aforementioned time management activity could be applied with the CU framework and utilized by all key stakeholders connected to Black male HSPs such as parents, coaches, teachers, mentors, etc. (Collective Uplift, 2018). The CU framework involves the intentional cultivation of the following identities:

(a) personal/self-identity,
(b) social identities,
(c) cultural identities,
(d) learner and thinker identity,
(e) physical health identity,
(f) psycho-emotional health identity,
(g) gender identity,
(h) global citizen/agent of change identity,
(i) spiritual identity,
(j) professional/career identity, and
(k) financial/fiscal identity (Collective Uplift, 2018)

Specific partnerships could be established with various entities in the community and globally (via digital platforms or in-person when feasible) with an expertise in these areas and information dissemination can be normalized in all types of educational and sporting spaces. Since sports are a place that attract Black males and the conditions therein keep them engage, then I recommend utilizing these areas first for holistic indoctrination. The next steps can involve the transmission of these environments/cultures into traditional classroom spaces as well as in community-based pedagogical spaces (e.g., recreation centers, religious organizations, barbershops, etc.) (Douglas, 2016). In addition to the adoption of these frameworks, as previously suggested, I encourage all social institutions to adopt terminology that signifies the valuing of young people's holistic identities (i.e., talented holistic person) versus one identity (i.e., athlete). I recommend replacing select time spent on traditional academic coursework and/or athletic skill development with activities designed to increase awareness and appreciation of culturally empowering artifacts, histories, and resources. One example is incorporating the seven principles of Kwanzaa into standardized curriculum and programming efforts to achieve this aim (Karenga, 1978).

In a related vein, organizations can use awards and recognition to indicate the value of these holistic development efforts and outcomes above and beyond athletic accomplishments. Currently, young athletes receive awards such as Most Valuable Player (MVP), Most Improved Player (MIP), Best Offensive or Defensive Player, Sportpersonship Awards, All-Tournament team, and team awards (e.g., 1st place, 2nd place, 3rd place, etc.). These awards recognize young athletes for their athletic accomplishments and reinforce the validation of their athletic identities. A paradigm shift towards holistic development would celebrate the development of young people's growth beyond sport-specific skill proficiency and performances (e.g., academic grade improvement and achievement, positive behavior report, completing a short report researching a positive Black role model outside of sport, saving money for investment goals, community uplift/we-reach engagement, participating in enrichment activities in and beyond traditional educational spaces, demonstrating cultural empowerment growth, etc.). This idea would differ from the current paradigm in that often times these type of recognitions do not occur in sporting spaces. However, given the reality that many Black males have unique attraction towards and affinity for sport, it is incumbent upon those interested in their holistic well-being to transform these spaces from cultivating a single identity (athlete) to an affirmational space for multiple identity validation and nurturance (holistic). If more Black males involved in youth sport begin to experience positive identity affirmation for their prowess beyond their athletic skills, then they could begin to internalize and actualize their potential in different areas of society such as law, sciences, politics, education, business, etc. Early indoctrination of this type of identity validation and awareness of transferable skills acquired through sport would positively enhance Black males' holistic development. Consistent multi-faceted messaging, reinforcement, and support regarding holistic development undergirds all of these recommendations.

Recommendations for Secondary (Mis)Education and Interscholastic Athletics

At the interscholastic level, there must be major reform to current practices to improve the holistic development outcomes for Black males. First, I recommend the establishment of CU type organizations at the interscholastic level (Collective Uplift, 2018; Cooper, Corral, et al., 2018; Cooper, Nwadike, & Macaulay, 2017). Several organizations such as *Crossroads: Pathways* to *Success, Inc.* in Greensboro, North Carolina, *T. Alexander Foundation* in Charlotte, North Carolina, and *Catch Education* in Dallas, Texas actively recruit and cultivate CCW (Yosso, 2005) for Black males (Catch Education, 2018; Crossroads, 2018; T. Alexander Foundation, 2018). Building on the success of intercollegiate holistic development support programs such as CU, current and former athletes, educators, and mentors could coalesce to utilize the CU or related frameworks (Bimper, 2016, Carter-Francique, 2013; Kelly & Dixon, 2014) for programming. Connecting Black males with same race and gender role models who identify with their plight racially and culturally is a direct counter-action to the prison industrial complex (PIC; Alexander, 2012). When Black male adolescents have positive Black male role models who demonstrate care, interest, support, and accountability they are more likely to experience positive developmental outcomes. If formal CU organizations are not feasible, then utilizing the framework in an informal capacity and/or integrating it within current practices is a viable alternative.

Regarding college readiness, as previously stated, there are critical areas such as literacy and basic mathematical skills that cannot and should not ever be overlooked or neglected. The story of Kevin Ross in Chapter 4 outlines the dire consequences associated with the academic neglect of Black males. Therefore, schools and athletic teams must establish strict policies that limit participation and matriculation unless the student meets academic proficiencies. In terms of academic support, organizers can establish more strategic partnerships with postsecondary institutions to provide high school students with role models, mentors, and supports for their cognitive development. These partnerships can include academic and athletic departments as well as student organizations. In order to incentivize college students to serve in these roles, institutions can offer academic credits similar to credit-bearing internship opportunities. In addition, each school and team culture should incorporate recognize and celebrate Black male HSPs for progress, success, and engagement beyond sport. Along with MVP and other sport related awards, organizations need to recognize Black males for academic progress and achievement, mastery of social justice concepts/events/histories and engagement in related efforts both within and beyond sport, etc. In addition, organizations should recognize and encourage participation in student organizations beyond sport (particularly culturally relevant mentoring programs), involvement with professional development activities, learning a foreign language, engaging in community we-reach, and creating innovative projects for societal improvement.

Adopting and/or creating holistic labels similar to the HI, HSP, and HA recommendations listed earlier is also recommended at this level.

At this level, the concept of multiple intelligence theory should also be introduced and critically discussed as well as different activities developing these areas can be adopted (Gardner, 1983). According to this theory, multiple intelligences include visual-spatial, linguistic-verbal, logical-mathematical, bodily kinesthetic, musical, interpersonal, and naturalistic (Gardner, 1983). The empirical examination of these intelligences has begun to emerge in the sport education literature as it pertains to Black male college athletes (Nwadike, 2016). It is important to teach these concepts so Black males can understand the breadth and width of their talents rather than being socialized to view intelligence and proficiency in myopic ways. Regarding career exploration, schools could invest in allowing students to complete personality, interests, values, and career matching assessments to provide them with a range of possibilities for their futures that are culturally relevant as opposed to Eurocentric based. For example, Monique Cooper has developed a *Culturally-Responsive Career Development Services for School Counselors* syllabus that would serve as a useful foundation for secondary and postsecondary educators and counselors (Cooper, 2018). Furthermore, these assessments could be required for athletic participation and programming before, during, and after seasons to aid in their continuous career development.

In related vein, incorporating social justice workshops and trainings with organizations such as 100 Black Youth and BLM with Black males in general and Black HSPs more specifically is recommended. The value of cultivating critical consciousness about ecological systems and dominant ideologies is vital for holistic empowerment. Thus, transforming hegemonic socialization spaces into empowering spaces must be pursued intentionally. Additionally, I recommend the theories[4] outlined in Chapters 2 and 3 as well as the Black male holistic (under)development through sport and (mis)education models (ISSM, EALM, TRM, P2EPGM, and HEM) outlined in Chapters 4 through 8 be discussed formally and informally with Black males from an early age through their young adulthood particularly at the secondary and postsecondary levels. Introducing them to the socialization models in this text and including various presentations from different professionals could expand their perception of what is possible for them in the short term and long term through consciousness, empowerment, and engagement in counter-actions (Cooper, 2016b; Cooper & Cooper, 2015). Requiring the readings of influential legendary scholar-activists such as Dr. Harry Edwards among others as well as the viewing of the documentaries listed in Chapter 4 and related films are highly recommended at this level as well.

Similar to the previous recommendation about transforming community based and youth sporting spaces into holistic development spaces, I recommend interscholastic athletic programs establish new criteria for excellence beyond athletics performance and nominal community service. Every athletic program could have explicit programming and evaluative strategies for cultivating CCW (Yosso, 2005), CRP (Ladson-Billings, 1995), EBA HDPs (Cooper, 2016b), and/or CU holistic identities (Collective Uplift, 2018). For example, each high school athletic team could have partnerships with non-sport based student organizations and community and professional groups such as the ones mentioned earlier (e.g., 100 Black Youth Project, BLM, NAACP, Urban League, Pan-Hellenic organizations, Pan-African organizations, etc.) and organize different activities and events specifically geared towards developing holistic identities. As previously noted, it must become the new norm that building critical consciousness, internalized empowerment, and engagement in counter-actions is a part of Black males' socialization processes regardless of their background (Cooper, 2016b; Cooper & Cooper, 2015). If Black males can learn about sport, music, and certain types of masculinities, then they can also learn about holistic concepts including productive masculinities (Martin & Harris, 2006), progressive Black masculinities (Mutua, 2006) as well as Afrocentric masculinities (Asante, 1990, 2003; Hilliard, 1998; Karenga, 1978).

Recommendations for Postsecondary (Mis)Education and Intercollegiate Sports

The disconcerting trends outlined in Chapter 2 indicate the broken system of postsecondary miseducation and intercollegiate athletics as it pertains to Black male athletes' holistic development. In previous work, my colleagues and I asserted that colorblind racism was at the root of policies and practices that have disparate impacts on Black male college athletes (Cooper, Nwadike, & Macaulay, 2017). With the exception of HBCUs, a majority of the athletic programs at HWIs were established at a time when Blacks were excluded from participation and thus their unique needs were not considered. Subsequently, throughout the 20th and 21st century, policy reforms have promulgated deficit-based perspectives of Black male college athletes' academic competencies and potential for growth. The exploitative structure of intercollegiate athletics values Black male college athletes for their revenue generating abilities while concurrently neglecting their holistic development and personal well-being.

One recommendation for improving the holistic development of Black male college athletes is to foster the establishment of culturally relevant organizations, programs, and support spaces. Programs such as Rambition at Colorado State University (CSU), Zest for Excellence in Athletics and Learning (ZEAL) at the University of New Mexico (UNM), and Collective Uplift (CU) at the University of Connecticut (UConn) are exemplar culturally responsive programs. These culturally relevant mentoring (CRM) programs have demonstrated the invaluable outcomes that manifest when the participants themselves are actively engaged in the ownership of program development, connection with former Black male college athletes, and strategic partnerships on campus. For example, former Black male college athletes created the ZEAL program at UNM in 2005 and the African American Student Services office houses this program. This intentional location enhances Black male college athletes' integration into the broader Black community on campus as opposed to be physically, psychologically, and socially isolated from their non-athlete peers (ZEAL, 2018).

Similarly, a group of five Black male college athletes and myself co-founded CU at UConn in 2014 in an effort to create an empowering space exclusively focused on their holistic development (Collective Uplift, 2018). Recent research on seven alumni of the CU program revealed benefits included mental health improvement, cultural empowerment, career readiness, and identity development beyond athletics (Cooper, Corral, et al., 2018, Cooper, Nwadike, & Macaulay, 2017). Similar to activist predecessors, culturally responsive groups could coalesce and organize efforts to demand change in intercollegiate sport related to racial diversity in leadership positions in sport, Black student enrollment and specific supports for retention and quality educational and social experiences in college, improving racial campus climate issues, college athlete unionization efforts, etc. Activating this power to leverage for better conditions should be pursued by any means necessary including the use of boycotts and protests of specific athletic events whether small (e.g., practice, media session, regular season game, etc.) or large scale (e.g., bowl games, March Madness tournament, etc.) (Edwards, 1980). Studying the history of previous efforts would assist in these organizational efforts (Cooper, Macaulay, & Rodriguez, 2017; Cooper, Mallery, & Macaulay, forthcoming; Edwards, 1980, 2016). Utilizing their platform to demand change as a collective is a powerful asset that should never be forgotten, unknown, underestimated, or underutilized.

In addition, it is imperative to normalize that Black college athletes engage in community we-reach efforts with local predominantly Black communities to foster a sense of collectivism and serve as positive role models and mentors for the younger generation (Cooper, 2016b). Career development programming for all college athletes should include strategic partnerships with Centers for Career Development and incorporate sequential programming whereby students have specific benchmarks to meet starting in the first year through graduation similar to current academic eligibility requirements for athletic competition (Cooper, 2016b). In concert with the secondary education recommendation, personality, interests, values, and career matching assessments could also be an athletic eligibility requirement (Cooper, 2018). In addition, every athletic department should have formal partnerships with African American and/or Black Alumni Associations, Cultural Centers, and African Diasporic-based academic departments to foster career exposure and relationship building. These efforts would greatly benefit Black male college athletes who have been found to experience career under preparedness because of athletic role engulfment and identity foreclosure (Beamon, 2008, 2010, 2012; Northcutt, 2013).

Another recommendation is to improve and expand culturally responsive mental health supports for Black male college athletes. The research documented throughout this book has detailed the significant mental health issues facing Black male college athletes due to miseducation, exploitative sporting systems, and a general lack of attentiveness and appropriate intervention. As a result, I propose intercollegiate athletic governing bodies mandate athletic departments establish formal partnerships with Counseling and Mental Health Services on campus, academic departments such as Social Work, Psychology, Counseling, and culturally relevant services off campus (this recommendation was offered by a CU alumni—see (Cooper, Corral, et al., 2018). If these changes are not incorporated by intercollegiate governing bodies, then Black college athletes, particularly those involved in organizations mentioned in the previous paragraph should take the onus to demand change. The lack of adequate attention towards the mental health of college athletes, particularly Black college athletes, is a form of a neglect and must be addressed in a formal systematic manner.

Moreover, the principle of amateurism, which prevents college athletes from economically benefitting from their athletic status, should be abolished

(Cooper, Nwadike, & Macaulay, 2017). The origins of the term "student-athlete" in terms of being widely used throughout the NCAA manual dates back to the 1960s, when then NCAA president, Walter Byers, sought to avoid worker's compensation claims from athletes who were injured while competing for their respective universities and colleges (Byers, 1995). In his memoir, *Unsportsmanlike Conduct*, Byers (1995) himself explained how this policy of amateurism was unjustifiable and denied college athletes their rights to benefit from their own likeness, images, and skill sets. Recent National Labor Relations Board (NLRB) ruling by Judge Claudia Wilken with the Northwestern football unionization effort in 2014 further indicated the lack of rationale for prohibiting college athletes from receiving employee benefits based on the conditions of their athletic involvement (Nocera & Strauss, 2016). This policy has the most disparate impact on Black male college athletes at major Division I institutions where they constitute the majority of participants on the highest revenue generating sports of football and men's basketball (Cooper, 2012; Harper, 2018; Hawkins, 2010; Smith, 2009).

A culturally responsive recommendation for redressing this inequity is to allow Division I college athletes the option of receiving equitable compensation during their athletic eligibility and/or accessing earned wages upon graduation (i.e., educational trust fund or payout) (NCPA, 2018; Schwarz, 2011; Schwarz, Volante, & Bayne, 2017). The fact that every entity surrounding Black male college athletes can generate revenue from their athletic abilities in a multi-billion dollar industry (e.g., universities and colleges, athletic departments, sponsors, local businesses, etc.) reflects gross exploitation. Equitable compensation would benefit Black male college athletes at the Division I level, but the abolishment of the amateurism principle would allow college athletes (including Black males at various other institutional types and levels) to generate revenue from their own image, likeness, status, and skill set (i.e., endorsements) (Cooper, Nwadike, & Macaulay, 2017). This policy reform would enable college athletes to have the same rights as their peers and professionals in the U.S. more broadly. In concert with the aforementioned reform, postsecondary institutions should incorporate financial management, entrepreneurship, and sport agent courses for college athletes. These courses could be coordinated with academic departments and financial businesses beyond the university and focus on financial literacy, contracts, taxes, and sport agents among other relevant topics (Cooper, Nwadike, & Macaulay, 2017).

Relatedly, the unionization of college athletes particularly at the Division I level should be promoted and supported. Several critics of big-time college sports have noted that if college athletes were able to negotiate the conditions under which they work, then targeted improvements would ensue (Finkel & Martin, 2013). As such, the current Student-Athlete Advisory Committees (SAAC) have limited power to change rules and the majority of them do not have a significant representation from Black male or female college athletes. Thus, increased diversity and inclusion efforts in this area are encouraged as well. The NCAA should initiate discussions with current professional players' associations to work with current and former college athletes in the formation of a union. The National College Players Association (NCPA) and College Athletes Players Association (CAPA) that has been established should be formally recognized and allowed by NCAA rules to empower college athletes to engage in more meaningful reform efforts (CAPA, 2018; NCPA, 2018). At levels beyond Division I, similar college athlete based advocacy organizations should be encouraged and supported by respective governing bodies (e.g., National Association for Intercollegiate Athletics (NAIA), National Junior College Athletic Association (NJCAA, etc.).

Academic reforms should also be pursued to shift away from deficit based polices towards more culturally responsive standards. Culturally relevant pedagogy (CRP) should be adopted by all athletic departments whereby academic success, cultural competence, and critical consciousness are integrated in policies and programming (Cooper, Nwadike, & Macaulay, 2017; Ladson-Billings, 1995). I recommend the NCAA, NAIA, NJCAA, and all intercollegiate governing bodies consider adopting the socialization models outlined in this text within their marketing materials and include more research from equity minded and race-based scholars as cited throughout the book so college athletes are knowledgeable about research in these areas (i.e., student athletes human rights project (SAHRP)) (SAHRP, 2018). Regarding eligibility, institutions need to monitor special admissions where explicit measures of improvement in terms of cognitive and intellectual gains for those admitted under these terms are benchmarks. The academic scandals revealing Black male college athletes' illiteracy is an indictment on postsecondary institutions (as well as the entire K-20 schooling system in the U.S.) (Donnor, 2005; Smith & Willingham, 2015). In addition, penalties for programs that have significant graduation and academic progress gaps should reflect the prioritization of racial equity (Cooper, Nwadike, & Macaulay, 2017). For example, in 2013, the NCAA enforced a post-season ban on the UConn men's basketball team for persistently low APRs. If the NCAA and/or other institutions administer similar enforcement for programs where Black males consistently graduate at lower rates than their peers do, then the seriousness of the message would be communicated regarding academic progress for all college athletes regardless of race, gender, and sport type.

It is imperative for institutions to adopt growth and proficiency metrics especially with students who are special admits so that reasonable progress is assessed (Cooper, Nwadike, & Macaulay, 2017). Based on my research on Black male college athletes' experiences, in college, my colleague and I proposed a conditions, relationships, and expectations (CRE) criteria that institutions could adopt to ensure a multi-faceted culturally responsive approach for improving this sub-groups' experiences and outcomes (Cooper & Cooper, 2015). The CRE criteria involves racial diversity of staff, time spent on educationally purposeful activities, formal expectations and incentives for meaningful engagement with professors and staff on campus beyond athletics, involvement in internships, research opportunities, study abroad experiences, and increased academic standards and supports to name a few (Cooper, 2016b; Cooper & Cooper, 2015). Institutions should also be required to document the extent to which their practices are data-driven (Comeaux, 2015). Academic departments and third parties outside of athletics should construct the creation of various instruments for data collection. For example, questions about academic major selection could be asked to determine explanations from college athletes themselves their experiences (or lack thereof) with clustering trends covered in Chapter 2. These assessments could be conducted by an outside third-party (e.g., academic departments on campus, off-campus services, etc.) to ensure anonymity of participants' responses, optimize comfort level with participants regarding providing honest responses, and monitor potential backlash from athletic department staff. Key areas of improvement can be documented to inform policy changes as opposed to the current top down approaches that are not data-driven, which are commonplace within athletic departments (Comeaux, 2015; Cooper & Dougherty, 2015; Cooper, Nwadike, & Macaulay, 2017).

Regarding graduation data, I recommend the adoption of metrics that allow for comparisons that are more accurate across peer groups who are non-athletes. Southall , Nagel, Wallace, & Sexton (2016) created an adjusted graduation gap (AGG) metric to compare college athletes with their full-time peers who are non-athletes. The instrument design assesses more clearly if and to what extent academic progress gaps exists between these groups. The authors asserted the NCAA's propaganda efforts rely on a GSR metric that does not allow for accurate comparisons with peers who are non-athletes. Thus, utilizing these metrics would hold institutions and their athletic programs more accountable. Related to career readiness, intercollegiate athletic governing bodies should mandate sequential career development programming with campus wide career services, which would signal the value of integrating college athletes with their peers (Cooper, Nwadike, & Macaulay, 2017). In addition, culturally responsive counseling and career programming and assessments should be adopted, created, and/or adapted (Cooper, 2018). Another recommendation is that the minimum term GPA for athletic competition should be 2.5 in the preceding academic semester excluding summer sessions to facilitate greater academic achievement among Black male college athletes. In conjunction with this recommendation, institutions should allow reduced course loads during the athletic season and provide athletic-grant-in-aid through graduation. For HBCUs who are disproportionately penalized by NCAA APR penalties, my colleagues and I propose a Title IX type three-prong approach to replace the current structure. The three prongs would include comparisons between college athlete sub-groups and their peers in the general student body, demonstration of growth over time, and achievement compared to peer institutions with similar resources (Cooper, Nwadike, & Macaulay, 2017).

Another major issue at the intercollegiate level is the lack of racial diversity in athletic leadership positions. As such, my colleagues and I offered the following recommendations: (a) recognize and promote institutions that enact a Rooney/Eddie Robinson type Rule for hiring (e.g., athletic director, coaching, faculty athletic representatives, athletic department staff, and college athlete academic support staff), (b) require institutions with perpetual racial disparities between college athletes and athletic administration and staff to create comprehensive diversity and racial equity action plans, and (c) require the creation of athletic chief diversity officer positions (Bimper, 2017; Cooper, Nwadike, & Macaulay, 2017). In concert with the racial underrepresentation of Blacks in leadership positions at HWIs, there is also a lack of formal on-going cultural competence trainings for athletic staff. My colleagues and I recommended the adoption of a multi-tiered CRP training (Ladson-Billings, 1995; Lynch, 2011) for institutional, personal, and instructional development regarding cultural empathy and responsiveness (Cooper, Nwadike, & Macaulay, 2017). Creating and strengthening partnerships with Diversity and Inclusion offices, Cultural Centers, Pan-Hellenic groups on campus as well as race-based organizations in the broader community such as the NAACP, the Urban League, and those who promote Pan Africanism could lead to improve supports for Black male college athletes.

Recommendations for Broader Society

There is a need for more research on the experiences and outcomes of Black male HSPs across their lifespans. There is an expansive body of literature on Black male college athletes, but a dearth of scholarly research that exists on Black males who participate in athletics at the primary and secondary levels. Thus, I recommend a National Longitudinal Study of Black Male HSPs (or currently referenced as Athletes). The government, private funders, institutions of higher education, sport-governing bodies, and/or African Diaspora-based organizations or entities could fund this research. The benefit of collecting and analyzing this data will enable a more comprehensive understanding of the interplay between multi-level systems and Black males' experiences and outcomes within and beyond sport and educational spaces.

Franklin and Resnik (1973) outlined four objectives for Black economic and community development particularly among the working class:

1. To create ghetto-based enterprises to absorb some portion of the black unemployment and underemployment.
2. To improve the potentially competitive performance and quality of existing enterprises in the ghetto owned by black capitalists.
3. To establish a ghetto-planning agency, that is, a community development corporation, to implement plans.
4. To acquire sufficient political power and autonomy to control the flow of resources out of the ghetto, as well as to extract resource transfers from "foreign" exploiters (p. 191).

Aside from the use of the term ghetto and the unquestioned endorsement of capitalism, I support these objectives because they focus on maximizing internal resources within the Black working and middle classes for a collectivist aim. Related to sport and education, I recommend we build elite sport and educational institutions in working class Black communities instead of exporting talented Blacks to prep schools and JUCOs, which are typically operated by Whites and are located in predominantly White economies. Corporate sponsors such as Nike, Under Armour, and Puma along with major big-time college athletic programs have demonstrated that they will go where the talent in located. Thus, I surmise as a Black collective, we maintain ownership over our resources and establish a stronger leveraging position akin to a political voting bloc. As a community, we would outline certain non-negotiables regarding our resources and only work with groups who are willing to engage with us as equity partners as opposed to the traditional oppressor-oppressed relationship (Freire, 1968).

For example, within WRC, the creation of multi-million dollar Black capitalist athletes such as LeBron James and Kevin Durant works in the systems favor because it maintains the illusion of singular success (ideological myth of meritocracy) and sustains widespread structural inequalities. I purport it also reinforces the notion of colorblindness and liberalism (negating the permanence of racism and Whiteness as property tenets of CRT) (Bell, 1980, 1992; Bonilla-Silva, 2010; Harris, 1993) and separates these individuals from the Black masses economically, psychologically, and physically (Rhoden, 2006). Hence, with the TSE blueprint (also known as the Black collectivist holistic development model), these talented Black male HSPs would possess socio-political consciousness, internalized empowerment, and commitment to engagement to counter-actions and racial uplift by negotiating with sponsors for specific concessions towards Black communities that have been unjustly impoverished. Until an Afrocentric worldview is adopted in the U.S. and globally, these *leverage capitalists with collectivist inclinations* (LCCIs) can fulfill an important role in uplifting the Black community. Well short of reparations, these LCCIs could utilize their wealth acquisition to shift power dynamics within a society founded upon and structured by WRC. Since direct reparations are unlikely to be provided on moralistic appeals (Curry, 2017), I argue that both *strategic responsiveness to interest convergence (SRIC) over time* as well as *direct confrontation via radical revolutionary actions* (i.e., collective sustained boycotts and divestment in sporting structures grounded in WRC) could lead to sustained transformative change in the Black community so as long as a baseline commitment to collective racial uplift is upheld. The aim could be to start small and work on establishing local sustainability and then duplicate while concurrently supporting more radical alternatives. Rather than an *either or* I propose a *both and* approach for optimizing short-term and long-term goal attainment.

When seeking to transform the current ISSM and EALM, which are embedded in the broader WRC structure, it is important to acknowledge the reality expressed by Douglas and Peck (2013) in their study of Black Bermudian males' educational challenges:

> … far less than thriving, some Black people are merely surviving, and too many others are being deprived of the necessary tools and opportunities (educational and otherwise) to challenge this reality. Sadly, the mantra "education by any means necessary" is often replaced by the bottom line: "survival by any means necessary." (p. 85)

Ownership of resources such as property is essential to the disruption of WRC and the establishment, strengthening, and sustainment of a Black Afrocentric collectivist culture and systems. Harris (1993) postulated that Whiteness as property manifests in society through the rights of disposition, rights to use and enjoyment, reputation and status property, and absolute right to exclude. Historically, Whites have violently taken from groups such as Blacks, Indigenous People/Native Americans, Latinx, and Asians and concurrently protected these rights for themselves. This reality is conspicuous in sporting and educational arrangements. In sport, the presence of White owners controlling sport leagues and associations while Blacks comprise the athletic labor force is an example of Whiteness as property in action. The recent exclusion of Kaepernick from the NFL based on his peaceful protest and political views is an example of the right to exclude. Educationally, the representation in leadership at the policymaking, administration, and educator levels across the U.S. (national, state, and local) in concert with the ideological and pathological beliefs that undergird policies and enforcements, curricula, and economic arrangements (i.e., property tax for public school funding) represent the various components of the Whiteness as property tenet of CRT.

As such, in order for Black liberation and sustained empowerment in society to occur Blacks must possess ownership and control over various types of property (e.g., land, intellectual, economic, etc.). The strength of the Negro Leagues in the early and mid-20th century existed because of the presence of Black ownership and management of the teams and leagues in partnership with Black owned businesses in the community (Lomax, 2003, 2014). This strength remains presence in the 21st century with HBCU athletics (Cooper, Cavil, & Cheeks, 2014; Hawkins, Cooper, Carter-Francique, & Cavil, 2015). However, a weaknesses of both entities is the lack of complete ownership of facilities, apparel brands, endowments/financial assets, and status reputation beyond a limited geographical scope. In addition, efforts to mimic their White counterparts as opposed to optimizing their unique racial and cultural assets is another weakness across these leagues, conferences, and athletic programs. These circumstances are byproducts of systemic racism (Feagin, 2006). These factors resulted in the demise of the Negro Leagues and continued subordination of HBCU athletics in the college sport landscape. As such, in order to fulfill collective racial uplift, I recommend we build and sustain Black owned businesses in every facet of our human existence including sporting leagues across all levels (youth to professional), apparel brands, athletic associations and conferences (see Cooper, Cavil, and Cheeks (2014) for a detailed overview of the HBCU secession from the NCAA plan), etc. This approach does not mean that we do not work with White owned organizations or not include individuals who are not Black in our business plans, organizational staff, and/or consumers. However, it does mean that ownership is Black, collective racial uplift is the top priority, and any and all engagements with races outside of Black are viewed as a strategic partnership that must involve at a minimum symbiotic benefits for our ultimate purpose/mission. In order to eradicate systemic oppression, we must own and control as many resources as possible (e.g., land, property, fiscal, etc.). In a similar vein, I recommend we build African Diasporic Alliances in all vital areas and geographical locations of African existence in particular on the continent of Africa. Building youth to professional Black sport and educational alliances is one recommendation for consideration. Holistic development and collective racial programming could be embedded within these events that stimulate economic commerce, information sharing, and cultural bonding for all parties. This Pan-African recommendation focuses on information exchange, economic interdependence, and symbiotic partnerships.

A core aim of the TSE blueprint is to deconstruct WRC in all its forms and replace it with a Black Afrocentric/Pan-African communal system in all facets of society (e.g., spiritual, political, economic, legal, cultural, etc.) including sport and education. In this regard, *the ultimate goal of holistic empowerment through sport and education is a revolutionary act connected to the broader global Black/Afrocentric/Pan-African struggle*. In contrast to aspiring capitalists including leverage capitalists, which are cultivated through the ISSM and EALM, the HEM and TSE blueprint is intended to cultivate Black revolutionary action through sport. Carmichael (1971/2007) conceptualized this notion of Black revolutionary action in the broader society: "… But a black revolutionary is an angry young man who wants to tear down and destroy an entire system that is oppressing his people and replace it with a new system where his people can live like human beings" (p. 159). As noted in Chapter 1, in order to fully attain the goal of holistic development (holistic excellence) and empowerment for Black males, we must seek to adhere to Edwards' (1984) charge for a systems change and Rhoden's (2006) recommendation for creating new models that more adequately serve the collective interests of the Black community as opposed to a select few individuals and families. Ultimately, securing and building more Black owned institutions including sport organizations that work in concert with broader Afrocentric/Pan-African based entities will lead to sustained empowerment beyond liberation.

Chapter Summary

In sum, the goals presented in this chapter reflect the Black Afrocentric worldview and collectivist values and strategies that I surmise are a solution for *transformative sustained empowerment* (TSE). The adoption, transmission, and manifestation of a clear communal mission, goals, and strategies is important for racial and cultural uplift. Frameworks such as Kwanzaa principles (Karenga, 1978), Afrocentric worldviews (Asante, 1990, 2003; Carruthers, 1999; Hilliard, 1998), culturally relevant pedagogy (CRP; Ladson-Billings, 1995), community cultural wealth framework (CCW; Yosso, 2005), critical race theory (CRT) in education (Bell, 1992; Crenshaw et al., 1995; Delgado, 1995; Delgado & Stefancic, 2001; Ladson-Billings & Tate, 1995) and sport (Bimper, 2016, 2017; Bimper, Harrison, & Clark, 2012; Cooper & Hawkins, 2014; Hawkins, Carter-Francique, & Cooper, 2017; Hylton, 2009; Singer, 2005, 2009), athletic role theory and identity foreclosure (Adler & Adler, 1991; Beamon, 2012; Brewer & Petitpas, 2017) and an emerging theory of Black male athletic identity and foreclosure, African American male theory (AAMT; Bush & Bush, 2013a, 2013b), anti-deficit achievement framework in education (Harper, 2010, 2012) and progressive and productive Black masculinities (Martin & Harris, 2006; Mutua, 2006), excellence beyond athletics (EBA; Cooper, 2016b), Collective Uplift framework (Collective Uplift, 2018), and Black male holistic (under)development through sport and (mis)education socialization models presented in this book (ISSM, EALM, TRM, P²EPGM, and HEM) are all recommended for review and strategic implementation in resistance and empowerment building processes. Each of these theories, frameworks, and models informed the creation of the TSE blueprint. Replacing oppressive systems with transformative sustained empowerment systems is the core aim of this text. Thus, in concert with the Sankofa bird, our collective progress as a people is predicated on our ability to learn and grow from our past as we continue on our journey towards our promising future. It is in this struggle and pursuit of this vision that we advance *past exploitation back to our empowerment roots and divine destiny*.

Notes

1. Influences referenced here include, but not limited to, developmental stage, time, space, frequency, nature, quality, type, and context of internalizations, relationships, expectations, resources, and supports.

2. I do not intend to imply that traditional charitable giving and community service efforts are futile or less valued, but rather I surmise that in order for more expansive liberation and empowerment to be achieved there must be an increase in concerted counter-hegemonic efforts that name the problem (i.e., WRC and its systems) and actively work to disrupt, deconstruct, and replace it with a collectivist equity-minded system.

3. The term "we-reach" is used as opposed to commonly used terms of outreach and service, which have acquired punitive or disingenuous connotations (see Douglas (2016) for similar rephrasing of terms to reflect more culturally endearing and empowerment connotations).

4. The following theories are recommended for discussion: (a) critical race theory in education (Bell, 1992; Crenshaw et al., 1995; Delgado, 1995; Delgado & Stefanic, 2001; Ladson-Billings & Tate, 1995) and sport (Bimper, 2016, 2017; Bimper et al., 2012; Cooper & Hawkins, 2014a; Hawkins, Carter-Francique, & Cooper, 2017; Hylton, 2009; Singer, 2005, 2009), (b) community cultural wealth (Yosso, 2005), (c) strategic responsiveness to interest convergence (Cooper & Cooper, 2015) and excellence beyond athletics (Cooper, 2016b), (http://coe.tsu.edu/?page_id=1815d) athletic role theory and identity foreclosure (Adler & Adler, 1991; Beamon, 2012) and an emerging theory of Black male athletic identity and foreclosure, (e) cool pose (Majors & Billson, 1992), (f) gender racist theories such as the mandingo, survival of the fittest, genetic, psychological mismatch, and dumb jock theory (Edwards, 1973, 1984; Sailes, 2010), (g) stereotype threat (Steele, 2010; Steele & Aronson, 1995), (h) racial microaggressions (Sue et al., 2007), (i) racial battle fatigue (Smith, Allen, & Danley, 2007), (j) racial socialization (Stevenson, 1994), (k) social reproduction theory (Beamon, 2008; Singer & May, 2010; May, 2008), (l) athletic identity foreclosure (Beamon, 2012; Brewer & Petitpas, 2017; Murphy, Petitpas, & Brewer, 1996), (m) progressive and productive Black masculinities (Mutua, 2006) and in particular in sport (Bimper, Harrison, & Clark, 2012; Cooper, 2016a, 2017; Cooper & Cooper, 2015a; Cooper & Hawkins, 2014a; Fuller, Harrison, Bukstein, Martin, Lawrence, & Gadsby, 2016; Harris, Hines, Kelly, Williams, & Bagley, 2014; Harrison, Martin, & Fuller, 2015; Martin & Harris, 2006; Martin, Harrison, & Bukstein, 2010; Smith, Clark, & Harrison, 2014), (n) Black male vulnerability (Curry, 2017) , (o) African American male theory (Bush, 2013a, 2013b), (p) Afrocentric worldviews and theories (Asante, 1990, 2003; Asante & Mazama, 2005; Hilliard, 1998; Karenga, 1978; Mazama, 2001; Jackson & Sears, 1992), (q) anti-deficit achievement framework in education (Harper, 2010, 2012) among other relevant theories, concepts, and frameworks that can contribute to Black male holistic development and racial and cultural empowerment.

References

Adler, P. A., & Adler, P. (1991). *Backboards and blackboards: College athletics and role engulfment.* New York, NY: Columbia University Press.

Alexander, M. (2012). *The new Jim Crow: Mass incarceration in the age of colorblindness.* New York, NY: The New Press.

Armstrong, K. L., & Jennings, M. A. (2018). Race, sport, and sociocognitive "place" in higher education: Black male student-athletes as critical theorists. *Journal of Black Studies, 49*(4), 349–369.

Asante, M. K. (1990). *Kemet, Afrocentricity and knowledge*. Trenton, NJ: Africa World Press.

Asante, M. K. (2003). *Afrocentricity: The theory of social change*. Chicago, IL: African American Images.

Asante, M. K., & Mazama, A. (2005). *Encyclopedia of Black studies*. Thousand Oaks, CA: Sage Publications.

Beamon, K. K. (2008). "Used goods": Former African American college student-athletes' perception of exploitation by division I universities. *The Journal of Negro Education, 77*(4), 352–364.

Beamon, K. K. (2010). Are sports overemphasized in the socialization process of African American males: A qualitative analysis of former collegiate athletes' perception of sport socialization. *Journal of Black Studies, 41*(2), 281–300.

Beamon, K. K. (2012). "I'm a baller:" Athletic identity foreclosure among African American former student-athletes. *Journal of African American Studies, 16*(2), 195–208.

Bell, D. A. (1980). Brown v. Board of Education and the interest-convergence dilemma. *Harvard Law Review, 93*(3), 518–533.

Bell, D. A. (1992). *Faces at the bottom of the well: The permanence of racism*. New York, NY: Basic Books.

Bensimon, E. M. (2004). The diversity scorecard: A learning approach to institutional change. *Change: The magazine of higher learning, 36*(1), 44–52.

Beyer, J. M., & Hannah, D. R. (2000). The cultural significance of athletics in U.S. higher education. *Journal of Sport Management, 14*(2), 105–132. doi:10.1123/jsm.14.2.105

Bible. (2011). The book of Matthew. Chapter 25: Verse 40 (pp. 1639–1640). New International Version. Grand Rapids, MI: Zondervan.

Bimper, A. Y. (2016). Capital matters: Social sustaining capital and the development of Black student-athletes. *Journal of Intercollegiate Sport, 9*(1), 106–128.

Bimper, A. Y. (2017). Mentorship of Black student-athletes at a predominately White American university: Critical race theory perspective on student-athlete development. *Sport, Education and Society, 22*(2), 175–193.

Bimper, A. Y., Harrison, L., & Clark, L. (2012). Diamonds in the rough: Examining a case of succesful Black male student athletes in college sport. *Journal of Black Psychology, 39*(2), 1–24. doi: 10.1177/0095798412454676

Bonilla-Silva, E. (2010). *Racism without racists: Color-blind racism and the persistence of racial inequality in the United States* (3rd ed.). Lanham, MD: Rowan & Littlefield.

Brewer, B. W., & Petitpas, A. J. (2017). Athletic identity foreclosure. *Current Opinion in Psychology, 16*, 118–122.

Bush, L. V., & Bush, E. C. (2013a). Introducing African American male theory (AAMT). *Journal of African American Males in Education, 4*(1), 6–17.

Bush, L. V., & Bush, E. C. (2013b). God bless the child who got his own: Toward a comprehensive theory for African-American boys and men. *The Western Journal of Black Studies, 37*(1), 1–14.

Byers, W. (1995). *Unsportsmanlike conduct: Exploiting college athletes*. Ann Arbor, MI: The University of Michigan Press.

CAPA (2018). College Athletes Players Association website. Home page. Retrieved from http://www.collegeathletespa.org/

Carmichael, S. (1971/2007). *Stokely speaks: From Black power to Pan-Africanism*. Chicago, IL: Chicago Review Press.

Carruthers, J. (1999). *Intellectual warfare*. Chicago, IL: Third World Press.

Carter-Francique, A. R. (2013). Black female collegiate athletes experiences in a culturally relevant leadership program. The National Journal of Urban Education & Practice, 7, 87–106.

Catch Education. (2018). Home page. Retrieved from http://www.catcheducation.org/

Cavil, J. K. (2018). Faculty home page. Retrieved from http://coe.tsu.edu/?page_id=1815

Coakley, J. (2017). *Sports in society: Issues and controversies* (12th ed.). New York, NY: McGraw-Hill Education.

Collective Uplift (2018). Goals page. Retrieved from http://www.collectiveuplift.com

Comeaux, E. (2015). *Making the connection: Data-informed practices in academic support centers for college athletes*. Charlotte, NC: Information Age.

Cooper, J. N. (2012). Personal troubles and public issues: A sociological imagination of Black athletes' experiences at predominantly White institutions in the United States. *Sociology Mind, 2*(3), 261–271.

Cooper, J. N. (2013). A culture of collective uplift: The influence of a historically Black college/university on Black male student athletes' experiences. *Journal of Issues in Intercollegiate Athletics, 6*, 306–331.

Cooper, J. N. (2016a). "Focus on the bigger picture:" An anti-deficit achievement examination of Black male scholar athletes in science and engineering at a Division I historically White university (HWU). *Whiteness & Education, 1*(2), 109–124.

Cooper, J. N. (2016b). Excellence beyond athletics: Best practices for enhancing Black male student athletes' educational experiences and outcomes. *Equity & Excellence in Education, 49*(3), 267–283.

Cooper, J. N. (2017). Strategic navigation: A comparative study of Black male scholar athletes' experiences at a historically Black college/university (HBCU) and historically White institution (HWI). *International Journal of Qualitative Studies in Education*, doi: 10.1080/09518398.2017.1379617.

Cooper, J. N., Cavil, J. K., & Cheeks, G. (2014). The state of intercollegiate athletics at historically Black colleges and universities (HBCUs): Past, present, & persistence. *Journal of Issues in Intercollegiate Athletics, 7*, 307–332.

Cooper, J. N., & Cooper, J. E. (2015). Success in the shadows: (Counter) narratives of achievement from Black scholar athletes at a historically Black college/university (HBCU). *Journal for the Study of Sports and Athletes in Education, 9*(3), 145–171.

Cooper, J. N., Corral, M. D., Macaulay, C. D. T., Cooper, M. S., Nwadike, A., & Mallery, Jr., M. (2018). Collective uplift: The impact of a holistic development support program on Black male former college athletes' experiences and outcomes. *International Journal of Qualitative Studies in Education*, DOI: 10.1080/09518398.2018.1522011.

Cooper, J. N., & Dougherty, S. (2015). Does race still matter?: A post bowl championship series (BCS) era examination of student athletes' experiences at a Division I historically Black college/university (HBCU) and predominantly White institution (PWI). *Journal of Issues in Intercollegiate Athletics, 8*, 74–101.

Cooper, J. N., & Hawkins, B. (2014). An anti-deficit perspective on Black male student athletes' educational experiences at a historically Black college/university. *Race, Ethnicity and Education, 19*(5), 950–979. doi: 10.1080/13613324.2014.946491

Cooper, J. N., Macaulay, C., & Rodriguez, S. H. (2017). Race and resistance: A typology of African American sport activism. *International Review for the Sociology of Sport*, 1–31. DOI: 10.1177/1012690217718170.

Cooper, J. N., Mallery, M., & Macaulay, C. D. T. (forthcoming). African American sport activism and broader social movements. In D. Brown (Ed.). *Passing the ball: Sports in African American life and culture* (pp. 35–51). Jefferson, NC: McFarland & Company.

Cooper, J. N., Nwadike, A., & Macaulay, C. (2017). A critical race theory analysis of big-time college sports: Implications for culturally responsive and race-conscious sport leadership. *Journal of Issues in Intercollegiate Athletics, 10*, 204–233.

Cooper, M. S. (2018). *Culturally-responsive career development services for school counselors.* Unpublished paper.

Crenshaw, K., Gotanda, N., Peller, G., & Thomas, K. (1995). *Critical race theory: The key writings that formed the movement.* New York, NY: The New Press.

Crossroads (2018). Crossroads: Pathways to success offers programs for triad youth. Retrieved from https://www.wfmynews2.com/article/syndication/facebook-instant/crossroads-pathways-to-success-offers-programs-for-triad-youth/83-536529703

Curry, T. J. (2017). *The man-not: Race, class, genre, and the dilemmas of Black manhood.* Philadelphia, PA: Temple University Press.

Delgado, R. (1995). The imperial scholar: Reflections on a review of civil rights literature. In K. W. Crenshaw, N. Gotanda, G. Peller, & K. Thomas (Eds.), *Critical race theory: The key writings that formed the movement* (pp. 46–57). New York, NY: New Press.

Delgado, R., & Stefancic, J. (2001). *Critical race theory: An introduction.* New York, NY: New York University Press.

Diop, C. A. (1974). *The African origin of civilization: Myth or reality.* Westport, CT: Lawrence Hill.

Donnor J. K. (2005). Towards and interest-convergence in the education of African-American football student athletes in major college sports. *Race, Ethnicity and Education, 8*(1), 45–67.

Douglas, T. (2016). *Border crossing brothas: Navigating race, place, and complex space.* New York, NY: Peter Lang.

Douglas, T. M., & Peck, C. (2013). Education by any means necessary: Peoples of African descent and community-based pedagogical spaces. *Educational Studies, 49*(1), 67–91.

Edwards, H. (1973). *Sociology of sport.* Homewood, IL: Dorsey Press.

Edwards, H. (1980). *The struggle that must be: An autobiography.* New York, NY: Macmillan Publishing Co., Inc.

Edwards, H. (1984). The Black "dumb jock:" An American sports tragedy. *College Board Review, 131*, 8–13.

Edwards, H. (1988). 'The single-minded pursuit of sports fame and fortune is approaching an institutionalized triple tragedy in Black society ...' Ebony Magazine, 43(10), 138–140.

Edwards, H. (2016). *The fourth wave: Black athlete protests in the second decade of the 21st century.* Keynote address at the North American Society for the Sociology of Sport (NASSS) conference in Tampa Bay, Florida.

ETS. (2011). *A strong start: Positioning young Black boys for educational success a statistical profile.* Washington, DC: Educational Testing Service.

Feagin, J. (2006). *Systemic racism: A theory of oppression.* New York, NY: Routledge.

Finkel, R., Martin, T., & Paley, J. (2013). *Schooled: The price of college sports.* [Documentary]. Makuhari Media: Strand Releasing.

Franklin, R. S., & Resnik,. S. (1973). *The political economy of racism.* New York, NY: Holt Rinehart and Winston.

Freire, P. (1968). *Pedagogy of the oppressed.* New York, NY: The Seabury Press.

Fuller, R. D., Harrison, C. K., Bukstein, S. J., Martin, B. E., Lawrence, S. M., & Gadsby, P. (2016). That smart dude: A qualitative investigation of the African American scholar-baller identity. *Urban Education,* 1–19. doi: 10.1177/0042085916668955

Gardner, H. (1983). *Frames of mind: The theory of multiple intelligences.* New York: Basic Books.

Gladwell, M. (2011). *Outliers: A story of success.* New York, NY: Back Bay Books.

Harper, S. R. (2010). An anti-deficit achievement framework for research on students of Color in STEM. *New Directions for Institutional Research,* 148, 63–74.

Harper, S. R. (2012). *Black male student success in higher education: A report from the national Black male college achievement study.* Philadelphia, PA: University of Pennsylvania, Center for the Study of Race and Equity in Education.

Harper, S. R. (2018). *Black male student-athletes and racial inequities in NCAA Division I college sports: 2018 edition.* Los Angeles, CA: University of Southern California, Race & Equity Center.

Harris, C. (1993). Whiteness as property. *Harvard Law Review,* 106(8), 1707–1791.

Harris, P. C., Hines, E. M., Kelly, D. D., Williams, D. J., & Bagley, B. (2014). Promoting the academic engagement and success of Black male student-athletes. *The High School Journal,* 97(3), 180–195.

Harrison, C. K. (1998). Themes that thread through society: Racism and athletic manifestation in the African-American community. *Race, Ethnicity and Education,* 1, 63–74.

Harrison, C. K., Martin, B. E., & Fuller, R. (2015). "Eagles don't fly with sparrows": Self-determination theory, African Americna male scholar-athletes and peer group influences on motivation. *The Journal of Negro Education,* 84(1), 80–93.

Hawkins, B. (2010). *The new plantation: Black athletes, college sports, and predominantly White NCAA institutions.* New York, NY: Palgrave-MacMillan.

Hawkins B., Cooper J. N., Carter-Francique, A. R., & Cavil, J. K. (eds.). (2015). *The athletic experience at historically Black colleges and universities: Past, present, & persistence.* Lanham, MD: Rowman & Littlefield Press.

Hawkins, B., Carter-Francique, A. R., & Cooper, J. N. (2017). *Critical race theory: Black athletic sporting experiences in the United States.* New York, NY: Palgrave Macmillan.

Henderson, E. B. (1939). *The Negro in sports.* Washington, DC: The Associated Publishers.

Hilliard, A. G., III (1998). SBA: *The reawakening of the African mind.* Gainesville, FL: Makare Publishing.

Hodge, S. R., Burden, J. W., Jr., Robinson, L. E., & Bennett, R. A., III. (2008). Theorizing on the stereotyping of Black male student-athletes: Issues and implications. *Journal for the Study of Sports and Athletes in Education, 2*(2), 203–226.

Howard, T. C. (2014). *Black male(d): Peril and promise in the education of African American males:* New York, NY: Teachers College Press.

Hylton, K. (2009). *'Race' and sport: Critical race theory.* New York, NY: Routledge.

Jackson, A., & Sears, S. (1992). Implications of an Africentric worldview in reducing stress for African American women. *Journal of Counseling & Development, 71*(2), 184–190.

Karenga, M. (1978). *Essays on struggle: Position and analysis.* San Diego, CA: Kawaida Publications.

Kelly, D. D., & Dixon, M. A. (2014). Successfully navigating life transitions among African American male student-athletes: A review and examination of constellation mentoring as a promising strategy. *Journal of Sport Management, 28*(5), 498–514.

Ladson-Billings, G. (1995). Toward a theory of culturally relevant pedagogy. *American Educational Research Journal, 32*(3), 465–491.

Ladson-Billings, G., & Tate, W. (1995). Toward a critical race theory of education. *Teachers College Record, 97*(1), 47–68.

Lomax, M. E. (2003). *Black baseball entrepreneurs, 1860–1901: Operating by any means necessary.* Syracuse, NY: Syracuse University Press.

Lomax, M. E. (2014). *Black baseball entrepreneurs, 1902–1931: The Negro National and Eastern Colored Leagues.* Syracuse, NY: Syracuse University Press.

Lynch, M. (2011, December 14). What is culturally responsive pedagogy? *The Huffington Post.* Retrieved from http://www.huffingtonpost.com/matthew-lynch-edd/culturally-responsive-pedagogy_b_1147364.html

Majors, R., & Billson, J. M. (1992). *Cool pose: The dilemmas of Black manhood in America.* New York, NY: Lexington Books.

Martin, B., & Harris, F., III. (2006). Examining productive conceptions of masculinities: Lessons learned from academically driven African American male student-athletes. *The Journal of Men's Studies, 14*(3), 359–378.

Martin, B., Harrison, C. K., & Bukstein, S. (2010). "It takes a village" for African American male scholar-athletes: Mentorship by parents, faculty, and coaches. *Journal for the Study of Sports and Athletes in Education, 4*(3), 277–295.

Maslow, A. H. (1943). A theory of human motivation. *Psychological Review, 50*(4), 370–396.

May, R. A. B. (2008). *Living through the hoop: High school basketball, race, and the American Dream.* New York, NY: New York University Press.

Mazama, A. (2001). The Afrocentric paradigm: Contours and definitions. *Journal of Black Studies, 31*(4), 387–405.

McMillan, D. W., & Chavis, D. M. (1986). Sense of community: A definition and theory. *Journal of Community Psychology, 14*(1), 6–23.

Moore, C. (2018, January 17). Caylin Moore speech. *The Power of Race in College Athletics: 2018 Black Student Athlete Summit* at the University of Texas at Austin. Retrieved from https://www.youtube.com/watch?v=NF1ASdrVPQU&t=24s

Murphy, G. M., Petitpas, A. J., & Brewer, B. W. (1996). Identity foreclosure, athletic identity, and career maturity in intercollegiate athletics. *The Sport Psychologist, 10*(3), 239–246.

Mutua, A. D. (2006). *Progressive Black masculinities.* New York, NY: Routledge.

NCPA (2018). Home page. *National College Players Association website.* Retrieved from https://www.ncpanow.org/

Newton, H. P., & Seale, B. (1967, March 15). 10-point program. *The Black Panther: Black Community News Service.* Retrieved from http://www.blacklivesmattersyllabus.com/wp-content/uploads/2016/07/BPP_Ten_Point_Program.pdf

Nocera, J., & Strauss, B. (2016). *Indentured: The inside story of the rebellion against the NCAA.* New York, NY: Portfolio/Penguin Random House.

Noguera, P. (2008). *The trouble with Black boys ... and other reflections on race, equity, and the future of public education.* San Francisco, CA: Jossey-Bass.

Northcutt, J. (2013). *The dilemma: Career transition of African American male football players at Division I institutions.* Dissertation. University of Mississippi.

Nwadike, A. (2016). *Uncovering the mediating variable between athletic identity and academic performance in revenue-sport student athletes* (Thesis). Athens, GA: University of Georgia.

Rhoden, W. C. (2006). *40 million dollar slaves: The rise, fall, and redemption of the Black athlete.* New York, NY: Crown Publishing Group.

Sage, G. H. (1998). *Power and ideology in American sport* (2nd ed.). Champaign, IL: Human Kinetics.

SAHRP (2018). Student-athletes' human rights project website. Retrieved from https://www.facebook.com/Student-Athletes-Human-Rights-Project-308323092530148/

Sailes, G. (2010). The African American athlete: social myths and stereotypes. In G. Sailes (Ed.), *Modern Sport and the African American experience* (pp. 55–68). San Diego, CA: Cognella.

Schwarz, A. (2011). Excuses, not reasons: 13 myths about (not) paying college athletes. In S. Barbieri (Ed.), *Selected Proceedings of the Santa Clara University Sports Law Symposium* (pp. 46–74).

Schwarz, A., Volante, R., & Bayne, B. C. (2017). *The HBCU League Business Plan.* Unpublished document. 1–22.

Shopkorn, A., Noah, J., Safdie, J., & Safdie, B. (2013). *Lenny Cooke* [Documentary]. New York, NY: Shopkorn Productions.

Singer, J. N. (2005). Understanding racism through the eyes of African American male student athletes. *Race, Ethnicity and Education, 8*(4), 365–386.

Singer, J. N. (2009). African American football athletes' perspectives on institutional integrity in college sport. *Research Quarterly for Exercise and Sport, 80*(1), 102–116.

Singer, J. N., & May, R. A. B. (2010). The career trajectory of a Black male high school basketball player: A social reproduction perspective. *International Review for the Sociology of Sport, 46*(3), 299–314.

Smith, E. (2009). *Race, sport and the American dream* (2nd ed.). Durham, NC: Carolina Academic Press.

Smith, J. C. (1994). *Black firsts: 2, 000 years of extraordinary achievement.* Detroit, MI: Visible Ink Press.

Smith, W. A., Allen, W. R., & Danley, L. L. (2007). "Assume the position ... you fit the description" Psychosocial experiences and racial battle fatigue among African American Male college students. *American Behavioral Scientist, 51*(4), 551–578.

Smith, M. P., Clark, L. D., Harrison, L., Jr. (2014). The historical hypocrisy of the Black student-athlete. *Race, Gender & Class, 21*(1–2), 220–235.

Smith, J. M., & Willingham, M. (2015). *Cheated: The UNC scandal, the education of athletes, and the future of big-time college sports.* Omaha, NE: University of Nebraska Press.

Southall, R. M., Nagel, M. S., Wallace, A., & Sexton, M. (2016). *2016 Adjusted graduation gap report: NCAA FBS football. College Sport Research Institute.* Retrieved from http://csri-sc.org/wp-content/uploads/2016/10/2016-Football-AGG-Report_Publish_Final_10-19-2016.pdf

Steele, C. M. (2010). *Whistling vivaldi: And other clues to how stereotypes affect us.* New York, NY: W. W. Norton & Company.

Steele, C. M., & Aronson, J. (1995). Stereotype threat and the intellectual test performance of African Americans. *Journal of Personality and Social Psychology, 69*(5), 797–811.

Stewart, J. C. (1996). *1001 things everyone should know about African American history.* New York, NY: Doubleday Dell Publishing Group.

Sue, D. W., Capodilupo, C. M., Torino, G. C., Bucceri, J. M., Holder, A. M. B., Nadal, K. L., & Esquilin, M. (2007). Racial microaggressions in everyday life: Implications for clinical practice. *American Psychologist, 62*(4), 271–286.

T. Alexander Foundation (2018). T. Alexander foundation home page. Retrieved from https://talexanderfoundation.org/

Williams, C. (1974/1987). *The destruction of Black civilization: Great issues of a race from 4500 B. C. to 2000 A. D.* Chicago, IL: Third World Press.

Woodson, C. G. (1933/1990). *The mis-education of the Negro.* Trenton, NJ: Africa World Press.

Yosso, T. J. (2005). Whose culture has capital? A critical race theory discussion of community cultural wealth. *Race, Ethnicity and Education, 8*(1), 69–91.

ZEAL. (2018). Brief history of ZEAL. *University of New Mexico African American Student Services website.* Retrieved from https://afro.unm.edu/signature-programs/zeal/index.html

INDEX